$f\mathbf{P}$

BETWEEN
WAR AND PEACE

How America Ends Its Wars

EDITED BY

COL. MATTHEW MOTEN

FREE PRESS

New York   London   Toronto   Sydney

FREE PRESS
A Division of Simon & Schuster, Inc.
1230 Avenue of the Americas
New York, NY 10020

First Free Press hardcover edition January 2011

FREE PRESS and colophon are trademarks of Simon & Schuster, Inc.

For information about special discounts for bulk purchases,
please contact Simon & Schuster Special Sales at 1-866-506-1949
or business@simonandschuster.com.

The Simon & Schuster Speakers Bureau can bring authors to your live event.
For more information or to book an event, contact the Simon & Schuster Speakers Bureau
at 1-866-248-3049 or visit our website at www.simonspeakers.com.

DESIGNED BY ERICH HOBBING

Manufactured in the United States of America

2   4   6   8   10   9   7   5   3   1

Library of Congress Cataloging-in-Publication Data

Between war and peace : how America ends its wars / edited by Matthew Moten.—
1st Free Press hardcover ed.
p. cm.
1. United States—History, Military—Case studies.
2. War—Termination—Case studies. I. Moten, Matthew.
E181.B56 2011
355.00973—dc22
2010031613

ISBN 978-1-4391-9461-4
ISBN 978-1-4391-9463-8 (ebook)

Maps courtesy of the Department of History, United States Military Academy,
Frank Martini, Cartographer.

Contents

Foreword

No one looks more fervently toward the end of a war than professional soldiers. All their exertions seek the day when the issues that sent them to war are settled and their objectives finally attained.

Between a war's beginning and its ending, all sides wage a grim contest in an environment marked by uncertainty. The most successful soldiers have not been those who avoided war's uncertainty, but rather those who embraced it so that it worked in their favor.

History isn't suspended during war. Over four bloody years the Civil War unfolded in ways no one could have predicted, and the manner in which it ended was not only the product of all the successes and failures on the fields of battle but also the product of the changes the war had wrought in the Union and the Confederacy alike. Nor was history fixed in place thereafter. What followed Appomattox was as unpredictable as the war itself, its outlines detectable only with the passage of time.

Yet there are patterns to how history unfolds during war. These patterns, so evident in the Civil War, can be detected in all of America's major conflicts and indeed in every war. For professional soldiers and the armies that follow them into war, a clear and unsentimental understanding of what awaits them can be one of the most powerful weapons in their arsenal. Come what may, the soldier must provide advice to civilian leadership and must act on the field of battle consistent with the guidance he receives in return. Obviously that advice is most useful and that action most effective when it is guided by knowledge.

For centuries soldiers have turned to military history as the foundation of professional knowledge. Far more than simply a collection of arid facts and dates, military history has the power to develop the professional imagination.

No American reader needs to be reminded of the importance of understanding the nature and conduct of modern war. Libraries are well supplied with books to guide the way. However, few among these works contribute to our understanding of the manner and consequence of how wars—especially America's wars—have been brought to conclusion.

It is for that reason that in the summer of 2009 the U.S. Army commissioned some of our nation's leading military historians to examine this question. The essays in this volume are not the product of a few months' work. They represent a lifetime of learning in the face of a persistent challenge facing America's statesmen, strategists, and operational commanders. The collective result is a wholly original and important contribution to military history and theory.

—Gen. Martin E. Dempsey, U.S. Army*

*The views presented are those of the author and do not necessarily represent the views of the Department of Defense or its components.

Introduction

America passed a sad milestone in the middle of 2010: the war in Afghanistan became the longest conflict in U.S. history. The war in Iraq, a year and a half younger, was not far behind. Many Americans strained to see just when and how these wars might end.

War is never—or never should be—an end in itself. Wars are fought to achieve results that political leaders decide cannot be gained by persuasion, negotiation, or threat. But not all wars in the past—in the American past—have begun as a last resort, a desperate roll of the dice when no other alternative was in view. And rightly or wrongly, nations go to war expecting to succeed, and invest their lives and treasure toward that end.

So it is curious that in all the hundreds of thousands of books on war and military history, the manner and results of war's end have seldom been addressed in a rigorous and systematic fashion. Historians and theorists have dissected armed conflict from a myriad of perspectives, examining war's essential nature, origins, purposes, and conduct. Library stacks bulge with treatments of particular wars, campaigns, battles, generals, and armies. Yet historians have largely neglected the course of events leading to a given war's conclusion and its consequences for the peace that followed. Indeed, even Clausewitz, that most preeminent of war's philosophers, rarely followed war to its very end.

The animating purpose of *Between War and Peace* is to examine how America's major conflicts have ended. The issue is of immense political and strategic import. For most of its history, the United States has been successful in its wars, but the endings of those conflicts have brought about unforeseen and unwanted consequences; the aftermath has seldom resembled the peaceful future the nation's leaders had imagined and hoped for when they first decided for war.

Witness the consequences that followed two unequivocal victories.

In 1865, Union armies decisively defeated their Confederate opponents, but rapid demobilization left the postwar army incapable of effective occupation, and little political will remained to achieve a complete reconstruction of the South. After a dozen years of halfhearted efforts to achieve political and social reform, leaders north and south agreed to end reconstruction, returning the heirs of the southern aristocracy to power and leaving African Americans disfranchised, destitute, and more racially segregated than they had been before the war. Most of a century would pass before the civil rights movement began to right the wrongs of a failed ending to a successful war.

A half-century after the Civil War, the United States joined the Allies and provided the additional strength necessary to win the Great War. Then, in 1919, diplomats overreached with the Treaty of Versailles, insisting that Germany accept moral responsibility for starting the war, imposing humiliating limitations on its military strength, and demanding burdensome reparations that galled the German populace. Those Allied recriminations helped to bring about worldwide economic depression and stirred German nationalist resentment that brought Hitler's Nazi regime to power and led to the Second World War.

In the first instance, neglect of postwar responsibilities squandered many of the gains of a victorious war. In the second, draconian terms of peace fostered the grievances that gave rise to an even broader and more brutal conflict. In both cases, and many others, the circumstances of ending the war were as important as the conduct of the war itself, and those endings sowed the seeds of later tragedy.

Policymakers are often faulted for underestimating the costs of war. A more probing criticism is that they fail to grasp its complexities. Once begun, war often takes on a life of its own, making unpredictable turns along paths of its own choosing. Presidents and prime ministers may find themselves following rather than leading along those paths, changing their war aims, expanding their commitments, struggling to explain their decisions. Ending war is, if anything, a problem more complex than war itself. It forces political and military chieftains to contemplate two actions that might previously have seemed incomprehensible: arresting the progress of an unwieldy beast called war, and coming to some form of agreement with the enemy, an entity known to be disagreeable, probably irrational, and perhaps implacably evil. Furthermore, what is often lost in the throes of terminating war is careful attention to the postwar era—consolidating the gains of victory or ameliorating the costs of defeat, and in either case repairing the damage wrought by conflict. In the time between war and peace it is easy to lose sight of the objectives for which one embarked upon war in the first place, and to forfeit the grasp on accomplishments bought at great expense to the treasury and the lives and health of the nation's soldiery.

Between War and Peace is a historical study of those complexities. It is not an exercise in commentary or punditry. Nor is it an anti-war screed. At the outset the fundamental purpose of the project was to contribute to historical knowledge, especially in the American experience. That remains the principal aim, but we have also found that concentrated study has afforded us an opportunity to expand the horizons of strategic and military thought. Thus, this volume also offers a novel contribution to the understanding of warfare: six general propositions on the problem of ending war.

This project began with a broad question: "How has the United States ended its wars, and how well has it accomplished its political aims and strategic goals in the past?" We chose to examine fourteen American conflicts, beginning with the American Revolution and ending with the Persian Gulf War of 1991, the last major U.S. war that reached its conclusion. We began searching for historians with recognized and particular expertise in each of those wars. The overarching question elicited enthusiastic interest, and we enjoyed enormous success in recruiting a most distinguished and accomplished group of scholars, as the list of contributors attests. Serendipitously, we also managed to gather a most collegial and generous cohort. It has been an honor and privilege to work with all of them.

In January 2010 we gathered at Chapel Hill, North Carolina, to discuss the project. That conference was vitally important in producing a consensus about our objectives. We agreed to focus our study at the political and strategic levels of war, looking forward to the aftermath of war and its implications for future American policy. We wrote to inform an audience of policymakers, military leaders, strategists, opinion shapers, and the well-informed public about the importance of clear strategic thinking, the uncertainties of war termination, and the unforeseen and unintended consequences of war and its aftermath.

Our contributors agreed to pursue a common set of questions as they approached their separate topics. What were the origins of the war? What were the war aims of each side, keeping in mind that political objectives are not static, but change over time? How did the war progress to the final campaign? How did that campaign affect the ending of the war? *How and why* did the war end? Where did the United States, its allies, and its enemies stand politically and strategically at war's end? How did those end states differ from those envisaged by the original political aims? Then, looking as far into the future as necessary, what were the consequences of the war on the subsequent peace? What were the ramifications of the war's termination for the nation and its military forces?

As editor, I imposed no further framework and certainly no outline for authors to follow. The reader will see that our contributors have tackled their assignments in creative and imaginative ways that are as different as the wars they explore. There was certainly no requirement that they agree with one another in their interpretations or their general conclusions; and, indeed, they do not.

We made one final commitment as we began this endeavor: we agreed to try to avoid analyzing the problems of the past through the lens of current concerns. Historians know that "presentism" invariably skews the results. In other words, we agreed, insofar as possible, to resist the temptation to view these American wars through the prism of the current conflicts in Iraq and Afghanistan. The reader, however, is under no such obligation. Indeed, this work can provide important context for public debate about national security policy. National leaders, civilian and military, may profit from these essays as they craft policy and strategy. Our immodest hope is that some future president, confronted with threats to American national interests and needing time to think, will tuck this volume under his arm as he departs for a weekend of reading and reflection at Camp David before making the awful decision between war and peace.

—Col. Matthew Moten, U.S. Army
West Point
August 2010

ROGER J. SPILLER

Six Propositions

For years the Corinthians had been storing up resentments against the Athenians, whose power was great, and growing. They were aggressive. The Corinthians said that the Athenians "possess a thing almost as soon as they have begun to desire it, so quickly with them does action follow upon decision."[1] As if preparing for war, the Athenians had fortified their city and closed to the Corinthians the market at Athens and all the ports in the Athenian Empire. They had taken possession of Corcyra and were even now laying siege against Potidaea, both Corinthian colonies. The Athenians were insufferable, arrogant. They falsely claimed the privilege of their arrogance by right of having defeated the Persian invasion years before, when everyone knew, the Corinthians said, the real reason for Persia's defeat was a mistaken policy by the Persians themselves. Far from beneficent, the Athenian Empire was rapacious, and it endangered the peace.

And so the Corinthians mobilized opinion among the lesser city-states of the Peloponnesus and laid their grievances before Sparta's governing assembly, the Ekklesia. If the Spartans could be convinced of the injustices Corinth suffered, a coalition to oppose the Athenians might be raised to defend their liberties behind Spartan shields. The Spartans, nursing resentments of their own, were receptive to these complaints. The Ekklesia seemed almost certain to declare for war against Athens.

A group of Athenians already in Sparta tending to other affairs learned of the Corinthians' maneuvers and petitioned to address the Ekklesia, hoping to dissuade Sparta's leaders from giving in to Corinth's demands for war. The Athenians were not defensive, and they did not apologize for their power. "We did not gain this empire by force," they declared. "We have done nothing extraordinary, nothing contrary to human nature in accepting an empire when it was offered to us and then in refusing to give it up."[2] The Athenians' message was blunt: a war against Athens would be both unworthy and unwise. Athens would fight. Regardless of the confidence that might propel Sparta into war, Sparta was taking a risk. Who could predict how a war might end? The Athenians concluded their brief with a warning: "Think, too, of the great part that is played by the unpredictable in war: think of it now, before you are actually committed to war. The longer a war lasts, the more things tend to depend on accident. Neither you nor we can see into them; we have to abide their outcome in the dark."[3]

The Athenians' warning was to no avail. Sparta declared war on Athens, igniting thirty years of tragedy, "death in every shape and form" that spread beyond the confines of ancient Greece from Sicily to Macedonia.[4] The Athenians' defiant confidence did not protect them from disaster, however. They lost the war, suffered the dismantlement of their empire, and saw their mother city reduced to a shadow of its former glory, its golden age brought to a definitive end.

The Athenians were not wrong to have been confident. History had been kind to them, and they saw no reason it would not continue to be so. Their leaders did not imagine victory would be won easily, but they were sure Athens would win in the end. Had they been less certain of their power they would have mollified the Spartans and their allies, relaxed their markets, and lifted their sieges. They would have relinquished the power they had attained, but this they would not, or could not, do. Yet in all their calculations they had not foreseen how their strategies would go awry, how successes would lose their potency and lead to reverses, how nature itself might intervene with a cruel plague, and how their leaders, thinking more of their own fortunes than those of their fellow citizens, would squander their advantages. The Athenians had failed to heed their own warning.

The way we commonly see war and how it ends comes to us from the world of the soldier. This world is highly utilitarian and quite simple in its most basic form: *If I kill enough of the enemy, the rest will stop fighting and I can live.* In this way the soldier means to impose control over events that are fundamentally unpredictable and chaotic. The chain of command from which he and his comrades receive their orders not only describes how this control is managed; it is also a *chain of knowledge,* prescribing how military ideas are organized.

In its ideal form this chain of military thought is hierarchical and deductive, proceeding from the general to the specific. Strategy sets the terms and objectives; campaigns are designed to meet those terms and objectives by means of engagements and battles, which are themselves composed of smaller unit actions and minor tactical events.

This is a world in which causes are meant to be translated into effects, in which decision is to lead as directly as possible to action. Successful actions are supposed to result in successful engagements whose sum will produce successful campaigns leading to the attainment of final victory. The ideal map has one straight road to victory. It is somewhat amazing that for some time the world's armies, great and small, have fought in consonance with this worldview, especially as it has so often proved to have little relevance to real war.

This highly structured world is also suffused with a unique value system, built upon good and practical reasons. In earlier days war was a blunt instrument, no more fit for surgery than an axe. Orchestrating the use of military power was very difficult even in ideal conditions, and soldiers regarded with a jaundiced eye any scheme that required them to reserve or limit their strength. Even now the principle of economy of force is sometimes seen as subtracting from an army's main effort. Soldiers everywhere have always preferred to be stronger than their enemy, so strong that the outcome of their war will be in no doubt. If one is *very* much stronger, so much the better; the enemy may be compelled to surrender without a fight, or he may be defeated quickly and thoroughly, thus sparing lives and treasure on both sides. For these reasons a soldier is bound to regard *any sort of limitation* on his strength as playing with his life.

But we outside the soldier's world are not obliged to see war in this way. To do so would make us like physicians who see an illness only from the patient's point of view. The soldier's perspective might serve him well, but that is not to say it advances our knowledge of war equally well.

This essay addresses the conduct of war and how it ends, seen from the perspective of the American military experience. Although its chief concern is how America's most important conflicts drew to a close, it is based on the premise that the actions of all wars and the conclusions they produce cannot be separated from one another or indeed from the influences of the world beyond the battlefield. To that end I advance six general propositions about the history of American war termination and its implications for the conduct of modern limited war, propositions that may at first glance seem counterintuitive from the soldier's perspective:

1. Wars are defined not by their extremes but by their limitations. The concepts of absolute war, total war, and total victory are theoretical abstractions whose function is to depict an ideal case against which real war can be understood and conducted.
2. War's original aims and methods, no matter how unyielding or uncompromising they may seem at first, are constantly revised by the stresses and actions of war.
3. In every war the aims of all sides, no matter how opposed at the beginning, gradually converge toward an agreement to stop fighting.
4. This convergence of aims is not produced on the battlefield alone. It is also driven by wider influences beyond the battlefield, only some of which may be manipulated by policymakers, strategists, or operational commanders.
5. The public face of war is ever more cosmopolitan, and so therefore is the conduct of war itself, which can no longer be quarantined from the influence of the world beyond, if it ever could.
6. Within the confines of war itself, a war's terminal campaign exercises the greatest influence over the manner in which it ends, and therefore is not always a war's final campaign. This suggests that the concept of a decisive campaign or victory is not as useful as orthodox military thought has traditionally assumed.

In 1965 the U.S. Army's dictionary of military terms defined *doctrine* as "the best available military thought that can be defended by reason." This definition was admirably idealistic. If reason controls military doctrine, it is the sort of reason that is a creature of the moment, for military doctrine is above all a modern army's way of thinking out loud about what it must do next. For one who studies doctrine but doesn't have to act on it, doctrine therefore is valuable for what it reveals about the state of military thought and practice at a particular point in time.

Current American military doctrine refers to *war termination* as the conclusion of "operations on terms favorable to the United States." Defense strategists and operational planners are enjoined to keep the question of how a conflict might end uppermost in their minds as they go about their work. The doctrine makes clear that strategies and plans should aim toward a certain "end state," which must be in accord with the goals of the conflict as set by national policy. Once the course of action has been decided, the doctrine recognizes that plans may well be interrupted by "unforeseen events" that force a "reassessment" of the terms on which hostilities will be concluded. Doctrine is less definitive about how all this might actually be accomplished.

That the subject of war termination is addressed at all is somewhat surprising. As a term of art *war termination* is of fairly recent vintage, having made its appearance during the First World War. There was no serious work on the subject between the two world wars, and although there was official and scholarly interest in the termination of a hypothetical nuclear war during the Cold War years, it was overshadowed by developments in nuclear arms control. Among social scientists toward the end of the war in Vietnam the subject attracted academic interest that persisted to the end of the century.[5] Only a few military theorists and historians paid any attention to the problem, and the subject does not seem to have found its way into professional military thinking. Now the term is not frequently heard in war or staff colleges, and over the past twenty years professional military journals have offered but two essays on the subject.[6] It is not difficult to understand why. The term implies something less than the ideal outcome of a war: reservation, equivocation, ambiguity, limitation—substitutes for victory.

Victory: for centuries statesmen, soldiers, and scholars have made do with this simpler, more encompassing concept of how wars end. The nature of victory seemed so self-evident it was seldom if ever examined. In its classical, ideal form, victory meant the triumph by force of arms over one's enemy, the kind of success to which the enemy cannot reply by force and which rewards the victor with complete freedom of action. This was the only proper goal of war. To aim for less or to settle for less was to expose oneself to the enemy's actions and to squander the sacrifices in blood and treasure war always demands. How a war ended was seen as the logical result of battlefield successes and failures, a final reckoning toward which all sides struggled. Every battlefield success contributed to final victory, and every failure subtracted from the possibility of attaining it. Victory settled all questions, one way or another. Indeed professional soldiers could hardly afford the luxury of thinking any other way. They would react instinctively against any suggestion that the course of a war toward its conclusion is a more complex process than treasuring up successes or guarding against reverses. "Man does not enter battle to fight," one soldier wrote, "but for victory. He does everything that he can to avoid the first and obtain the second."[7]

Soldiers are likely to recoil at the thought that a battlefield defeat might in some way contribute to their ultimate goal. The American survivors of Japan's victory at Pearl Harbor would not take kindly to the suggestion that their defeat exercised a far greater influence over the outcome of the Pacific War than if they had successfully repelled the attack with little loss of life or damage to the Pacific Fleet. Yet the defeat at Pearl Harbor drove the United States to declare war sooner than it might have. The vulnerability of its battleships forced the United States to create a new fleet of aircraft carriers that would carry the burdens of its war far more effectively. And for Americans on the home front as well as the fighting front, Pearl Harbor served as a powerful incentive for retribution until the day the *Enola Gay* appeared over Hiroshima. But if you were to ask a veteran of Pearl Harbor whether any of these results lessened the sting of his defeat, you need have no doubt about the answer.

Today you will search in vain for any definition of *victory* in American military doctrine. Exactly when the classical ideal of victory disappeared from official doctrine is an open question, but its absence invites the thought that at some time in the recent past, victory, which so long dominated military thought and practice, lost some of its official appeal. Regardless of its present status in public discourse or as a doctrinal term, however, victory has by no means gone out of fashion, and there is no reason to think that *war termination,* with its vaguely clinical, antiseptic feel, is likely to supplant it anytime soon. The ideal of victory still exerts a powerful hold over modern war making. This ideal was what General Schwarzkopf had in mind when he recalled the end of the First Gulf War. "Our side had *won,*" he wrote, "so we were in a position to dictate terms." His meeting with Iraqi commanders at Safwan that halted the fighting, he insisted, was in no way a transaction. "I'm here to tell them exactly what we expect them to do," he told reporters at the time.[8] A dozen years later, under a banner on the USS *Abraham Lincoln* proclaiming "Mission Accomplished," President George W. Bush declared victory in the second Iraq War, just as his secretary of defense had done after the initial campaign in Afghanistan had overthrown the Taliban. These are only the latest instances across the long expanse of the American military experience in which the ideal of victory met its limits. As Carl von Clausewitz wrote long ago, once one moves "from the abstract to the real world, the whole thing looks quite different."[9]

* * *

Since the American Revolution the world has seen more than 650 wars, more than a third of which have occurred since the Second World War.[10] The American military experience, according to the neat divisions of history, includes twelve major conflicts, from revolution and civil war to colonial and imperial wars, wars against other nations as well as irregular wars. Some of these, such as the Mexican War, the 300-Years War against the Native Americans, and the Spanish-American and Philippine Wars, have been blatantly aggressive; others have been less so. In some cases aggression is very much defined by the mind of the beholder. How one classifies the Mexican War, for instance, depends on the credence one grants President Polk's view that Mexico started the war when its troops intruded on disputed territory along the Texas border. And American readers are not likely to see the Pacific War as anything but a defense against Japanese aggression, but it was launched in part because of Japan's long-standing concerns about an antagonistic American foreign policy that encroached on its strategic sphere of influence.

Seeing these wars as self-contained events, with distinct beginnings, coherent, sequential battle actions, and distinct endings, can pose other questions. The War of 1812, for instance, can be seen as a continuation of a war for independence that left issues unsettled, some of which persisted even years after the Treaty of Ghent, which formally ended the war. If one were to include southern social and political resistance that followed the surrender of Lee's army at Appomattox, the Civil War, often depicted as the most complete victory in American history, had a very long denouement that ended in the political resurgence of the defeated. And given the less-than-complete victory sealed by the Treaty of Versailles after the First World War, there is reason to expect that historians of the future, instead of seeing the Second World War as distinct from the First, will see these together as another Thirty Years War.

In nine of its major conflicts America did not fight alone, but in the company of allies, and in the Civil War both sides contended for either direct military or diplomatic support of other nations. None of America's allies entered war for America's sake, but in pursuit of their own goals, some of which were barely in consonance with America's. The nation's World War II alliance with Great Britain, the Soviet Union, China, and France, often depicted as a model of cohesion, was beset by strategic and operational disagreements from beginning to end, disagreements that not only influenced the peace that followed but carried on for years afterward.

In the War of 1812, the Korean War, the Vietnam War, and the Cold War, diplomatic maneuvers between allies and enemies alike exercised a critical role in setting terms for the cessation of hostilities.

Seen in detail, America's major conflicts have produced far more limited victories than is often supposed. And in this the American military experience is by no means unique. In its abstract, ideal, most extreme form, victory is the result of an enemy's complete moral and physical collapse produced by force of arms. But real war, as Clausewitz recognized long ago, is a resistant medium. From inception to conclusion those who direct and conduct war are fighting not only the enemy but the dynamic nature of war itself. As the Athenians warned, the kind of victory so often imagined at the onset of war rarely if ever survives intact at war's end.

However one may imagine war in the abstract, in reality all wars are defined not by their extremes but by their limitations. America's wars, like all real wars, have been creatures of their place and time. The purposes for which they have been fought, the manner in which they are fought, the ways they have ended, and their lasting results arise from their social, political, and material circumstances, *and their influences are not held in suspension as the war is being fought.*[11]

Even in wars in which the United States aimed for an unlimited victory, the practicalities of translating its social and material strength into military power intervened. No two antagonists could have pursued aims more diametrically opposed than the North and the South during the Civil War: the South would not remain in the Union, and the North could not let it go. Despite early hopes that the actual fighting would be far more constrained than its aims, the operational course of the war eventually became just as uncompromising. But the transformation of both sides' social power into military power was far from comprehensive. In its fight for independence the Confederacy mobilized more than 80 percent of its white males of military age, but intentionally did not recruit its huge slave population. For social and political reasons the South willingly paid a very high price that President Davis would try to rectify very late—too late—in the war. With war aims no less demanding, the North, beset by a clumsy and poorly administered system for getting its citizens into uniform, did far worse.[12]

Even when American society was far better organized than in the Civil War and more easily managed, social mobilization was far less than total. In pursuit of Germany's and Japan's unconditional surrender during the

Second World War, the United States mobilized more extensively than any time before or since. But the nation reserved much of its potential social strength for industrial mobilization, with the result that only one-sixth of its male population served in the armed forces. Even at that, more than six million draftees were rejected for service on grounds that, according to one authority, would not have excused them from serving in other armies.[13] America's calculations of the number of men needed on the fighting lines were so fine that the army came close to running out of infantrymen during the critical last year of the war.

The limits imposed on war by material resources are even more pronounced. The state of science, technology, and industry directly influences a war's geographic scope, its pace of operations, and the effectiveness with which these resources are employed from the strategic to the tactical level. Moreover the mere existence of such resources is no guarantee that their potential can be fully exploited. The theoretical foundations necessary to construct an atomic bomb were well understood by physicists before the onset of the Second World War, but only after four years of the most expensive engineering project in American history could an operational bomb be produced. Even when America's industrial capacity hit its stride after two years of war, the global logistics essential for bringing equipment into action at the right time and place were strained. Americans produced 82,000 landing craft and ships in the war, but to the very end America and its allies struggled with the strategic effect of shortages in one theater or another. In these and many other instances the practicalities of war acted as a check on the full expression of military power.[14]

To all these limitations one must add those exacted by the actions of the enemy. Yet the list of America's wars in which its statesmen, strategists, and generals have embarked with only the dimmest understanding of their enemy's intentions and capacities is depressingly long. The common conceit is that if one is strong enough, if one's plans are well designed, and if one's operations are well generalled, how the enemy responds is of secondary importance, perhaps of little relevance at all. In the opening pages of *On War* Clausewitz famously described war as a duel, but he wisely chose not to take this metaphor, with its connotation of sequential action and thrust and parry, too far. Instead he wrote later on of war as "a *continuous interaction* of opposites."[15] In practice, from the moment war is declared the interactions of the two sides are increasingly more, not less, intimate, no matter how intense their hostility toward one another, as the war goes on their relations will become more intimate than ever. As the ancient Chinese theorist Sun Tzu wrote, "Leaders who are able to rise above the passions of the moment will enjoy an advantage over opponents who cannot."

The reciprocal, evolving, intimate nature of war is perhaps the single greatest challenge for leaders to comprehend and act upon. During the Vietnam War, President Johnson and Secretary of Defense McNamara occasionally took notice of the enemy and found their knowledge lacking. Rather than attempting to learn as much about their enemy as they could, their solution was to imagine what *they* would do if they were Ho Chi Minh. The historian Douglas Pike found in the writings of Aldous Huxley the perfect term for this conceit: "vincible ignorance," or "that which one does not know and realizes it, but does not regard as necessary to know."[16] This attitude prevailed in the general public at the time as well. Informed Americans might have known the names of Ho Chi Minh and General Vo Nguyen Giap or, if pressed, Ho's close advisor Le Duc Tho, but otherwise the most important field commanders of the North Vietnamese Army and the National Liberation Front might as well have been invisible. Americans in World War II were accustomed to hearing of Emperor Hirohito and Gen. Tojo Hideki, usually as targets of official ridicule. The three army officers who succeeded General Tojo after his resignation in the summer of 1944, however, had nothing like his official or public visibility. And now few Americans, official or otherwise, could name the commander of the Iraqi Army's most capable formation, the Republican Guard, in either of America's wars with Iraq.

Yet even if such a thing as perfect knowledge of the enemy ever exists, it is no protection against war's unpredictability. The Civil War was to all intents and purposes a West Pointer's war: Academy graduates commanded on both sides in fifty-five of the sixty largest battles, and on one side in the rest. Although concerns were voiced on both sides that their generals were all too familiar to their enemies, a common professional background and personal acquaintance in themselves were no guarantee that their strategies and operations would benefit. On the contrary, an officer's professional reputation could be misleading. When General Grant took command in the East in 1864, General Lee's staff officers were skeptical that he would pose much danger to their cause. By the time they surrendered to him at Appomattox they had been disabused of this notion.

Wars begin not by accident, but with an agreement to fight, deliberately and with purpose; that is how they are fought and that is how they end.

All too often a state of war is assumed to create such an impenetrable wall of enmity that the adversaries have no relation to one another except when they meet in battle. But even if such absolute hostility were possible, the interactions of the war itself would constantly redefine their relationship. Moreover even the most vicious of America's wars have been shot through with shared assumptions, traditions, treaties, and formal or informal understandings with the enemy. As both sides prosecute their war these interactions intensify until their interests converge toward terms for ending the war that each will accept.

One might think this convergence is somehow nullified in wars where the nature and purposes of the adversaries are so remote from one another that they seem to belong to separate universes. This indeed seemed to be the case in America's war with Japan. Depths of enmity not present in the war against Germany, fed by racial animosity that was intensified by Japan's surprise attack on Pearl Harbor and its conduct in the campaigns that followed, sustained the Americans to the very end of the war. Most Americans would not have minded if Japan had been erased from the face of the earth. Any sort of concession or accommodation with this enemy was unthinkable. For their part Japan's most powerful leaders could not countenance the idea of surrender in any form until the last days of the war. Even the atomic attacks against Hiroshima and Nagasaki were not enough to dissuade some in Japan's Supreme War Council from fighting on. Scholars now believe that the use of atomic weapons against Japan, rather than delivering the knockout blow that led to Japan's unconditional surrender, exercised less influence over its decision makers than the Soviet Union's belated entry in the Pacific War.

From the first days of that war, President Roosevelt aimed for the unconditional surrender of his Axis enemies. Judged by the actions of war alone, all signs pointed to a Carthaginian peace: the utter destruction of Japan as a nation and the subjugation of its people. Yet currents of official opinion for a far less draconian peace emerged on both sides even as the war reached a white-hot intensity.

The redefinition of what unconditional surrender meant to both sides ran a slow, convoluted course. In the United States this process of moderation toward a convergence of purposes began as early as 1942, when the war's end was far from view. In Japan two years of strategic and operational reverses were required to move some officials to consider how their nation might manage to survive the war.

The intersection at which the two sides would finally meet turned critically on the question of what the Japanese knew as *kokutai:* the irreducible nature of Japanese culture itself, and the emperor who was its living embodiment. Thus the postwar fate of the nation and its emperor were inseparable. On this point at least, all parties on both sides—even the most militant and unforgiving—agreed.

Judged by the actions of war alone, the course of the Pacific War seemed straightforward, yet the strategic landscape in which they occurred was far from fixed. As the war advanced, whether or when the Soviet Union might join the war came to dominate Japan's strategic calculations. To this was added, for the few Americans who knew of it, the question of whether or how to use the atomic bomb and the result it might produce.

Nor was the convergence of interests that eventually produced Japan's surrender guided by calculations in airless conference rooms or by their enactment on the fields of battle. Policymakers and strategists were careful to consider the opinions of their fellow citizens. Japanese leaders, including the emperor himself, were by no means isolated from domestic opinion, especially that of the powerful military constituency, which had a long history of reacting violently to national policies. For their part American policymakers were well attuned to public opinion, which polls showed was as uncompromising in 1945 as the day the war began. President Truman, having been sworn in after Roosevelt's untimely death, understood very well what his secretary of state meant when he warned that Truman would be "crucified" if he showed any signs of appeasement toward the Japanese.

At this distance it is easily enough forgotten that Japan emerged from the war having preserved many of its most important conditions for surrender. Japan was not destroyed as a nation. Although stripped of his godhood, the emperor was not brought to account for his part in the war. Relatively few leading political or military leaders were prosecuted, and still fewer were executed. Japan did not suffer the partitioning that Germany did, and Soviet incursions on Japanese territory were checked by the United States. Ultimately Japan took the place of China as the mainstay of American strategy in East Asia. The shadow of Pearl Harbor and the draconian American war aims it inspired had faded as all sides moved toward war's end.[17]

The age of modern limited war began with the dropping of the atomic bomb. War, limited as always, was now more constrained than ever. The bomb's unprecedented expression of power, and the prospect of a nuclear war between the United States and the Soviet Union, created a new strategic context that exercised a commanding influence over America's conflicts for more than four decades.

Many believed the new weapon threatened to overturn the sum of military knowledge. Above all, the traditional relationship between ends and means in war was curiously inverted: the means of future war were in place well before the policy that might require their use was articulated. No one could confidently describe the process by which a nuclear war might be ignited, nor the vital interests—save national survival itself—for which such an apocalyptic war might be fought. Still less could anyone imagine how to prosecute such a war or how to end it.[18] Classical military theory seemed obsolete, and dangerously so. Lt. Gen. James Gavin, the World War II airborne commander who was to play an important role in postwar weapons development, said of the bomb, "Military thinking seemed, at the outset, to be paralyzed by its magnitude."[19]

Historical knowledge, which had long served as the foundation of military thought, seemed of little use in a world that to all appearances transcended history itself. Few if any strategists looked back to the war just finished for any guidance about the atomic future. Although the bomb was an integral part of the Second World War, the history of the atomic bomb was abstracted from the history of the war itself, as if it belonged to a separate time, untouched by the context in which it was created or the circumstances in which it was first used. The dramatic role of the bomb in terminating the war was so compelling that the rest of the war seemed almost incidental to the Allies' final victory. The effect of the bomb appeared to be so definitively war-ending no one thought to consider, as Geoffrey Blainey did many years later, what its effect would have been had it been used a year or two earlier, before Japan's military power was so depleted. In that case the Japanese reaction might well have been to *intensify* their resistance.[20]

Strategic thinking during the Cold War years thus became highly speculative, theoretically remote from the real conflicts that entangled the United States. A new class of strategic thinkers emerged during this period, drawn not from the uniformed ranks but from academia. Undeterred by their lack of military experience, confident of their intellectual powers, and openly contemptuous of those in uniform who might be called upon to execute their theories, these new strategists helped frame the nation's defense policies for more than two decades after the end of the Second World War.[21]

One of the most important consequences of this trend in strategic thought was the devaluation of the role of battle in the prosecution of war. The atomic bomb was not only a strategic weapon; it was above all a *policy weapon*. If traditional tools of war such as ground combat were susceptible to all sorts of limitations, the atomic bomb—theoretically—was not. The bomb was above all an efficient weapon; there could be a seamless line between executive command and employment that no other instrument of military power could match.[22]

Further, the advent of the atomic bomb called into question the traditional roles and missions of the American armed forces. Not only the awesome power of the weapon itself, but the means of employing it seemed to open a new chapter in American war making. Whereas the expression of power on land had been the foundation of American statecraft since its inception, airpower became the strategic tool of choice during the Cold War. In the hypothetical nuclear war that dominated strategic thought, the use of ground combat to achieve the nation's aims seemed a quaint relic of wars gone by. Modern war could be made into a more precise instrument of statecraft.

No strategic thinker advanced this new concept of war more effectively than Thomas C. Schelling. Schelling's understanding of war was resolutely ahistorical. His insights, inventively and closely argued, were drawn not from the American experience of war but from the field of economics, in which he was an accomplished, prominent figure. From this frame of intellectual reference Schelling argued that the management of war was little different from the management of markets, especially markets dominated by a small number of corporations. Elite managers dealt with one another in a closed, self-referential system, where "winning" meant "gaining relative to one's own value system . . . by bargaining, by mutual accommodation, and the avoidance of mutually damaging behavior." Strategy as traditionally defined seemed beside the point to Schelling; instead strategy should not be "concerned with the efficient application of force but with the exploitation of potential force." Seen in this way strategy could prevent us "from becoming exclusively preoccupied either with the conflict or with the common interest."[23]

Schelling's theories would be put to the ultimate test during the war in Vietnam, when the air campaigns of Presidents Johnson and Nixon against North Vietnam were specifically designed to persuade Hanoi and its allies in the South to negotiate an end to the war. Events on the ground were seen to count for less in this process of bargaining. Had the new strategists been so inclined they would have seen that America's military experience had long anticipated their theories and in many ways invalidated them. That some aspects of their concepts had come to life in the War of 1812 would have seemed scarcely creditable. In what was America's first and only "cabinet war," as Wayne Lee has observed, "every military move was accompanied by a diplomatic initiative" meant to secure by negotiation each side's territorial ambitions. Far from being irrelevant to the outcome of the war, gains and losses in battle served as the engine that moved both sides toward the peace table at Ghent.[24] But the new strategists need not have consulted their history books to find instances in which processes of negotiation and battle were so interdependent. All they needed to do was look over their shoulders to the Korean War.

The war for the dominance of the Korean peninsula is in many respects the quintessential modern limited war, and nowhere more so than in its results. North Korea invaded South Korea in 1950 with the objective of unifying the peninsula under the Communist banner. For the Koreans themselves the war was much like our own Civil War, in which the adversaries fought to define their people's future. But the war was not Korea's alone, and there is reason to doubt that the fighting would have ended the way it did if it had been. Instead Korea was the first major armed conflict of the Cold War and a test of the long-term strategies of the Western alliance and the Communists. China and the Soviet Union stood behind North Korea; the United States intervened at the head of a hastily formed United Nations Command, whose original mission was to defend South Korean territory and sovereignty. The determining question for both coalitions was to what degree the Korean conflict would advance their strategic purposes. Thus from the outset military actions were strictly subordinated to grander strategy. Even when successes on the ground met traditional definitions of victory, the larger strategic context commanded the war's progress toward mutual accommodation, however distasteful.

To American military leaders such as the UN commander Douglas MacArthur, such an outlook flew in the face of his professional upbringing and long personal experience, which had convinced him that only success in battle made strategy possible. He disagreed with his civilian and military superiors on the most fundamental premise of American strategy: that beyond the security of the United States itself the defense of Europe against Soviet aggression was paramount. The way President Truman and his national security advisors saw strategy meant that the war MacArthur commanded was not the main effort at all, but an exercise in economy of force. This crisis in strategic outlook deepened after MacArthur's counteroffensive in the fall of 1950 erased the gains made by the North Korean People's Army the preceding summer and drove it north of the 38th Parallel. Although China threatened to intervene in the war, MacArthur, citing his victories at Inchon and advances into North Korea, successfully lobbied for an escalation of the UN's war aims to reunify the peninsula by completely defeating the Communist North. When the Chinese made good on their threat, President Truman reversed the objective of the war, aiming once again for the status quo ante bellum. This, MacArthur would not accept, and his public defiance of political direction by insisting that East Asia was the true cockpit in which the struggle with Communism would be decided led to his relief of command in the spring of 1951. MacArthur could not imagine a form of warfare in which his battlefield successes counted for less than his career of soldiering had taught him.

By the summer of 1951 the main line of resistance stabilized along the 38th Parallel after a last UN offensive, and from that point forward in the conflict the sounds of battle along a static front served as a background to diplomatic wrangling over the negotiating table at Panmunjom. By then the North Koreans and their Chinese allies were incapable of launching another offensive, and the UN Command, more capable than ever, was unwilling to.

Although the ground war continued during these negotiations, the Joint Chiefs of Staff came to believe that America's air supremacy over the peninsula offered a channel through which the North could be persuaded to terminate the war. After months of futile peace talks and stalemate on the ground, senior commanders in the Far East Air Force mounted an air campaign in the spring of 1952 against targets specifically selected to influence the talks at Panmunjom. Having spent its energies in the first phase of the war on interdicting enemy supply lines, the air force turned to a highly orchestrated campaign of destruction against hydroelectric dams close to the Chinese border. But from the outset of the campaign the air force was hard-pressed to identify targets sufficiently critical to advance the peace talks. It became clear that if their sorties were sending a message, it was not at all clear who would receive it and, still less, whether the receiver would respond as the sender wished. This "signal-sending approach" was to be repeated during the war in Vietnam with similar results. Signals sent but not received were, if anything, worse than no signals at all.[25]

More than half a century after the Korean War began, peace still has not been concluded. Although the peace negotiations that began in 1951 produced an armistice two years later, the purposes of the two sides had converged only in a barely tolerable mutual dissatisfaction, separated by a demilitarized zone that is anything but. The age of modern limited war had begun, and with it a new definition of victory and a new role for the battles that once gave it meaning. Battles could no longer be thought of as important in and of themselves, capable of producing results without reference to the purposes that set them in motion; the relationship between strategy and battle seemingly had become more tenuous.

As the United States began its long strategic retreat in the aftermath of its war in Vietnam, the historian Russell Weigley concluded his history of American strategy in a way that reflected the nation's disappointments and frustrations with the war. "The history of usable combat," he wrote, "may at last be reaching its end."[26]

For the first time in its history the United States had lost a war, failing to attain any of the objectives for which it fought. The miscalculations that led the United States into the war persisted throughout the war and poisoned any chance for a favorable conclusion. If the results of America's earlier wars did not exactly correspond to their original aims, the results were sufficiently consoling; if not examined too closely, some measure of victory could always be claimed. But several of these earlier wars had also left rough edges that could not be smoothed over by the passage of time. In every case they revealed the limits of what war could accomplish.

In the hard mathematics of war, military action had no greater purpose than to drive war toward a final campaign that would crown the nation's efforts with victory, its interests at war's end satisfied in every particular. Yet on closer inspection the course of the major conflicts and the effects they produced are not so simply measured. War's dynamic nature does not follow such a logical course, no matter how determined our efforts to make it do so.

Traditions of military thought tell us that the final campaign is the most decisive of all; its proximity to the cessation of hostilities naturally leads to the assumption that it has the most to do with the character and conditions of the peace that follows—that is, that the final campaign is also the terminal campaign. In real war, however, the two are not synonymous.

The difference between a decisive campaign and a terminal campaign lies in the effects they produce. A decisive campaign may be won at any point of a conflict, and by either side, regardless of whether that side was losing or winning when it was fought. Any side can fight a decisive campaign or even a succession of them and still be defeated. The true measure of its decisiveness lies in the degree to which it drives the war in a different course than it would have taken had it not been fought. Although historians still wage battles over how decisive the Gettysburg campaign was, there is no question that the rest of the war was different than it would have been without it. Furthermore, however positive the outcome of a decisive campaign, the results are not necessarily permanent. They do not suspend the action of war. They do not fix the future on an unalterable course. However decisive Gettysburg may seem in retrospect, the war still continued for nearly two years. The results of the Gettysburg campaign were not sufficient to convince hundreds of thousands of soldiers and the governments that commanded them to stop fighting.

By contrast a terminal campaign may exercise an influence over the outcome of a war *neither side intends,* nor does it derive from military action alone. A terminal campaign is strategically important; it plays a role in educating both sides about how much—or how little—their efforts can accomplish. Chronologically, North Vietnam's offensive of 1975 was the last campaign of the Vietnam War. Seen from the present, however, North Vietnam's Tet Offensive some seven years earlier exercised the greatest influence over how the war would end. Although North Vietnam and their National Liberation Front confederates in the South suffered heavy losses, Tet's strategic effect was profound, convincing President Johnson that he should not stand for reelection, leading to the replacement of his principal field commander, General Westmoreland, and a sea change in public attitudes toward the war at home and around the world.

From Tet onward the United States was on the strategic defensive, and not in Vietnam alone. Although in 1968 the nation was more deeply and powerfully engaged in Vietnam than ever, the war had eroded America's strategic will. Politically and socially in disarray, the readiness of its armed forces in Europe and Korea reduced to a state of dysfunction, America's response to an aggressive turn in Soviet policy in Eastern Europe was muted. The North Koreans' seizure of the USS *Pueblo* that year caught the United States unprepared to respond, when in earlier days it might have reacted far more aggressively.

The immediate, tactical results of the Tet Offensive certainly gave

North Vietnam's leaders little cause for optimism, while they encouraged American commanders in the field. But operational and tactical successes, then or later, were not enough to forestall the fundamental change in the strategic environment that Tet had achieved, and it was on that wider stage that the interests of the several sides in that war intersected at the peace table in Paris. At Paris and in its aftermath the United States would learn that if the end of a war is badly handled the consequences can be every bit as damaging as losing the war itself.[27]

If military action still plays a crucial role in moving a war toward its termination, of what value is it to redefine the terms of victory that have sustained armies for centuries? The answer is that modern war, no less than any other, is a creature of its unique place and time. The terms by which war was understood in the past have been overturned by the view that modern war must be more precisely attuned to the limited objectives for which it is being fought—limited objectives that must be precisely defined as well.

The demands made on those who direct war today are therefore substantially different from those of the past. The use of military power in pursuit of national objectives in the age of modern war is more a question of its efficient employment than use of its full potential. That today the United States accepts these limitations at risk to its interest means that its enemies benefit from advantages they might not otherwise enjoy, including the deliberate protraction of conflict as well as the expansion of the scope of war well beyond its immediate operational zones to regions that seem to have no direct involvement in the war. Under these circumstances the immense military power of the United States is no guarantee that it can seize and sustain the strategic and operational initiative, and steering a war toward a desirable end is no small task even in the most favorable circumstances. The policymaker who decides for war must *at the same time* understand that there *will* be mutually acceptable terms in the end, that these terms may bear little resemblance to those originally envisioned, and that in any case no single nation or party to the conflict will be the sole arbiter of the peace. Thus every war should be designed so that the strategic effect it produces contributes to the nature of the peace that will inevitably follow, and *on no other basis*.

Gen. George C. Marshall once wrote that the art of war has no traffic with rules. No book of rules on the art of ending war is likely to grace the bookshelves of the Oval Office or the doctrinal libraries of the Pentagon. The propositions advanced in this essay derive from America's own military experience. Although these propositions may appear to be self-evident, it is nevertheless true that every one of America's major conflicts has been fought in ignorance—or defiance—of one or more of them. Seen together they bid us to understand that the course by which a war ends, if embarked on without care, can be as dangerous to a nation's vital interests as the war itself, regardless of the war's military results. It is for that reason that the essays in this volume are now offered as aids to the judgment of the policymaker and the soldier as they face the test of ending America's wars in the future.

IRA D. GRUBER

Yorktown: The Final Campaign of the War for American Independence

In early August 1781 the principal armies of the United States were camped more than 600 miles apart. There were 2,000 men under Gen. George Washington at Dobbs Ferry on the east bank of the Hudson River about 20 miles north of New York City; slightly fewer than 2,000, under Gen. Nathanael Greene, were in the High Hills of Santee, about 75 miles northwest of Charleston, South Carolina. These Lilliputian armies were watching the main British garrisons in North America, at New York City and Charleston, and awaiting orders for the remainder of the campaign. They were not the only forces of the United States fighting for their independence from Great Britain that summer; there were state and local troops in Virginia and the Carolinas opposing 7,000 British troops fortifying posts within Chesapeake Bay and smaller British detachments garrisoning Savannah, Georgia, and Wilmington, North Carolina. As in every year since 1778, the Americans had the support of French allies: 4,000 troops who were with Washington's army along the Hudson, eight ships of the line and a siege train at Rhode Island, and twenty-eight ships of the line with another 3,000 troops that were en route from the West Indies to the Chesapeake. It remained to be seen whether Washington, Greene, and the French commanders could make better use of their forces in 1781 than in the past, whether they could make the campaign of 1781 decisive in a war that had dragged on for more than six years and that had escalated from a colonial rebellion into a world war. How had that war begun and spread? What did the allies propose to do with the remainder of the campaign of 1781? And how would that campaign affect the outcome of the war?

The War for American Independence began when British soldiers exchanged fire with Massachusetts militia on Lexington Common in April 1775. The fighting that morning was the result of long-festering differences between American colonists and British imperial officials. In nearly a century and a half of living in North America the colonists had learned to govern themselves, evade imperial restrictions, and protect their rights and liberties. Relations between the colonists and the British imperial government had deteriorated sharply after the British victory in the French and Indian War. In 1763 the British had a larger North American empire to pacify, govern, and defend, an empire that now included former French and Spanish colonists as well as some very dissatisfied Native peoples on its frontiers. To keep the colonists from encroaching on Native lands and to damp the Native uprising that came at war's end, the British decided to close the frontiers to further European settlement and increase the strength of British regular forces in the colonies. They also decided to tax the colonists to defray some of the costs of empire. However reasonable these measures might have seemed to the king and Parliament of Great Britain, they were alarming to colonists who had borne more than three-fifths of the cost of the French and Indian War and who saw efforts to control and tax them as conspiracies against their liberties. In 1765, when Parliament imposed a Stamp Tax on them, the colonists reacted with constitutional objections, mob violence, and economic sanctions. Parliament repealed the Stamp Tax but asserted its right to make laws to bind the colonies in all cases whatsoever. For a brief period this compromise allowed both the colonists and the British to ignore the fact that they fundamentally disagreed about who held ultimate power in the empire.

These differences surfaced once again when the British imposed the Townshend Duties of 1767, a new set of duties on trade with the colonies, and gradually moved their army from frontier posts to colonial ports, particularly to Boston in the fall of 1768. Because some colonists had acknowledged Parliament's right to regulate trade, the British decided to raise revenue by imposing duties on goods imported into the colonies. The colonists objected much as before, and as before, economic sanctions brought repeal—in this case, of all the duties save that on tea. But British troops remained in Boston, where in 1770 they fought with and killed colonists. That "massacre" was all too vividly remembered when in 1773 the British offered tea, duty paid, at a price lower than that for smuggled tea—tempting the colonists to give up their constitutional objections to Parliamentary taxation for inexpensive tea. The people of Boston chose to destroy the tea instead. Parliament responded with acts designed to uphold its sovereign power and punish the people of Boston. Other colonists made common cause with Boston, convening a Continental Congress that denied Parliament's right to tax the colonists or interfere in their domestic affairs, imposed further economic sanctions, and resolved to fight should the British use troops to support the authority of the king and Parliament. The king and his ministers, deeply offended by the rebellious behavior of the colonists, ordered the commander of British forces at Boston to act in support of the imperial government. He did, sending troops to destroy military stores at Concord and precipitating the fighting at Lexington that started the War for American Independence.

In deciding subsequently what they were fighting for—in establishing war aims—both sides were to be influenced as much by the disputes that had disrupted the empire since 1763 as by the fighting after 1775. The British began the war determined to sustain the sovereignty of Parliament throughout the empire and to end the rebellion in North America. Some ministers and members of Parliament—and some senior officers of the army and navy as well—thought reconciliation should be part of any restoration of royal government. But clear majorities of the ministry and Parliament insisted that the colonists should submit to Britain before any grievances were discussed. For more than two and a half years and particularly after the colonies declared themselves to be the independent United States in 1776, the British government relied on fleets and armies to destroy rebel forces, disperse revolutionary congresses and committees, restore royal officials, and break the spirit of rebellion. The British commanders in chief, who also served as peace commissioners, could offer pardon to anyone who would take an oath of allegiance; they could not begin negotiations until the colonies had surrendered. Not until the British lost an army at Saratoga, New York, in the autumn of 1777 did they change their war aims. Thereafter they fought to retain the colonies and to combat the European states that had entered the war as allies of the United States. The British sent out a new peace commission in 1778 empowered to grant the colonies almost anything except independence: freedom from parliamentary taxation for revenue, withdrawal of the British Army, restoration of trade, and security in their colonial charters.

Although there was little prospect that the United States would accept such terms after France recognized their independence and entered the war, the British fought on for another four years in a desperate effort to keep their American colonies and hold off France, Spain, and the Netherlands in a world war.

American war aims also reflected events before and after 1775. When fighting first began, representatives of the colonies sought mainly redress of grievances, specifically freedom from parliamentary taxation and control of their domestic affairs. For more than a year they relied on militia and short-term volunteers organized into a Continental Army under George Washington to resist the British at Boston and New York and sustain their petitions to the crown. But when their petitions were rejected, when it became clear that Britain would rely on force to support the supremacy of the king and Parliament throughout the empire, the colonies decided they could no longer be secure in their liberties within the empire. In 1776 they declared their independence and began defining fresh war aims. Above all the new United States wanted independence, republican governments, and a national domain under a loose central government that would make war and conduct foreign affairs. So averse were Americans to a strong central government, taxes, and a standing army—to what they saw as instruments of British oppression—that they could scarcely bring themselves to do what was necessary to win their independence. Only when they saw that militia and short-term volunteers could not hold their own against the British at New York did they agree to create an army of men serving for at least three years and under strict discipline. But the states refused to give the central government the power to tax, and the United States had to fund the war with loans from Europe and contributions from the states. The states, ever reluctant to burden their citizens with taxes and conscription, only fitfully provided money, men, and supplies for the Continental Army; and soldiers, suffering from repeated neglect, deserted or mutinied, especially after France entered the war and Americans, anticipating victory, became preoccupied with local and private affairs. Even when in 1780 British forces won victories in the South, the states continued to neglect the army and to deny the central government greater powers to wage war.

With such complicated and shifting war aims both sides had trouble developing strategies that promised victory in the War for American Independence. The British had marched to Lexington in 1775 hoping that a show of force would restore royal government. That and subsequent efforts to intimidate the colonists of New England having failed, the British decided to shift their army to New York, add substantial reinforcements, and adopt a strategy to crush the rebellion in New England. The ministry and the new commander in chief, Gen. William Howe, agreed both to seek a decisive battle with rebel forces holding New York City and, in conjunction with another British army advancing from Canada via Lake Champlain, to isolate and conquer New England. Yet before General Howe could open the campaign, his brother, Admiral Lord Howe, arrived with a peace commission and clear preference for a negotiated settlement. Together the Howes combined force and persuasion throughout the campaign of 1776, recovering Long Island, New York City, and much of New Jersey before rebel forces won small, dramatic victories at Trenton and Princeton—victories that spoiled the Howes' hopes for peace and blighted the ensuing campaign. In 1777 General Howe sought alternatively to draw the Continental Army into a decisive battle and to recover territory in Pennsylvania as a haven for Loyalists. So preoccupied was Howe with Pennsylvania that he not only failed to cooperate with a British army from Canada in conquering New England but left that army, unsupported, to surrender at Saratoga in October 1777. The surrender of the Canadian army brought France into the war and effected a complete change in British strategy. With fewer troops and a wider war to wage, the British decided to rely on the Royal Navy and Loyalists to prosecute the American War. The navy would blockade and raid the Atlantic seaboard from New England to the Chesapeake, while detachments from New York would recover the South, restoring Loyalists to power gradually from Georgia to the Carolinas to Virginia. By the late summer of 1780 this new strategy seemed to be succeeding better than anyone might have expected: the British had captured Savannah and Charleston, established posts in the interior of Georgia and South Carolina, enlisted Loyalists, and destroyed the principal Continental forces in the South. But would the new strategy continue to flourish? Would the British have the Loyalists' support as well as the patience to build upon their success in the lower South?

That would depend in part on the forces that opposed them, who had had their own troubles developing strategies to suit their war aims. In 1775 the colonists had fought almost reflexively to sustain their grievances, hoping that an army of militia and volunteers would be able to defeat the British at Boston and persuade the ministry to reverse its imperial policies. That summer, Congress took control of colonial forces at

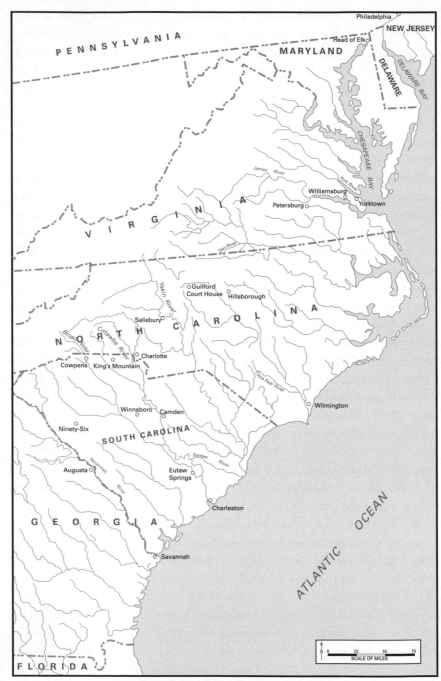

THE SOUTH IN THE WAR FOR
AMERICAN INDEPENDENCE

Boston—now the Continental Army—and appointed George Washington commander in chief. Washington, a steadfast republican and experienced soldier, gradually shaped his strategies to suit the army, Congress, and the American people. He knew that he was expected to defend the territory and republican governments of the states and, beginning in July 1776, the independence of the United States. He also knew that many members of Congress wanted him to make the war short and decisive, to forestall the development of an oppressive central government and standing army and the need for burdensome taxes. Yet to achieve those aims he would have to risk the destruction of the army on which the revolution depended, an army of inexperienced men who could not do all that Congress expected. After forcing the British from Boston he shifted his army to New York City, expecting the British, when reinforced, to try to capture the city and gain control of the Hudson River. He subsequently fought mainly on the defensive in dangerous and unsuccessful efforts to hold Long Island and Manhattan during the summer and fall of 1776. By December he had withdrawn to Pennsylvania, his army disintegrating and the British occupying New Jersey. In desperation he struck back, winning small victories at Trenton and Princeton that saved his army, and evicted the British from all except eastern New Jersey. During the following year he fought mainly in defense of Philadelphia, resisting members of Congress who prodded him to attack the enemy and significantly delaying the British capture of the city. His stubborn defense of the Delaware River contributed indirectly to the success of another American army that trapped British forces advancing south from Canada at Saratoga, New York, in October 1777.

The surrender of a British army at Saratoga, together with improvements in the Continental Army and France's entry into the war, encouraged Washington to consider changes in his strategy. By the spring of 1778 the Continental Army had, for the first time, the benefits of long enlistments, firm discipline, and systematic winter training. And when in June the British evacuated Philadelphia and started overland for New York, Washington followed closely enough to precipitate battle and fight the British to a draw at Monmouth Court House. Later that summer he urged a French squadron to cooperate in attacking the British garrison at Newport, Rhode Island. But when that attack miscarried he was unable to undertake any significant offensive operations for nearly three years. The French Alliance had the paradoxical effect of diminishing American support for the war. Congress, lacking the power to tax, had to rely on loans from Europe and contributions from the states to pay, equip, and supply the Continental Army. When the states failed to meet their quotas, when they kept the army from impressing food and fodder, and when they refused to give Congress an impost and Washington authority to coerce defaulting states, the soldiers deserted or mutinied (at least four times in 1780 and 1781). With ever declining numbers of Continentals, Washington had to rely on militia, partisans, and state troops to supplement his regulars—troops who lacked the discipline and training for offensive operations. Except for an occasional raid he remained on the defensive throughout 1779 and 1780, even when French forces were present; indeed the French, seeing the startling weakness of the Continental Army, declined to cooperate until 1781, when they assembled a fleet that could dominate North American waters.

While Washington could do little more than think of attacking the British at New York City, Gen. Nathanael Greene succeeded in liberating large portions of the southern states. Greene was appointed to command in the South in the autumn of 1780, after the British had captured Charleston, destroyed a Continental Army at Camden, and established outposts throughout the backcountry of Georgia and South Carolina. His forces were fewer and no better supplied than Washington's, a mixture of Continentals and militia, supported by independent partisans. But unlike Washington, Greene had an enemy that was scattered in detachments and garrisons over hundreds of miles of sparsely populated countryside, and he had the imagination to draw that enemy into a series of destructive battles that in little more than seven months (January to July 1781) restored Americans to power in all of Georgia and the Carolinas except for three ports: Savannah, Charleston, and Wilmington. By early August 1781 Greene was able to rely on his cavalry and partisans to contain the British in their ports while he rested his army outside Charleston. Expecting the arrival of a powerful French fleet from the West Indies and knowing that his forces controlled the interior of South Carolina and Georgia, Greene urged patriot leaders to reestablish the republican governments of those states. He anticipated that the French would join in capturing New York City, Lord Cornwallis's forces in the Chesapeake, or Charleston, forcing the British to abandon the American War and accept a diplomatic settlement. In any case Greene wanted to be sure the British would have little claim to territories within the United States and that American diplomats would not be tempted to sacrifice some states to secure the independence of others.

Although Greene had liberated the interior of South Carolina and Georgia, and although a French fleet was expected that summer, the allies were slow to develop a plan of campaign for 1781. Washington had long preferred an attack on New York City; his French counterpart, the Comte de Rochambeau, advocated capturing Lord Cornwallis's army of about 7,000 men in the Chesapeake. In late July, Washington began to change his mind. He had inspected the formidable defenses of Manhattan and received a letter from Nathanael Greene arguing that a French fleet could be used most effectively in the Chesapeake, that it would be easier to trap Cornwallis in Virginia than to capture New York City or, for that matter, Charleston. Washington remained undecided until August 14, when he learned that the Comte de Grasse, who commanded the French West Indies fleet, was bound for the Chesapeake for a limited stay. Washington agreed at once to take his and Rochambeau's troops from New York to Virginia. He could not yet decide whether the allies should campaign in Virginia or in South Carolina. He had no doubt that the French squadron at Rhode Island, some eight ships of the line under the Comte de Barras, should join de Grasse in the Chesapeake to ensure that the French fleet would be superior to any that the British might assemble. He ordered the Marquis de Lafayette, who was commanding American forces in Virginia, to keep Cornwallis from escaping overland to the Carolinas. On August 20–21 Washington's army crossed to the west bank of the Hudson at Kings Ferry and began its march south, Rochambeau's army following close behind.

It would take the allies six weeks to move their forces the 400 miles from Kings Ferry on the Hudson to Yorktown, Virginia. When they set out they could not be sure that they would be able to trap Cornwallis in his fortified base on the York River: that de Grasse would be able to join forces with Barras to seal the Chesapeake against the British fleet assembling at New York or that Cornwallis would remain on the York. They could hope to move along rapidly, overland through New York and New Jersey and then mainly by water on the Delaware from Trenton to Christiana and, after a short portage, on the Chesapeake from Head of Elk to Williamsburg. Washington planned the marches and embarkations carefully, asking Congress and the states to provide the boats and wagons as well as the provisions that the armies would need on the way; appealing to de Grasse for a naval escort and transports for the voyage down Chesapeake Bay; and ordering Lafayette to prepare the horses and wagons to shift the armies from Williamsburg to Yorktown. But there were not boats enough to carry the army down the Delaware, forcing some units to march, and when the allies reached the Head of Elk they had to delay their embarkation until they were sure that the French fleet had control of the Bay. De Grasse had reached the Chesapeake on August 30, put to sea to engage a British fleet that arrived on September 5, and, after scattering the British and joining the French squadron from Rhode Island, returned to the Chesapeake by September 15. By then, Washington had reached Williamsburg and promptly arranged to have transports sent to bring his and Rochambeau's armies from Head of Elk to the James River. Those armies arrived between September 22 and 27, disembarked, and marched from Williamsburg to Yorktown on September 28. The allies had managed, with some cooperation from the enemy as well as their own excellent timing and good luck, to trap a British army.

The ensuing siege was brief, not just because the allies had overwhelming force and skilled engineers but especially because Cornwallis's defenses were unusually shallow. His base sat astride the York River, including Yorktown on the south bank and Gloucester Point on the north. Both positions were fortified, but even the main works on the south bank were built very close to the river, at most 700 yards from the water and little more than a mile long. Soon after the allied armies appeared, Cornwallis gave up his outlying works and withdrew into the main line of fortifications and redoubts about the town. The allies occupied the abandoned outworks on September 30 and began digging their way toward the main lines on October 6. By October 10 they had completed a first trench parallel to the southeast end of the British line and constructed six batteries facing the town. Those batteries made portions of the enemy lines untenable and destroyed or drove their ships across the river to Gloucester. Four days later the allies, having opened a second parallel trench only 300 yards from the main British line and captured two redoubts on their flank, were able to place batteries that enfiladed nearly the whole of Cornwallis's defenses and commanded his communications across the river. Washington remained anxious that Cornwallis would escape up the York. But Cornwallis, having tried unsuccessfully to attack the allied lines and to flee his own, showed little tolerance for being under sustained bombardment. On October 17 he offered to surrender. Washington, remembering the terms that the British had granted the garrison at Charleston in 1780, made few concessions. He required the British to become prisoners of war in the United States and give up their ships, artillery, arms, stores, horses, and plunder (including slaves). The formal surrender took place on October 19. The allies, well aware of what they had accomplished, lost no time in sending the news directly to Europe. Washington made clear to American diplomats not just that he had captured an army of 7,000 men and over 200 cannon but also that he and Nathanael Greene had driven the British from all of the southern states except for enclaves about Wilmington, Charleston, and Savannah and that on September 8 Greene had defeated the most recent attempt by the British to establish themselves at Eutaw Springs outside of Charleston.

Washington could not be sure what effect Cornwallis's surrender would have in Europe. He could hope that it might lead to a diplomatic settlement favorable to the United States. But he knew that he could best advance American interests by prosecuting the war, exploiting the victories that the allies had won in 1781, and preparing for the campaign of 1782. Even before sending news of Cornwallis's surrender to France he was pressing de Grasse to join in attacking Charleston or, at least, to assist the Americans in recovering Wilmington. De Grasse declining, Washington sent 2,000 men overland to capture Wilmington and become a part of Greene's army in South Carolina. Greene was soon able to report that the British had evacuated Wilmington and that he was not only pushing ever closer to Charleston but also conciliating the Loyalists. Washington devoted the remainder of the fall and the following winter to preparations for 1782. He urged de Grasse to return to the Chesapeake in May for an attack on either New York City or Charleston. He asked Lafayette, who was en route to France for the winter, to remind his government that French ships and money could win the war in one more campaign. Above all he pushed Congress and the states to do their parts. Congress should send prominent officers to New England to ask for men, money, and supplies. The states should meet the quotas that Congress had set for recruits and money—altogether some $8 million for 1782. When spring came Washington was very disappointed that he did not have the forces he needed for an offensive and that de Grasse, having been defeated in the West Indies, would not be returning to North America that summer. There was better news from the South: the British had begun redeploying their troops from Charleston to the West Indies in April, would give up Savannah in July, and would be completely out of the South by the end of the year. In August, Washington learned that Britain was prepared to grant America independence.

Even so, American diplomats would have considerable trouble turning Cornwallis's surrender into a peace that realized American war aims:

independence, generous boundaries, republican governments, and a loose confederation of the states. In 1779 Congress had defined hopes for peace around independence and a national domain that stretched from the Atlantic to the Mississippi and from Florida to the St. Lawrence and the Great Lakes. Congress had also appointed able men to represent the interests of the United States in Europe and instructed them to be guided by the French Alliance, their French and Spanish allies, and their own judgment. But the allies were not reliable guides; they regularly put their own interests before those of the United States. The Spanish, averse to supporting a colonial rebellion, were unwilling to recognize the United States, lend them money, support their claims to independence, or protect them from partition. Even the French sought to control American diplomats and, as the war became increasingly expensive, to constrict their claims to independence and land. Other European states, particularly Austria and Russia, who offered to mediate the differences between the belligerents, were contemptuous of the United States and their republican pretensions. Cornwallis's surrender did increase the standing of American diplomats, but they still served under great disadvantages. The men representing the United States—Benjamin Franklin in France, John Jay in Spain, and John Adams in the Netherlands—were never able to correspond quickly or safely with Congress; they remained in the awkward position of trying to act in the best interests of the United States while soliciting loans from and listening to the advice of their allies. Until peace negotiations were well under way they were rarely able to meet or work together.

Under these circumstances it would take Franklin, Jay, and Adams more than six months after receiving news of Cornwallis's surrender in November 1781 to launch meaningful negotiations with Britain—to discover who represented the British government and what might be essential for peace. In March 1782, after Parliament voted to abandon the American War, the king accepted a new ministry and the prospect of granting independence to the rebellious colonies. But not until late June did the ministry decide who should conduct negotiations with the United States, whether the Earl of Shelburne, at the colonial office, or Charles James Fox, the foreign secretary. Both Shelburne and Fox sent representatives to Paris to begin talks with Benjamin Franklin. Franklin came to prefer Shelburne's agent, Richard Oswald, and the ministry eventually chose Oswald to conduct the negotiations. By early July Shelburne was leading the government and, after Fox resigned, telling Parliament that he did not like giving the colonies independence and would do so only from necessity. By then, Franklin and Oswald had come to some understanding of the issues that would have to be solved before any peace could be made. To divide the allies, Oswald sought separate negotiations and a separate peace with the United States. Franklin, with the approval of France, agreed to separate negotiations but not a separate peace; any Anglo-American treaty would have to be linked to treaties between both Britain and France and Britain and Spain. Although the ministry authorized granting the colonies their independence before negotiating peace, Shelburne instructed Oswald to make independence the price of peace, to withhold independence until the colonists had agreed to a treaty that allowed Britain to retain all of her 1763 empire except for a United States limited to the Atlantic seaboard and provided reparations for Loyalists whose lands had been confiscated. Franklin replied that the United States required much more: independence before negotiations, a national domain that went well beyond the seaboard, and reparations for patriots as well as Loyalists.

The representatives and the issues having been identified, it would take the United States and Britain another five months to settle on the terms of peace. During that time the American commissioners, discovering that France and Spain were working against them, had the independence to ignore their instructions and to work apart from their allies in negotiating a most favorable peace. Once they learned that France and Spain would sacrifice their interests on the fundamental questions of independence and land, the Americans felt fully justified in negotiating bilaterally with the British. The British, sensing the divisions among the allies, moved to reach an agreement with the Americans before France or Spain could intervene. Together Franklin, Jay, and Adams worked with Oswald and Shelburne through three draft treaties to find a peace that was acceptable to both countries. Jay suggested a solution to the difficult questions of when and how to grant American independence. If Britain would explicitly empower Oswald to negotiate with the United States—thereby recognizing the new nation—the Americans would be satisfied with the granting of independence as the first article in a treaty of peace. The Americans had less trouble getting the national domain that they wanted because Shelburne wished to divide the allies and seemed to care more about trade, debts, and reparations than land and because Jay proposed opening the Mississippi to both British and American people. The final draft of the treaty gave the United States nearly all the land Congress had sought and far more than Spain or France intended: from the Atlantic in the east to the Mississippi in the west and from the Georgia frontier in the south to the St. Lawrence watershed, Great Lakes, and headwaters of the Mississippi in the north. The American commissioners did make concessions on some issues. They agreed to support the payment of all debts owed to British merchants, to recommend that the states make reparations to Loyalists whose lands had been confiscated, and to accept fewer North Atlantic fishing rights than they had at first claimed. Although the Anglo-American treaty was not to go into effect until Britain made peace with France, the Americans did not tell the French what they had done until they were ready to sign the preliminary peace treaty on November 29. The French were shocked but agreed to support the treaty and give the United States an additional loan, ostensibly to keep the British from thinking they had divided the allies. The Anglo-American treaty went into effect with the signing of preliminary treaties between Britain and France and Britain and Spain on January 20, 1783.

With the Peace of Paris the United States realized its most important war aims: recognition of its independence, its government, and its national domain. Beginning in 1776 the United States had fought to gain its independence from Great Britain and establish itself as a separate nation. Although France had made a treaty of commerce and an alliance with representatives of the United States in 1778, many European states refused to receive American diplomats or recognize their government until Great Britain formally acknowledged the independence of the colonies. The Peace of Paris—specifically, the Anglo-American treaty of November 1782—gave the most fundamental and formal diplomatic recognition to the United States, to a loose confederation of republican states that had remarkably little political or military power even after gaining its independence. Perhaps just as important, the Peace of Paris gave the United States claim to a vast national domain stretching from the Atlantic to the Mississippi and from Florida to Canada. The Peace made no mention of the Native peoples living within the new nation and their traditional use of the land, and it left many boundaries to be defined. Yet by ending hostilities and providing for the withdrawal of British forces and the restoration of all conquests, the Peace gave the new United States title to an abundant land. It also gave Americans the expectation of access to the seas around that land, specifically to the navigation of the Mississippi and the fisheries off Newfoundland and Nova Scotia as well as the unsettled beaches of Labrador and Nova Scotia that were used for drying fish.

There were two provisions in the Anglo-American treaty and one in the Anglo-Spanish treaty that threatened the territories of the United States. According to the Anglo-American treaty, American citizens were required to pay their British creditors and Congress was to recommend that the states restore the rights and property of the Loyalists. Should Americans fail to meet either of these requirements, Britain would have cause for refusing to honor its commitments; it could then refuse to withdraw all of its forces from the United States. Beyond that, after agreeing to guarantee Americans free navigation of the Mississippi, Britain had ceded Florida to Spain. Now Spain controlled the entire Gulf Coast and could close the Mississippi to citizens of the United States. These were potential problems, but the Peace of Paris had gone far toward satisfying America's principal war aims.

There were other war aims, and as fighting wound down, Americans made sure that they would not sacrifice those aims in a rush toward peace. Disbanding the Continental Army created serious problems for the weak central government of the United States. The states had refused to give Congress the power to tax, and Congress remained dependent for revenue on contributions from the states and loans from abroad. Without adequate revenues Congress was unable to pay the army, and the army, unpaid, was so near mutiny that Washington chose to remain with his troops through the winter of 1782–83 at Newburgh, New York. In December 1782 senior officers of the army went to Congress asking for pay for the officers and men. Members of Congress who wished to strengthen the national government encouraged the officers to put more pressure on Congress, to say that they would not go home until paid. In March, when some Continental officers sought to say as much, Washington reminded them of their duty, promised to plead their case, and persuaded the officers to express their faith in Congress and ask for less than the half pay for life, which they thought their due. Congress, pleased with what Washington and the officers had done, responded by voting to commute the officers' half pay for life, to full pay for five years and to ask the states to provide the national government with the power to tax foreign imports. The officers were satisfied, and although the states eventually refused to give Congress the power to tax, Congress managed to pay the officers and neglect the rank and file, who went home disgruntled in the fall of 1783. In disbanding the army (officially in the summer of 1784) Americans had achieved additional war aims. They had kept the central government weak and dependent on the states, sustained republican governments, restricted taxation to representatives of the people within the states, and freed Americans from a standing army.

Congress went beyond disbanding the Continental Army. It also refused to create another national army to defend the United States once the war was over. Washington and many of his senior officers had little confidence in state militia. He had always found the militia, except in very special circumstances, to be expensive, wasteful, and ineffective; he repeatedly urged Congress and the states to recruit men for periods of service that were long enough to turn civilians into reliable soldiers. The American people did not share Washington's opinion of militia; some went so far as to say that the militia had won the War of Independence and that the Continental Army had been expensive and dangerous, a threat to the liberties of the people. No wonder that in 1783, when Washington recommended that the United States create a national army, he got little support in Congress. Washington had in mind an expansible army of 2,600 men to defend frontiers against Native peoples and neighboring European colonists, prepare for war, establish magazines and arsenals, and train state militias to a national standard. Congress, remembering that standing armies were expensive and potentially oppressive and that the British Army had killed Bostonians before it marched to Lexington and Concord in 1775, rejected Washington's proposal. The United States would rely in the future, as it had in the past, on the militia for defense and on volunteers and draftees from the militia for offensive operations.

Congress soon learned how vulnerable the United States was as an independent nation with a weak central government, heavy debts, and inadequate revenues and armed forces. The United States made commercial treaties with France, the Netherlands, Sweden, and Prussia, but those treaties did little to free Americans from the domination of British merchants; nearly half of postwar American exports and nearly all imports continued to flow to and from Britain. When Britain issued Orders in Council discriminating against Americans trading with the British West Indies and, subsequently, with Canada, Great Britain, and Ireland, Congress was too weak to provide relief for the merchants, farmers, fishermen, and shipbuilders suffering from the restrictions. Congress was just as ineffectual when Barbary privateers seized American merchantmen in the Mediterranean, when Spain closed the mouth of the Mississippi River to American shipping, and when Britain refused to give up its posts north of the Ohio River until Americans paid debts owed to British merchants and compensated Loyalists for property confiscated during the war. The United States could not even enforce its national and state laws. When Americans migrated west, squatting on unoccupied lands and provoking conflict with Native peoples, Congress could do no more than call upon Connecticut, New York, New Jersey, and Pennsylvania to provide 700 militia for a year's service. This regiment, the beginnings of a national peacetime army, was poorly equipped, poorly supported, and undisciplined—a force that was wholly inadequate to restoring order on the sprawling frontiers of the northwest and south. Most important, when efforts to manage national and state debts provoked popular resistance, when a Revolutionary War officer named Daniel Shays led some 1,100 debt-ridden Massachusetts farmers to stop the seizure of their property for payment of debts and taxes, Congress was simply unable to take effective action. Congress first called out local militia who, sympathetic with Shays's followers, refused to act. Congress then asked the states to raise 1,340 troops to crush the rebellion. Virginia alone responded, and Congress could do no more.

Shays's Rebellion added a sense of urgency to those citizens who had long argued that the United States needed a stronger national government. Nationalists knew that it was nearly impossible to strengthen the government by amending the Articles of Confederation. Yet Americans had learned to make their state governments more effective without sacrificing republican principles or endangering the liberties of the people; in 1785, Virginia and Maryland had shown that states could work together to improve interstate commerce. When representatives of five states meeting in Annapolis invited all the states to send delegates to Philadelphia in May 1787 to render the constitution of the federal government "adequate to the exigencies of the Union," twelve states responded favorably. Most of the fifty-five delegates who came to Philadelphia were determined to do more than amend the Articles. They wanted a more powerful central government for the United States, a government that received its authority from the people, that could act directly on the people, and that was free from the domination of the states. They succeeded in creating a government with the power to tax, regulate commerce, raise armed forces, wage war against enemies foreign and domestic, and call out the militia of the states to enforce federal laws, maintain civil order, and repel invasions. They also denied the states the authority to make war, conduct foreign affairs, issue currency, and tax imports. But while increasing the authority of the national government, they made sure that that government would be checked in its use of power: intermingling executive, legislative, and judicial branches so as to keep any one branch from dominating the others; setting national and state governments in tension against each other; and making all governments dependent upon the people. Authority over armed forces, for example, was balanced not only between executive and legislative branches of the central government (the president as commander in chief had to work with Congress, which had the authority to declare war and appropriate funds for the armed forces) but also between the central and the state governments (each had some authority over the state militias, which were to be an integral part of the forces of the United States). The new Constitution, which was accepted by the people of the states in 1788, made power compatible with liberty.

But the Constitution did not automatically solve the problems that had burdened the United States under the Articles of Confederation and threatened the nation's self-respect, if not its security. The United States remained in debt, its western lands occupied by British garrisons, its frontiers disordered by a population surging onto lands used by Native peoples, its elected officials reluctant to create a peacetime army, its citizens morbidly averse to taxes, its militia ineffective, and its national legislature torn by local and regional interests, including Spain's having closed the lower Mississippi to American shipping. The new nation did have a popular and able first president, George Washington, as well as some unusually talented men in the cabinet and legislature. But even they were hard-pressed to solve the nation's lingering problems. When Washington took office in April 1789 he and his secretary of war, Henry Knox, were faced with a crisis in the northwest territory between the Ohio River and Lake Erie, territory contested by American squatters and Native peoples (supported by British garrisons). Washington and Knox, knowing that their army of 1,200 men was far too small to be effective in such a region and that militiamen were unreliable, hoped that a show of force and negotiations would pacify the Ohio country. Gen. Josiah Harmar tried to do more. In the autumn of 1790 he led a force of 1,500 regulars and militia over 150 miles north from Cincinnati on a punitive expedition to the Maumee River Valley. He burned villages, enraged the Natives, and, after his militiamen were defeated, retired to Cincinnati under severe criticism from Washington and members of Congress. Fighting had preempted negotiations. Congress voted money for raids and another expedition to the Maumee. The raids were effective, but the second punitive expedition, led by Governor Arthur St. Clair, ended in disaster and near universal criticism (900 of his 1,400 men were killed or wounded).

Washington and Knox continued to prefer a negotiated settlement to the disorders in the northwest, but they were also determined to have adequate force to sustain negotiations. Their preference for negotiations was the result of a keen appreciation that American citizens had caused much of the trouble on the frontiers and that the rest of the country was reluctant to raise and support the forces needed to restrain frontiersmen or fight Native peoples. Washington was particularly intent on having public support for any use of force. He now proposed sustained diplomacy together with a substantial increase in the size and quality of the regular army and the militia. The diplomacy did not go well: four American emissaries were killed while under a flag of truce, and others found their way to the Natives blocked by British soldiers. But the administration persuaded Congress to create a peacetime army of 5,000 men, serving for three years and organized into four separate legions, each containing infantry, cavalry, and artillery. The administration also managed to pass a militia act that obligated every white, male, able-bodied citizen from 18 to 45 to be equipped at his own expense and trained by the states for service for up to three months a year. Although Congress did not provide for enforcing the militia act, it did establish an individual citizen's obligation for military service to the United States. Drawing upon this new congressional legislation, Washington's administration created an army to support its diplomacy or, if necessary, to gain control of the Ohio country. That army, under an able veteran of the Revolutionary War, Gen. Anthony Wayne, was not ready for action until 1794. By then negotiations had clearly failed, and the American people, frustrated by British meddling in the northwest and impressing American sailors in the Atlantic (Britain was at war with revolutionary France), were ready to support the use of force. Well supported and well prepared, Wayne took the offensive in the summer of 1794, defeated a Native force of 1,000 at Fallen Timbers in the Maumee Valley, and destroyed all nearby Native and British storehouses and crops. He retired to Greenville, where the United States made peace the following year with the Natives of the northwest.

Washington employed much the same combination of diplomacy and force in sustaining the law within the United States and settling longstanding differences with Britain and Spain. In the summer of 1794, while Wayne was mounting his offensive in the northwest, Washington was faced with a tax rebellion in western Pennsylvania. When negotiations failed to persuade citizens to pay an excise tax on whiskey and when public opinion had come to support the government, Washington and the governor of Pennsylvania led a force of militiamen that emphatically dispersed the rebels and upheld the law. That November, after Congress had begun construction of a navy and of coastal fortifications to protect the United States in the event of war with Britain, John Jay negotiated a treaty with Great Britain to resolve problems created by the Peace of Paris and the wars of the French Revolution. Jay's Treaty provided that Britain would remove its garrisons from American territory, that unpaid debts to British merchants would be settled by a joint commission, and that the northeastern boundaries of the United States and illegal seizures of American vessels would also be resolved by an international commission. The treaty did not consider compensation for Americans whose slaves had been captured by the British or for Loyalists whose property had been confiscated during the War for Independence, or for American seamen impressed by the Royal Navy since 1793. Although Jay had settled long-standing disputes with Britain, many Americans with lingering grievances opposed the treaty that was ratified by the Senate in 1795 and was narrowly supported in the House of Representatives the following year. In late 1795 the United States also negotiated an end to its boundary and navigational disputes with Spain. By the Treaty of San Lorenzo (Pinckney's Treaty) Spain recognized the Mississippi River and the 31st parallel as boundaries of the United States and gave Americans free navigation of the Mississippi as well as the right to deposit goods at the mouth of the river.

By the end of his second administration Washington had resolved some of the most persistent problems from the War for Independence. The final campaign of that war, the Yorktown campaign of 1781, had allowed the United States to achieve its war aims. With the decisive support of French forces and loans, the Americans had been able to win the kind of victory that drove Britain to abandon the war and make a peace that was most favorable to the United States. Americans won their independence, a vast national domain, and recognition of their loose confederation of republican governments. They also emerged from the war with a central government that was as weak as the most ardent republican could have wished—a government without the power to tax or regulate commerce, without a regular army to protect its frontiers and enforce its laws, and without a realistic prospect of reforming itself. So successful were Americans in achieving their war aims that they soon found some of those aims in jeopardy. They could no longer expect European states to sustain them with armed forces and loans; indeed Europeans could all too easily discriminate against their commerce, prey upon their ships and seamen, and encroach on their lands. Americans had to find solutions within themselves. They had to strengthen their national government without sacrificing the republican principles for which they had fought. They did: in the Constitution of 1787 and in the governments they formed under that Constitution. By the end of Washington's second term he and Congress together with American diplomats and regular armed forces had given the new nation just enough power to meet its minimal needs—not enough to become a power in a European sense but enough to sustain its republican governments in an abundant land with great natural security.

SUGGESTED READING

The Yorktown campaign is best understood within the larger political, diplomatic, and constitutional history of the American Revolution. Gordon S. Wood, *The Creation of the American Republic 1776–1787* (Chapel Hill: University of North Carolina Press, 1998) connects the causes of the Revolution to subsequent efforts to create republican governments in the United States; Piers Mackesy, *The War for America, 1775–1783* (Lincoln: University of Nebraska Press, 1993) analyzes the development of war aims and grand strategies in a colonial rebellion that became a world war; and E. Wayne Carp, *To Starve the Army at Pleasure: Continental Army Administration and American Political Culture, 1775–1783* (Chapel Hill: University of North Carolina Press, 1984) shows how difficult it was for Americans to win their independence while inhibited by fears of a strong central government, a standing army, and taxes. Jonathan R. Dull, *The French Navy and American Independence . . . 1774–1787* (Princeton: Princeton University Press, 1975) and Richard B. Morris, *The Peacemakers: The Great Powers and American Independence* (New York: Harper and Row, 1965) explain that American victory—the realization of American war aims—depended to an unusual extent on European politics and diplomacy. Richard H. Kohn, *Eagle and Sword: The Federalists and the Creation of the Military Establishment in America 1783–1802* (New York: Free Press, 1975) and Russell F. Weigley, *History of the United States Army* (Bloomington: Indiana University Press, 1984) link postwar efforts to secure the United States to the development of a national government and the preservation of liberty. As Marcus Cunliff, *George Washington, Man and Monument* (Boston: Little, Brown, 1958) makes clear, Washington had an indispensable part in nearly every phase of the Revolution, from the creation of the Continental Army to the Yorktown campaign and from the adoption of the Constitution to the establishment of a viable national government and domain.

WAYNE E. LEE

Plattsburgh 1814:
Warring for Bargaining Chips

In the summer of 1814, the divisive and so far inconclusive war with Britain began to take an ugly turn for the United States. The endless Napoleonic wars had seemingly wrapped up, and although Britain was eager to end the distracting American war as well, they were determined to do so on their own terms. The Earl of Bathurst, British secretary for war and the colonies, ordered veteran regiments from France and the Mediterranean to North America. They were to continue to ensure the security of the Canadian provinces, but now the balance of forces had shifted and the British could take the offensive. The war's campaigns had long ceased to bear much relation to its original causes, and as the beginning of peace negotiations loomed, both sides hoped to gain and hold the territorial chips necessary to dominate the bargaining table at Ghent, in Belgium. It was there that the war's end would be determined, not in the capture of a capital or in the final defeat of a field army. For the summer and fall campaign season of 1814 the main British effort followed a path familiar from their previous war in North America: Gen. John Burgoyne's route, from Montreal, down Lake Champlain, and then along the Hudson River. Such a route could even threaten New York City and thereby force territorial concessions from the Americans. Burgoyne's 1777 campaign had ended in disaster at Saratoga. In the 1814 plan there was no hope to reconquer the United States, but with a British army firmly ensconced in the interior of New York, amid what the

British yet again assumed was a sympathetic population, the Americans might have to concede a more southerly border for the Canadian provinces, if not in New York, then perhaps in Maine. To support this main effort Bathurst arranged for diversionary attacks all along the eastern seaboard, while British and Native American forces farther west would hold the line. On September 1, 1814, as many as 12,000 British troops, the largest field army North America had seen since 1782, crossed the border south of Montreal and marched along Lake Champlain, shadowed by a newly built frigate, the *Confiance,* and her sister vessels, designed and built with the intent to immediately establish naval dominance on the lake. Waiting for them at Plattsburgh was a scratch force of 1,700 regular troops, 700 New York militiamen, and 2,500 militiamen (technically volunteers) from Vermont, commanded by Brig. Gen. Alexander Macomb, and a small, hurriedly expanded squadron of ships under the command of Cdr. Thomas Macdonough. Macdonough flew his flag on the *Saratoga*. It would need to live up to the promise of that name.

Plattsburgh determined much about how the war ended, but the story of the British plans for the summer of 1814, their movements down the lake, and the American defense of Plattsburgh also presents a microcosm of the war's strategic challenges at both operational and policy levels. Operationally the logistical challenges of campaigning in North America dominated the War of 1812, and often the only solutions lay in the mutual support of land and naval forces. And so it was at Plattsburgh: the British needed to control the lake to keep their army fed, supplied, and moving forward. At the policy level, by 1814 diplomatic negotiations, or at least predictions about those negotiations, dominated many operational choices. Armies and navies were dispatched with the peace table in mind, not in a quest for some ultimate or decisive military victory. In the balance of offer, counteroffer, and compromise that would dominate the peace talks, Plattsburgh would loom large. Understanding what made Plattsburgh so crucial, however, requires backing up and examining how the war erupted and how it had progressed from 1812 to the summer of 1814.

I

The historian Gordon Wood has called the War of 1812 the "strangest war in American history." Much of that strangeness derives from the confusion and paradoxes associated with how it began. A certain level of Anglo-American antagonism persisted in the decades after 1783, but British naval arrogance combined with their long-running attempt to cut off trade to Napoleon's France greatly aggravated relations. In practice this meant that British naval vessels stopped American vessels (including men-of-war), searched them for presumed British citizens, and then pressed those men into service—to the great outrage of a nation seeking to assert itself as a full member of the international system of sovereign states. It also meant that Britain imposed ever stricter conditions on America's (and other neutrals') trade with France and its allies. The paradox is that these maritime grievances affected primarily the New England states, which were dominated politically by Federalists opposed to the war and which feared its potential impact on their maritime economy, and they generally voted *against* going to war. The most enthusiastic war hawks came from the southern and western states. The final vote in Congress for war was close, and this divided sentiment hampered the American war effort throughout. In hindsight it makes sense to blame the outbreak of war on two separate arenas of Anglo-American friction. British maritime policy clearly infringed on American sovereignty, while at the same time the western frontier remained a turbulent zone of competition between American settlers and the Indians. Westerners blamed the British for stirring up the Indians, most recently the Shawnees, defeated at Tippecanoe in November 1811, or at least for giving the Indians hope for British support in their efforts to stem the westward expansion of the United States. If it is too much to blame the war on western land hunger and greed, it is not too much to blame it partly on the western states' collective sense of insecurity.[1]

Reinforcing the sense of the strangeness of the war, at least in the way that Americans now think of war as the product of some catastrophic or defining event, there was not really a last straw. Tension between the two nations had ebbed and flowed continuously, and war had nearly come in 1807 after a particularly egregious incident at sea. Britain did not want war, and indeed made several concessions in the years and even weeks prior to the final American declaration of war in June 1812.

II

For a misbegotten war that relatively few seemed to want, the War of 1812 proved difficult to end. There were various reasons for this stubborn resistance to resolution. The British truly did not need this sideshow in the midst of their titanic struggle with Napoleon, who, in the same month as the American declaration of war in 1812, invaded Russia with 600,000 men. For the British the primary aim was to preserve the status quo in North America while fighting Napoleon in Europe and elsewhere; particularly crucial was to maintain the territorial integrity of the Canadian provinces. They also pursued the somewhat less critical goal of propping up a Native American independent territory on the northwestern periphery of the United States, which might in the long run form a buffer between the two Anglo nations. These aims clashed with American operational options and emotional inclinations. American naval weakness meant that the only way the United States could truly pressure Britain was by threatening the Canadian provinces, which was the one thing guaranteed to keep Britain's attention and to draw its resources. Unexpected early American victories in frigate-on-frigate actions in the Atlantic, although strategically insignificant (since America had no true ships of the line), succeeded both in emotionally investing the British population in the war and in providing the American public with a false sense of confidence in its ultimate outcome. Meanwhile the American western and southern states seized the war as an opportunity to cement their territorial control of the frontier at the expense of the Indians. Although internally divided, the Indians naturally turned to the British in a last-gasp effort to confine American expansion in the northwest. Anglo-Indian cooperation, however, only opened up well-established American bugaboos about the violence of an Indian war; even Thomas Jefferson linked the war to those emotions, arguing in June 1812, "[To take] possession of that country [Canada] secures our women & children for ever from the tomahawk & scalping knife, by removing those who excite them." This kind of thinking justified campaigns against the Indians that often had little or nothing to do with the war against the British.[2]

In this sense the war followed a common pattern: the aims changed as the conflict progressed. For many in the United States the war increasingly became one for territory, or at least for the freedom to expand westward. For Britain preserving Canada remained central, but with the defeat of Napoleon looming in 1814 they were able to commit resources on a new scale. Both sides thus escalated their hopes for the meaning and outcome of the war, but they did so based on unrealistic assessments of the possibility for meaningful conquest on a continental scale. The British, for example, continued to believe reports of widespread sympathy among the Americans in the northeast. They therefore calculated that a successful regional invasion could find local support sufficient to convert limited territorial occupation into a partial reconquest. The Americans, on the other hand, who may have let their territorial ambitions carry them away in 1812 and 1813, by 1814 found themselves facing the full power of an undistracted Britain. Military successes and failures could affect regional military control but were unlikely to change dramatically the demographic and political integrity of the two nations (although the Indians suffered more substantially, largely because they lacked the demographic resilience to militarily challenge the United States).

Under these circumstances each side increasingly pursued military operations with the aim of improving its bargaining position. President James Madison had begun the war calling for the preservation of national honor, for "manly resistance" to avert the "degradation of our best and proudest hopes." But immediately after declaring war Madison also communicated the terms on which it could end, and he made clear the nation's diplomatic "readiness to concur in an honorable reestablishment of peace and friendship." In 1814, as the Americans began to fear the ending of the Napoleonic Wars and as the British faced domestic war weariness after two decades of struggle, both sides returned to this vision of war as negotiation. In this sense the War of 1812 continued an old European tradition of "cabinet wars," in which every military move was accompanied by a diplomatic initiative, and in which territorial successes had meaning as much in their value for bargaining purposes as they did in and of themselves. Americans had seen the consequences of such wars in their colonial past, when their local victories against the French in Canada were traded away in the final treaty for places considered by the ministry to be more valuable. For the United States as a nation, however, this was the first, and really the only cabinet war. But calling something a cabinet war when it was fought by a democracy at the beginning of the nineteenth century does not do justice to the power of public opinion and conceptions of national honor. Public opinion and amorphous definitions of honor affected operational choices as well as the peace negotiations. Although it was an unpopular war with shifting goals, Americans nevertheless proved unwilling to let it end on a sour note. Fortunately for them, 1814, and especially Plattsburgh, would provide just enough success to bring the war to a close, and then the otherwise irrelevant victory at New Orleans in early 1815 fully salved the national sense of honor.[3]

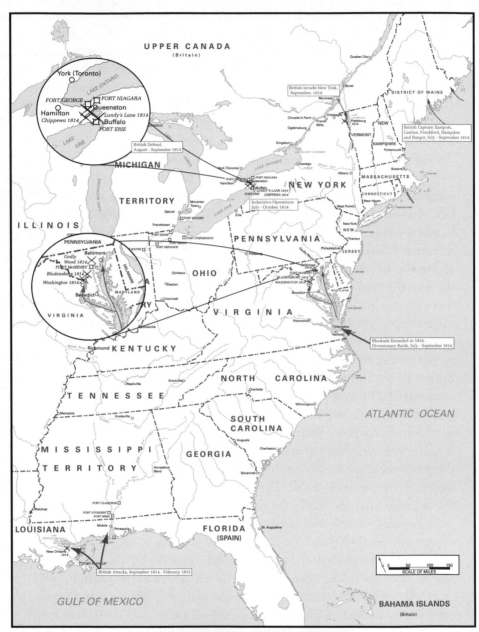

THE EASTERN UNITED STATES
British Movements in 1814

III

The War of 1812 was a vast, sprawling, poorly managed affair, with little obvious strategic logic. But that seeming lack of logic followed from the lack of clear political aims for the war, the asymmetry of the two sides' relative power, and the huge, continental scope of land operations conducted by forces generally too small to assert territorial control as invaders. The asymmetry generated ironies as well. Britain's overwhelming naval power at first seemed to bring them little advantage. American frigates in single-ship actions inflicted several startling defeats on the British, the strategic impact of which was merely to fire the outrage and stiffen the resolve of the British public. Meanwhile the length of the American coastline initially frustrated the British naval blockade, although the blockade gradually inflicted substantial economic pressure. On the other hand, the United States could not seem to bring to bear its ostensible demographic advantage in North America, as mismanagement, weak government, even weaker finances, and the logistical challenges of moving men in a continent-size wilderness undermined or mooted American invasions of Canada.

There were some key successes and failures in the first two years of the war, however. They are best broken down theater by theater: northwestern, southwestern, north central (essentially the Niagara region), lower Canada (the approaches to Montreal), the Atlantic seaboard, and the open ocean. In the far northwest, comprising western Ohio and the Indiana, Illinois, and Michigan Territories, the Americans battled an Anglo-Indian alliance, with Tecumseh serving as the nominal leader for the northwestern Indians. American commanders in 1812 attempted several advances in the region; all were thrown back. But then on September 10, 1813, Capt. Oliver Hazard Perry defeated the British fleet on Lake Erie and established American control over the lake. That control prevented the British from supplying their forces, or their Native allies, farther west. Gen. William Henry Harrison followed up with a victory at the Battle of the Thames in October 1813 (between Lakes Erie and Huron, northeast of Detroit), at which Tecumseh was killed. These successes, however, merely reversed earlier American losses in the region. From a purely British perspective, the seesaw fighting had maintained the U.S.-Canadian frontier. From a Native American perspective, it constituted a major long-term defeat.

In the southwest, operations from 1812 to June 1814 were similarly decisive for the Indians, although primarily in the absence of British forces. In early 1813, American Gen. James Wilkinson, commanding in the Gulf of Mexico, received permission to seize Mobile from the Spanish, who were then allied with the British. He did so virtually without resistance. Meanwhile an internal struggle in the Creek Indian nation eventually pulled in American forces, who campaigned against the traditionalist "Red Stick" faction. Gen. Andrew Jackson defeated them at the battle of Horseshoe Bend in March 1814, whereupon he forced the Creek nation to cede twenty-three million acres of Alabama and Georgia to the United States.

Although it could not be known for certain until the war had ended and the treaty had been negotiated, these victories over the Indians in the northwest and the southwest constituted perhaps the most important legacy of the war. They removed the Indians' European allies as players in the struggle over American westward expansion. The United States would fight again in the nineteenth century to define its southern boundary, and it would threaten to fight to determine its northern boundary, but the essential freedom to expand westward without further European-based interference was now clear.

Other theaters proved less decisive. In the north-central theater around Niagara the British also defeated the initial American invasion in 1812 (at Queenston Heights). In 1813 both sides frantically built ships on Lake Ontario while trading ugly destructive raids on the towns on either side of the lake. By 1814 American regular army forces had begun to improve, and the campaigns in the summer of that year seemed to promise a more decisive outcome. Gen. Winfield Scott defeated a British force at Chippewa and then fought another to a draw at Lundy's Lane. In strategic terms, however, these actions meant little. The Americans soon retreated back to Fort Erie, where they withstood a British siege later that summer. As in the northwestern theater, the essential nature of the U.S.-Canadian frontier remained unchanged.

In many ways the war on the oceans and along the Atlantic seaboard should have been more consequential. It certainly generated drama. The possibility for decisiveness derived from the serious asymmetry in potential naval power. The U.S. Navy started the war with seven frigates, two corvettes, two brigs, four schooners, and 5,025 officers and men. The navy did not own a dry dock, and the British burned the only U.S. Navy yard (at Norfolk) early in the war. In contrast the Royal Navy had over 1,000 warships, with 150,000 officers and men. However, it was tied up containing the French and protecting a worldwide empire, and the long American coastline proved far harder to blockade than France's. In 1812 the most spectacular naval actions fell in favor of the Americans, as their more heavily built and gunned frigates defeated several British frigates in single-ship actions. The U.S. government also encouraged privateers to join the small navy in preying on British trade, eventually issuing 500 privateering commissions who took some 1,300 prizes. Although the single-ship defeats shocked the British, such actions were barely pinpricks against the full scope of their naval might, and over the course of 1813 and 1814 they tightened their blockade of American ports. In accord with divided American opinion about the war, and in the finest tradition of war profiteering, however, for much of the war the British allowed New England ports to ship the provisions that helped supply Wellington's army in Spain and France. Even with such exceptions (closed in 1814), American export trade dropped from $130 million in 1807 to $25 million in 1813 and then $7 million in 1814.

There is little doubt that by 1814 British naval power was exerting potentially decisive economic pressure on the United States, but it had not yet achieved any clearly decisive victories to parallel Trafalgar, the Nile, or even Copenhagen. British naval superiority in this war had been latent, quietly growing through the blockade, but unable to land a heavy, telling blow. The most consequential naval actions up to that point had been on the Great Lakes, where both sides built fleets from scratch, obviating British superiority. Indeed the American victory on Lake Erie in 1813 can reasonably be called the most decisive battle of the war up to the summer of 1814. All that was set to change. In the spring of 1814 Napoleon retreated into France. Pressed from the east and west, he finally abdicated in early April. Britain immediately looked to end its war with America, and to do so quickly and decisively. With the army and navy freed up, a whole new array of options emerged that combined Britain's heretofore slumbering naval superiority with veteran regiments from the European theater. This new accession of military power led to the most spectacular moments of the war: the burning of Washington and the American defense of Baltimore at Fort McHenry. Ironically, as spectacular as they were, they were but diversions within the overall British plan for the summer of 1814.

IV

In June 1814, Bathurst wrote to George Prevost, governor and commander of British forces in Canada, to outline the summer's campaign plan. He promised Prevost some 3,000 men immediately, with 10,000 more to arrive in waves. Prevost was to use those forces to commence offensive operations, although he was not to risk the loss of his force. His primary mission remained protecting the security of Canada, but such security demanded clearing the American threats on Lakes Erie, Ontario, and Champlain. Prevost could dispose the forces as he chose, but Bathurst expected him to go on the attack. To support such an attack in the interior Bathurst assured him, "It is also in contemplation . . . to make a more serious attack on some part of the Coast of the United States. . . . These operations will not fail to effect a powerful diversion in your favor."[4]

This scheme turned Prevost's troops and ships gathering in Quebec and Montreal into the British main effort. First they would establish superiority on Lakes Champlain and Ontario, and then they could roll down into Lake Erie and reestablish control stage by stage as far as Detroit. British forces to the west, whether around Fort Niagara or as far away as Mackinac in northern Michigan, would have to hold the line until Prevost could reinforce them, which they did successfully. Meanwhile as Prevost gathered his forces and constructed his fleet on Lake Champlain, the diversions began. In July 1814 Adm. Thomas Hardy captured Eastport on disputed Moose Island off the Maine coast. Then, on September 1, Rear Adm. Edward Griffith carried in 2,500 British troops, who rapidly captured Castine, Maine, and then sailed and marched up the Penobscot River, capturing Frankfort, Hampden, Machias, and Bangor—essentially all of Maine east of the river. In one way this small diversionary attack was the most successful of all: British forces took and held a slice of American territory and asserted their sovereignty there, successfully forcing the locals to swear allegiance to the British government. Many of them did so with every evidence of eagerness.

More famous were the British raids that summer along the Chesapeake. British blockading forces had been harassing the coast with small raids for over a year, but the end of fighting in Europe allowed for a more ambitious raiding program. Bathurst sent Gen. Robert Ross 3,000 veteran troops from Europe with orders to conduct such raids, although he specifically ordered Ross to consider them diversionary attacks, and that he should never progress too far inland nor seek to hold territory.

Although these were diversions, the British military and political leadership agreed that the raids would also serve as retaliation for the American burning of York in 1813, and they believed that a particularly spectacular victory might press the Americans to end the war. Ross and the British naval commander, Adm. Alexander Cochrane, agreed that Washington was just such a target. They sailed up the Chesapeake and then the Potomac River, landed on August 20, brushed aside the local militia at the infamous Battle of Bladensburg (opprobriously nicknamed the "Bladensburg Races" on account of the militia's rapid flight), sacked Washington, burned most of the public buildings, including the White House, and then returned to their ships to seek their next target. On September 7, after some debate, the combined British army and fleet proceeded against Baltimore, a major American commercial harbor and privateering base. The expedition failed after the garrison at Fort McHenry successfully resisted a two-day bombardment on September 13 and 14. The Americans at Fort McHenry fired no shots, but their unwillingness to surrender, combined with a stout American resistance ashore (which killed General Ross), convinced the British to withdraw.

In one sense these diversions, as well as other distractions, accomplished their mission, and in the case of the burning of Washington, a great deal more. Prevost's force gathering in Montreal in late August faced almost token levels of American forces along Lake Champlain. His plans and preparations in that respect had gone almost perfectly. American forces farther east faced threats along the Atlantic, and remained there. Prevost's forces on the Niagara peninsula had bent but had not broken, and even now (from August 1 to September 21) were laying siege to the Americans at Fort Erie. His reinforcements were streaming in, and he successfully deceived the American high command into thinking that he intended to attack into Lake Ontario (and especially toward the American naval yard at Sacket's Harbor). The American commander at Plattsburgh, Maj. Gen. George Izard, doubted those intentions, but his superiors ordered him to march most of his army west, leaving behind the token force under Brig. Gen. Alexander Macomb described earlier. Finally Prevost pushed through the rapid building of a full-size frigate on Lake Champlain. The *Confiance* had thirty-one long guns and six carronades; the latter were short-range, large-caliber guns that had proved extremely useful in the narrow waters of the lakes. He was confident that the *Confiance* would immediately establish British naval supremacy on the lake, and with it a truly decisive territorial bargaining chip.

He should have been right, but a divided command, rushed construction, a lack of transports, and an inspired American naval defense set the stage for ending the war. The British advance would proceed through Clinton County, New York, a region scantily populated at best, home only to about seven people per square mile. A near-contemporary military writer in Europe suggested that an army without prepositioned supplies could not feed itself from a population less than about ninety-one people per square mile. Clinton County's population produced neither the subsistence nor the roads adequate to the movement of a major force. Burgoyne had foundered in this same wilderness in 1777 with barely 7,000 men; Prevost was bringing 12,000. Although American smugglers in the region had been providing provisions to his smaller army in Montreal for some time, this larger mobile army required waterborne logistics and close cooperation with his naval forces. Unfortunately, Prevost and the regional naval commander, Cdr. James Lucas Yeo, did not get along, and their commands were literally divided. Yeo answered to the Admiralty in London, not to Prevost, and the Admiralty tasked him to "cooperate with" Prevost. They agreed on the necessity of a frigate to command the lake, but at several other points, especially the last-minute change in command of the Lake Champlain fleet from Capt. Peter Fisher to Capt. George Downie, their inclinations clashed. Fisher had supervised the building of the *Confiance,* and then Yeo appointed Downie to command that ship and the lake fleet mere days prior to its launching. Worse, the *Confiance* was green in timber and crew. Her new captain barely had time to practice his gun crews (many pressed from the infantry) before he and his fleet were ordered to cover Prevost's march into New York. The building effort that had almost miraculously produced the *Confiance* had not allowed for the preparation of transports to carry the infantry. Instead they would have to trudge south along the poor roads that paralleled the lake. One British officer reported during their march, "[The roads are] worse than you can imagine and many of our wagons are broken down— the road through the woods at Beatville [Beekmantown] is impassable therefore our only dependence is upon water communication." This kind of conjoined land and water movement in a narrow corridor followed an entirely predictable path, one for which the Americans could plan.[5]

On the American side Major General Izard had long anticipated a summer offensive of some kind, and he assumed that Plattsburgh would be the first stop in a British advance. Most of the town lay north of the Saranac River gorge and could not be defended, but the river itself presented a fine line of defense, and Plattsburgh Bay was a complex, shoal-filled harbor from which an American naval force could bombard a marching British column while sheltered from the lake's weather. Izard dug in south of the river. Even better, the reports of the construction of the *Confiance* had led the U.S. secretary of the navy to speed carpenters and a shipbuilder to Vermont. There, within a remarkably short span, they built the sloop *Saratoga* (eight long guns, eighteen carronades), the *Ticonderoga* (twelve long guns, five carronades), and the *Eagle* (eight long guns, twelve carronades) and rehabilitated ten gunboats (oared ships with one gun each). Like the British ships, these ships, plus the extant *Preble* (seven long guns), had inexperienced crews, but their commander, Commodore Macdonough, had had more time to train them and to consider his defensive position. Izard and Macdonough jointly formed their plans for the defense of the town, and by most accounts were entirely in agreement on the necessary steps.

Unfortunately the War Department swallowed Prevost's feint and ordered Izard with most of his force to march west. Izard resisted and delayed, but in the end he departed Plattsburgh, leaving Macomb with 1,700 assorted regulars and orders to raise the militia. The American militia in the War of 1812 has a deservedly poor reputation (especially compared to several successful actions by the Canadian militia). They repeatedly refused to march across state boundaries (much less the U.S. border), they were extremely unreliable on the tactical offensive, and they were not especially trustworthy even in a defensive role. In their one main action at Plattsburgh, a delaying action north of town, they performed poorly. As an institution, however, the militia had the great virtue of showing up when called. Whenever British forces landed or invaded, American commanders, faced with a nearly infinitesimal regular army, repeatedly called for militia. They never got as many or as good men as they wished, but the militia represented a kind of demographic resilience on a continental scale that meant that serious or expansive British conquest was unlikely. In this case Macomb raised 700 New York men, and at the last minute 2,500 Vermont men crossed the lake, technically not militia since they had crossed state lines, but volunteers in federal service.

The *Confiance* slipped off the stocks on August 25, and on September 1 Prevost marched across the border into New York. He hoped to win the population to him, and he carefully ordered that there be no plundering and that all provisions be paid for. Such care flew in the face of reports arriving that week about the burning of Washington. Prevost

quickly pushed through the American delaying effort north of Plattsburgh, moved into the town, and began seeking a way across the river
while the two sides commenced bombarding each other.

Macomb lacked the forces to defend the town north of the river,
but feeling the "eyes of America" upon him, he also felt he could not
retreat farther south. The river had only two bridges, and Macomb could
cooperate more easily with his own naval forces while beside the bay.
Meanwhile Macdonough moved his fleet into an anchorage designed to
cover the American position at Plattsburgh, while also forcing the longer-
gunned British fleet to enter the bay almost within range of his shorter
guns and having to approach him head-on—the worst possible position
for a ship in the age of sail.[6]

From Prevost's perspective all the American eggs were now in one bas-
ket. He had the main American force in front of him and an inferior
American fleet locked up in the bay. To his surprise, on September 8 Captain Downie objected that the *Confiance* was not yet ready, even claiming
that the American fleet was "considerably superior in force." Nevertheless, within two days Downie reassured himself and coordinated a plan
with Prevost to simultaneously attack the American land and lake positions, the navy's guns to signal the start of the mutual attack. Prevost
planned to hold the Americans' attention in central Plattsburgh while a
flanking column marched three miles upstream to a lightly guarded ford.
Meanwhile Downie was to sail in and dominate the American fleet with
his longer-range broadside.

Instead the British fleet rounded Cumberland Head to enter the bay,
with their bows facing the Americans' broadsides. As they came around,
the head the wind died, and they slowly drifted toward the American line,
absorbing the blows first of the few American long guns, and then of their
carronades, all without being able to answer effectively in return. As the
distance closed, the British ships finally turned and a brutal broadside-to-
broadside combat ensued. The Americans fought from an anchored line,
blocking the center of the bay, and Downie had sailed in to concentrate
the fire of the *Confiance* and two other, smaller ships first on the *Eagle*
and then on the *Saratoga*. Within the first fifteen minutes of fighting an
American shot dismounted a British cannon, which flew into Downie's
chest and killed him. Damaged but continuing to fight, the *Confiance*
poured heavier broadsides into the *Saratoga* and nearly evened the contest by taking out virtually all of its guns on one side. Macdonough then
used his preset kedge anchors to spin his ship around in place and bring

his other broadside to bear. The *Confiance* attempted the same maneuver, but lacking Macdonough's careful prebattle preparations, she became fouled and struck her colors at 10:30 a.m. The smaller British ships either grounded or surrendered, and the gunboats fled.

Without a covering fleet the British land advance was probably doomed, but matters were made worse by a failure to properly coordinate the timing of the two attacks. Downie commenced the fleet attack between 7:30 and 8:30 a.m., but Prevost's flanking column was under orders not to attack before 10:00 a.m. By that time the British fleet was on the verge of defeat, and as Prevost realized that his fleet was fleeing or captured, he recalled his advancing flank attack. Prevost almost immediately began a wholesale retreat, covered by a heavy rain, although Macomb lacked the forces to pursue at any rate. Prevost had been steadily stockpiling stores, especially artillery ammunition, and now he lacked the transport to bring them back to Canada. One artillery officer complained, "Several Wagons & Carts from being Overloaded (in order to remove as much as possible) and the extreme badness of the Roads broke down, leaving no alternative but to destroy them and their Contents." As for the retreat itself, Prevost later explained to Bathurst, "Your Lordship must have been aware . . . that no Offensive Operations could be carried out within the Enemy's Territory . . . without Naval Support. . . . The disastrous and unlooked for result of the Naval Contest . . . rendered a perseverance in the attack of the Enemy's position highly imprudent as well as hazardous." Prevost also blamed the poor state of the roads and the growing threat of a militia "raising En Masse around [him], desertion increasing & the Supply of Provisions Scanty." Without "the advantage of water conveyance" both problems were insoluble.[7]

V

The Battles of Plattsburgh, on land and lake, generated relatively few casualties and represented only one campaign among many that summer and fall of 1814. Furthermore the British had yet one more major diversionary campaign already under way against Mobile and New Orleans. So what made Plattsburgh the key to ending the war? By late 1814 both sides' war aims had shifted, and with the shift in war aims, strategies had shifted as well. Strategy had become focused on achieving bargaining chips for and honor in an inevitable peace. While Napoleon fought, the British had merely sought to contain the American war and the Americans' trade with France. In 1814, with Napoleon gone, they sought to end it quickly, perhaps with some territorial advantage, especially in eastern Maine, and certainly with an independent Indian state in the west. To get those things, however, they needed negotiating leverage. The Americans had given up any hope of keeping large parts of Canada, something arguably never an official war aim, while ironically, with Napoleon's abdication the maritime issues that had started the war were no longer relevant. President Madison's administration also wanted an end to the war, but they felt compelled to end it in a way consistent with popular demands and the public's sense of "national honor." The United States therefore also needed a bargaining chip, something that could force some honorable concession from the British, or at least a striking symbolic victory to present to the public. What they got instead was a burned capital, indecisive operations around Niagara and farther west, a prostrate and occupied eastern Maine, and finally a defensive victory at Plattsburgh. It was just enough. When Henry Clay, one of the American peace commissioners at Ghent, summed up the treaty agreed to there in December, he reflected on America's minimalist goals by the summer of 1814:

> The terms of this instrument [the peace treaty] are undoubtedly not such as our Country expected at the commencement of the War. Judged of however by the actual condition of things, so far as it is known to us, they cannot be pronounced very unfavorable. We lose no territory, I think no honor. . . . Judged of by another standard, the pretensions of the enemy at the opening of the negotiation [on August 8, 1814], the conditions of the peace certainly reflect no dishonor on us.[8]

In Clay's mind a great deal had changed in British "pretensions" between early August 1814 and December. In August, as the British summer offensives were getting under way, the British commissioners offered terms about which Clay could only say, "The prospect of peace has vanished. . . . It would be offering an unpardonable insult to our Government to ask of them any instructions [regarding those terms]." Plattsburgh made the difference, although other American defensive efforts contributed, especially the defense of Baltimore. The British had not exactly put all their effort into one roll of the dice at Plattsburgh, but it had been their main effort, and it was the one *designed* to acquire that territorial bargaining chip needed to tilt the peace talks to their advantage. In late October news of Plattsburgh arrived to officials in England and to the American peace commissioners in Ghent. Bathurst then offered the North American command to the Duke of Wellington, who declined, commenting that control of the northern lakes was essential for taking any territory from the United States, and that the failure at Plattsburgh had ended any further chance to do so. Henry Goulburn, one of the British peace commissioners, later agreed: "If we had either burnt Baltimore or held Plattsburgh, I believe we could have had peace on our terms." Coming to this realization in the wake of Plattsburgh, the British ministry lost interest in fighting to hold New Orleans or other American territories, and instead moved decisively to end the war at the peace table. Literally on the same day (November 26) that the *London Gazette* published Prevost's letter reporting the defeat at Plattsburgh, the British commissioners shifted from demanding a peace in which both sides held the territory currently in their possession (*uti possidetis*) to one accepting the prewar status quo. With that admission the negotiations began to make real progress. The two nations' representatives signed the treaty of Ghent on December 24, 1814. The Battle of New Orleans occurred in January 1815, before the news of the treaty arrived in North America, and it had no effect on its terms.[9]

VI

For such a muddled ending, determined by a less than spectacular defensive battle, a battle whose course was shaped as much by logistics as by tactics, the consequences of the war for the United States were dramatic, if not immediately obvious. That lack of initial clarity derived from the mismatch between the Americans' original war aims and the eventual results. The United States had declared war on Great Britain in 1812, while the latter was heavily engaged in a war with Napoleon. They had done so ostensibly over grievances about Britain's maritime policies and its treatment of American ships and citizens. (Ironically, none of those grievances were mentioned in the final treaty.) In translating a desire for war into strategic action the United States lacked any other way seriously to damage Britain other than invading Canada. Even against a distracted Britain, U.S. forces quickly faced the practical, political, and especially the logistical problems of exercising any sort of territorial control in the interior of Canada, despite gaining naval dominance in Lake Erie in 1813. The Canadians, many of whom had been Loyalists during the American War of Independence, had no interest in being folded back into the United States, and they fought with grim determination against periodic American invasions that lacked the capacity to hold ground without local support. Then in 1814 American policymakers faced a Britain freed from the threat of Napoleon and an increasingly effective naval blockade. American strategic vision rapidly narrowed to ending the war in a way compatible with domestic public opinion. Fortunately, despite the burning of Washington and the loss of eastern Maine (which was returned in the treaty), enough American defenses held (at Plattsburgh, Fort Erie, Baltimore, and Mobile) that the equally weary Britain agreed to a status quo peace.

If the war began with American strategic overreach, it ended with newly stabilized borders to the north and south and an apparently wide-open western expanse, still filled with Indians but now largely free of the likelihood of European interference. One of Britain's goals at the outset of peace negotiations had been the creation of a western Indian buffer state that, supported by communications with British Canada, could hem in American expansion. By mid-September 1814 British ministers were already abandoning that hope, and the final treaty virtually ignored the Native Americans. This new western freedom was the most decisive legacy of the war—ironically created by a naval battle in a bay in upstate New York. The United States became convinced that the conquest of Canada was not feasible and that repeating a war with Britain would not be in the national interest; some other form of relationship with Britain was essential. At the same time, however, western expansion could now proceed without threatening British interests. To be sure, American expansion did eventually generate a war with Mexico, but it did so after Mexico's independence from Spain and after American settlers had become a significant demographic presence within Mexican-claimed territories, as they never had in Canada.

The war had a relatively minor impact on the U.S. government (although it did result in the dissolution of the antiwar Federalist Party). The historian Gordon Wood argues that this restrained impact was the deliberate policy of President James Madison. Architect of the Constitution and a believer in constrained federal power, Madison had sought to manage the war in a way that avoided the usual wartime expansion of governmental powers. Often seen as an inept wartime leader who failed to deliver the resources necessary for a more impressive victory, Madison succeeded in, and was praised at the time for, containing the size and reach of government. In Wood's words, "Better to allow the country to be invaded and the capital burned than to build up state power in a European monarchical manner." Ironically the citizens of that burned capital praised Madison after the war for fighting it without infringing on "civil or political liberty." According to them, Madison had "restrained the sword 'within its proper limits,' [and] . . . had directed 'an armed force of fifty thousand men aided by an annual disbursement of many millions, without infringing a political, civil, or religious right.'"[10]

The implications for the U.S. Army and Navy, and for U.S. military and strategic policy, were somewhat more mixed. In many ways Plattsburgh faded from institutional and popular memory in favor of other, more spectacular events whose imprints were more lasting, if sometimes contradictory. At the strategic level the abysmal failure to defend Washington and the near-run defense of Baltimore convinced many military thinkers that the country needed both a new coastal defense system and an expanded navy. In April 1816, Congress approved an eight-year program to build nine ships of the line, twelve large frigates, and three steam-powered port-defense batteries. As for the army, coastal fortification and defense became a major part of its institutional structure and thinking. President James Monroe repeated the supposed lessons of 1814 in an 1824 address to Congress, in which he pleaded the vulnerability of American port cities and argued that it was necessary to "stop the enemy at the coast. If this is done, our cities, and whole interior, will be secure. For the accomplishment of this object, our fortifications must be principally relied on." Behind that speech lay a vast program of fortification that dotted the eastern and southern seaboard with still-surviving coastal artillery forts (now mainly national parks). This fixation on a European naval threat was such that of the $8,250,000 spent on fixed defenses between 1816 and 1829, only $200,000 was spent on the border with Canada, where in fact the majority of the war had been fought. This expenditure limited the amount of money that could be spent on personnel, and the regular army remained minuscule (6,000 men in 1821, 8,500 in 1846). That small size also derived from the impact the Battle of New Orleans had on the American public's perception of itself and of the militia. Although the battle did not affect the nature of the peace treaty, Andrew Jackson's destruction of a substantial and professional British invasion force convinced Americans not only that they had won the war, but that they had done so on the backs of militiamen like those under Jackson's command. Forgetting the militia's many failures, especially the "Bladensburg Races" in front of Washington, Americans reaffirmed their belief in the military tradition of the "gifted amateur." In contrast, for the regular army, now a permanent institution seeking a professional identity in the postwar years, the defining events became the battles at Chippewa and Lundy's Lane in 1814 in the Niagara peninsula. There the regular army had come closest to successfully copying the European standard of linear warfare and discipline under fire. The probably apocryphal quote attributed to the British commander at Chippewa—"Those are Regulars, by God"—continues to appear in the U.S. Army's instructional materials and celebrations of its heritage as an affirmation of the birth of a professional American army. Ironically, Chippewa was a defensive battle, and after stopping the British assault, the Americans were unable to pursue, while Lundy's Lane was arguably a draw. Neither was decisive to the outcome of the war. Institutionally the army also sought greater command coherence than it had displayed in the war, a process that started with Col. Sylvanus Thayer's reforms of officer training at West Point. Although West Point was founded in 1802, it was only after his reforms (beginning in 1817) that the academy acquired the traits of a professional training program. At a higher level, in 1821 Secretary of War John C. Calhoun tried to solve the problems of a divided and sometimes contradictory command structure by creating the office of commanding general. Calhoun also tried to push through Congress the idea of an "expansible army," essentially a skeleton regular force that could readily absorb a wartime influx of personnel. Congress denied the specifics of his plan, but his vision became the de facto army mobilization system through the beginning of the Civil War.[11]

In the aftermath of the war the nation celebrated the amateurs at New Orleans, mourned but rebuilt Washington, and made the defense of Baltimore eternal by adopting "The Star-Spangled Banner" as its anthem. That the war actually ended in a quest for territorial bargaining chips much like the European wars of the ancien régime was a lesson lost. In one sense forgetting that lesson proved irrelevant because the United States would not again fight this kind of cabinet war (although the war with Mexico retained aspects of that diplomatic system). On a cultural level the war entered a pantheon of American wars won, helping cement the myth of American exceptionalism and fostering an imagined virtuous invincibility. Popular and institutional memories also ignored the real operational lessons of Plattsburgh: the strategic resilience of a professional army when supported by an expansible militia; the necessity of close interservice cooperation; and the necessity for expeditionary-capable logistical support when operating in lightly populated wilderness.

SUGGESTED READING

Despite a long-held reputation as a "forgotten war," the War of 1812 has been well served by historians in recent decades. The older classic accounts by John K. Mahon, *The War of 1812* (1972), and Reginald Horsman, *The War of 1812* (1969), retain their value, as does the even older naval history by Alfred Thayer Mahan, *Sea Power in Its Relation to the War of 1812* (1919). More recent overviews of the war have been provided by Donald R. Hickey, *The War of 1812: A Forgotten Conflict* (1989), J. R. Elting, *Amateurs to Arms! A Military History of the War of 1812* (1995), and Robert S. Quimby, *The U.S. Army in the War of 1812: An Operational and Command Study* (1997). J. C. A. Stagg fully embeds the war in the American political context in *Mr. Madison's War: Politics, Diplomacy and Warfare in the Early American Republic, 1783–1830* (1983), and Jeremy Black places the war in an international perspective in *The War of 1812 in the Age of Napoleon* (2009). For the Plattsburgh campaign itself there is a campaign study by David G. Fitz-Enz, *The Final Invasion: Plattsburgh, the War of 1812's Most Decisive Battle* (2001), which also reprints the crucial document discussed in the text. Older but more carefully narrated is Allan S. Everest's *The War of 1812 in the Champlain Valley* (1981).

JOHN W. HALL

"A Reckless Waste of Blood and Treasure": The Last Campaign of the Second Seminole War

By mid-February 1838, Maj. Gen. Thomas S. Jesup had done as much as any one man could do to end the Second Seminole War. "The Florida War," as he and his contemporaries called it, had already dragged on for over two years, and Jesup had been the senior U.S. commander for the past fourteen months. In that time he had used every resource and ruse at his disposal to defeat an implacable, irregular foe who, although fielding no more than 2,000 warriors, had managed to tie down 9,000 American troops. In the previous March, Jesup had secured the surrender of more than 800 Indians and thought that victory was at hand—only to face censure and embarrassment when the militant chief Osceola made off with both the captives and the prospects for an early peace. Embittered, Jesup resorted to aggressive offensive operations and treachery, securing 850 prisoners as well as an ignominious historical legacy. But as these operations drew to a close, he and his officers concluded that the absolute removal of the Seminoles from Florida was as impossible as it was imprudent. On February 11, 1838, he wrote the War Department to recommend a modification of U.S. war aims and a cessation of hostilities. "To persevere in the course we have been pursuing for three years past," he added later, "would be a reckless waste of blood and treasure." Four and a half years, three commanders, and two presidents later, the government agreed, permitting the remaining Seminoles to stay in Florida and thereby ending the longest "Indian war" in U.S. history.[1]

Among the hundreds of wars and lesser conflicts the United States has waged against Native Americans, the Second Seminole War is remarkable not only for its length but for its cost and ambiguous legacies. The conflict demanded the expansion of the regular army from twelve to fourteen regiments, more than half of which were in Florida for most of the war. The supplemental operating costs of their operations ran as high as $40 million—an unprecedented and intolerable sum at the time. But the human toll was greater yet. Of the roughly 10,000 army regulars who served in Florida, 1,466 died, making the Second Seminole War one of the most hazardous wars in American history. It was also among the most tragic. The true number of Seminole casualties is unknowable, but most of those who perished were noncombatants; many died in the course of a forced migration that affected 4,400 people. Framed by morally contentious issues, the conflict was subject to a bitter partisan debate that only intensified as the war's costs multiplied. The army's senior commanders—seven of them during a seven-year war—became unwilling parties to this political dispute, and three asked to be relieved of their command. Under other circumstances so might have the war's final commander, Col. William Worth. Like his predecessors he came to appreciate the limits of force and urged the United States to accept something less than victory. Politically and ideologically this was unconscionable to Presidents Andrew Jackson and Martin Van Buren, who directed the war's first six commanders—but not Worth, who answered to President John Tyler. Only when those who had committed the United States to the war had left office could the government consider subordinating principle to national interests. Only then was it possible for Colonel Worth to wage the war's last campaign.

I

The origins of the Second Seminole War are nearly indistinguishable from the origins of the Seminoles themselves. For the most part they were Creek Indians who, over the course of the eighteenth century, had migrated from Georgia and Alabama to Florida, intermarried with other Indians residing there, and developed distinct identities. The last significant migration of the Creeks occurred in the course of the War of 1812, after the 1814 Battle of Horseshoe Bend, in which Andrew Jackson lent decisive weight to one party in a Creek civil war. The defeated "Red Stick" Creeks, including a child named Osceola, took refuge in Spanish Florida, where they continued their war against the Americans. But Jackson was done neither with the Red Sticks nor with their Seminole neighbors, who for some time had offered refuge and arms to runaway slaves from the southeastern United States. In 1818, Jackson invaded Florida to eliminate these threats to American interests, shattering black and Indian resistance. Without orders Jackson then turned his army on the Spanish colonial capital at Pensacola. Although embarrassed by Jackson's audacity, the James Monroe administration was quick to capitalize on it, entering a treaty with Spain by which the United States acquired Florida in exchange for financial considerations and portentous territorial concessions in the Southwest.

Following the organization of Florida as a U.S. territory in 1822, white settlers moved in, bringing with them African slaves and a hunger for Indian land. And the Seminoles, rattled but somewhat united by Jackson's invasion, occupied some of the best real estate in northern Florida. For slaves any land was preferable to the plantation, and they took every opportunity to escape a life of bondage to live as "Black Seminoles" among the Indians. Slave catchers and strife followed, and by 1823 the Seminoles were eager to sign a treaty guaranteeing them a refuge in central Florida. But the slaves remained a contentious issue, and many Indians refused to relocate to a reservation that Florida's governor described as "the poorest and the most miserable region I ever beheld." The only permanent solution, many whites argued, was the complete removal of the Indians from Florida.[2]

Andrew Jackson agreed. Elected to the presidency in 1828, he championed passage of the Indian Removal Act of 1830, which authorized relocation of Indians from the eastern United States to reservations west of the Mississippi. By its letter the law demanded consent of the Indians, but government agents exploited loose Native political structures to find some chiefs willing to sign a removal treaty—or resorted to fraud, as was almost certainly the case with the Seminoles. In 1832, fifteen Seminole leaders signed the Treaty of Payne's Landing, agreeing to leave Florida contingent upon inspection of their new reservation in the West. Seven chiefs made this trip the following year and found the circumstances entirely unsatisfactory but, according to army officers who witnessed the proceedings, were nevertheless cajoled into signing another treaty that stated otherwise. The Seminoles never ratified this treaty, but the United

States did, and in 1835 it prepared to relocate approximately 5,000 Seminoles to Indian Territory (present-day Oklahoma).

Anticipating that it would have to resort to force, the War Department assigned Brig. Gen. Duncan Clinch operational control of the Seminole removal, placing fourteen companies under his command by the end of October 1835. But only six of these were stationed among the Seminoles, and the local commander warned of the probable consequences of attempting "too much with inadequate means." On December 28, 1835, the Seminoles vindicated his fears in spectacular fashion, simultaneously assassinating U.S. officials at Fort King and ambushing two companies marching to that post under the command of Maj. Francis Dade. At the end of the day 111 Americans were dead and the Second Seminole War had begun.[3]

For militant Seminole leaders the attacks of December 28 represented the latest and most emphatic proclamation of their intent to remain in Florida. By design they left no room for equivocation or compromise, neither among the various Seminole bands nor with a stunned United States. Lest the Americans somehow misconstrue their meaning, the firebrand war leader Osceola afterward sent Clinch a message, vowing to resist "till the last drop of the Seminole's blood has moistened the dust of his hunting ground." Such a prospect did not trouble Andrew Jackson, whose determination matched that of Osceola. He forbade General Clinch from negotiating with the Seminoles "till they are unconditionally subdued, and till they consent to an immediate embarcation [sic] for the country west of the Mississippi." As it became clear that these aims were beyond Clinch, Jackson escalated the stakes. On January 21, 1836, Maj. Gen. Winfield Scott received orders to assume command of operations against the Seminoles and to call upon as many state militia forces as he deemed necessary. Jackson's earlier guidance stood, but Scott acquired the additional responsibility of securing "every living slave in their possession." The caveat "belonging to a white man" was meaningless, as ownership was impossible to determine and nearly all of the Black Seminoles preferred death to bondage.[4]

II

Absolute and unyielding, Jackson's war aims would have been virtually unobtainable even for the most versatile of operational commanders—which Winfield Scott was not. He was nevertheless an obvious choice.

A hero of the War of 1812, Scott was one of the army's three senior officers and the commander of its Eastern Department, which encompassed most of Florida. Jackson needed a senior officer to ensure unity of command over state militia officers, and he knew from past experience that Maj. Gen. Edmund Gaines, commander of the Western Department and Scott's nemesis, was too sympathetic toward the Indians. Yet if Scott could be counted on to pursue unconditional surrender, he was ill-suited to fight Indians or manage citizen soldiers.

As the war unfolded, Americans had yet to resolve their sixty-year dispute over the respective roles of the militia and the regular army in national military policy. Citing the fighting prowess of the frontiersman and America's isolation from European threats, militia advocates argued that a professional army was unnecessary, expensive, and offensive to republican values. Modern warfare was too sophisticated for amateurs, countered the professionals, who envisioned trained regulars as the nucleus for an expanded wartime army. At the conclusion of the War of 1812, army officers were certain they had proven their point, only to resume the inglorious duties of a frontier constabulary. Nevertheless a coterie of officers dedicated themselves to casting their army in a European mold and distinguishing their troops from the contemptible citizen soldiery. Crucial to this movement was Winfield Scott, who based the army's general regulations and its tactical drill manual on French models. Yet even in emulating European doctrine Scott displayed an indifference to light infantry tactics, perhaps because they reminded him of the sort of American warfare and warriors he disdained.

Scott's operational concept for subduing the Seminoles was similarly constrained. Without knowledge of the terrain or the enemy, he devised a grand scheme involving the synchronized movements of three columns over uncharted wilderness. After painstaking logistical preparation he arrived in theater to learn that the incorrigible Gaines had swooped into Florida, fought one indecisive battle, and promised the Indians they could stay. Having in his mind won the war, Gaines went home, leaving a fuming Scott in his wake. Predictably Scott's plan and its sequel foundered, much to the satisfaction of his critics. While Gaines mocked his bête noire's "visionary plans . . . according to the Napoleon tactics," a militia officer sneered that Scott had used "the shreds and patches of the obsolete system of European tactics where they could not possibly work."[5]

Scott blamed his disappointments not on his methods but on Gaines's meddling and the troops at his disposal. The next campaign, he advised the War Department, would require the employment of "3,000 *good troops, (not volunteers).*" Soon afterward he rebuked Florida's citizens for cravenly fleeing their homes and sowing panic among their neighbors. His words were as poorly chosen as they were ill-timed. Earlier, Duncan Clinch had blamed Florida volunteers for an embarrassing defeat on New Year's Eve, and Scott's comments touched a raw nerve. Some Floridians burned his effigy; others simply demanded his recall. Disgusted by a war without prospects of success or glory, Scott was happy to oblige. "I have no particular desire to conduct the operations of the new forces," he had already informed his superiors. "That is a duty which I shall neither solicit nor decline." On May 21, 1836, Scott left Florida in search of better fortune. Many officers went further; in 1836 alone, 17 percent of the army's officers resigned their commissions. Most of them simply sought opportunities in the booming civilian economy, but their exodus, like that of Scott, gratified critics of the regular army.[6]

As did elevation of Florida's governor to overall command of the war. An old Jackson crony and self-styled Indian fighter, Richard Keith Call proposed to do what the regulars thought impossible: launch a summer campaign into the heart of the Seminole country. But he was beset by manpower shortages, a hostile climate, and an intractable foe, and the Americans had abandoned the interior by August 1836. Call finally launched his "summer" campaign in September, but his inadequacies as a logistician cost his army more than 600 horses and the initiative. By the time Call engaged the enemy in the Battle of Wahoo Swamp on November 21, Andrew Jackson had already lost confidence in his former protégé and named a new commander.

On December 9, 1836, Maj. Gen. Thomas Jesup assumed direction of the war. The army's longest-serving quartermaster general also proved to be one of its most capable—if controversial—Indian fighters. Initially pessimistic, Jesup eventually devised an effective methodology of gathering intelligence, establishing a network of supply depots, and using mobile columns and small detachments to maintain pressure on known enemy strongholds. By March 6, 1837, many Seminoles agreed to westward removal on the condition that all Black Seminoles go with them. Certain that they, not the Indians, posed the greatest threat to U.S. interests, Jesup agreed. In addition to their forming "a rallying point for runaway negroes from the adjacent States," Jesup feared that the Black Seminoles would assist any foreign power that chose to invade the United

States via Florida. Jackson's determination to return runaway slaves to their "rightful" owners, moreover, made the Black Seminoles among the most determined of the army's antagonists. Presented an opportunity to neutralize this threat, Jesup took it—and invited wails of protest from indignant Floridians. Jesup waffled, entertaining claims of ownership and permitting slave catchers to enter the camp of Seminoles awaiting removal at Tampa Bay. By June 2, this camp teemed with more than 800 Seminoles; the following morning fewer than 150 remained. Alarmed by the general's prevarication, the others may not have resisted when Osceola and 200 warriors stole into the camp the night before and led them back to hostility.[7]

Ridiculed in the press, Jesup first requested relief and then resolved to clear his name. It proved a futile endeavor. The first order of business remained prying the Black Seminoles from their Indian allies. He eventually settled on a very effective (if contentious) program that guaranteed Black Seminoles freedom in the West. Although it created various legal problems, within a year it eliminated the Black Seminoles as an appreciable military force. Jesup thought the Indians might be permitted to remain in Florida, but Martin Van Buren thought otherwise. Jackson's vice president had succeeded to the presidency in March 1837, and he tolerated Jesup's concessions regarding the Black Seminoles only as means of expediting the principal goal of Indian removal. Embittered by recent experience, Jesup resorted to treachery: inviting parlays with militant chiefs, then seizing them and threatening death to ensure the surrender of their followers. The seizure of Osceola on October 21, 1837, was the most infamous instance of a program that netted many of the Seminoles' most important leaders, transforming Jesup into an Anglo-Floridian hero and a nationally divisive figure. In December, he threw 9,000 soldiers, volunteers, marines, and sailors against the Seminoles in a massive offensive that produced two of the war's most significant battles, at Okeechobee and Loxahatchee. Never again would the Seminoles mass hundreds of warriors as they did in these engagements. If Jesup had any say in the matter, neither would the Americans.

In early February 1838, Jesup's officers began to impress upon him the futility of further pursuing removal by armed force. Already of a similar mind, Jesup sent envoys among the Seminoles and granted them a reservation in southern Florida. He informed the administration of this initiative afterward, explaining that the land the Seminoles coveted so dearly was worthless to whites. "The only means of terminating, immediately, a most disastrous war, and leaving the troops disposable for other service," he argued, was to let the Indians have it. Otherwise, he warned, "the war will continue for years to come, and at a constantly accumulating expense." Secretary of War Joel Poinsett responded that a reappraisal of strategic objectives was out of the question; the Senate had ratified the Treaty of Payne's Landing, "and the constitutional duty of the president requires that he should cause it to be executed." Five days after receiving this response Jesup seized more than 500 Indians who thought they had a deal. It was a fitting coda to Jesup's tenure, which ended three weeks later. In less than eighteen months and by whatever means expedient, Jesup had killed or secured for removal nearly 3,000 Seminoles, making him by far the war's most effective commander and its most reviled villain.[8]

But his achievements came at tremendous moral and fiscal cost. The economic prosperity that had lured officers away from the service in 1836 was the product of a speculative bubble that burst in May 1837, and the nation entered a severe recession that lasted five years. The Whigs naturally blamed the Democrats and President Van Buren, who had been in office only a month when the crisis struck. Abolitionists and humanitarians had opposed the Florida War on moral grounds, and the rest of the Whig Party exploited the unpopular conflict as a political foil. Although Van Buren refused to revisit the war's aims, his administration could no longer spend lavishly to achieve them. The easiest way to reduce costs was to curtail militia call-ups; this suited the army fine but galled Governor Call, who urged Poinsett to muster more of Florida's militia and pestered Jesup's successor with unsolicited advice regarding troop dispositions.

The successor, Brig. Gen. Zachary Taylor, was unreceptive. He had already outraged militia advocates by impugning the performance of Missouri volunteers at the Battle of Okeechobee, and he generally kept his distance from Call. Meanwhile the Seminoles successfully kept their distance from Taylor. Despite scouring "every hammock and swamp" in Florida, he could not find the enemy. Frustrated, he devised a plan to divide all of Florida into 20-mile squares, each patrolled by half an infantry company. One officer later observed charitably that the plan might have worked with 30,000 or 40,000 regulars, but Taylor had fewer than 2,000. Nevertheless, Secretary of War Poinsett approved Taylor's scheme in January 1839.

Although historically regarded as one of the nation's most capable secretaries of war, Joel Poinsett was preoccupied with potential European foes and volatile border disputes, and he treated the Seminole War as a distraction. As congressional pressure "to terminate the war in Florida by pacific measures" and the threat of war with Great Britain mounted in early 1839, Poinsett hoped to shed this distraction. He sent the army's commanding general, Alexander Macomb, to Florida to broker a settlement with the Seminoles. Macomb made the only deal he could—letting them stay—and on May 18, 1839, he crowed, "[I have] this day terminated the war with the Seminole Indians." He was not the first officer to make such a claim, and he would not be the last. Anglo-Floridians howled in renewed protest and Poinsett dissembled, but it did not matter after July 23. Not privy to the settlement, a band of southern Indians attacked a party of dragoons and workers, killing or capturing eighteen. Relations with Britain had by this time improved, and the government immediately disavowed Macomb's settlement.[9]

It is doubtful that the administration would have upheld Macomb's pledge under any circumstances, but Poinsett never again brooked retreat from the goal of absolute removal. "The experience of the last summer," he declared in November, "brings with it the painful conviction that the war must be prosecuted until Florida is freed from these ruthless savages." No one agreed more than Florida's new governor, Robert Reid. Like the war itself, Call's carping had become a nuisance to Poinsett, who asked the president to find a more cooperative territorial governor. Poinsett found his man in Reid, whose loyalty to the Jacksonian Democrats matched his hatred for the Indians and their sympathizers. The Seminoles, he claimed, should be hunted like *"Wild Beasts,"* and he presented the army with imported bloodhounds to do the job. The dogs found only controversy, however, as they proved worthless in the field. Taylor was scarcely more effective. Denied a request for relief the previous spring, he dutifully launched a second winter campaign but had little to show for it. The only accomplishments he could claim—roads built, rivers spanned, and posts erected—were virtually meaningless. A year too late Poinsett granted Taylor's relief.[10]

His successor, Brig. Gen. Walker Keith Armistead, fared little better. "There is a fair prospect from appearances," one officer observed in October 1840, "of this protracted contest with a handful of naked savages [lasting] until the next century be ushered in." Congress agreed, and it voted Armistead more than $1 million to bribe the remaining Seminoles into emigrating voluntarily, but to little avail. Maj. Ethan Allen Hitchcock was not surprised. The army's foremost expert on and critic of U.S. Indian policy, he damned Armistead's habit of wielding "the olive branch in one hand and the sword in the other," which undermined the Indians' faith in his intentions. According to another officer, "this fatal paralysis, neither peace nor war," also devastated the army's morale. Eventually, Armistead advocated negotiations as the surest way to end the conflict, but by then he too had been relieved of command at his own request. On May 31, 1841, he handed the war to its final commander.[11]

<h1 style="text-align:center">III</h1>

This was not, however, the only important change of command. Armistead relinquished his post only two months after Van Buren surrendered the White House to the Whigs, and only one month after the new president, William Henry Harrison, died of pneumonia. His successor, John Tyler, had fixed opinions on neither the war nor Indian policy, but his secretary of war did. In John Bell's view, the previous administration had been committed to the war's aims but indifferent about its execution. And although he inherited a war that his party had generally opposed, Bell was one of the architects of the Indian Removal Act that had occasioned the conflict. For Bell the most appropriate way to rid his president of this albatross of a war was to win it as quickly and cheaply as possible. He entrusted this task to Col. William Jenkins Worth.

Despite his monumental ego, Worth was the right man for the job. A veteran of nearly thirty years' service, he was among the army's most experienced officers and had commanded the 8th Infantry Regiment in Florida since the previous autumn. "My head quarters are in the saddle, sir," he reportedly said when he took overall command, and his troops soon discovered that this was more than bluster. Befitting his experience more than his rank, Worth assumed control of eight of the army's fourteen combat regiments, totaling some 5,000 soldiers; they would know little rest under their new commander. Expensive civilian contractors and volunteers, conversely, could no longer count on work; Bell discouraged the former and all but forbade the latter. Worth diligently implemented the government's "retrenchment" program, eliminating civilian jobs under his quartermaster department and otherwise making do with less. In his first order as commander he prohibited the construction of new barracks. The cost was unwarranted, and Worth's troops would have little need for barracks in the months ahead.[12]

Worth immediately prepared for a summer offensive against the roughly 1,500 Seminoles remaining in Florida. The army chronically underestimated their strength, but Worth understood that those bands remaining were the most intractable and the hardest to find. Inspired by the legendary Seminole spiritual leader Sam Jones (Arpeika), hundreds had taken refuge in the Everglades, where they eked out austere but fiercely independent lives. No less determined, bands under Halleck Tustenuggee, Octiarche, Tiger Tail, and others found refuge in the hammocks of northern and central Florida. Ranging from Tallahassee to St. Augustine, they attacked settlements and travelers and kept the most populous part of the territory in perpetual turmoil. For Worth to make any significant progress he would have to subdue these bands, and he directed his summer offensive against those residing along the Withlacoochee River.

There was nothing novel about the location; many of the war's earliest and most significant engagements had occurred on the labyrinthine margins of this waterway. But thus far the army had generally confined large-scale operations to the temperate months of November to April, adhering to Winfield Scott's edict that the rest of the year was "too hot or too sickly to be endured." Consequently the Seminoles had learned to regard the summer as a time of respite during which they could raise their crops and families in relative peace. Worth determined to disrupt this pattern, whatever the risks to his soldiers. On June 25, 200-man columns departed Forts Brooke (Tampa), King (present-day Ocala), and Harrison (present-day Clearwater) to canvass the country surrounding the Withlacoochee River. Each supported by mounted detachments to aid in communications and (hopefully) pursuit, the columns conducted aggressive patrols in their respective zones. In the words of Worth's aide, operations took on a "partisan character," as twenty-man detachments scoured assigned areas of interest, seeking engagements and destroying villages and supplies where they found them. Elsewhere post commanders across Florida stepped up the intensity, duration, and range of their patrols, mounting pressure the likes of which the Seminoles had not seen in several years—and had never encountered in the dead of a Florida summer.[13]

As Scott anticipated, the twenty-five-day offensive took a toll on Worth's troops. More than a third of those involved took ill, and almost a quarter ended up in the hospital. Out of fewer than 5,000 troops more than 2,000 were unfit for duty at some point during the offensive. By conventional standards they had little to show for their sacrifices: five prisoners and a litany of huts and fields laid to waste. But Worth's troops were not fighting a conventional war, and their destruction of thirty-two fields, some as large as twenty acres, meant much more than blows traded. Thanks to Florida's long growing season and natural bounty, the Seminoles were less susceptible than most Indians to the tactics of crop destruction that Europeans had traditionally employed against Native Americans. Yet the Seminole economy remained fragile and somewhat dependent on an unmolested summer growing season. While it prostrated his own force for a time, Worth's offensive shattered the sense of security that had pervaded Seminole camps every summer. On the last day of June and in the very midst of the forces hunting them, four chiefs and 120 warriors resolved to continue resistance and execute any who subverted their policy. Taken in one light as a sign of undaunted resolve, the council actually bespoke the vulnerability of Seminole will. Their people had borne much already, and Worth's offensive dimmed their prospects of a better future. Presented with a credible alternative, the chiefs feared, many of their followers would take it.

Worth determined to offer that alternative by whatever means necessary. For several years the Americans had used Indian envoys brought back from Indian Territory to induce the remaining Seminoles to emigrate. But after interviewing the envoys about conditions in the West many Seminoles concluded that it was better to live on the run in Florida. Worth's summer offensive compelled many Seminoles to revisit this assessment, and throughout the fall they proved more receptive to the appeals of the reservation Indians. Others remained reluctant to emigrate. In such cases Worth turned to the opprobrious but proven methods of Thomas Jesup. Shortly after Worth assumed command his subordinates seized the important chief Coacoochee under a white flag of truce. After threatening to hang Coacoochee to secure the surrender of his followers, Worth used him to lure chief Hospetarke and his band into a similar trap. By means fair and foul Worth was able to secure more than 200 Seminoles by early fall, and he optimistically suggested to the War Department that it could accelerate the redeployment of combat regiments.

Worth's optimism was not shared by Florida's new governor, the recently reinstated Richard Call. Fired first from command and then from office by Jacksonian Democrats, Call changed his party affiliation but not his conviction that the defense of Florida depended on mobilization of the territorial militia. Worth disagreed emphatically. "It will be with extreme reluctance, and only in the last resort, that I shall muster in militia," he informed Call, further explaining that a desire to bilk the government "enters largely in to every panic." If armed Floridians could be of any service, Worth contended, it was by establishing and defending homesteads in the backcountry. In this regard he was following the lead of President Tyler and Senator Thomas Hart Benton of Missouri. Since 1839, Benton had been pressing for legislation that would provide land and guns to settlers willing to make homes in Florida's hinterlands, theoretically securing the countryside from Indian attacks. The House had yet to entertain the scheme, but Tyler liked it and directed Worth to implement it with money Congress had already voted to relieve Florida's "suffering inhabitants." The obedient colonel assigned the project to two officers and suggested that these militant homesteaders be paid as soldiers—even if he adamantly refused to use them as such.[14]

Worth's refusal to employ the militia was highly satisfactory to Winfield Scott, who became the army's commanding general following Alexander Macomb's death in July 1841. Submitting his first annual report in this capacity, Scott praised both Worth's accomplishments and the fact that "not a company of volunteers or militia was engaged in those operations." A faithful steward of his fourteen-regiment service, Scott added without a hint of irony, "Sixteen regiments is the *minimum* regular force now absolutely required by the country [in times of peace]." The man receiving Scott's report was also relatively new to the job. In August Tyler revealed himself to be a states' rights Democrat by vetoing a bill that would have reestablished a national bank. All but one member of the cabinet he had inherited from Harrison resigned in protest, including John Bell. In his stead Tyler appointed John C. Spencer, a New York lawyer and politician with little military experience but a principled stance on Indian policy. He implied as much in his own annual report, characterizing the war in Florida as a regrettable affair and writing of "pity, not far removed from contempt, for an inglorious foe." However subtle, such language hinted at a significant shift in the strategic direction of the war.[15]

In the meantime, Worth shifted his attention to southern Florida and the second phase of his first (and final) campaign. After months of preparation, in early December, U.S. forces plunged into the Everglades in three columns from both coasts. From Fort Dallas (present-day Miami) Navy Lt. John McLaughlin advanced with 150 canoe-borne sailors and marines, while Maj. Thomas Childs's 3rd Artillery advanced from Fort Lauderdale with similar numbers and conveyance. From the Gulf coast Worth's main force of thirteen infantry and dragoon companies entered the Big Cypress Swamp by way of the Caloosahatchee River and pre-staged depots. Meanwhile supporting forces moved into a blocking position between Lake Okeechobee and the Atlantic coast. For the next two months a third of Worth's total force and elements of all three armed services scoured every known or suspected enemy camp in one of the war's most ambitious operations.

It was also singularly inconsequential. Producing a single firefight on December 20, 1841, the campaign taxed the stamina of the troops and the credulity of their officers. "Eleven hundred men against a handful of savages!" one company commander wrote a friend. "You will say, how ignoble and pitiful a service! And so it is." Worth might not have disagreed. Shortly before launching the expedition, he advised a regimental commander that there were more effective methods of waging this war "than in cutting down a solitary Indian, who may have been guilty of the indecency of defending his own country in his own way." A week into the operation, Worth realized that decision was not to be found among the cypress stumps and alligators. On December 9, he delegated command and returned north to close the campaign on its decisive diplomatic front.[16]

That Worth regarded the Everglades expedition as superfluous was made clear by his first report from Tampa, on December 15. Despite the recent assassination of two of his western Indian envoys, negotiations with the northern bands had proceeded apace, and Worth boldly predicted that his first campaign would be the war's last. On December 20, however, Halleck Tustenuggee's band attacked an unsuspecting white settlement in northeastern Florida, and on January 21, 1842, the recently surrendered chief Tiger Tail subverted nearly two months' worth of negotiations before fleeing to the enemy's camp. "This war has been so often over, and it has been told to the world so often," one journalist observed sardonically, "that it requires nerve to say it is not . . . and we must submit calmly to disappointments, and hope for the best."[17]

Yet Worth remained undaunted, if for no other reason than that the end of the war remained as fixed in his view as the means of reaching it. In the wake of these disappointments he resumed active patrolling to track down the offending bands and recalled all but four companies from the Everglades, relegating that watery region to McLaughlin's "mosquito fleet" of canoes and borrowed revenue cutters for the balance of the war. But the experience of the previous eight months had convinced Worth and his officers—as it had their predecessors—of the futility of force. Toward the end of his Everglades duty one company commander commended the "wiser and more humane policy" of sending Indian envoys among the Indians' camps, where they could work upon the sentiments of Seminole women, who had stoically borne so many of the war's costs. Only by such appeals, Worth had come to believe, could he finally end the war.[18]

Every commander since Thomas Jesup had, in his own course, reached the same conclusion, and yet the war continued. Confident he could do little more in the field, on February 10, 1842, Worth headed to Tallahassee in search of a political ally. Perhaps because it shifted responsibility for Florida's security back to its citizen soldiery or simply because it made sense, Governor Call "generally . . . concurred" with Worth's position.[19] Soon afterward and doubtless on cue, Tallahassee's Whig newspaper exalted Worth and suggested that peace was at hand. With local support secured, Worth turned his attention to the administration that appointed him.

On February 14, he wrote Winfield Scott a letter strikingly similar to one Thomas Jesup had written four years earlier. The logic and proposal were nearly identical; the conditions were not. Only 301 Seminoles remained in Florida, Worth claimed, and the previous campaign had convinced him of "the utter impracticability of securing them by main force." Like Jesup, Worth suggested that they be left in peace, but he took great pains not to overstep his bounds as operational commander. Of the 301, Worth argued that 120 were not signatories to the Treaty of Payne's Landing, implying that neither national honor nor law demanded their removal. As for the rest, he argued not for *abandonment* of the goal of complete removal but rather its pursuit by "pacific and persuasive measures." The only way to win the war, in Worth's postulation, was to stop fighting it.[20]

His senior colleagues were unconvinced. Upon receiving Worth's proposal, Secretary Spencer convened a council of the army's senior generals to weigh its merits. According to Ethan Allen Hitchcock, most officers had already acknowledged the propriety of letting the Seminoles remain in Florida, but many feared that anything less than victory would tarnish the army's reputation. This fear likely operated on the council of generals, few of whom had any firsthand knowledge of the war; all but one of them rejected Worth's proposal. The lone dissenting vote came from Jesup, whose own proposal had been rejected out of hand. But Joel Poinsett was no longer the secretary of war, and the Seminoles were much reduced. Spencer appeared receptive but lacked the military credentials to contest the judgment of the army's senior officers. Rather than overrule or bow to them, he pocketed the proposal, withholding a definite decision until the balance shifted.

Worth did not receive a formal reply to his recommendations for three months. Instead, rumor arrived that the army's senior generals had voted him down. In the absence of positive instructions he followed his conscience, maintaining military pressure on those bands unwilling to treat and diplomatic pressure elsewhere. In mid-April he launched a concerted hunt for Halleck Tustenuggee, catching up with him on the April 19 near Lake Ahapopka. The war's last battle was reminiscent of many of its earliest, as Worth led 400 men against a well-prepared defensive position yet failed to contain an outnumbered foe. Nevertheless, Worth captured most of Halleck's supplies as well as his father-in-law. By this agent Worth opened negotiations with Halleck; by Jesup's methods the Americans ensnared the indignant chief and 114 of his followers. Estimating that he had nearly halved the number of Indians remaining at large and acting on his own authority, Worth sent them word that they could remain in southern Florida. He characteristically sent the message via Halleck, but the chief was too embittered either to be an effective envoy or to remain in Florida. "I have been hunted like a wolf," he complained before embarking for his new home, "and now I am sent away like a dog." Few officers relished such scenes, but they suppressed their refined notions of military honor in the interests of speeding the conclusion of a dishonorable war. "The ends *must* justify the means," Capt. George McCall explained to his father. "They have made fools of us too often."[21]

Whether or not the means were justified, Halleck's capture was a tipping point. Favorable news out of Florida and the end of the traditional campaign season at last swayed Scott, and on May 10, 1842, John Tyler acknowledged what many army officers had maintained for years. "The further pursuit of these miserable beings, by a large military force," he apprised Congress, "seems to be as injudicious as it is unavailing." The president announced Worth's proposal as administration policy and reserved for the colonel the honor of declaring hostilities ceased "as soon as he shall deem it expedient." Thenceforth the security of Florida would rest not on soldiers but on hardy settlers, who would "defend themselves and their houses, and thus relieve the Government from further anxiety or expense for their protection." To encourage their migration Tyler urged Congress to provide them with land, rations, arms, and ammunition. Senator Benton picked up the charge and resubmitted his Armed Occupation Bill the following month. When it cleared both houses the guns were gone, but a toothless Armed Occupation Act became law on August 4.[22]

Worth meanwhile passed the summer in negotiations, offering financial inducements to those Seminoles willing to migrate west and peace to those who would consent only to moving south. Based on favorable responses in all quarters, on August 14, 1842, Worth declared the war over and went on leave. *"Jubilate,"* George McCall wrote home, *"the war is closed!"* Recalling past disappointments he added prudently, "At least it so is by *proclamation."* Indeed, within a month an isolated band attacked a homestead in the western panhandle, and Chiefs Octiarche and Tiger Tail temporized into the winter. Disinclined to risk his accomplishments on their goodwill, Worth, newly promoted to brigadier general, returned from leave, reopened negotiations—and seized them. In Worth's view they and their followers had forfeited their opportunity to remain in Florida. He loaded them aboard steamers and sent them west. By the end of February 1843 he had shipped to Indian Territory approximately 900 Seminoles. Only 600 remained, and relative quiet returned to Florida. For a time.[23]

IV

Whether such a peace might have been possible earlier is impossible to know. Florida's supposedly uninhabitable southern peninsula was capacious enough to accommodate the 3,000 Seminoles Jesup would have left there in 1838. But American will—like that of the Seminoles—had only begun to be tested at that early juncture. Indeed even when opposition Whigs assumed the presidency in 1841 it was unclear whether they were willing to forsake a war they had opposed. This much was clear in Bell's initial guidance to Worth and Spencer's hesitancy in accepting Worth's peace plan. Moreover, both secretaries retained Ethan Allen Hitchcock as a special advisor yet disregarded his persistent advice to seek a negotiated settlement. Nursing a bruised ego, Hitchcock failed to appreciate how remarkable it was that an avowed critic of the war even had a voice in the administration. For if Tyler's war secretaries were not at liberty to abandon the war, neither could they chase victory regardless of its costs. This willingness to consider not merely the ways and means but the *ends* themselves as a variable in the formulation of strategy distinguished Tyler from his predecessors (especially after July 1839) and made possible a negotiated settlement. From the beginning Tyler entertained the possibility of letting the Seminoles remain and replacing the army with his vaunted farmers-in-arms. The trick was demonstrating enough progress to make a negotiated settlement politically feasible. In this regard Worth fulfilled his role admirably. The actual number of Seminoles remaining in Florida arguably mattered less than the fact that a leather-tough combat officer had waged an exhausting campaign that demonstrated progress in the abstract. This accomplished, Tyler found the space he needed to terminate the "unhappy warfare" that plagued Florida. Ironically—and ominously—only Anglo-Floridians raised serious objections.[24]

Transfixed by the promise and problems of territorial expansion, most Americans, army officers included, were eager to forget the unfortunate war; they were not too particular about how it ended. They should have been. Far from securing the peace, Tyler's armed settler program exacerbated the root cause of the conflict: incompatible conceptions of land and the Indians' place upon it. Having spent the past quarter century enforcing an uneasy peace between Indians and unruly frontiersmen, few army officers could have predicted otherwise. Yet they wanted out of Florida so dearly that they suspended disbelief long enough to make good their escape. Once Worth declared hostilities ended, ugly reality intruded. On September 29, 1842, Col. Josiah Vose warned that the "vagabond class of citizens of this Territory" had threatened war against peaceable Indians. One wonders whether Tyler second-guessed the armed settlement scheme when he authorized Vose to repel attacks on the Indians with deadly force. Tyler at least had little reason to worry that *his* armed settlers might upset the peace, at least in the short term. Vose's "vagabond class" actually represented Florida's better established settlers; those lured to Florida by the Armed Occupation Act and its military precursor were barely capable of feeding themselves, let alone of launching an offensive. In November 1843, Worth reported that they had "neither weapons, nor the disposition to use them; not one in ten appeared with arms of any description." He was not complaining. "Though a practical satire upon the purpose and policy of the law, it may be regarded as fortunate. There will be some caution and hesitation in the indulgence of hostile feelings toward the Indian." Yet such feelings required little indulgence, particularly after Florida gained statehood in 1845 and its population swelled. Pressure to complete the removal of the Seminoles revived, producing a Third (albeit much smaller) Seminole War in the late 1850s. Once more the United States attempted to remove every last Indian from Florida, and once again it failed—this time leaving only 300 Indians in their homes.[25]

Because it failed to produce an enduring peace, historians may judge Worth's final campaign a failure. Even in 1842 many of his contemporaries were inclined to agree. To the Jacksonians any concession to the Indians was a shameful stain on national honor. Northeastern humanitarians, conversely, regarded the war itself—methods and ends—as an abomination. Indeed no one was truly happy with the outcome, least of all the Seminoles. Yet in retrospect it is difficult to conceive that the interests of either the United States or the Seminoles might have been better served by prolonging the war. And if Worth did not establish the conditions for an enduring peace it was because such conditions required a cultural transformation on the part of one or both antagonists and were beyond his control.

But the passage of time has accomplished what Worth could not. Following the final Seminole war the Indians remaining in Florida receded from view and restored their population in the midst of an increasingly tolerant Anglo-American society. Today more than 3,500 Seminoles live in Florida, and 17,000 Seminoles (Black and Native) reside in the West. No longer vilified, they are revered for their perseverance and have become symbols of national pride. The war's greatest hero is not Worth but Osceola, whose name graces more than twenty municipalities as well as counties, lakes, mountains, and a national forest. The U.S. government's campaign to remove the Indians, conversely, is justly remembered as one of the more regrettable episodes in American history. Waged too long in the name of national honor, the Second Seminole War was ultimately a self-defeating affair.

Of course most officers knew better than to expect glory or an enhanced reputation from their service in Florida. The final campaign merely affirmed convictions they brought into the war about the superiority of professional soldiers, as well as their proper roles and missions. In the eyes of its officers, the army had broken free from the corrupting influences of militiamen and the demagogues who led them, ending the war and reducing its costs to boot. If militia advocates refused to acknowledge the army's superiority in Indian warfare, the officer corps was not inclined to protest. Instead it feigned adherence to the myth of a virtuous American frontiersman long enough to win reprieve from Florida and turn its energies to the sort of warfare it preferred.

Although a prescient, young Lt. William T. Sherman observed that valuable lessons were to be derived from the Florida War, "as the Indian is most likely to be our chief enemy in times to come," few of his elders concurred. Fixated on the threat (and fancy) of a European invasion, the only peninsular war that interested them involved Wellington and Napoleon. It yielded valuable lessons on siegecraft, whereas Florida offered nothing they wanted to know. Even as Worth mounted his final offensive, an officer in Kansas complained that "a long peace" had dulled the army's war-fighting edge. The soldiers of the 3rd Artillery Regiment, who buried more than 200 of their comrades in Florida, might have scoffed, but they could not wholly disagree. For over six years they had known only the duty of infantrymen, none of it according to Scott's drill manual. A frustrated Scott had tried to remedy this by running troops through Napoleonic drill as they rotated in and out of Florida, but as the war drew to a close he more usefully established a crash gunnery course for the 3rd Artillery. In large measure these efforts to restore conventional capabilities reflected sincere concern for the nation's defense. But they also bespoke officers' profound dissatisfaction with a thankless, inglorious brand of war. Willfully they left the hard-won lessons of seven years' irregular warfare where they had found them in the fantastic hope that they would not be needed again and that an armed citizenry could take on the army's unwanted constabulary role. When tasked with the subjugation of the Plains Indians, officers fell back only on their individual experiences, for the army had no doctrine to offer. Indeed it had scant institutional memory of Florida and looked once more to archetypal France for lessons in colonial warfare.[26]

But not before John Tyler did the army's officers another favor. Already he had relieved them of the war they detested; three days before leaving office he annexed Texas and created the conditions for the one they coveted. In Mexico, Scott, Taylor, and Worth at last found the sort of antagonist—and glory—the Seminoles could not provide. National honor remained elusive.

SUGGESTED READING

More than forty years after its initial publication John K. Mahon's *History of the Second Seminole War, 1835–1842* (revised, 1985) remains the authoritative secondary source on this conflict. Another indispensible work is John T. Sprague's *Origins, Progress, and Conclusion of the Florida War* (1848; reprinted with an introduction by Mahon, 2000). Among the many memoirs of the Second Seminole War, Ethan Allen Hitchcock's *Fifty Years in Camp and Field* (1909) and George McCall's *Let-*

ters from the Frontiers (1868) are among the most relevant to the war's final year.

Solid biographies exist for most of the war's U.S. commanders, but a paucity of sources had discouraged scholarly treatment of most Seminole leaders. Although Osceola has not lacked attention, much of it casts him in the tragic-romantic mold of "noble savage" and overstates his significance within Seminole society. Theda Perdue succinctly addresses this phenomenon in "Osceola: The White Man's Indian," *Florida Historical Quarterly* 70, no. 4 (1992): 475–88. For more general examinations of Seminole history, see J. Leitch Wright's *Creeks & Seminoles* (1986) and James Covington's *The Seminoles of Florida* (1993).

A tremendous field of scholarship addresses the tragic policy of Indian removal, but Grant Foreman's classic *Indian Removal* (1932) and Ronald Satz's *American Indian Policy in the Jacksonian Era* (reprinted with a new preface in 2002) are particularly attentive to the War Department's role. The historiographic themes of Indian policy and early-nineteenth-century U.S. military history come together masterfully in the work of Francis Paul Prucha; all of it is invaluable, but *The Sword of the Republic* (1968) is a good place to begin. Other important works on the early-nineteenth-century army include the relevant chapters of Edward Coffman's *The Old Army* (1986), William Skelton's *An American Profession of Arms* (1992), Robert Wooster's *The American Military Frontiers* (2010), and Samuel Watson's *Frontier Diplomats* (2011).

JOSEPH G. DAWSON III

The U.S. War with Mexico: The Difficulties of Concluding a Victorious War

Maj. Gen. Winfield Scott triumphantly led the way through the streets of Mexico City, followed by row after row of his mounted troops. Lining the route through the Alameda, a massive public park, were Brig. Gen. William J. Worth's division of regulars, while Brig. Gen. John Quitman's veteran soldiers walled the passageway through the Grand Plaza to the National Palace. Bands blared out "Yankee Doodle" and other favorite tunes in celebration of Scott's extraordinary campaign, seizing the port of Veracruz and marching 250 miles overland to defeat the larger Mexican army and capture Mexico City.

Yet Scott's objective for holding this garish display was more than simply honoring his soldiers for their excellent service. The general was deeply concerned about problems after the conventional fighting ended. Throughout the campaign, Scott's army had been subject to guerrilla harassment, and the commanding general correctly assumed that the grand parade would generate wide interest among the local inhabitants. His forces had been so successful in the campaign that they routed the Mexican army and forced the collapse of the Mexican government. It would take some time for Mexico to assemble a responsible body and negotiate a peace treaty with the United States. In the meantime, Scott's army would be compelled to perform occupation duty, procure supplies, and maintain communications along that 250-mile corridor. The general intended the grand parade to be the first in a series of steps to prevent a massive partisan uprising. He hoped this exhibition of military strength might intimidate at least some of those who would be tempted to snipe at Scott's troops and undercut his authority. Ever the thoughtful commander, Scott nonetheless feared the worst.

I

Disputes over Texas caused the war. Texas claimed to win its independence from Mexico in 1836, but Mexico never acknowledged losing the state. Moreover, in contrast to Texas's circumscribed borders as a Mexican province, Texans asserted grandiose boundaries along the entire Rio Grande, from the Gulf of Mexico into Colorado. Dismissive of such assertions, Mexicans argued that even if Texas were independent, its southern boundary must be the Nueces River. Of course this question was moot as long as Mexicans contended that *all of Texas* still belonged to Mexico and denied that America could annex the state. In major steps leading to war, in July 1845 U.S. President James K. Polk approved the annexation of Texas with the Rio Grande boundary and made it official in December 1845. Both sides spurned mutual concessions or continued diplomacy necessary to avoid war.[1]

Texas sparked the war, but controversies over Manifest Destiny and Anglo-American racial attitudes fueled international antagonism. According to the concept of Manifest Destiny the United States was destined with the help of God to expand across North America. America's purchase of Louisiana from France in 1803 and Florida from Spain in 1819 garnered popular support for the idea. By the terms of the Adams-Onis Treaty in 1819 Spain and the United States drew a transcontinental boundary line from Louisiana westward to the Pacific. Only two years later, Mexico won its independence from Spain and inherited that transcontinental boundary. In 1844 many Democrats, led by Polk, endorsed Manifest Destiny, and negative racial stereotypes of Mexicans spurred many Americans to favor buying or annexing parts of Mexico.

Even if Mexico had relinquished Texas, America's aggressive attitudes left other matters unresolved. Intensifying prewar enmity, Polk had insulted Mexico by trying to buy the Mexican provinces of California and New Mexico (including modern Arizona), but Mexicans refused to sell. Other irritants were U.S. citizens' demands that Mexico's government pay them millions of dollars in disputed claims. Both nations recognized that the alternative to diplomacy was war.

To control Texas, President Polk ordered 3,400 U.S. regular troops (about 40 percent of the army) into the state in March 1846. This action all but assured war: Mexicans viewed the arrival of U.S. troops anywhere in Texas as an invasion of Mexico. In April, Mexican President Mariano Paredes announced that Mexico was in a state of "defensive war." On April 25, regular soldiers from the two nations' armies fought a skirmish north of the Rio Grande, resulting in casualties on both sides. This skirmish was followed by two substantial battles on May 8 and 9 in Texas. Polk called on Congress for a declaration of war, which came on May 13.[2]

II

Each side advocated starkly contrasting war aims. Polk had deployed U.S. Army units to verify annexing Texas with the Rio Grande boundary, and he also grasped at further national expansion. Rather than create a European-style empire, he adhered to the concept that any added lands would become equal states in the Union. Hastily designing expeditionary forces to take the offensive, Polk planned to deploy "a competent force into the Northern Provinces [New Mexico and California] and seize and hold them until peace was made." Despite the transcontinental breadth of Polk's aggressive aims, he expected to conduct a limited war. He had no plans for a national draft and did not seek to conquer all of Mexico. He intended to employ the small U.S. Army already on duty (fewer than 8,000 regular soldiers who had enlisted for five years) and thirteen warships of the U.S. Navy, supplemented by 20,000 state volunteers signing up for one year of service. Making an important decision, Polk and Secretary of War William Marcy declined to depend on state militia units that had demonstrated problems in the War of 1812. Instead individual soldiers enlisted in new state volunteer regiments (about 1,000 soldiers each) with the express purpose of fighting in Texas and Mexico. Congress temporarily increased the regular army, but it would take months to organize those units. In a prewar cliché, Polk expected a short, victorious war lasting a few months.[3]

Mexico's war aims were equally clear. Mexicans planned to defend their entire nation, including its northern provinces, but also strongly supported an offensive to regain Texas. To carry out these aims Mexico's army officially enrolled 29,000 men but probably fielded 20,000—still more than twice the size of the U.S. Army's 8,000 soldiers.

Mexican politicians, military officers, and newspaper editors seemed united and belligerent, but privately many were ambivalent about their nation's ability to turn back U.S. attacks. Only a few small naval vessels patrolled Mexico's vulnerable coasts. To defend a large country, national conscription was necessary, but supplying soldiers was difficult because Mexico's treasury was almost empty. Other factors undercut national military efforts, including political unrest in the outlying provinces and discord between government leaders and the Catholic Church. One more factor was less widely appreciated: economic damage caused by Comanche Indians, who carried out raids far below the Rio Grande. Some even argued that the Comanche raids had weakened the national government's authority in northern Mexico.

On the other hand, a few points seemed in Mexico's favor. With good reasons, Mexicans doubted U.S. military capabilities. Assignments scattered the U.S. Navy's few ships around the world. It appeared questionable whether ships could coordinate with army units that would have to go overland to a distant theater of war in California, more than 1,600 miles from the Mississippi Valley. To get there the Americans would need to march across formidable deserts and through high mountain ranges. Drawing on public information, such as statistics published annually in the U.S. secretary of war's annual reports, some Mexicans wondered if America's small army could even conduct transcontinental campaigns. America had displayed problems against Britain in the War of 1812: unenthusiastic state militiamen had refused to leave U.S. territory, and ineffectual generals failed as combat leaders. Furthermore, vocal American critics of Polk and Manifest Destiny encouraged Mexicans to believe that antiwar opponents were numerous. Mexicans counted on their army to make the war more unpopular in America by deterring invasions and inflicting U.S. casualties.

III

Polk possessed no military experience, but he was an aggressive commander in chief. He knew that Mexico allocated most of its army near Mexico City, leaving northern Mexico almost undefended. This strategic imbalance remained glaringly obvious in the decade after Texas's independence. Overconfident that America's small army and navy would make a quick end to the war in 1846, Polk proposed a cordon offensive of multiple invasions. Launching nearly simultaneous attacks would make it difficult for Mexico to respond. Polk's risky plans depended on resourceful American commanders moving adequately supplied troops across great distances to overcome weak Mexican defenses. If Americans captured Mexico's northern provinces, Polk believed, Mexico should recognize the fait accompli and be willing to negotiate.[4]

To Mexico's dismay, aggressive American forces fulfilled Polk's cordon strategy. Leading nearly half of the soldiers in the U.S. regular army, Brig. Gen. Zachary Taylor won two battles, at Palo Alto and at Resaca del la Palma on May 8–9, 1846, driving Mexican regular army units out of Texas. Moving south of the Rio Grande in September Taylor's army attacked and controlled the city of Monterrey in the state of Nuevo León. Commanded by regular Brig. Gen. Stephen W. Kearny and volunteer Col. Alexander W. Doniphan, Americans marched nearly 1,000 miles from Fort Leavenworth, near Independence, Missouri, and in August captured Santa Fe, New Mexico. Kearny took a few hundred regulars overland to California. Leading volunteers, Doniphan fought his way across the Rio Grande near El Paso in December.

On the Pacific the Americans perpetuated their success. Assisted by the navy, by August 1846 about 1,000 U.S. troops had seized San Francisco and Los Angeles. Reaching California with some reinforcements, Kearny suffered a tactical defeat near San Diego in December, but took the town when the Mexicans retreated so that U.S. officers were able to establish a military government in California.

Army expeditions had seized the lands Polk sought, but Mexicans rejected negotiations and united across party lines. In an unexpected development, a former president, Gen. Antonio López de Santa Anna, returned from exile in Cuba in August 1846, took command of the army, and assumed Mexico's leadership. Instead of conceding the war's outcome, as Polk had hoped, Santa Anna inspired Mexican resistance, conscripted more soldiers, extended the length of the war, and counterattacked.

In response Polk authorized another aggressive offensive but, alienated by Zachary Taylor's budding political candidacy, picked Winfield Scott to lead it. Scott had an excellent combat record from the War of 1812 and as commanding general of the U.S. Army displayed a sophisticated understanding of military matters. However, Scott had also dabbled in politics, seeking the Whig Party's presidential nomination. Nevertheless Polk ended Taylor's campaigning in northern Mexico and sent half of his army to Scott. He ordered Scott to capture Veracruz as a base on the Gulf of Mexico. Scott could then march on the National Highway to Mexico City and win victories to demonstrate that Mexico must capitulate. Having been wrong about terminating the war in 1846, Polk decided to widen its geographic scope and called for more military resources. American politicians, newspaper editors, and the president also introduced the prospect of greatly expanding the war by annexing all of Mexico rather than limiting American conquests to Mexico's northern provinces.

Capturing a messenger carrying an outline of American plans, Santa Anna decided to risk a bold counterattack. The outline revealed that Polk had assigned several units from Taylor's army, near Monterrey, to Scott's landing in the Gulf. Santa Anna wanted to win a galvanizing victory by defeating Taylor's weakened army before Scott invested Veracruz. Making a desperate winter march across a nearly waterless desert, Santa Anna's army attacked Taylor's camp at Buena Vista on February 22–23, 1847. Defeated, the Mexicans suffered severe losses. Santa Anna touted nationalism, suppressed internal critics, drafted another army around the nucleus of Buena Vista veterans, and prepared to oppose Scott.

IV

Before Santa Anna could reach the coast, Scott began America's next offensive. In a well-designed amphibious operation he landed his troops below Veracruz on March 9. He laid siege to the city and accepted its surrender twenty days later.

To administer Veracruz and offset the bitter reaction it was logical to expect from Mexican civilians, Scott took several steps. Continuing a policy set by Secretary of War Marcy and implemented by Zachary Taylor, Scott's army paid fair market prices for supplies. Furthermore, Scott got the attention of both his troops and the Mexicans when he issued General Order No. 20. This order stipulated that when convicted, American soldiers would be severely punished for murder, rape, assault, and robbery or any crimes against priests or Catholic churches. U.S. military courts would judge accused soldiers. Scott enforced his promises of punishment for American soldiers who committed crimes against civilians. Most of the perpetrators were in fact volunteers, whom Mexicans detested because of their loose discipline. In Scott's opinion, however, his orders produced "the highest moral deportment and discipline ever known in an invading army."[5]

Worried that disease could cripple his army if it stayed on the coast, Scott left a small garrison in Veracruz and advanced inland on April 8. His forces numbered less than 12,000. In another move to placate Mexican civilians, his "Proclamation to the Good People of Mexico" on April 11 introduced the political tactic of condemning Mexico's national leaders but befriending its populace.[6]

To stop the invaders' advance, Santa Anna entrenched in a substantial blocking position at Cerro Gordo. On April 17–18 the Americans won a battle by outflanking the trenches. The Mexicans suffered 3,000 casualties; the Americans lost 420. When the invaders reached the city of Jalapa the Mexican Congress prohibited Santa Anna from seeking a diplomatic opening, though Scott wrote Taylor that this was the right moment for "a *peace,* or an *armistice.* As yet no such overture has been heard of."[7]

More than halfway to Mexico City, Scott's army next halted in mid-May at Puebla, a substantial city of 80,000. The one-year enlistments of many volunteers would expire soon, and he waited for replacements. In the meantime the Americans policed Puebla, instituted sanitation procedures to head off fevers capable of decimating the army, and punished U.S. soldiers convicted of crimes against civilians. Pesky guerrillas prompted Scott to issue another proclamation, this time threatening to penalize civilian leaders for guerrilla attacks. Having built his credibility among Mexicans by enforcing his previous orders, Scott contended that Americans "desired[d] peace [and] friendship."[8]

Because Santa Anna refused to negotiate, Scott resolved to attack the capital. His force numbered around 10,500 after he left 2,500 others in hospitals in Puebla. He had kept his losses at a minimum by relying on flanking movements, turning the Mexicans out of strong defensive positions, and not making major operational errors. Consolidating most available troops, he closed some depots on the National Highway. Britain's Duke of Wellington supposedly commented unfavorably on Scott's decision to cut his line of communications so deep in enemy country. Scott knew that the campaign could go against him and yet forged ahead.

Nicolas Trist, a U.S. State Department diplomat, had traveled with the army since it took Jalapa. Though Scott and Trist had been at odds, their relationship improved. They both sought an opportunity for negotiations to end the war.

THE U.S. ADVANCE ON MEXICO CITY
August - September, 1847

V

Nearing the outskirts of Mexico City from the east on August 12, Scott found that Mexican officials continued to show no interest in negotiating. So he examined the capital's defenses. Extensive marshes and multiple lakes bridged by causeways complicated any approach to the city. Relying on the causeways to channel Americans along certain routes, Santa Anna deployed more than 30,000 soldiers and designed the city's defenses in the east. He hoped that the Americans would exhaust themselves attacking El Peñon, a cannon-studded fortification. Scott had other ideas. Reposing great confidence in an unofficial staff composed of engineer officers who were graduates of the Military Academy, notably Capt. Robert E. Lee, Lt. George B. McClellan, and Lt. P. G. T. Beauregard, he directed them to scout ahead and assess Mexican dispositions.

Disposing his units, Scott made it appear that he was going to attack from the east. On Scott's order, Brig. Gen. William Worth, a regular officer, marched his division to the southwest, first around Lake Chalco and then around Lake Xochimilco. With his division, Brig. Gen. Gideon Pillow, a volatile volunteer officer, supported Worth. Other brigades followed, sidestepping the best Mexican defenses, but it remained to be seen if a southern path would lead to victory.

American operations in the south got under way on August 18. This approach required either outflanking or assaulting a sequence of defended villages and towns: San Antonio, Churubusco, and Padierna (near Contreras). Reconnaissance confirmed that the southern defenses were also strong and it would take multiple attacks to breach them. Finding a rough path along a lava bed called El Pedrégal, Scott's engineers confounded Mexican defenders, who had assured themselves that the Pedrégal was impassable. Supported by artillery laboriously brought along the jagged pathway, American infantry divisions marched on Mexican positions near Padierna (north of Contreras). Beginning with a dawn attack by Col. Bennett Riley's brigade of regulars on August 19, Americans fought a bitter engagement at San Gerónimo. There, had they exercised better coordination, Santa Anna and a subordinate general might have trapped about 3,000 Americans. Instead the Mexicans failed to seize the moment and American units smashed through and proceeded up the road. Scott watched as his battle lines successfully swept into the Mexican defenses at Coyoacán.

After three days of combat, with 800 wounded and 130 killed, the

Americans found themselves in an increasingly dangerous position. The Mexican defenders had proved themselves better than expected. Nothing about this operation was turning out to be an easy victory for the Americans.

As the fighting tapered off south of the city, Scott and Santa Anna arranged for a cease-fire on August 24; Scott was hopeful that this cessation would lead to the negotiations he and Nicholas Trist had sought since the spring. As a gesture of goodwill (and removing the need to care for them) Scott returned Mexicans who had been taken prisoner. While the Americans foraged for food, Santa Anna redistributed soldiers along the city's defensive perimeter. After a week of meetings addressing disputed points, such as declaring the Nueces River rather than the Rio Grande as the boundary of Texas, Trist's stab at diplomacy failed. The cease-fire terminated on September 6.

Although some of his subordinates favored resuming assaults by the southern route, engineer officers' scouting reports led Scott to decide to maneuver west of the capital. The Americans found that imposing defensive works also guarded Mexico City's western approaches. Uncertain which avenue Scott would take, but still focused on the south, Santa Anna was reluctant to shift additional veteran units to Chapultepec, a castle-like edifice housing the Mexican Military College. Scott worried that multiple failures in either leadership or unit determination could lead to high American casualties and catastrophe.

At dawn on September 8, after a hasty reconnaissance, General Worth's division assaulted Molino del Rey ("the King's Mill"), the rumored location of a cannon factory. Masked Mexican batteries poured a fierce cannonade, catching Worth unaware and cutting swaths through his troops. Torrents of Mexican musketry, described by Lt. Ralph Kirkham as coming "like the roll of drums," killed and wounded more Americans. Multiple units faltered and turned back. Then the attackers renewed their assaults and captured the complex of buildings composing the Molino, only to find no cannon foundry there. More than 800 attackers had been killed or wounded. Looking across the way, Scott and his troops saw Chapultepec, and two miles beyond, the castle blockhouses defended city gates. No matter the losses at the Molino, more hard fighting lay ahead.[9]

Engineers, including Lee and Beauregard, scouted ahead. At a conference some engineers and generals reemphasized the southern route. Scott called on all to speak their mind. In contrast to others, Beauregard favored the western approach. After hearing several opinions, Scott committed them by declaring, "Gentlemen, we will attack by the Western gates!"[10]

Looming over open fields from a prominence 200 feet high, Chapultepec drew everyone's attention. Mexican military engineers supplemented the castle with entrenchments and cannon emplacements, but for an adequate defense Santa Anna needed to double the troops he had assigned there. Instead of bypassing Chapultepec, Scott resolved that a feint on September 12 by Bennett Riley's brigade would keep Mexicans' attention on the south and precede the main attack on the castle by a combined force of volunteers, regulars, and marines. An early-morning cannonade on the castle opened the action the next day. Some Americans rushed forward, carrying ladders to scale walls and parapets. After two hours of bitter combat Americans gained control of the castle from its resolute defenders, including young college cadets, the "heroic boys." The number of Americans killed or wounded again totaled more than 800. Scott recognized that his army could not afford any more such casualty lists.

If Scott meant to get into the city itself his soldiers had to breach Mexican fortifications at two well-defended *garitas* (gates): Belén Gate and San Cosme Gate. Maj. Gen. John A. Quitman, another headstrong volunteer, urgently pointed his division toward Belén, worried that Scott would deprive him of pressing home his attack. Scott hoped that capturing Chapultepec was the last step needed before negotiations. Ignoring messengers from Scott ordering him to delay and refusing to let him give the honor of the final assault to a favored regular general, Quitman took matters into his own hands.

The battles for the gates began. Quitman sent his troops rushing to the Belén Gate, and found that its defenders had not been demoralized by the fall of Chapultepec. They let loose deadly blasts of musketry into Quitman's column. As American cannon shots silenced some of those defenders, a Mexican artillery shell exploded near where Quitman, two other generals, and their staffs had assembled. Several of them were "severely stunned," but amazingly the shell caused no serious wounds. Americans breached the Belén Gate around 1:20 p.m.[11] Later in the afternoon William Worth and his division stormed the San Cosme Gate, where Mexicans held up the American advance for more than four hours. Inspired by junior officers such as Lt. Daniel H. Hill and Capt. Ulysses S. Grant, the attackers took the gate that evening.

Scott now issued ultimatums to the Mexicans: surrender the city and provide money to offset the costs of maintaining the American army or face urban warfare and civilian casualties. Influenced by the city council, Santa Anna decided not to subject his capital to destruction. He and his demoralized army abandoned the capital, and the general resigned the presidency.

VI

The Mexico City campaign terminated the conventional war, leaving Mexico exhausted and bankrupt. Santa Anna's resignation opened a tremendous void in Mexico's leadership, and no one replaced him as generalissimo. For several weeks U.S. diplomat Nicholas Trist sought a Mexican counterpart with authority to negotiate an official end to the war.

Scott established a military government to police and supervise the capital, procedures that helped to terminate the war. Worried about the safety of his small army, he also aimed to restore routine for civilians—or life as normal as possible with 8,000 foreign troops occupying the capital. Creating the office of military governor of Mexico City, he appointed General Quitman, a lawyer in civilian life, to the post. For several days numerous Mexicans, including convicts who had been released from jails and prisons, shot at American soldiers and committed crimes against civilians. Persuading the Catholic hierarchy to open its churches, Scott symbolically attended mass. Americans protected cathedrals and churches; priests were sacrosanct, but religious leaders were not allowed to use church property to give sanctuary to guerrillas. Mindful of civic order, Scott set up five city military police districts, and U.S. soldiers carried out patrols. Scott emphasized the dangers in the enemy capital, "cautioning soldiers against leaving their quarters, unless in small parties or well-armed." Soon stores reopened and Mexicans began to accommodate themselves to the presence of the occupying army.[12]

In the weeks to come, the American army supervised elections, administered public health, and regulated markets, businesses, taverns, and gambling. These activities naturally involved Americans in Mexican domestic politics at the city, province, and national levels. Mexican civil courts handled crimes between Mexicans but also adjudicated cases of Americans arrested on minor charges. U.S. military courts dealt with major crimes by American soldiers. Scott declared, "I will tolerate no disorders of any kind, but cause all [violators] to be rigorously punished. No officer or man, under my orders, shall be allowed to dishonor me, the army, and the United States with impunity." His design for military occupation worked remarkably well.[13]

The U.S. occupation plan relied on Americans controlling major cities, such as Puebla and Jalapa, but also a series of depots on the National Highway. Although it received reinforcements, America's small army was unable to blanket the provinces with troops, pointing out the truism that there are seldom enough troops available during postwar occupations. Protecting wagon trains was the key. Secretary of War Marcy had advised Scott to strike guerrillas in their "haunts and places of rendezvous," but the general decided to *react* to guerrillas rather than seek them out.[14]

At the same time that Scott supervised central Mexico, American military governments also functioned in New Mexico and California. Those governments were similar to Scott's, but Polk designated no general or staff officer to coordinate the three regions. American army officers also administered California and New Mexico in order to annex them into the United States. Rumors circulated among Mexicans and in the United States that America was annexing all of Mexico.

Prior to September 1847, Americans viewed guerrillas as pests, but even Scott had worried that they were capable of extending the length of the war. The general also anticipated that capturing Mexico's capital might not force the enemy to capitulate, as Polk wished. Writing to Zachary Taylor, Scott had postulated, "The enemy, without an army, would still hold out and operate against our trains, small parties, and stragglers . . . on the guerrilla plan." After Mexico City fell, the guerrillas grew increasingly active. For instance, a month after the capital fell, Captain Lee wrote, "So beset is the road [to Veracruz] by robbers and Guerilleros, that it is difficult for even a courier to steal through." Mexican troops and irregulars posed serious threats to U.S. depots, especially at Puebla.[15]

Guerrillas haunted American couriers and troops moving outside of cities in less than company strength (about 100 soldiers). Neither American regulars nor volunteers had prepared for or were interested in fighting a guerrilla war, particularly not one of indefinite duration. Guerrilla attacks were troublesome to U.S. wagon convoys, mounted patrols, town garrisons, and supply depots. Notable guerrillas took pride in obtaining official military commissions from Mexican authorities, keeping alive the spirit of resistance against the American occupation.

Aside from the guerrillas, self-interested bandits added to Scott's woes. Out for their own profit, bandits accosted individual American soldiers as well as foreign merchants along the National Road and in northern Mexico, where Zachary Taylor initiated punishing counterstrikes. Sometimes Americans found it difficult to distinguish garden-variety robbers from guerrillas, which one American veteran acknowledged caused "a good deal of trouble." Showing the strains in the fabric of Mexican society, some guerrillas and bandits also preyed upon their fellow countrymen, alienating support vital to the irregulars' operations.[16]

Americans took steps to counteract the guerrillas, especially after diplomatic negotiations got under way between Trist and Mexican officials in December. Scott announced that no quarter would be given to guerrillas and that civilians harboring them would have their property confiscated or destroyed. U.S. officers assigned several hundred soldiers to escort big wagon convoys on major roads. In late September one American officer likened swarming guerrillas to "a beehive overturned." Later he specified that guerrillas were noisy "without doing us much harm."[17]

It is notable that although guerrillas appeared in many locations they never captured one of Scott's depots or cut his supply lines. One Mexican officer later contended, "War made systematically by guerrillas would in the long run have ruined the enemy and given success to the Republic." But Mexicans were unable to prevent Americans from traveling on any Mexican roadway that U.S. officers decided to use, much less push the occupying army out of central Mexico.[18]

When treaty negotiations proceeded during January 1848, each nation adjusted to the realities of the situation, and guerrilla activities declined in some areas. Mexico completely abandoned its original war aims. With Santa Anna no longer the nation's leader, Manuel Peña y Peña, a senior judge on Mexico's Supreme Court, acted as temporary president. He persuaded Mexicans that terms they had rejected in 1846 must be accepted, including U.S. annexation of Texas with the Rio Grande boundary. Peña also convinced them to relinquish the northern provinces.

The diplomat Nicholas Trist maintained the original American war aims and refused Polk's orders to return to Washington. Polk had announced to Congress in December 1847 that he was opposed to annexing all Mexico, opening the way for Trist to produce an acceptable treaty. Polk rejected annexation for three reasons: the modest size of the U.S. military forces could not dominate the country; it was too expensive and controversial to maintain an army in central Mexico; and many Anglo-Americans opposed bringing millions of Hispanics into American society.[19]

For political reasons Polk replaced Scott as commander, but Scott's occupation procedures remained in effect. Mexican attacks declined after authorities announced on February 2, 1848, that a treaty was ready and that U.S. occupation forces would begin withdrawing from Mexico. A month later U.S. and Mexican military officers reached an arrangement to restore the capital to Mexican control.

The U.S. Senate ratified the Treaty of Guadalupe Hidalgo on March 10 and the Mexican Congress approved it on March 25. Mexico acknowledged the loss of Texas and its northern provinces of California and New Mexico. The United States paid an indemnity of $15 million to Mexico and also paid American citizens $3 million, which they claimed the Mexican government owed them. As the departure of U.S. forces came into view, Mexico's internal political rivalries intensified, leading to many violent incidents between Mexicans, though these rivalries didn't blow up into full-scale civil war.

Following a ceremony to hand over authority, American units evacuated Mexico City on June 12. Guerrillas had not caused U.S. forces to withdraw prior to the negotiation of the Treaty of Guadalupe Hidalgo or in the ten weeks after the treaty was ratified. For nine months Americans had maintained a firm hand over the capital. Some Mexicans predicted chaos when the U.S. occupation ended, but the last American troops returned home in August leaving a fairly peaceful Mexico in their wake.

VII

Strategically, operationally, and tactically the War with Mexico represented improvements for the United States, in contrast to the War of 1812. Americans had not relied on state militias, and no volunteer regiments refused to serve outside the United States. Unlike President James Madison during that earlier war, President Polk demonstrated superior attributes in formulating strategy, functioning as commander in chief and achieving his war aims. During eighteen months of successful campaigning against the Mexican regular army, the United States had raised and deployed military forces to four theaters of war: Texas and the southern Rio Grande, New Mexico, California, and central Mexico. Three of the four theaters were at considerable distances from the eastern United States and the Mississippi River Valley and therefore presented notable logistical challenges, which America met or overcame. This was the first war in which the U.S. Navy fought with a superior strength over its enemy. The navy effectively carried out all actions: blockades, convoys, and troop landings. On the other hand, there was no tradition of joint operations and no established expectation that a single officer would be assigned to joint command, which sometimes caused tension between army and navy officers. One secretary of war, William Marcy, brought consistency and competence to the War Department, a notable improvement over the failures of William Eustis and some of his successors in the War Department from 1812 to 1815. From 1846 to war's end America's top generals and expeditionary commanders—Taylor, Kearny, and Scott—were far better than U.S. senior officers William Hull, Henry Dearborn, and James Wilkinson in the War of 1812.

Nevertheless the ultimate U.S. victory glossed over some of the war's important features.

Underestimating their opponent, Americans usually failed to credit the efforts of Mexican soldiers and Santa Anna's leadership. Several Mexican units fought well, notably around Mexico City and at Buena Vista, where Taylor's victory was narrow. In Scott's campaign the outcome of battles resulted from well-executed American flanking attacks rather than direct breaching of Mexican defenses. When Scott's regiments conducted frontal assaults, U.S. casualties were heavy.

Antagonisms within the military impinged on American success. As had been evident with Continental officers in the American Revolution and regular officers in the War of 1812, regular army officers again disagreed with volunteers about military fundamentals, including camp regimens, basic discipline, and training units for combat. Scott pointed out to Secretary Marcy that regulars routinely set up a well-laid camp at the end of a day's march, but volunteers "neglect[ed] all those points" necessary for a healthy and orderly bivouac; as a result, diseases killed more volunteers than Mexican bullets. Leadership among volunteer officers was very uneven; only a few were effective or remarkable. Given such contention, regulars and volunteers often distrusted each other, and tension between them was routine.[20]

Victory submerged the distress caused by American violence against Mexican civilians, mostly committed by volunteers. Volunteers often violated the bounds of decency and the U.S. Army's official Articles of War, threatening to ruin the careful arrangements made by Taylor and Scott to win cooperation from Mexico's populace, local officials, provincial leaders, and the Catholic Church. The volunteers' unlawful behavior further alienated the regular army and reinforced senior officers' mistrust of volunteers.

By the summer of 1848 the strength of the U.S. regular army had grown to approximately 47,000, supplemented by thousands of volunteers. After ratifying the Treaty of Guadalupe Hidalgo, Congress began reducing the army's strength. Naturally volunteers mustered out rapidly. Soon new regular units were also disbanded. The army's postwar regular strength leveled off at around 11,000, some 3,000 higher than prewar levels. Even after incremental additions were made in the 1850s, increasing the number of soldiers to about 16,500, the U.S. Army did not come close to matching the armies of Britain, France, Prussia, Russia, or Spain. Furthermore, because France had easily intervened in Mexico in 1838 some observers downplayed the American victory over Mexico. In the end Europeans found no reason to fear U.S. military prowess after 1848.

A major change in the U.S. strategic situation after 1848 was the nation's transcontinental reach. Seizing, occupying, and annexing California, with its ports on the Pacific, conclusively ended any possibility that Britain would gain possession of that state or exercise influence there. Soon California's ports handled increased traffic due to the Gold Rush of 1849. Observers recognized that America's national potential had greatly increased but that American military strength did not match its geographic size.

VIII

The war's outcome had many ramifications for the United States. It expanded the size of the nation by more than 25 percent, brought the slave state of Texas into the Union, and increased disputes over the expansion of slavery into the regions captured from Mexico. Slavery already functioned in the trans-Mississippi in the states of Missouri, Louisiana, and Arkansas. Disputes over slavery had surfaced during the war when Democratic congressman David Wilmot of Pennsylvania introduced a resolution that no slavery be allowed in any land taken from Mexico. Although Congress never approved Wilmot's Proviso, it aggravated sectional tensions. Later Congress passed the Compromise of 1850, an omnibus measure containing several parts designed to quiet sectional disagreements. One part was statehood for California, a result of the Gold Rush. Statehood ended the U.S. Army's military government of the California territory and foreclosed slavery on the Pacific Coast. Between 1850 and 1860 controversy intensified over slavery in other territories and was a major cause of America's Civil War.

The war also had long-lasting ramifications for relations between the United States and Mexico. Mexico lost 50 percent of its land area (including Texas), and was significantly weaker as a result. The discovery of gold in California in 1848 confirmed Mexican expectations that the Pacific Coast was Mexico's "national patrimony," an area of untapped resources and future national growth. The Gold Rush obviously benefited the United States instead of Mexico, and in subsequent decades important commercial seaports thrived at San Diego, San Francisco, and Long Beach, while petroleum in California and Texas became highly prized. All of these facts produced among Mexicans regrets and recriminations over what might have been if California had remained a Mexican province.

Not only did the war slash Mexico's access to resources and future growth, but its outcome drastically decreased Mexico's prospects as a rival to the United States. For instance, in 1853, when the United States wanted to add a strip of Mexico along the Gila River to support a railroad route, the Mexican government agreed to sell the land without raising a hint of war to block the Gadsden Purchase.

Strained relations with Mexico continued far into the twentieth century. The years before and after the Great War of 1914–18 were particularly tense, and the United States intervened militarily twice. In 1914, U.S. forces occupied Veracruz, and in 1916–17 Brig. Gen. John J. Pershing led an expedition to capture Pancho Villa. In March 1917 the British revealed the controversial "Zimmerman Telegram," which indicated that Mexico might join an alliance with Imperial Germany in order to retrieve California and other provinces lost in 1848. In April 1917 the U.S. Congress declared war against Germany, but Mexico did not enter the war.

One of the less appreciated results of the war was related to a provision of the Treaty of Guadalupe Hidalgo calling on the United States to guard against attacks by Native American tribes, particularly Comanches and Apaches. The United States was too weak militarily to live up to this provision. The tribes, the armies, and civilian residents on both sides of the border fought a forty-year conflict that eventually led to the tribes' defeat when they were pushed onto reservations in the 1880s.

American subjugation of Indians and territorial expansion reinforced the contention made by Mexicans and others that America was an empire, and like other imperial powers it acquired land, subordinated people, and exploited resources. Adding territories had been a hallmark of an expansionist America since 1787. But instead of war, purchase brought major acquisitions, such as Louisiana from France, Florida from Spain, and Alaska from Russia, and diplomacy equitably divided Oregon with Britain. European and Asian imperialism subjugated colonies distant from the home country, and the legal and economic standing of colonial peoples was well below citizens'. In contrast, U.S. policy declared that all contiguous lands it added would be divided into states admitted to the Union on an equal footing with the original states of 1776; citizens of new states were supposed to have rights equal to those of citizens of older states. The year 1898 marked a notable break in this policy, when the United States gained control of noncontiguous islands, acquiring Wake, Guam, and Puerto Rico as a result of the Spanish-American War and separately annexed the Hawaiian Islands. Fitting the traditional definition of imperialism, the United States treated those islands as colonies that were unlikely to become states and discriminated against their populations.

The Treaty of Guadalupe Hidalgo added thousands of Hispanic citizens to the United States. In contrast to official U.S. policy and in violation of the Treaty of Guadalupe Hidalgo, those Hispanics found it difficult or impossible to gain legal status or equal rights with Anglo citizens. Anglos took numerous steps to discriminate against Hispanics, depriving them of their land titles and discouraging or preventing them from voting. Federal authorities delayed statehood for New Mexico and Arizona, areas with large Hispanic populations, holding them in territorial status until 1912. Hispanics residing in the captured provinces joined Native Americans and African Americans to become a third major minority group in the diversifying U.S. population. The Hispanic population later ballooned and by the year 2000 surpassed that of both Indians and blacks.

IX

The war with Mexico also had numerous ramifications for the U.S. military. It was the first time Americans fought mostly outside their own country, placing new demands on America's military, naval, and political leaders. Few of them showed evidence of giving careful consideration to the long-term consequences of the war. The war strained America's haphazard logistics; U.S. troops invading Mexico often ate reduced rations and purchased supplies from the Mexicans. One way or another America raised and supplied enough troops and deployed them to win campaigns in four war zones, and then occupy or annex large parts of Mexico. In several instances the Americans overcame hazards and demonstrated that they were capable of marching great distances—notably Kearny and Doniphan to Santa Fe, Kearny to California, and Scott to Mexico City. Any of those campaigns could have failed due to inadequate food and water, diseases, Mexican resistance, or attacks by Native Americans. One failed campaign could have pushed Polk to call for more troops, probably lengthened the war, and potentially increased antiwar opposition.

After the war, Congress recognized the need to boost the size of the U.S. regular army to patrol and garrison the lands taken from Mexico. Stationed in Texas and throughout the trans-Mississippi region, soldiers attended to road building, exploring, enforcing federal laws, protecting settlers, patrolling international borders, garrisoning coastal fortifications, and guarding the perimeters of Indian reservations. Given the many duties its soldiers performed, the United States could have used an army five times larger than it was in 1845. As always, cost played the primary role in Congress's refusal to approve a larger peacetime constabulary for the West.

The conduct of regular army officers between 1846 and 1848 greatly improved the reputation of the U.S. Military Academy and its graduates. Scott praised his "West Pointers" as intelligence gatherers, especially R. E. Lee, who in Scott's judgment stood "far above that of any other officer in the army." Taylor complimented the Academy's artillery officers. The low-ranking Academy graduates were unlikely to influence presidents or secretaries of war in the 1840s, but the enhanced standing of the Academy helped it become a political and military fixture in American life. Criticisms of the Academy and West Pointers would be reignited during and after the Civil War.[21]

Conducting successful military campaigns put generals in the national spotlight. Taylor's battlefield victories made him a national hero, and the Whig Party nominated him for president. He won the election of 1848, demonstrating that successful generals made appealing contenders for high political office. The successes of Scott's military campaign were often studied by students of the military arts; his use of turning movements appears to have influenced some Union and Confederate officers during the American Civil War. Enhancing Scott's reputation were compliments from Britain's Duke of Wellington and analysis by the Swiss military writer Antoine Henri Jomini, who pronounced that Scott had conducted a "brilliant campaign." Politically active before the war, Scott personified "the man on horseback," and he naturally hoped that his wartime victories would lead to political office. The Whig Party did nominate him for president in 1852, but he lost to Democrat Franklin Pierce, one of Polk's volunteer generals during the war.[22]

While some generals gained political fame, wartime disputes between Polk and his senior commanders revealed strains in civil-military relations. Polk distorted his presidential authority and used blatant political favoritism to appoint only Democrats, most of whom did not have much military experience, to become volunteer generals commanding brigades and divisions. Thus, Polk politicized the army, putting some ineffective officers in high command and reconfirming many Americans' belief that high-ranking military posts were political plums for presidents to dispense rather than serious assignments that should go to professional officers. Adding insult to injury, after Scott commanded the army to victory Polk recalled him to Washington and embarrassed him with groundless accusations, thus attempting to reduce Scott's political appeal. Polk's political machinations reflected badly on him but also demonstrated that in America civilian leaders controlled the military, even when presidents or members of the cabinet manipulated the military for partisan purposes.

The war confirmed the focus of most U.S. Army officers on conventional warfare. Despite the fact that Americans had employed guerrilla tactics against the British in the War for Independence and against Native Americans, most U.S. regulars dismissed guerrilla warfare as dishonorable and disreputable. Regular officers shared the opinion of Secretary of War Marcy: "The [Mexican] guerilla system . . . is hardly recognized as a legitimate mode of warfare." American regulars into the twentieth century preferred to concentrate on conventional operations used by European armies.[23]

The Mexican War failed to convince U.S. Army officers and political leaders that it made sense to establish a military government after a war, although the army and its political leaders created military governments after the Civil War and the Spanish-American War and after World War I U.S. soldiers occupied part of Germany. During World War II the U.S. General Staff finally initiated plans for American military governments and set them up in Germany, Austria, Japan, and Korea.

By the measurements of the nineteenth century the Mexico City campaign ended with a decisive American military victory, but the United States was to discover that victory brings its own challenges. From 1846 to 1848 President Polk encountered one problem after another trying to terminate the war, upholding the argument that it is more difficult to end a war than it is to start one. The war proved to Polk that no matter his goals and expectations, war can go in unexpected directions and bring about unanticipated results. After capturing Mexico City, the American army confronted guerrilla warfare inside a foreign nation far earlier than is usually recognized. At the same time, the military governments that the army operated in California, New Mexico, and Central Mexico demonstrate that the United States has allocated postwar efforts to civil-military relations, including what came to be called "nation building," earlier and more extensively than is usually acknowledged. Fighting a guerrilla war while occupying enemy states and attending to complex civil-military relations in a foreign capital, the U.S. Army produced underappreciated but successful results.

SUGGESTED READING

Surveying the war's causes are David M. Pletcher, *The Diplomacy of Annexation: Texas, Oregon, and the Mexican War* (Columbia: University of Missouri Press, 1973); Gene Brack, *Mexico Views Manifest Destiny, 1821–1846* (Albuquerque: University of New Mexico Press, 1975); Reginald Horsman, *Race and Manifest Destiny* (Cambridge: Harvard University Press, 1981). Timothy D. Johnson, *A Gallant Little Army: The Mexico City Campaign* (Lawrence: University Press of Kansas, 2007) effectively analyzes both the conventional battles and guerrilla warfare. Timothy D. Johnson, *Winfield Scott: The Quest for Military Glory* (Lawrence: University Press of Kansas, 1998) puts the campaign in the context of Scott's life. *Memoirs of Lieut. General Scott* (New York: Sheldon, 1864) gives his personal views. A broader work that also includes the U.S. Navy's role is K. Jack Bauer, *The Mexican War, 1846–1848* (1974; Lincoln: University of Nebraska Press, 1992). For Mexican perspectives, see Ramón Alcaraz, *The Other Side, or Notes for the History of the War* (1850; New York: Burt Franklin, 1970); Cecil Robinson, trans. and ed., *The View from Chapultepec: Mexican Writers on the Mexican-American War* (Tucson: University of Arizona Press, 1989); William A. DePalo Jr., *The Mexican National Army* (College Station: Texas A&M University Press, 1997); Irving W. Levinson, *Wars within War: Mexican Guerrillas, Domestic Elites, and the United States of America, 1846–1848* (Fort Worth: Texas Christian University Press, 2005). On the U.S. military governments, see Neal Harlow, *California Conquered: The Annexation of a Mexican Province, 1846–1850* (1982; Berkeley: University of California Press, 1989); Joseph G. Dawson III, *Doniphan's Epic March* (Lawrence: University Press of Kansas, 1999). An introduction to an extensive historical literature on American expansionism is Thomas R. Hietala, *Manifest Design: American Exceptionalism and Empire*, revised ed. (Ithaca, NY: Cornell University Press, 2003).

JOSEPH T. GLATTHAAR

The Civil War:
A New Definition of Victory

As he had done since 1861, Union president Abraham Lincoln pored over military telegrams from the field to the War Department. Much of the news over that span of time had been disheartening. On this day, April 7, 1865, things were different.

Two and a half weeks earlier Lt. Gen. Ulysses S. Grant had cabled Lincoln to visit him in City Point. "I would like very much to see you," the general-in-chief had telegraphed, "and I think the rest would do you good." Grant was ready to make a great push to force Confederate general Robert E. Lee and his Army of Northern Virginia out of their works around Richmond and Petersburg and then crush them before Lee and his soldiers could escape. Four long years of massive bloodshed, staggering destruction, and vast treasure had been expended. Finally the end might be near. Grant wanted the president, who had borne so much of the burden during the war, to be there to savor the moment.

The morning after Lincoln arrived, but before Grant could deliver his culminating blow, Lee took action. On March 25 he struck Union troops east of Petersburg at Fort Stedman. The attack, Lee hoped, would force the Federals to pull back, enabling his army to steal a march westward. The only Confederate chance in the East, he believed, rested in the hope that his Army of Northern Virginia could escape intact and merge with Gen. Joseph E. Johnston's small army in North Carolina. Initial reports of the predawn attack were favorable, but by sunrise the strength and depth of Union lines proved too difficult for Confederate troops to over-come. The plan failed.

Four days later Grant launched a powerful turning movement around Lee's right flank, threatening the Southside Railroad. Lee's men could not halt the Union onslaught. As the fighting commenced, Grant moved closer to the front and relayed news regularly to the president, who analyzed and assessed each telegram as it arrived. Grant was right. Lincoln relished every moment of it. After four years he truly felt a part of the ultimate conquest.

The president felt a twinge of guilt over his absence from Washington. "I begin to feel that I ought to be at home," he admitted to Secretary of War Edwin M. Stanton on March 29, "and yet I dislike to leave without seeing nearer to the end of General Grant's present movement." Stanton suggested that the president's responsibility was there with the army. Compared to urging the Union troops onward, "No other duty can weigh a feather," he counseled the president. "A pause by the army now would do harm; if you are on the ground there will be no pause." The words reassured Lincoln that his proper place was there with the army.[1]

With Lee's right flank turned, he had only one alternative besides surrender. He abandoned his works, yielding Richmond and Petersburg to the Federals, and made his army's escape westward.

On the morning of April 3, Lincoln caught a train to Patrick's Station, where an escort took him to Grant's field tent. The two men then rode into Petersburg, which had withstood Union efforts since the previous June. Lincoln thanked his general warmly for a job well done. That same day Federal troops occupied Richmond.[2]

While Grant returned to the work of capturing Lee's army, Lincoln decided to visit the Confederate capital. He boarded a gunboat and chugged up the James River, escorted by Adm. David Dixon Porter in his flagship. As he stepped onto the dock, crowds of rejoicing freedmen and freedwomen rushed around him. Lincoln wandered the streets, touring the city and examining the debris from a recent fire as joyous former slaves cheered him. At the Confederate White House, Lincoln, with considerable satisfaction, held meetings in President Jefferson Davis's office.

Soon back in City Point, Lincoln resumed the job of scrutinizing telegrams from Grant. He could not resist them. Lee had broken for Lynchburg, with Grant in hot pursuit. Maj. Gen. Philip Sheridan, commander of the Union cavalry, pursued rapidly with his horsemen and five infantry corps. All along the march Federal troops picked up stragglers from Lee's army, men so badly weakened from months of inadequate diet that they could not keep up with their comrades. On April 6 at Sailor's Creek, Union forces carved out a sizable chunk of Lee's army. That night Sheridan announced his triumph to Grant, closing with the assessment, "If the thing is pressed I think Lee will surrender." The next day, April 7, Lincoln scanned Sheridan's victory telegram and injected pithily to Grant, "Let the *thing* be pressed."[3]

The Civil War culminated more than four decades of dispute on the national scene over slavery and its expansion. Neither the northern nor the southern states could come to an accommodation. An attempt in October 1859 by John Brown and his twenty-one men to seize the U.S. Arsenal at Harpers Ferry and arm slaves in a massive uprising heightened sectional tensions. In November 1860 the election of Republican presidential candidate Lincoln triggered secession by the states in the Deep South. Within three months of the presidential election, seven states had left the Union. Mississippi justified its decision to abandon the United States by asserting, "Our position is thoroughly identified with the institution of slavery—the greatest material interest of the world." Georgia declared, "For twenty years past, the abolitionists and their allies in the Northern States have been engaged in constant efforts to subvert our institutions and to excite insurrection and servile war among us." By the time of Lincoln's inauguration in March 1861, those states had already formed a separate country, the Confederate States of America, and had undertaken a strong lobbying campaign to bring the other eight slave states in the Union into their new government.[4]

With twisted logic, President James Buchanan believed that the Constitution permitted no state to leave the Union but that the president, who took an oath to uphold and defend the Constitution, had no authority to keep them in the Union. His successor, Lincoln, viewed matters in a different light. In his First Inaugural Address on March 4, 1861, he attempted to reassure the seceding states that he had no intention of threatening slavery where it existed, but the Union was perpetual and he had a constitutional obligation to execute the laws of the Union in all the states. As Federal property and installations fell into Confederate hands, Lincoln decided after extensive consultation to make a stand at Fort Sumter in Charleston Harbor. By declaring publicly that he would send only humanitarian aid to the troops and no reinforcements or weapons and ammunition, he skillfully shifted the onus to President Davis. Either Davis would allow the shipment to land, thereby extending Union control over property the Confederacy claimed as its own, or he would have to use force to prevent resupply, thereby instigating violence. Davis ordered the shelling of Fort Sumter, which began early on April 12. Thirty-three hours later the fort fell. Lincoln responded by calling for 75,000 militiamen to put down the insurrection. Free states rejoiced, yet four more slave states, Virginia, North Carolina, Tennessee, and Arkansas, seceded from the Union and joined the Confederacy. The war was on.

The eleven seceding states formed the Confederacy to protect slavery. The war, however, would compel them to preserve from invaders not only their new government but also hearth, home, and other property. They mobilized on a massive scale, tapping over 80 percent of all white males between the ages of 17 and 45, with those between 46 and 50 in a reserve. When this proved insufficient, a desperate Confederacy authorized the enlistment of slaves in 1865, but only a few hundred entered the ranks before Lee's army evacuated the Richmond-Petersburg line.

Against the larger and more industrialized northern states the Confederate government understood that it had to utilize its population and resources efficiently. To offset the huge manpower loss at home, the Confederacy would have to rely on blacks, more than 90 percent of whom were slaves, and white women. Confederates hoped to use cotton as a means of purchasing necessary wartime supplies that its infant industries could not produce and as a fulcrum to leverage European assistance against the more populous and industrial Union. They also counted on their belief in the superiority in character, manhood, and military arts of southern whites over their northern counterparts.

Even though the Confederacy intended to import vital war materials, develop industry and agriculture, and seek recognition and intervention from European powers, it would rely mainly on its military forces for defense. Davis designed a military strategy that encouraged his commanders to seize the initiative and strike at the enemy to counterbalance Union superiority. If his armies could dictate the areas of fighting, they could shield citizens better and secure and utilize resources more effectively. The president called on his armies to deliver heavy blows against invaders as close to the border as possible, to protect citizens and property and to discourage the Union from persisting in efforts to conquer the Confederacy. They would suffer heavy losses, to be sure, but Davis believed the Confederate people would endure tremendous hardship and sacrifice for independence.

Federal aims changed during the war. Initially northerners rallied around the flag to preserve the Union. By mid-1862 Lincoln had come to the conclusion that the war had already exacted an enormous amount of blood and treasure and would continue to do so for some time. If the Federals were to win and restore the Union, they must remove the single great division between the two sections: the institution of slavery. That decision also opened the door for exploitation of the single greatest untapped resource: African Americans. Thus, Lincoln expanded the war's aim to save the Union and destroy slavery. Federals originally fought the war to preserve the Union, but if they won the war they would be creating a Union that was substantially different from the old one. Some two thousand years earlier Thucydides had warned of just such a thing when he wrote, "For war, least of all things, conforms to prescribed rules; it strikes out a path for itself when the moment comes."[5]

Although the Federal government would have to defeat a nation with some 750,000 square miles of land, it possessed overwhelming resources. Compared to the Confederacy, the Union had four times as many white people, twice as many farms, nine times the industrial power, a navy, and an economic base to expand all of these areas dramatically. During the war the Union placed 2.25 million men in uniform (more than one million at peak) and at the same time fed, clothed, and equipped its soldiers and population at home and exported vast amounts of foodstuffs. As the war extended into its second, third, and fourth years the Union also tapped the black population, particularly slaves, for almost 180,000 soldiers, at least 18,000 sailors, and tens of thousands of teamsters, stevedores, and laborers. Moreover, by freeing slaves the Union removed laborers from the Confederate cause and placed weapons in their hands or hired them to work on behalf of the Union armies. That step also placed a moral roadblock before European powers that were considering intervention or military support for the Confederacy. Lincoln boasted that the combination of emancipation and black recruitment "works doubly—weakening the enemy and strengthening us," but "triply" might have been more accurate.[6]

The Lincoln administration embarked on a policy to choke the Confederacy economically. A blockade of Confederate ports grew increasingly more effective, so that by 1865 the Union had captured about half of all supply runners, while the number of ships that tried to run the blockade had declined precipitously. Vigorous and skillful diplomatic efforts ensured European neutrality, thereby limiting the economic aid those nations provided the Confederate States. And by 1864 the Union embraced an official policy to draw supplies from Confederate territory as much as possible, to ease demands on northern logistics and augment the burdens on Confederate civilians.

During four years of war the Union altered its military approach several times. In 1861, once Federal authorities had trained their troops satisfactorily, Commanding General Winfield Scott proposed as his initial phase a blockade and a drive to seize the Mississippi River and selected port cities. Scott feared a destructive war would engender such hatred that the Union would have to occupy the seceding states for years, but that slow, steady pressure might bring them back to the negotiating table. Lincoln rejected this strategy, instead yielding to public pressure from the "On to Richmond" media campaign. This naïve approach resulted in a disaster at the Battle of First Manassas.

As Lincoln became more educated in military matters he sought simultaneous advances by his armed forces, utilizing their superior numbers and resources, with Confederate armies as the principal target. By 1863 Grant and his trusted subordinate Maj. Gen. William T. Sherman had developed a raiding strategy, which would operate in conjunction with traditional campaigns. Grant and Sherman sought the devastation of the Confederacy's economic and transportation base and the destruction or seizure of all property, including slaves, that would be useful militarily. These giant raids into the interior would demonstrate the Confederacy's inability to protect its people and property and force Confederate soldiers to choose between fighting for their fledgling country and returning home to look after the welfare of their loved ones. Although the Lincoln Administration was reluctant to embrace the strategy, Grant and Sherman pushed the issue so hard that by late 1864 the Union began implementing it with considerable success.

In the final ten months of the war, overwhelming Federal resources squeezed Lee's army to the breaking point. Throughout the second half of 1864 and into 1865, Grant extended his lines around Richmond and Petersburg, severing vital rail lines to those cities. In November 1864, Lincoln won reelection. That same month Sherman's army began its destructive march through Georgia and into the Carolinas, destroying railroads, consuming supplies, and spurring Confederate desertions. By early March 1865, Sherman's command had crossed into North Carolina, where it merged with another Union force to become 100,000 strong and was poised to press on into Virginia.

With limited railcar space to haul cargo, Lee had to pay soldiers to pick up and recycle battlefield lead. Animals nearly starved. Confederate soldiers subsisted on a pint of corn meal, a quarter pound of beef, and an occasional cup of sorghum per day. That diet, consisting of approximately 900 calories daily, lacked the vitamins and minerals that would have allowed the soldiers' bodies to break down the meager nutrition they consumed. Underfed, overtaxed by hardship, with many of their families overrun or on the verge of falling under Union control, Lee's army was trapped in a downward spiral. By March 1865, on average, one hundred soldiers per day deserted. Lee could no longer hold his lines, and he bolted westward in hopes of uniting with the Confederate force that fronted Sherman's massive army.

If Lincoln had any fear that Federal commanders might not press Lee aggressively enough, it was misguided. The elevation of Grant, Sherman, and Sheridan to positions of high command marked a turnabout in the conduct of war. Their predecessors had only boasted of making war against civilians as well as soldiers and had largely failed to push their armies to achieve great results. These new Union leaders were hard on the enemy and demanding of their own troops. In the movement and successful attack at Five Forks on April 1, Sheridan believed a veteran corps commander had acted slowly and lacked aggressiveness; he removed him. Fair or not, this kind of decision reflected a new attitude among ranking Union commanders. They demanded much of their subordinates and soldiers and exhibited little tolerance for those who failed to measure up to those standards of aggressiveness.

By the night of April 8–9, Union cavalry had positioned itself ahead of Lee's columns. White and black infantrymen, who had marched twenty-five of the previous twenty-eight hours, arrived the next morning just in time to block Lee's attempt to break through the Federal mounted men. The Confederate escape route was sealed.

Twice before, Grant had found himself in an awkward position with Confederates who were authorized to seek an end to hostilities. Both times Lincoln extricated his general-in-chief. In February 1865, the president traveled to Fort Monroe and met with a group of negotiators, but nothing came of the gathering. At the beginning of March, during an exchange of prisoners, Confederate Lt. Gen. James Longstreet and Union Maj. Gen. E. O. C. Ord conversed about the possibility of a military convention to seek a termination of hostilities. With the Confederacy tottering on the brink of collapse, Lee immediately seized the opening and communicated to Grant that his government authorized him to discuss the prospects. Sensibly cautious, Grant requested instructions from

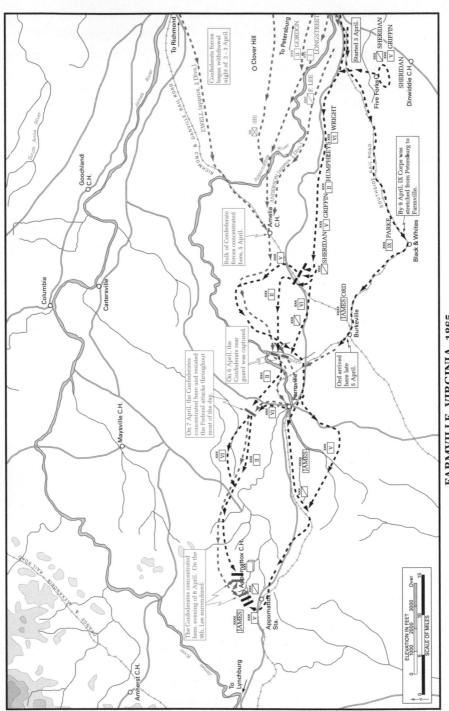

To Richmond

James River

South Anna River

Goochland C.H.

Columbia

Cartersville

RICHMOND & DANVILLE RAIL ROAD

Confederate forces began withdrawal night of 2 - 3 April.

EWELL (approx. 2 Divs.)

O Clover Hill

To Petersburg

[II] GORDON

[I] LONGSTREET

Started 3 April.

[XXX] SHERIDAN

[V] GRIFFIN

F. LEE

[III]

Appomattox River

ANDERSON (approx. 2 Divs.)

Amelia C.H.

[XX]

[V] SHERIDAN

[V] GRIFFIN

[II] HUMPHREYS

[VI] WRIGHT

Five Forks

SHERIDAN

Dinwiddie C.H.

Maysville C.H.

Bulk of Confederate concentrated here, 5 April.

[XXX] V

[XXX] II

[XXX] VI

SOUTHSIDE RAIL ROAD

By 9 April, IX Corps was stretched from Petersburg to Farmville.

[IX] PARKE

Black & Whites

[JAMES] ORD

Burkeville

On 7 April, the Confederates concentrated here and resisted the Federal attacks throughout most of the day.

On 6 April, the Confederate rear guard was captured.

[XXX] II

Farmville

[XXX] VI

Ord arrived here late 5 April.

[XXX] VI

[XXX] II

[JAMES]

[XXX] V

Appomattox C.H.

The Confederates concentrated here, evening of 8 April. On the 9th, Lee surrendered.

[JAMES]

[V]

Appomattox Sta.

ALEXANDRIA RAIL ROAD

ORANGE

River

Amherst C.H.

To Lynchburg

ELEVATION IN FEET
1000   2000   3000   Over
SCALE OF MILES
0   5   10   15
N

FARMVILLE, VIRGINIA, 1865
THE DEFEAT OF LEE
Pursuit to Appomattox Court House,
3 - 9 April 1865

authorities in Washington. The response, drafted by the president him-self, directed Grant "to have no conference with General Lee, unless it be for the capitulation of General Lee's army or some minor or purely military matter." Grant was "not to decide, discuss, or confer upon any political question. Such questions the President holds in his own hands, and will submit them to no military conferences or conventions." Lin-coln wisely set clear guidelines for negotiations: Grant could treat only for surrender. The next day, March 4, the Union commanding general informed Lee that the president alone possessed the authority to under-take such discussion.[7]

As guidance for the actual surrender proposal, Grant relied not only on Lincoln's directive but also on conversations that he, Sherman, Porter, and the president held in late March. Lincoln was uneasy that Lee might escape, and the thought of any more major battles pained him. If the armies of Lee and Johnston surrendered, however, the president believed the other Confederates would lay down their arms. Grant conceded that one more major battle might be necessary, but he assured the president that neither Lee's nor Johnston's army in North Carolina would escape. In the course of discussions Lincoln conveyed the impression that the surrender terms should be magnanimous, a notion that Grant incorpo-rated in the basic proposal that he offered Lee on April 8 at the Confed-erate general's request.

On the afternoon of April 9, 1865, at Appomattox Court House, Grant once again demonstrated the clarity of his thought and the skill-fulness of his writing when he crafted surrender terms on the spot. He required officers to sign paroles for themselves and regimental or battery commanders to sign them on behalf of their men. They could not take up arms again until they were properly exchanged. This was done in dupli-cate; one copy went to Lee's army and Grant's staff kept the other copy. Soldiers then stacked arms, artillery, and other public property. Terms permitted officers to take their side arms, and Confederates who owned horses were allowed to keep them, along with personal baggage. Grant concluded with a simple sentence that captured the essence of his com-mander in chief's intent. "This done," he wrote, "each officer and man will be allowed to return to his home, not to be disturbed by U.S. authority so long as they observe their paroles and the laws in force where they may reside." Lee signed a letter of acceptance, and the surrender was done.[8]

Grant forwarded the agreement to the secretary of war. By then Lin-coln was back in Washington, and if he objected to any of the terms he had ample time to intervene. There would be no persecution, no imprisonment for the men in Lee's army. They were to return home and pick up the pieces of their shattered lives, but they must abide by federal, state, and local laws. Lincoln's silence was an endorsement of the terms.

Prior to surrender, Lee considered a guerrilla campaign but eventually dismissed the idea. The day Lee surrendered, he conversed with Brig. Gen. E. Porter Alexander on the very subject. Grant had offered generous terms, merely seeking to parole the troops and to get them safely home, and Lee felt he could not refuse. To disperse forces would do little good, Lee explained, because only about 10,000 would get away, and most of them would head home to look after their families. His soldiers already had no rations and were demoralized in defeat. "They would have to plunder & rob to procure subsistence," the general detailed. "The country would be full of lawless bands in every part, & a state of society would ensue from which it would take the country years to recover." He insisted that the Union cavalry would pursue the men in hopes of catching the principal officers, and that would lead to "fresh rapine & destruction." It was spring and most of the men were farmers. They needed to go home to "plant crops & begin to repair the ravages of the war."[9]

Eleven days after the surrender at Appomattox Court House Lee reported to Davis that in his opinion, "an army can not be organized and supported in Virginia," and so far as he could tell, the people east of the Mississippi River had no stomach for more fighting. "A partisan war may be continued, and hostilities protracted," he counseled the president, "causing individual suffering and the devastation of the country; but I see no prospect by that means of achieving a separate independence." Of course, Lee reassured Davis respectfully, the decision was the president's. "To save useless effusion of blood, I would recommend measures be taken for suspension of hostilities and the restoration of peace." Other key advisors chimed in that further resistance was futile. Neither the soldiers nor the people at home had any interest in a drawn-out guerrilla war. The capitulation of the Army of Northern Virginia and its commander, the most highly regarded man in the Confederate government, triggered a series of surrenders, so that by the beginning of May the last major field command had accepted terms with the Union.[10]

Five days after Lee surrendered, John Wilkes Booth fatally shot Lincoln. Sherman and Johnston had already begun negotiations, and news of Lincoln's death increased the urgency of a resolution. Clearly, Sherman misunderstood Lincoln's intentions when he negotiated a surrender of all

Confederate troops under terms that gave tacit recognition to Confederate state governments and permitted Rebel soldiers to take home their weapons and deposit them at a later date at their state capitals. Had Lincoln survived he most likely would have corrected Sherman discreetly and the issue would have been forgotten. But in the panic after Lincoln's death the new president, Andrew Johnson, and his cabinet erupted in a firestorm over Sherman's terms. Secretary of War Edwin Stanton objected in writing so stridently that the *New York Times* interpreted his harsh words as an accusation that Sherman's conduct was traitorous. With the cabinet's support, President Johnson ordered Grant to travel to North Carolina, supersede Sherman, and offer General Johnston the same terms as he had given Lee. Grant did visit Sherman's headquarters, but he refused to humiliate his closest lieutenant. He left Sherman in command and informed him that his terms were unacceptable in Washington and instructed him to offer the Confederates the Appomattox terms. After some inconsequential wrangling General Johnston surrendered on that basis. The only lasting impact was the hatred that Sherman bore for Stanton.

Confederate soldiers, some under parole and others who simply abandoned the flag at the end, walked home. For those in Texas and elsewhere it would take months. Along the way Confederate veterans begged or stole food from civilians, worsening hardships in the wake of warfare. Union forces in the East held a grand review in Washington, D.C., on May 23 and 24, 1865. On the first day the spit-and-polish Army of the Potomac paraded to cheering crowds. On the next day Sherman's veterans marched along Pennsylvania Avenue, their scuffed shoes, well-worn clothing, and scratched rifle stocks reflecting the hardships of their long journey. The army sent them and other soldiers to their original muster locations, where the government issued back pay and had them sign muster-out rolls. Some soldiers grew frustrated with the wait and, having served faithfully for years, deserted. Decades later, when they sought their veteran's pension, their impetuousness would cause them considerable headache.

In less than a year the Union Army demobilized from more than 1 million strong to 80,000. Hardened veterans left the service first, with more recent recruits, many of them black, remaining in uniform until 1866 or early 1867. In mid-1866 Congress directed a drawdown to approximately 54,000, and by 1871 the total strength had fallen to fewer than 30,000 officers and men. Coping with great demands for protection from Indians along the Western frontier, the army assigned little more than token occupation forces in the South. Within a year and a half after the surrender at Appomattox, only 20,000 men oversaw Reconstruction across a domain that included nine million people in eleven former states covering three-quarters of a million square miles of land.

Reconstruction created awkward and sometimes dangerous problems for the army. At the time of surrender Confederate and Union war aims had merged. Confederates were no longer willing to fight for an independent Confederacy and slavery; they would rather exist in the Union in peace. Northerners achieved their goals: restoration of the Union and an end to slavery. But neither side had consented to full and equal rights for African Americans. Conservative President Andrew Johnson was pitted against the Radical Republicans, who increasingly demanded equal rights for blacks. For the first few years of Reconstruction, power shifted from the Johnson Administration to the Radical Republicans, and that transfer concomitantly increased the authority of the army and its officers in the South. Yet over the course of a dozen years, political control gradually, inexorably shifted from the national government back to the southern white aristocracy, largely because the preponderance of army officers implementing policy, whether at high levels or on the ground, were racially prejudiced and deeply conservative. Collectively, the officer corps, as a class and a profession, ultimately aided the restoration of southern whites to power.

In 1864, Lincoln had floated a mild reconstruction plan in Louisiana as an inducement to lure the state back into the Union. Congress responded with a much more rigid approach called the Wade-Davis Bill, which Lincoln blocked with a pocket veto. Lincoln was not so much offended by the terms; after all, his mild plan was a wartime scheme to chip away at the Confederacy, and once the Union conquered all resistance a harsher approach was more likely. Lincoln's true basis for opposition was flexibility. If Congress passed a law that he signed, he must implement it as the law read. If instead the president oversaw reconstruction policies, he could adapt them readily by executive order.

Yet Lincoln and the Radical Republicans were not necessarily at loggerheads. Both elements joined in the passage of the Freedmen's Bureau Act, a progressive bill that assisted blacks in the transition from slavery to freedom primarily by serving as a clearinghouse for information, overseeing labor contracts, and establishing schools. Lincoln had also come to the conclusion, along with many Radicals, that in order to protect their newfound rights blacks must be given the right to citizenship and the vote.

Lincoln's assassination could not have come at a worse time for Reconstruction. In 1864 he had chosen Johnson as his vice presidential candidate because he was a Democrat from Tennessee who, Lincoln assumed, would strengthen the Union ticket. Unfortunately, Johnson was ill-suited ideologically and temperamentally for the demands of the job. He was a white southerner, a slaveholder, a states' rights advocate, utterly inflexible, and self-righteous. As president he began pardoning secessionists and encouraged states to reenter the Union. Their proposed constitutions included black codes—laws that restricted blacks' civil rights—and they sent numerous prominent Confederate officials as new representatives to Congress. Congress blocked their readmission as states. When Congress passed the Civil Rights Act of 1866, granting former slaves citizenship and due process and equal protection of the law, Johnson vetoed it. He did the same with a new Freedmen's Bureau Act, which extended the organization until southern states were readmitted and established freedmen's courts to ensure justice for African Americans. In both cases Congress overrode the veto.

As the manifestation of the political will, the army was soon at the heart of the battle over control of Reconstruction. Again over the president's veto Congress passed the Military Reconstruction Act of 1867. It divided the South into five military districts headed by general officers with extensive powers to govern. The object was to oversee the formation of new state constitutions with full suffrage and participation of blacks. Southern people must also ratify the Fourteenth Amendment, granting blacks citizenship and due process and equal protection. At the same time Congress passed the Command of the Army Act, which restricted the president's authority as commander in chief by compelling him to issue orders through the commanding general of the army. Because Grant, who leaned toward the Radical camp, held that position, Congress perceived the law as a screen against conservative presidential directives. Congress also passed the Tenure of Office Act, which stated that the president required Senate approval before removing any civilian official the Senate had confirmed. Secretary of War Stanton had fallen into the Radical camp, and Congress did not want him replaced. When Johnson challenged the constitutionality of the Tenure of Office Act by removing Stanton and replacing him with a conservative Democrat and active-duty major general, John M. Schofield, the House of Representatives levied charges against Johnson. In a suspense-filled trial, the Senate failed by one vote to remove Johnson from office. Johnson survived but was almost powerless politically.

General officers oversaw much of the implementation of Reconstruction policies, and for the most part they hated the duties. Initially the officers naïvely assumed that whites would tolerate the new status of blacks. At times the consequences proved disastrous, as they did in Memphis and New Orleans in 1866, when white mobs rioted and murdered dozens of blacks and injured hundreds more. After passage of the Reconstruction Act of 1867 some conservative district commanders sympathized with southern whites; other conservatives tried to be fair, but blacks needed a level of vigilance and support that they failed to provide; and some commanders fell into the Radical camp, only to be removed or undercut by President Johnson.

In 1866, Grant directed officers to shield freedmen from unfair prosecutions and to arrest citizens who committed crimes against soldiers, Freedmen's Bureau agents, and others if local authorities failed to do so. In effect the army would protect civil rights. Yet at lower levels, where officers interpreted and enforced policies and issued important decisions on a daily basis, duties were even more complex. Most southern whites resisted efforts to provide blacks with rights and opportunities and vigorously and often violently opposed Reconstruction programs. The only protection blacks, Freedmen's Bureau agents, and a handful of white supporters living in the South had was the army and, in isolated instances, communities of black citizens. Freedmen's courts could issue all the rulings they wanted, but if the army did not enforce them they were meaningless. In some cases officers defended Freedmen's Bureau personnel and their decisions and actively protected blacks and their rights. Far too often, however, racial prejudice clouded officers' judgment and convinced them to look away or side with their former enemy. Many officers resented the fact that, especially in 1865 and 1866, a substantial portion of the occupation troops were black. They believed blacks were inferior and required southern white leadership to survive. It infuriated southern whites and gnawed at officers' moral sensibilities to side with blacks over whites. Those officers viewed blacks as a nuisance who should simply do as whites told them and quit battling against southern white efforts to resume authority. Many officers also resented their roles as pawns in the power struggle over control of Reconstruction.

It was not as if these duties were completely alien to army officers. Those who had served in the Regular Army on the frontier knew well that one of the principal missions of the army was to be the representative of the federal government and that they often had to enforce federal law against civilians there. They also served as a buffer between two feuding parties, civilians and Indians—not so different from refereeing between blacks and whites. But in this instance they had emerged from a long and bloody war, only to perform occupation duty amid bands of partisans who sought to undercut U.S. government policies and reestablish southern whites in power. They also found themselves responsible for defending blacks and their rights, a burden that required daily vigilance.

Service was especially dangerous for black soldiers and their white officers. Black soldiers were abused, beaten, and occasionally murdered by white vigilantes; for example, Lt. J. T. Furman, a white officer in the 33rd U.S. Colored Infantry, was assassinated by southern whites. In one instance an entire black regiment had entrained for Charleston to be mustered out of service when someone uncoupled the cars and isolated them on a high trestle bridge. Armed civilians then launched volley after volley into the train cars, until a black sergeant who was riding atop the locomotive compelled the engineer at gunpoint to back up the engine and remove the cars from that precarious position.

With the rise of the Ku Klux Klan and similar organizations in the South, Congress passed the Enforcement Acts in 1870 and 1871, authorizing the president to protect civil liberties in the South. Grant then ordered soldiers to crack down on acts of violence against blacks and selected whites in South Carolina, where Klan activities were the fiercest. Soldiers helped capture Klansmen, guarded jailhouses and courthouses when authorities prosecuted them, and demonstrated that the army would aid in enforcing federal laws. To prevent voter fraud, troops also guarded ballot boxes. Democrats howled over Grant's use of soldiers for these duties, and even some Republicans balked at its constitutionality. With growing opposition Grant had to ease up on his efforts, and the violence continued.

Time and power worked to the advantage of southern whites. Radical Republican leaders died off or lost their fervor for the cause of African Americans, and the northern public focused more and more on picking up the pieces of their lives after the war. With each southern state fulfilling congressional mandates and reentering the Union, fewer and fewer troops performed Reconstruction service. Democrats increased in strength in the federal government, and southern whites gained more and more control. The ultimate insult occurred when Democrats in the House, reacting to occupation in the South, failed to appropriate money for the army for 1877. As part of the Compromise of 1877 to resolve the disputed presidential election of 1876, President Rutherford B. Hayes barred all soldiers from interfering on behalf of blacks and Republicans in the South. Hayes's decision marked the triumph of southern whites. Essentially the army had no more troops in the former Confederate states than it did in antebellum times, and they occupied mainly coastal fortifications and arsenals.

The consequences of the Civil War were disastrous. More than 2 percent (620,000) of the entire population lost their lives in uniform, another 2 percent (more than 500,000) sustained wounds, and 2 percent more were debilitated permanently or in part from illness. All told, the war cost an estimated $20 billion. The South was a shambles. Union policy to destroy anything of military value left railroads and other elements of the transportation network a wreck. Livestock was depleted, wilderness had begun to reclaim lands that had been in cultivation, currency became valueless, and generations of hard work were lost. With the destruction of slavery and the creation of a free labor system, southern whites had lost control of their workers. They reestablished it through sharecropping and the crop lien system, which forced debtors to continue to do business with specific merchants; debts grew so large that black and poor white families could never escape from beneath them. Not until the third decade of the twentieth century did southern agriculture regain its 1860 level.

Turbulence marked the U.S. economy over the succeeding decades. During the war the Union fed its civilian and military population and still exported foodstuffs to Europe. After the war, hundreds of thousands of soldiers returned to farms, producing even more bountiful supplies of food. Manufacturing also benefited, not just in certain areas from war production but also from extraordinary managerial experience that veterans gained during their military service. Like agriculture, overproduction followed by shortage created a boom-and-bust economy. To make matters worse, the U.S. government embarked on a monetary policy of taxing wartime paper notes out of existence. A shrinking money supply at the time of huge population growth placed Americans on an economic roller-coaster over the next three decades.

In the aftermath of the war, the U.S. military's budget and size declined precipitously. The navy ended the Civil War with more than 600 vessels, arguably the best in the world. By 1880 it ranked eleventh worldwide, directly behind Turkey. Lost too were remembrances and techniques from those extraordinary joint operations under Grant, Sherman, and

Porter at Vicksburg in 1862–63 and Porter and Brig. Gen. Alfred H. Terry at Fort Fisher in 1865.

Occupation duty heightened sensitivity toward the use of the Regular Army. In 1878, Congress passed and the president signed into law the Posse Comitatus Act, which made it unlawful to use the Regular Army as a posse comitatus or for the enforcement of laws, except when its use was specifically authorized by the U.S. Constitution or by an act of Congress. Punishment included fines and imprisonment. The militia, later called the National Guard, would perform these duties for states.

At the close of the war, the United States possessed a truly extraordinary army: battle-hardened, well-equipped, innovative, and highly efficient. It would take years for any other nation to eclipse the army of 1865. Observing the Franco-Prussian War in 1870, Sheridan commented to President Grant that he had "seen much of great interest," particularly the battles of Beaumont, Gravellotte, and Sedan, but he added, "[I] have not found the difference very great, but that difference is to the credit of our own country." He insisted, "There is nothing to be learned here professionally, but it is a satisfaction to learn that such is the case." Sheridan commented that the European armies had "about the same percentage of sneaks, or runaways" as those in the Civil War, and that they fought in a disorderly fashion, resembling more a "deadly skirmish." Prussian troops had greater confidence in themselves and their leaders and regularly drove the French from position after position, confirming the importance of officers and morale. The American general boldly asserted, "There is much however which Europeans can learn from us." Federals and Confederates employed superior rifle pits, had vastly higher quality cavalry, and protected their lines of communication better. "There are a hundred things in which they are behind us—," Sheridan wrote in conclusion. "The staff Depts are poorly organized the Q.M. [Quartermaster's] Dept wretched &c &c. . . . ."[11]

Yet like the navy, the army soon declined rapidly from the finest land force in the world to a mere shell of its wartime status. From the early 1870s into the late 1890s the Regular Army averaged approximately 27,000 officers and men, a far cry from its wartime peak of more than one million citizen soldiers. The army dispersed into small units across the vast frontier, once again helping the nation to conquer Indian lands. As it had done before the Civil War, it largely manned forts, with only an occasional clash with Indians to interrupt a mundane existence.

Aside from Indians, the army's greatest enemies were politicians who attacked the institution itself. Democrats bore deep grudges against the army for its Reconstruction duties, and again in 1879 the House failed to appropriate funds in time. For two months officers had to borrow money to feed soldiers, until Congress got around to allocating funds to cover expenses. Other opponents of the military after the Civil War were former Union generals who felt they had been mistreated at the hands of Regulars. In the case of Congressman John A. Logan, a major general in the war who served superbly, the complaint was legitimate. Sherman had passed Logan over for command of the Army of the Tennessee, appointing instead Maj. Gen. Oliver Otis Howard, a West Point graduate. Other sharp critics, such as Maj. Gen. Benjamin Butler, sought the termination of the U.S. Military Academy. West Point was to them the root of all evil in the army, though Butler's poor military record gave him little standing in this debate. For years the army had to fend off attacks against West Point from a small but influential band of politicians.

Fortunately, a movement toward professionalism blitzed American society in the latter half of the nineteenth century, undercutting the arguments of wartime volunteers who criticized the army. In the face of reduced size, critical politicians, and unreliable budgets, the army focused inward on professional development, building on a prewar trend of its own. With the Indian wars winding down, the door opened for the army to embrace this powerful impulse and reevaluate its function in American society.

At the heart of the movement was the cerebral Sherman, who called for structural changes, established schools to train officers better, and encouraged and supported a corps of young, talented officers in a quest for improvement. Not long after Sherman assumed the position of commanding general, he sought control over the bureau chiefs, who functioned both independently of the army's highest-ranking officer and often without proper regard for the needs of the troops in the field. These staff officers had lifetime appointments in Washington and reported to the secretary of war, not Sherman. By coddling congressmen and senators they fended off assaults on their private domains until the early twentieth century. One of Sherman's acolytes, Schofield, recognized the significance of the problem and brokered a cooperative arrangement with his secretary of war, Redfield Proctor, in the early 1890s that helped pave the way for the passage of the General Staff Act in 1903, which theoretically placed the bureau chiefs under the commanding general, now called the chief of staff.

Despite difficulties in civil-military relations and command and control of the army, Sherman and his protégés were successful in reforming other areas of the army. They revived or established branch training for artillerists, engineers, and signal corpsmen. In 1881 the army opened the Infantry and Cavalry School, a two-year program that offered hands-on training of troops in all three branches—infantry, cavalry, and artillery. Students also received theoretical instruction, which, Sherman hoped, would be the springboard to a lifetime of professional development. The school struggled initially, but within a decade after it opened it had upgraded its faculty and curriculum; students now learned the methods of their profession, such as map reading, order writing, and war gaming.

The postwar army embraced important tactical changes that more accurately reflected wartime experiences and lessons. Against rifled muskets soldiers learned to construct field fortifications, so that in the last year or so of war, men built them skillfully and with little prodding from their officers. They also fought in more wooded areas, usually rejecting the rigid formations, elbow to elbow, that contemporary tactics manuals had dictated. Instead, soldiers advanced more in skirmish formation, taking advantage of trees and other means of protection. Emory Upton, a West Point graduate who commanded artillery, cavalry, and infantry units in combat, prepared a new tactics manual after the war that allowed for more dispersed formations and single as well as double ranks, thereby integrating valuable wartime lessons into standard infantry practice. Union artillerymen had become accustomed to firing over the heads of their advancing infantry, employing a means of indirect fire that would prove invaluable in the twentieth century and beyond. Union and Confederate cavalry fought less and less on horseback; in the last two years of the war they used horses mostly for mobility and fought dismounted. Once the Union armed its cavalrymen with repeating carbines this combination of firepower, speed, and mobility elevated the prowess of the mounted army and transformed the cavalry. Cavalrymen also launched deep raids, employing mobility and firepower to seize key crossroads and tactical positions and fend off enemy attacks until infantry could relieve them. Unfortunately, officer resistance and preoccupation with Indian troubles prevented a more effective tactical integration of the three branches of the army into a true combined arms organization.

Sherman and others also paved the way for more intellectual and analytical military undertakings. On War Department orders Upton traveled around the world, exploring various armies and drafting a comparative critique called *The Armies of Asia and Europe*. Later he wrote *Military Policy of the United States from 1775,* which was not published in book form until the twentieth century but nevertheless passed from one officer to another in manuscript. In it Upton criticized shortsighted government policies on preparedness for war, arguing that a bit more expense and effort in peacetime would save a tremendous number of lives in wartime. Another of Sherman's favorites, former corps commander William B. Hazen, studied in Europe and then wrote a book on military education, *The School and the Army in Germany and France*. Hazen called on officers to pay careful attention to the superior Prussian system and urged the United States to adopt policies that evaluated and promoted officers meritoriously and to create military schools to train them better. Other former Union officers followed suit, founding professional journals, taking staff rides to battlefields, reading books and tracts, and drafting their own articles to promote military improvement and engage in public and private debates. Inspired by the experience of the Civil War and reaping the benefits of a societal shift toward professional development that opened the atmosphere for discussion and debate, the army enjoyed an intellectual renaissance in the last decades of the nineteenth century.

The Civil War also left a vital legacy for the conduct of future wars. In 1863, Francis Lieber, LL.D., had drafted "Instructions for the Government of Armies of the United States in the Field." A board of officers modified the document and submitted it for Lincoln's approval. The president then directed the secretary of war to issue it as General Orders, No. 100. The order established rules of conduct in war by U.S. military personnel, covering such topics as martial law, retaliation, proper conduct toward enemy civilians and their property, and treatment of deserters, prisoners of war, and civilians who rise up in arms against occupation forces. General Orders, No. 100 became critical in advancing the rules of war internationally and guided U.S. military forces for nearly five decades.

As Civil War veterans grew older, former Union soldiers lobbied heavily for old-age pensions. Veterans of other major wars had received them, and disabled Union soldiers, widows, and orphans had been awarded monthly subsistence payments since 1861. In 1890, Congress offered pensions to veterans who claimed even a partial disability based on their wartime experiences, both illnesses and injuries. Widows and dependents also received pensions, even if the veteran's death was not from a war-related cause. Fourteen years later President Teddy Roosevelt ordered half pensions for veterans who reached the age of 62. Congress slightly modified the process over the succeeding decade, and when it created the Veterans Bureau after World War I, surviving Federal veterans were transferred under its umbrella. This massive pension program may very well have been the origin of a huge new welfare state in the United States.

As the years passed, Union and Confederate soldiers generally reconciled. Federals had won the war, but to bring the two sections together as one the northern public began to embrace southern postwar myths about the war. Secession over slavery, an enterprise that had become anathema around the world, was played down when the two sides met. Instead the Civil War was remembered as a struggle about states' rights. That way both sides could fight for an honorable cause, and Confederate losses were not for some misguided purpose. Defeat resulted in a loss of Southern honor; the Myth of the Lost Cause, as it has been called, restored it. As veterans passed away, succeeding generations embraced the myth. Thus to a great degree southern whites lost the war but won much of the peace.

For the army postwar experiences were both burdensome and a disguised blessing. Had Lincoln lived, the transition from war to peace and Reconstruction policies would most surely have been smoother. Racial prejudice among southern whites and many army personnel assured difficult times for African Americans in the postwar world and increasing danger and headaches for occupation forces, but Lincoln's standing as a victorious commander in chief and his exceptionally sound judgment suggest that he would have managed matters better than the narrow, rigid Johnson. Nevertheless, the army in the Civil War evolved from a stumbling, inefficient, and ill-disciplined volunteer force into a progressive, sophisticated, efficient war-making machine. The learning curve was extremely painful, costing hundreds of thousands of lives, but the experience left a lasting impression on thoughtful officers. A great army must always critique itself, always look for new ways of resolving problems and fulfilling its myriad missions more efficiently. Military professionalism, Sherman taught officers and men, must operate at its highest level, not just during war but also in peacetime.

SUGGESTED READING

For a discussion of the Army of Northern Virginia in the late stages of the war, see Joseph T. Glatthaar, *General Lee's Army: From Victory to Defeat* (2008). On the Appomattox campaign, see William Marvel, *Lee's*

Last Retreat: The Flight to Appomattox (2002). On Lee's consideration of a guerrilla war, the best source is Edward Porter Alexander, *Fighting for the Confederacy,* ed. Gary W. Gallagher (1989). On Reconstruction, Eric Foner's classic *Reconstruction: America's Unfinished Revolution* (1986) is still the principal source. Foner is more interested in free labor and freedmen. On occupation duties, see James Sefton, *The United States Army and Reconstruction, 1865 to 1877* (1967); Joseph G. Dawson, *Army Generals and Reconstruction: Louisiana, 1862 to 1877* (1982); and Joseph G. Dawson, "The U.S. Army in the South: Reconstruction as Nation Building," in *Armed Diplomacy: Two Centuries of American Campaigning* (2003). Some of the problems that black soldiers experienced in Reconstruction duty are included in Joseph T. Glatthaar, *Forged in Battle: The Civil War Alliance of Black Soldiers and Their White Officers* (1989). For a terrific book that develops the role of the army from a bird's-eye view, see Mark L. Bradley, *Bluecoats and Tarheels: Soldiers and Civilians in Reconstruction North Carolina* (2009). Edward M. Coffman, *The Old Army: A Portrait of the American Army in Peacetime, 1794 to 1898* (1986) covers the postwar professional movement. See also Timothy K. Nenninger, *The Leavenworth Schools and the Old Army: Education, Professionalism, and the Officer Corps of the United States Army, 1881 to 1918* (1978).

PETER MASLOWSKI

The 300-Years War

Wite settlers and miners were having problems with Snakes.
Not serpents, but Indians, for Americans referred to the Shoshonis, Northern Paiutes, and Bannocks who roamed the Great Basin
where Oregon, Idaho, and Nevada converged as "Snakes."

The Snakes were having problems too. They had lived in the area a
long time, whereas the Americans were newcomers, pressing in fast from
both the east and the west. Unfortunately for them, the Snakes were not
well prepared to contest the U.S. invasion. Harsh climatic conditions and
rugged topography compelled the Snakes to live in small, isolated, wan-
dering bands. Although temperatures soared to 100 degrees or more in
the summer in the Great Basin, they resided in a cold desert; the region
received fewer than ten inches of rain per year, and most of that fell as
snow, so water was scarce. Because antelope, deer, buffalo, and moose
were nonexistent, the Snakes subsisted on mice, jackrabbits, gophers, and
coyotes and supplemented their meager meat supply with seeds, nuts,
berries, and insects. Naturally if too large a group occupied any locale for
long, it exhausted the limited resources. Death was never far away even
in the best of times, and when whites began drawing on the Great Basin's
already strained food and water supplies, times got harder.

The Snakes' tribal structure was fragmented. Collectively numbering
about 16,000, the Shoshonis consisted of seven distinct groups, each of
which was further subdivided. The Northern Paiutes were a loose confederation of 8,000 living in a dozen different bands, and the Bannocks had
northern and southern divisions. Negotiating with the Snakes or defeat-

129

ing them in war was difficult because the leader of one band could not sign a peace treaty that was binding on other leaders, and subduing one faction in battle did not mean subduing all bands. Euro-Americans had to negotiate with or defeat each band, which often resulted in unpleasant surprises: all too often whites assumed, prematurely, that the war was over after one tribal leader signed a treaty or one band suffered a battlefield defeat.

Almost from the moment Euro-Americans arrived in the Great Basin sporadic violence became commonplace as the Snakes sought to defend their homeland. As deadly episodes escalated, Col. George Wright, who commanded the Department of Oregon in 1860, recognized that outright war loomed. The colonel was under no illusions: the conflict would be difficult, involving painful marches through daunting terrain as military expeditions chased a nearly invisible foe. On those rare occasions when the army cornered the enemy, Wright expected easy victories— easy, but rarely decisive. Conquering the Snakes, he predicted, would require patience and endurance.

Determining the precise event that ignited the war is nearly impossible, but the battle at Wildhorse Creek on April 7, 1864, seems an appropriate starting point. After riding some 20 miles from their base camp, Lt. James A. Waymire, who commanded fifteen men of Company D, 1st Oregon Cavalry, and Capt. Cincinnatus H. Miller with thirty horse-mounted citizens attacked a Paiute camp. Cooperation between the cavalrymen and Miller's horsemen was less than perfect, and the Indians were more numerous than either commander expected. The whites retreated in midafternoon, and by late that night most of the command had reassembled at the base camp, except for a four-man detachment Waymire had dispatched to investigate a large smoke signal. Despite a lot of shooting during the battle, only one white man was wounded, and Waymire estimated that five Indians were killed or wounded. However, the body count evened out when a search failed to locate the four men who investigated the smoke signal (which turned out to be billowing steam from a warm spring); they were presumed killed.

Colonel Wright's prediction of an easy victory whenever the army cornered its foe was wrong at Wildhorse Creek. Unafraid of the truth, Waymire admitted that the Paiutes had defeated him, though he was certain the blame fell on the citizen volunteers and not his cavalrymen.

Thus began the most deadly Indian war in the West, a sputtering guerrilla conflict in which expeditions were frequent, agony was commonplace, battles were few, and deaths for Euro-Americans at any one engagement were minimal. By war's end 378 soldiers, civilians, and Indian scouts were killed or wounded, while an estimated 1,254 Indians died or were wounded. Other, more famous Indian conflicts in the West were much less deadly; total casualties during the Great Sioux War were only about half the Snake War's number. Despite the high death toll the war received little public notice. No great artist, no George Catlin or Frederic Remington, painted scenes featuring the Snakes; only one war correspondent (he worked for the Idaho *Owyhee Avalanche*) covered the war, and no great battle akin to the Little Bighorn stirred the nation's imagination and indignation.

In part because the war occurred in dark shadows its salient characteristics remained largely unknown. When a new officer arrived he had a hard time recognizing the low-level violence as warfare and had to learn through hard experience that the absence of set-piece battles did not mean the absence of war. Through trial and error some officers became successful guerrilla fighters, particularly Lt. Col. George Crook. Men such as Crook relied on Indian allies who gathered intelligence, served as guides, and sometimes did most of the fighting. Because Snake warriors so rarely stood and fought, Crook and others grimly waged a war of attrition, wearing the Indians down day after insufferable day, staying on their trail, giving them no rest, and ultimately forcing them into the uncomfortable position of dying or surrendering.

Successful officers also learned that the best time to inflict damage was in winter. A surprise attack on Snake families huddled in a winter camp inevitably killed not just warriors, but old folks, women, and children, and often smelled more of a massacre than a battle. In five such cold weather assaults five whites and 270 Indians died. Unlike the bloody episodes at Sand Creek or on the Marias, none of these events became a cause célèbre among easterners. Those who learned about them were almost exclusively westerners, many of whom saw nothing wrong with exterminating Indians regardless of age or gender. Warring in the dark did have advantages.

Those who fought in the Snake War could not know they had inaugurated the final chapter in the long history of conflict between Euro-Americans and Indians. Resulting in the end of hostilities, this final stage lasted approximately twenty years and ensured that Euro-Americans enjoyed hegemony over the continental United States.

The death of half a dozen men at Wildhorse Creek was, of course, not the *cause* of the Snake War. For the cause of that particular war, and for the terminal phase in Indian-white conflict as a whole, one has to probe far more deeply into the past.

The United States, the general pronounced, had the distinction of fighting the longest war in history. That statement puzzled me and the other historians sitting in a small auditorium at the U.S. Army Command and General Staff College. We knew the United States never fought a Thirty Years War, much less a Hundred Years War. No, the best it could do was the Vietnam War, which lasted only a paltry eight years.

Then the general, who was from the history section of the Chinese People's Army, explained that he was referring to the nearly 300-year war against the Indians, which, he said, began in the early seventeenth century and continued until the late nineteenth.[1]

From the perspective of military historians this was a dubious assertion. Few of them viewed the Euro-Americans' struggle against the indigenous peoples as a single, continuous war of subjugation. Instead, whites fought a series of Indian wars, each a discrete event: the First, Second, and Third Tidewater Wars, the Pequot War, King Philip's War and Bacon's Rebellion, the Tuscarora War, the Yamassee War, Pontiac's Rebellion, and so on until the mid-1880s.

If at first glance the concept of an unbroken 300-year war seemed implausible to military historians, it was equally dubious from the perspective of the hundreds of tribes inhabiting North America. The indigenous peoples had no sense of a shared racial identity, and like Europeans—Germans, French, English, and so on—were ethnocentric, as exemplified by their self-perceptions. Virtually every tribe considered itself "the People"—*the* people, not *a* people. Whites called them Cherokees, Apaches, and Crows, but to themselves they were, respectively, the Tsulage, the People; the Nde, the People; the Absaroka, the People. So it went for tribe after tribe: *the* People.

And yet the general had a point: Euro-Americans did wage a protracted war to conquer the Indian nations in order to acquire their land and its resources. Although often cloaked in arguments emanating from religious zealotry, a sense of cultural superiority, or national security concerns, the whites' ultimate objective was always the same: to establish dominion over the indigenous peoples so that they could be dispossessed of their land and its bounty.

Standing in the way of these imperial ambitions were the Native inhabitants, who resisted in a prolonged anticolonial war, beginning with the first day of the first permanent English settlers at Jamestown. On April 21, 1607, Capt. Christopher Newport led about twenty men ashore. They explored for nearly eight hours, sweating profusely in the springtime warmth, without seeing a single Native. As they trudged back to the boat that brought them ashore, Indians sprang an ambush, wounding two men with arrows before blending back into the wilderness. Despite being taken by surprise, several Englishmen fired their muskets, but without hitting any of their attackers.

For the next three centuries warfare between whites and Indians followed the course of white settlement, which is why the last campaigns occurred on the Great Plains and in the Intermountain West rather than on the West Coast. After populating the eastern seaboard, whites moved steadily westward to the Mississippi River, inched across that mighty waterway to settle a belt of states running from Louisiana to Minnesota, and then leaped across the West's interior to settle California and Oregon. Only toward the end of the Civil War and afterward did Americans, approaching from both the east and the west, backfill the Great Plains and Intermountain West.

Whites unabashedly acquired Native lands through fraud, bribery, force, and the threat of force, but seldom by honest dealings. Treaty negotiations were typically a façade, a hollow formality for grabbing Indian land. For one thing, Indian leaders rarely understood a treaty's provisions because they did not comprehend the Euro-American concept of land ownership. In the Native worldview, land was something the community used and shared; when Indians signed treaties, they thought they were granting white people permission to share the land and its resources, not to "own" them. And Indians lived in an oral rather than a written culture. To them, speeches, ceremonies, and gift exchanges at a peace conference were of greater importance than the written record because they created a peaceful environment; to whites these rituals were only the prelude to a written agreement. Indians usually discovered that the words preserved on paper bore little relationship to their memories of the negotiations; sometimes these misunderstandings arose because interpreters were incompetent, but more often they resulted from the whites' deliberate deception.

Euro-Americans also insisted on negotiating with men whom they designated "main" chiefs, as if they were akin to European royalty. But such leaders never represented an entire tribe; indeed the very notion of a "tribe" was a Euro-American construct that bore little relationship to the complex ethnic reality of Indian societies. The Apaches never comprised a unitary state with a unified political structure. Instead they consisted of six independent tribal groups, each further subdivided by overlapping structures of family groupings, warrior societies, bands, and clans. Oftentimes intense factionalism sundered these nearly autonomous subunits, paralyzing decision making and united action and sometimes becoming deadly. The same could be said for Crows (Mountain, River, and Kicked-in-the-Bellies), Blackfeet (Piegans, Bloods, and Blackfeet), and virtually every other Native American society.

Among the Indians with the most complex structure were the Sioux. Of their Seven Council Fires, three—the Lakota-speaking Tetons and the Dakota-speaking Yanktons and Yanktonais—spearheaded the tribe's westward, imperialistic thrust onto the Great Plains that began in the early eighteenth century. Some of these Council Fires were subdivided into tribes: the Tetons included the Brules, Two Kettles, Oglalas, Miniconjous, Sans Arcs, Hunkpapas, and Blackfeet Sioux, and each of these was further splintered into bands and other, smaller entities.

At the Fort Laramie Treaty of 1851, U.S. negotiators believed they had made a treaty with the Sioux nation. In fact they had signatures from a few Brules, Two Kettles, and Yanktons, but none from the other five Teton tribes or any Yanktonais. Why should these groups consider themselves bound by the treaty? Even leaders who signed a treaty had little power to enforce it. Because Native peoples enjoyed an individualism that was beyond the ken of supposedly individualistic whites, no chief possessed anything approaching absolute authority; each of his followers was free to accept or reject his counsel. Warfare was such an integral part of Native culture—for young warriors, war was a rite of passage and the best route to wealth and status—that chiefs could not easily temper, much less eliminate, it. When tribal elements that had not agreed to a treaty "violated" it, or when young warriors refused to abide by a chief's wishes, whites depicted Indians as duplicitous savages. Such uninformed judgments were easier than trying to understand indigenous societies and provided ready excuses for seizing still more land.

A final reason why treaty making was nothing more than subterfuge was that farmers, traders, miners, speculators, and ranchers, unrestrained by any individual sense of morality or justice or by any concerted government action, violated treaty provisions with impunity. Federal officials pled that they lacked sufficient military force to rein in so many acquisitive whites, but in fact few had a genuine desire to do so. Their concern was not to slow "civilization's" advance, but only to keep it as orderly as possible. Thus boundary lines "guaranteed" to the Indians dissolved.

Dispossessing the Indians raised a subsidiary but still important war aim: What should be done with the Indians? One potential solution that received little serious consideration was protecting Indians in their ancestral homelands. From the beginning of the 300-Years War until its end, some whites advocated genocide: solve the "Indian problem" by exterminating the Natives. Others favored "civilizing" them and assimilating them into society as whites in everything but skin color. But where and when should this civilizing process occur? Few believed that it should take place in the midst of Euro-American society, or that it would be done quickly. For fifty years after 1800 most whites embraced a removal policy. In this regard the Louisiana Purchase was a godsend because Indians living on rich farmlands between the Appalachians and the Mississippi River could be "removed" to Indian Territory, which whites envisioned as a permanent Indian homeland. Removed Indians could then imbibe civilization—education, Christianity, farming—in the fullness of time.

Native peoples confronting removal pointed out that assimilation by segregation made little sense. If whites wanted Indians to become civilized, why isolate them from civilized society by sending them into the trans-Mississippi wilderness? Such logic had no impact on U.S. policy, and virtually all Natives in the Southeast and the Old Northwest were removed to a supposedly permanent Indian Territory by the mid-1840s. Ironically some removed tribes were already "civilized." Cherokees lived in a constitutional republic modeled after the U.S. government, and many wore European clothing, cultivated corn and cotton, held slaves, and were literate Christians. The truth was that American society, plagued by racial and cultural prejudices, never embraced acculturation and assimilation; most whites wanted the Indians warehoused somewhere out of the way and outside white society.

The idea of a permanent Indian Territory did not outlive the expansionist forces of the 1840s as the United States acquired Texas, Oregon Country, and the Mexican Cession, all topped off by the discovery of gold in California. As the Euro-American population in these areas exploded, the convenient expedient of moving Indians beyond the line of white settlement collapsed. The reservation policy emerged as an alternative to extinction or removal: save the remaining tribes or bands by colonizing them on small parcels of land "reserved" for their use. In these fixed, permanent (albeit small) enclaves Native culture could be extinguished and the transformation of Indians into sedentary, Christian agriculturalists could continue, forcibly if necessary.

"This is a delightful country," wrote Alexander Henry, who built a trading post on the Park River (a tributary of the Red River) in 1800, "and were it not for perpetual wars, the natives might be the happiest people on earth."[2] Perpetual intertribal wars: that was the fate of Native Americans, just as it was for Europeans. Archaeological evidence reveals that long before Euro-Americans arrived in the New World, warfare convulsed North America, with periodic upswings and downturns in its scope, magnitude, and intensity. Indians were not immune to Clausewitz's dictum that wars differ depending on the prevailing conditions and ideas and hence vary across time and geography.

Intertribal warfare remained commonplace even as Euro-Americans spread across the continent; during the nineteenth century more Indians perished in warfare against other tribes than they did fighting whites. Tribalism itself was a fundamental cause of warfare. Because each tribe considered itself "the People" it frequently harbored deep suspicions, even hatred, toward outsiders. Accentuating tribalism were more specific rationales: competition for hunting or fishing grounds; defense against aggressors; the expansion of trading opportunities; a pursuit of vengeance for insults or injuries, real or imagined; the acquisition of wealth by capturing animals, slaves, and other plunder; extortion; honor and social status; and at times survival. In short, Indians fought Indians because they were entangled in the human condition. As in many societies warfare was of such paramount importance that, as one white explorer wrote, "it is utterly impossible to be a great man amongst them [Indians] without being a distinguished warrior."[3]

When explorers and settlers first witnessed Native American warfare it seemed almost sporting or playful because it involved none of the mass slaughter so common in Europe. Roger Williams noted that wars among Indians were "farre lesse bloudy and devouring than the cruell Warres of *Europe*."[4] With more than a little contempt Capt. John Underhill wrote, "[Indians] might fight seven yeares [*sic*] and not kill seven men. . . . This fight is more for pasttime [*sic*], than to conquer and subdue enemies."[5] Two and a half centuries later a 2nd Cavalry trooper echoed his colonial forbearers when describing a battle between Lakotas and Crows: "After several hours of characteristic Indian warfare—bantering, blustering, showing off, and doing some occasional intermingled deadly work, [the Crows prevailed]."[6]

These observations about Indian-style warfare were not universally applicable. True, some wars consisted of little more than persistent low-intensity violence, primarily raids to inflict revenge, acquire plunder, or take captives. Raiding parties were small, well-organized guerrilla operations undertaken by individual volunteers who went to extraordinary lengths to avoid casualties. These more or less continuous raiding wars used limited means to achieve limited ends. Their purpose was not to gain control over an area or conquer rival groups, but to inflict a few enemy deaths or to capture horses, slaves, and other property.

Indians understood the difference between raiding and war. The Apaches' term for raiding meant "to search out enemy property," but their word for war meant "to take death from an enemy." *Individuals* conducted raids and fought for prestige and honors; *tribes* waged war to destroy an enemy, capture prime real estate, or at least establish hegemony over other peoples. Full-scale war could involve an entire tribe acting under centralized strategic guidance from political and military leaders. Such wars were so urgent that they temporarily overcame the individualism and fragmentation that were the norm in a tribe's social and political life. Strict military discipline, prolonged campaigns, pitched battles, fortified positions, sieges, the brutal slaying of women and children—all these were at times characteristics of Indian warfare.

When Native American peoples seized land from another tribe the wars were never sporting affairs. By 1750 the Comanches (in alliance with Utes) had established an empire on the southern Great Plains by obliterating a centuries-old Apache plains-based civilization in a ghastly half-century-long war. Having gained possession of the southern Plains the Comanches fought to preserve their conquest, not only from the Spanish but also from Pawnees, Arapahoes, Osages, Kiowas, Naishans, Wichitas, and Navajos. Simultaneously with the Comanches' expansion another warlike people conquered the northern Plains. Beginning in the early seventeenth century the Tetons, Yanktons, and Yanktonais pushed westward from the Great Lakes and the Mississippi Valley. With the Teton Sioux in the lead they ultimately dominated a region stretching from the Platte River to the Yellowstone. In alliance with two weaker tribes (Northern Cheyennes and Northern Arapahos) they held the Mandans, Hidatsas, and Arikara in virtual serfdom, and through near constant warfare dispossessed the Otos, Iowas, Missouris, Omahas, Poncas,

Pawnees, Kiowas, Shoshones, Assiniboines, and Crows of at least some of their territory.

In the latter part of the nineteenth century the Crows, who at one time had hunted as far east as the Black Hills, were in a harrowing situation. By 1860 the Sioux had driven them far to the west, all the way back to the Bighorn River in present-day Wyoming and Montana. In their shrinking domain the Crows endured permanent war, fighting for survival against the Tetons, who pressured them from the east, and the Blackfeet, Assiniboines, and Crees, who attacked from the north. Pretty Shield, a Crow, recalled, "[Enemy tribes] never let us rest, so there was always war. When our enemies were not bothering *us,* our warriors were bothering *them,* so there was always fighting going on somewhere."[7] White observers could not help but be impressed by the Crows' fortitude, while also lamenting what they perceived as the tribe's imminent extinction at the hands of Native American foes.

If warfare was widespread before Euro-Americans arrived, it became endemic afterward. White expansion transformed a continent already in flux. It crowded unfriendly or unfamiliar Native Americans into each other's territory, thus igniting conflicts, and ensnared Indians in the whites' market economy, which impelled Indians to joust for access to hides and furs and to barter for trade goods, such as weapons and alcohol. As the trading economy spread, Native Americans competed in ever compressed areas for ever dwindling resources. When the buffalo herds began to shrink in the 1830s, competition for them became white-hot; whenever tribes collided in the shrinking bison range, noted the Jesuit missionary Father Pierre-Jean De Smet, "it [was] war to the death."[8]

Also intensifying Indian warfare was the introduction of metal weapons, horses, and firearms, all of which seeped across the continent at unequal rates, with some tribes gaining access to them more quickly than others. Possession of these military innovations allowed a tribe to attack with relative impunity any foe that was still foot-bound and armed with Stone Age weapons. A deadly arms race developed as each tribe sought access to steel-edged hatchets, brass for making arrowheads, flintlocks, and horseflesh. Consequently the military advantage from utilizing Euro-American imports was usually short-lived; when an aggressive tribe's aggrieved neighbor found itself suitably armed and mobile it struck back—with a vengeance.

Intertribal enmity facilitated the Euro-American conquest in two ways. First, it allowed whites to divide and conquer, for they usually found Native

American allies who relished access to European weapons and trade goods and embraced Euro-American assistance in fighting traditional Indian foes. When Europeans paid Indian allies and provided them with weapons and reinforcements the recipients considered this an opportunity to strike at another tribe with which it was *already* at war. Understanding that escalating intertribal warfare with increasingly deadly weapons sapped the Indians' ability to resist their imperial ambitions, Euro-Americans jockeyed to keep Indians fighting one another. Rarely was warfare a matter of whites fighting Indians; instead Indians killed Indians, or whites and some Indians battled other Indians, or some whites and some Indians fought other whites and Indians. Of course sometimes it wasn't easy to discern who was exploiting whom, for self-interest determined diplomacy among Indians as much as among Euro-Americans. The former cleverly manipulated the British, French, Spanish, and (eventually) Americans against one another and against their Native enemies for their own purposes.

Second, intertribal discord worked against the development of pan-Indianism. For example, militant nativist Euro-Americans, who first arose in the late 1730s, believed in polygenesis, asserting that the Master of Life engineered separate creations of Europeans, Africans, and Indians and placed them on different continents. Indians, they argued, were a single people linked by common interests that transcended tribal rivalries and had a right to defend their continent from white avarice. But the concept of being an "Indian" was foreign to most Native Americans; only Euro-Americans lumped them all together. Natives did negotiate intertribal alliances, but these were usually local and transitory, changing as tribal interests diverged. Most Indians could not overcome their ethnocentrism, animosities, and fragmentation even when confronted by a menace as grave as the encroaching white empire. The fault line between nativists and accommodationists, between those wanting to resist and those who believed whites were too strong to fight, could prompt assassinations. In their debate over removal Cherokees splintered into an antiremoval National Party and an accommodationist Treaty Party; the latter prevailed, though its leaders—Major Ridge, John Ridge, and Elias Boudinot—later paid for this victory with their lives. Sometimes internal discord erupted into civil war, as it did in 1813–14 when the Red Stick War shattered the Creek nation.

The three Tidewater Wars between 1609 and 1646 and the Pequot War of 1636–37 were comparatively small, but they cast a long, dark shadow onto the future: every rationalization, strategy, and tactic the English employed in these conflicts remained in use during the final campaigns of the 300-Years War.

Although a few Euro-Americans proclaimed the Indians "noble savages," many more dehumanized and demonized them. Depriving Native Americans of their humanity and considering them the Devil's handymen allowed whites to rationalize terrorizing them and seizing their peltry, wampum, and—always—land. The conquerors assured themselves that their behavior, no matter how horrific, was God's way of punishing subhuman, heathen creatures.

Settlers waged war with remorseless, extravagant violence, though this was not unique to North America; the English perpetrated similar devastation in Ireland, and the Thirty Years War was hardly a model of Christian charity. Nor were Indians allied with the angels; ferocity, atrocities, and sadism were common on both sides. In America whites believed they had to resort to terror because Indians avoided battle and instead "skulked" in the woods and swamps, launched a raid or sprang an ambush, and then vanished back into the wilderness. These tactics frustrated and angered colonists, who endured nagging losses and yet could rarely strike back at enemy warriors. So they turned to unrestrained terror: attacking villages, preferably at dawn and during foul weather, when Native Americans were most vulnerable; indiscriminately slaughtering elders, women, and children; undermining the foundations of Native society by destroying lodging, food, crops, and fishing weirs, causing death from exposure and starvation; scalping and raping; pursuing fugitives ruthlessly; executing or enslaving captives. The objective was to exterminate a tribe in order to expropriate its land and, equally important, terrorize potential foes into remaining quiescent.

In an example of the Indians' strategic thinking, on March 22, 1622, the Powhatan chief Opechancanough orchestrated a simultaneous attack against English farms and villages scattered for 80 miles across the Virginia landscape, killing a fourth of the colony's men and women. Perhaps Opechancanough thought his masterstroke would impel the whites to withdraw. If so, he was mistaken. The Virginia Company called for a "sharp revenge upon the bloody miscreants" that would prevent them from "being longer a people upon the face of the Earth."[9] Enlisting the Potomack Indians' aid and often assisted by defectors from Opechancanough's forces, the English responded with macabre ferocity. For the next decade they campaigned relentlessly, striking at the foundations of Indian society year-round.

The Pequot War was equally instructive. Its turning point occurred at a Pequot fort along the Mystic River shortly after dawn on May 26, 1637. Leading ninety soldiers and hundreds of Mohegan and Narragansett allies who cast their lot with the whites rather than the Pequots, Capt. John Mason and Capt. John Underhill selected their target knowing that most enemy warriors were at another fort; that is, they chose the fort with the fewer combatants. The colonial plan was to kill the residents with the sword and then plunder the place. But Pequot resistance was so spirited that Mason decided, "WE MUST BURN THEM."[10] The English shot and stabbed those who fled the flames, but most Pequots were burned alive; at least 600 died, including 150 warriors. "We had sufficient light from the word of God for our proceedings," wrote Underhill in justifying the massacre.[11]

Mere victory did not satisfy the whites. Thirsting for annihilation, they pursued the vanquished foe ruthlessly, executing captured warriors and selling women and children to slave traders. If the English did not quite exterminate the once fearsome Pequots, they did reduce them to submission. Only a few hundred survived the war. And other tribes learned a lesson in what it meant to oppose the English.

Along with Indian allies and terror tactics, the whites had another advantage in the Pequot War, and in every Indian campaign thereafter: disease. Euro-Americans spread Old World diseases such as typhus, cholera, tuberculosis, measles, and smallpox throughout the New World. Because Indians had no immunity to these unseen killers, such diseases often reduced a tribe by 50 to 90 percent and left survivors demoralized. In 1633–34 a smallpox epidemic reduced the Pequots from about 13,000 to only 3,000, making the Puritan conquest much easier.

The seeds of extermination and terror that sprouted in Virginia and New England moved westward with white settlement, flowering anew on the moving frontier. In the mid-1860s Senator James R. Doolittle gave a speech in Denver in which he asked whether Indians should be placed on reservations and civilized, or exterminated. In response the crowd chanted, "Exterminate them! Exterminate them!"[12] No wonder Indian haters often failed to distinguish between hostile and friendly Indians or between the guilty and the innocent, and instead waged a race war, killing *all* Native Americans in the coldest of blood.

Responding to the U.S. Army's recent massacre of 173 Piegans (mostly women and children) on the Marias River in early 1870, *Harper's Weekly* published an editorial noting, "Undoubtedly, the feeling which led to the destruction of the Piegans was, at bottom, precisely the same as that which burned the Pequot fort upon the Mystic."[13]

At least the Pequots were hostile. The Piegans at the Marias were not.

Though it included operations against Snakes and Modocs in the Northwest, Apaches in the Southwest, and Utes, Sheepeaters, and Nez Perces in the Rocky Mountains, the terminal campaign's decisive theater was the Great Plains. There Indian opponents were more powerful than elsewhere; there they threatened the vital transcontinental routes of movement and communications; there the fighting occurred closer to major population centers, readily accessible to journalists whose accounts spurred interest; there the ultimate result was a grand imperial reorganization as the American empire supplanted the once great Comanche and Sioux empires.

Despite overwhelming advantages in wealth, population, disease immunity, and technology, the United States had a difficult time defeating the Plains tribes, in part because of its army's weaknesses and in part because of the Indians' abilities. The decisive campaign occurred against the backdrop of societal ambivalence toward Indian policy. As usually happened in the United States, war generated dissent because elements of the public questioned the conflict's justice and wisdom. Eastern humanitarians favored the reservation-civilization solution and thought that trying to solve the "Indian problem" with military force was absurd. They wanted no more massacres of old folk, women, and children, as occurred at Bear River (1863), Sand Creek (1864), and the Washita (1868). Their solution was to save Indians from extinction by removing them to reservations, where civilian agents, through benevolence and honest dealings, would induce them to abandon "savagery."

Preferring extermination, aggressive westerners thought humanitarians read too many James Fenimore Cooper novels exalting the "noble savage." They believed easterners spouted their pro-Indian nonsense only because they were isolated from the brutality by a thousand miles or more. "Here's seventy more reasons for those safely-located, chicken-hearted, high-toned-mealy-moral-suasion philanthropists to generally wail about, and we're glad of it," wrote a newspaper editor after he learned that Nevada and California volunteers had killed seventy Indians.[14] Although some regular army officers shared the humanitarians' concerns for the Indians' welfare, admired Natives as warriors, despised rapacious frontiersmen, and regretted the government's unbroken record of broken treaties, most sided with the westerners and thought "Indian lovers" were impractical visionaries, more feminine than masculine in their approach to problems.

Caught in the crossfire between paternalistic humanitarians and those wailing for extermination, the army was damned as butchers if it killed too many Indians and scorned as cowards if it killed too few. Its position was especially sensitive when President Ulysses S. Grant inaugurated his Peace Policy, which seemed to elevate the reservation-civilization approach to center stage. What many observers overlooked was Grant's pledge that Indians who did not readily accept reservation life would "find the new administration ready for a sharp and severe war policy."[15] Grant's policy promised peace on the reservations but war outside of them.

And war it was. Comanches, Sioux, and other tribes might avoid physical annihilation on reservations, but once confined they would confront the unappealing prospect of cultural extermination. The humanitarians' peace-loving platitudes and noble-sounding principles shattered on the granite of Indian resistance to reservation life.

In driving the Indians onto reservations the army faced numerous problems beyond enduring less than complete societal support. It fought at the outer edge of the American empire, where projecting military power was never easy. The army was small, yet the Plains were enormous, stretching from the Missouri to the Rockies and from the Rio Grande to Canada's coniferous forests. Much of the region was arid and plagued by horrendous weather. Vast distances and topographic and climatic extremes defeated more army columns than did Native Americans, if for no other reason than reconnaissance missions often failed to find the hostiles. As Gen. William T. Sherman acknowledged, locating hostiles was "worse than looking for a needle in a hay stack," and instead was "rather like looking for a flea in a large clover field."[16]

With an authorized strength of fewer than 50,000 officers and men between the late 1860s and mid-1870s, the army could rarely commit more than a few thousand soldiers to the Plains due to its other responsibilities: enforcing Reconstruction policies; garrisoning federal arsenals and seacoast fortifications; coping with natural disasters and civil disturbances; escorting scientific expeditions and railroad construction crews; and policing the other Indian frontiers. Many enlisted men were recent immigrants, inexperienced, and poorly armed, and personal disputes among hypersensitive officers often precluded effective cooperation. The army also contained a number of ignorant, arrogant officers who held Indians in contempt, thus underestimating them.

Also adversely affecting the army's performance was a lack of doctrine, a written guide to inform officers about the difference between conventional-style conflicts and unconventional warfare. Considering the Indians little more than a temporary nuisance, the army never developed any cogent guidance for Indian fighting. Instead each officer had to learn—often through haphazard and unfortunate experience—how to wage guerrilla-style warfare, and some learned more quickly than others.

Native Americans were thoughtful strategists, shrewd tacticians, and resilient warriors. Because they left few written records, their strategic thinking does not appear in triplicate in an archive; instead it must be inferred from their actions. Diplomatic negotiations demonstrated that Native leaders had an astute perception of their tribe's "national" interests and maneuvered (often without much success) to achieve long-range policy goals. Comanche leaders acted strategically in the 1830s and 1840s when they raided deep into Mexico with war parties numbering as many as 1,000 men. During such dangerous endeavors a warrior's individualism was restrained as specialized war chiefs enjoyed absolute authority. These raids established the Comanches' hegemony over northern Mexico, which they spared from utter ruin only because they wanted to exploit it systematically for horses and mules, supplies, and captives. Comanches also realized that shifting the geographic focus of the violence far to the south reduced the possibility of vindictive Mexican counterraids against their homeland.

The Oglala chief Red Cloud thought in strategic terms in the mid-1860s when he tried to force the army to withdraw from Forts Phil Kearny and C. F. Smith by disrupting their lines of supply and communication. And by the early 1870s Sioux and Northern Cheyennes living between the Yellowstone and the Black Hills purposefully shifted from an offensive to a defensive strategy. They would no longer attack whites outside this region, but would defend themselves if whites invaded. To give added weight to this strategy, the Sioux tinkered with a new form of centralized command to resist a sustained invasion. Sitting Bull became the foremost chief, with Gall and Crazy Horse selected as crucial subordinates. Perfect unity remained difficult to achieve, but strategic thinking underlay the effort.

Only in buffalo hunting and warfare, both vital to Plains Indians' survival, could leaders impose strict discipline on their followers. Moving under tight control, war parties traveled great distances in battle formation, with "wolves" (scouts) well in advance and decoys drawing enemy attention away from the main attack. When fighting began, Indian "officers" exercised tactical control much as whites did, by sight and sound. They communicated with flashing mirrors, flags, and signal fires and by blowing eagle-bone whistles. Of course war plans and battlefield command and control frequently unraveled; "friction" played no racial favorites.

Plains Indians were sophisticated tacticians who normally emphasized three military attributes: speed, stealth, and surprise. Many whites considered their skulking, sneaky way of war "unmanly" and treacherous. Others, such as Gen. Nelson Miles, knew better. "They employed the art of deceiving, misleading, decoying, and surprising the enemy with great cleverness," he wrote in praising them. "The celerity and secrecy of their movements were never excelled by the warriors of any country."[17] After a raid or ambush or if hard-pressed, Indians scattered and disappeared like ghosts, often to rendezvous at a designated assembly point some distance away; as they withdrew they burned the grass to impede pursuit, a tactic that caused many enemy mounts to starve. But hit-and-run tactics did not exhaust the Indians' tactical repertoire. Occasionally they fought it out, digging rifle pits and trenches or constructing fortifications out of rocks and logs that differed little from Civil War defensive positions. And sometimes Indians operated conventionally with what Sherman considered "almost scientific skill" by deploying advance and rear guards, skirmish lines, and well-aligned formations.[18]

Having been trained for war since childhood Plains warriors were formidable, especially those in elite warrior societies, which sustained a tribe's martial spirit and had their own officers and customs, including in some cases a duty to die rather than retreat and a responsibility to court one's own death. When an enemy tangled with Comanche Lobos, Cheyenne Dog Soldiers, Crow Lumpwoods and Foxes, Sioux Miwatani, or other warrior societies, it fought men of great courage and fortitude.

Although army commanders lacked an official doctrine, in the terminal campaigns they relied on widely accepted practices, most dating to the colonial era. By compressing Indians into an ever smaller area, converging columns negated their ability to flee. Native American ponies were scruffy-looking but had greater endurance than bigger army horses and lived on grass while the army's depended on grain and quickly weakened without it. When the grass was lush, Indians moved at will, but the army still needed burdensome supply trains. Although multiple converging columns reduced the Indians' ability to escape, poor communications made coordinating the columns difficult, and widely separated formations invited defeat in detail.

Converging columns in winter could be particularly effective. During the summer Indians ordinarily dispersed into small, mobile hunting and war parties, but in winter they huddled together in larger encampments. If the army surprised a winter camp the occupants were at a grave disadvantage since the snow and cold, the grass-fed ponies' weakened condition, and the presence of many women and children made fleeing difficult. Even escaping was often fatal because soldiers burned lodges, clothing, buffalo robes, and food supplies and slaughtered captured ponies. Starvation and exposure were as lethal as bullets. Of course winter campaigning was never easy on the army, as expeditions plowed through snow, savage winds, and temperatures that congealed the mercury in thermometers and men in the saddle.

Because the army's problem was not simply *finding* the Indians but also *surprising* them, Native American allies were invaluable. They negated the army's disadvantage of operating in enemy country by following trails that army officers could not see, locating an enemy camp without alerting the occupants, and guiding soldiers to the best positions during the night for a surprise dawn attack. They also carried a heavy combat load; in some encounters Indian allies represented at least half the army's strength, and in a few instances they were the *only* soldiers who engaged the foe. Yet officers whose mental habits were confined to the army's narrow orbit of military values hesitated to rely on Indians, who lacked "proper" discipline and a willingness to die in mini-Gettysburgs. Some officers believed that employing Native allies reflected badly on the army's capabilities and, fueled by racial anxieties, questioned Indian loyalty. (Only at Cibicu Creek in 1881 did Native allies turn on white comrades.)

Successful Indian fighters realized they had to fight in loose order, if for no other reason than that the rugged terrain demanded it. "The peculiar drill of men in masses, and the 'elbow touch' of the regular soldier, admirable as they are in ordinary warfare," wrote one general, "are utterly thrown away in contests with the Indians."[19] Maneuvering against Native Americans required practicality, not blind adherence to rote training.

Relentless campaigning was another operative concept. Hounding Indians during the summer made it difficult for them to hunt and prepare for the long winter ahead, and unremitting pressure after a winter attack intensified the physical and moral agony survivors endured. The army won the final campaigns not with spectacular victories but with a grinding persistence that resulted in numerous skirmishes, each chipping away at Indian strength and morale until even reservation life seemed preferable to being hunted and watching elders, women, and children suffer.

The Great Sioux War of 1876–77 displayed these concepts in practice. Two events precipitated the conflict. In 1873, a Northern Pacific Railroad surveying expedition penetrated the Yellowstone River region, and the next year gold was discovered in the Black Hills. These were lands the Fort Laramie Treaty of 1868 guaranteed to the Sioux, and Sitting Bull and other leaders vowed to defend them. The treaty negotiated at Fort Laramie failed because the chiefs from those tribes who signed did not understand all its terms, leaders from other tribes (especially Sitting Bull) refused to sign, and whites did not honor the provisions they disliked.

After the Panic of 1873, conquering the Black Hills became a national priority on the assumption that new gold would alleviate the money shortage and stimulate the economy. The Grant administration concocted a rationalization for violating the Fort Laramie Treaty so that it could seize the area. In a secret meeting on November 3, 1875, senior generals, high-ranking civilians, and the president made two decisions designed to provoke war: the army would no longer keep miners out of the Black Hills, and Sioux "hunting bands" that still roamed freely would be forced onto a reservation. To make the aggression seem less blatant, messages were sent to the hunting bands ordering them onto the reservation by January 31, 1876. Since no one expected them to obey, military officials secretly planned an offensive against the winter camps. Some bands never received the message, and those that did saw no reason to undertake a hazardous winter march; after all, they were at peace and had no way of knowing that Grant's administration was avidly seeking war.

The Sioux were stronger than many other tribes because their nomadic lifestyle protected them from the worst effects of epidemics that swept the Plains; in addition the government inoculated some Sioux bands against smallpox in 1832, mitigating that disease's impact. But their aggressive empire building alienated weaker tribes, and before the war ended, Crows, Assiniboines, Shoshones, Arikaras, Pawnees, Utes, and Bannocks fought for the Americans. Also, political rivalries so badly splintered some Sioux and Cheyenne bands and families that a few men from these tribes served the army.

The war's first battle occurred when 375 soldiers from Gen. George

Crook's command struck a Cheyenne village along the upper Powder River in March. Despite having been warned that soldiers were nearby and appointing ten men to stand guard during the night, the Indians were surprised and driven away from the camp. As soldiers torched the village, warriors counterattacked, saving about half their lodges, recapturing the pony herd, and forcing the whites to retreat. Still, as one warrior noted, "the Cheyennes were rendered very poor," and amid great misery they struggled down the Powder to find succor with Crazy Horse and Sitting Bull.[20]

With the winter offensive's failure to achieve decisive results, Gen. Philip H. Sheridan planned a summer offensive built around three converging columns. Commanding more than 1,000 troops and 262 Crow and Shoshone allies, Crook marched north from Fort Fetterman. Moving eastward from Forts Shaw and Ellis was John Gibbon with 450 soldiers and twenty-five (later reduced to nineteen) Crow auxiliaries. Thrusting westward from Fort Lincoln was Gen. Alfred Terry with 925 soldiers, including Custer's 7th Cavalry, thirty-seven Arikara scouts, and ultimately six Crows borrowed from Gibbon. Every commander focused on finding the Indians, not defeating them, because each column could deal with up to 800 warriors—far more than anyone expected to fight. After all, history proved (a phrase that usually portends a faulty history lesson) that Plains Indians dispersed in the summer, that the grass and food supply in an area could not sustain a large population, and that when Indians saw bluecoats they fled.

Such stereotypical thinking ignored an important consequence of the Powder River battle: it incensed the hunting bands. Without any provocation Americans had invaded their land. Cheyennes, Arapahos, and Sioux united in a powerful coalition to fight Sitting Bull's defensive war. As they concentrated in unprecedented numbers, including several thousand warriors, the Indians had no intention of fleeing. At the Battle of the Rosebud on June 17, some 1,000 warriors fought Crook's column for six hours in a furious battle of charges and countercharges. Crook's Indian allies played such a prominent role that some Sioux remembered the Rosebud as "the battle with our Indian enemies." Joseph White Bull, a Miniconjou, recalled that the battle "lasted all day, but when it was over 'Three Stars' [Crook] took his troops and hit the trail back to his base."[21]

After repulsing one column, a week later the Indians shattered another. Custer's Crow scouts found the enemy village but failed to convince him that it was too big to attack, and in a woeful command failure Crook did not alert the other columns about the Indians' strength and determination. As an experienced Indian fighter Custer believed the opportunity to strike a large group of hostiles was so fleeting he had to attack *now*, before they escaped. To increase the chances of trapping them he divided the 7th Cavalry into several detachments so he could attack from multiple directions. Except this time the Indians stood and fought, at one point jeering a portion of Custer's command that was retreating in panic, "You are only boys. You ought not to be fighting. We whipped you on the Rosebud. You should have brought more Crows or Shoshones with you to do your fighting."[22] When the Battle of the Little Bighorn (or the Battle on the Greasy Grass, as Indians referred to it) ended, more than 260 whites and Indian scouts were dead and Sheridan's summer campaign was in tatters.

The Indians' victories at the Rosebud and the Greasy Grass did not translate into strategic benefits (which may have been beyond their reach in any event, given the whites' enormous advantages). In accordance with their nomadic life they were unable to sustain a cohesive effort; separate bands drifted apart to find fresh grass and hunt bison in preparation for the coming winter. On the other hand army leaders, bent on retribution, poured troops into Sioux country. After the Custer battle, Black Elk remembered, "Wherever we went, soldiers came to kill us."[23] None of the many subsequent engagements was a pitched battle, but their impact was nonetheless dramatic, as several examples demonstrate. In early September a detachment surprised a camp at Slim Buttes. Most of the Indians escaped in the misty dawn, but they lost their shelter and possessions, leaving them destitute. Two months later another detachment, assisted by Pawnee and Shoshone allies, surprised Dull Knife's camp at dawn. The Indians improvised breastworks on nearby hillsides and fought back but could only watch helplessly as soldiers burned tepees, blankets, and sacred objects, destroyed tons of dried buffalo meat, and seized 750 ponies and a thousand buffalo robes. That night the temperature fell well below zero and a two-day snowstorm began. "Those were terrible days," Beaver Heart recalled. "The nights were alive with the cries of men tortured with wounds and women and children dying of cold."[24] Although a dozen babies froze to death, others survived by being warmed in the steaming entrails of butchered horses.

Mopping-up operations continued until May 1877. By then virtually all Indians, resigned to their fate, had moved onto reservations. Although scattered violence erupted throughout the West for another dozen years, the Plains Indians' defeat marked the end of the decisive, terminal campaign of the 300-Years War. The United States had humbled its most powerful Native American adversaries.

Military force simply hastened an outcome determined by more significant factors. As always Euro-Americans benefited not only from Indian disunity but also from diseases. Microbes, not bullets, killed Indians in ghastly numbers. Long before whites appeared in appreciable numbers in the West, smallpox, cholera, measles, typhus, and other diseases afflicted Native Americans with a biological catastrophe that eroded their ability to resist. Because the diseases recurred—in the northern Plains an epidemic occurred about every six years in the eighteenth and nineteenth centuries—a tribe never fully recovered before renewed death and suffering arrived. The Comanche population peaked at 40,000 in the 1770s and then, ravaged by smallpox and cholera, dwindled to no more than 10,000 by the 1850s. Sioux were lucky only by comparison since they too lost thousands. Societies woven together with bonds of kinship and clan were torn asunder, with some survivors so distraught after watching loved ones rot away that they committed suicide. Nor should alcoholism be forgotten as a disease. Introduced by Europeans, alcohol caused mayhem and demoralization among Indians, who seemed to have an insatiable appetite for liquor. Drunken binges led to fighting, maiming, and even killing, and the violence accentuated tribal, band, clan, and family factionalism.

Even without diseases the white population would have overwhelmed Native Americans. State and territorial governments vigorously promoted emigration, as did the federal government through the Homestead Act of 1862. Fertile prairies held an irresistible appeal for farmers, especially with the development of steel breaking plows (they cut prairie sod more easily than wooden or cast-iron plows) and improved harrows, seed drills, mechanical reapers, and threshing machines. Patented in 1874, barbed wire was also crucial. Eastern farmers fenced their fields with wood and stone, both in short supply on the prairies. Barbed wire, literally an armed fence, protected crops from unruly livestock. In 1866 fewer than two million whites lived in the West; a quarter century later 8.5 million resided there. Plains Indians imagined the whites as more numerous than blades of grass.

Railroads were essential in this immense migration because their boosters advertised the West, developed programs to settle farmers on railroad-owned land, provided cheap transportation to those who went elsewhere, and enhanced military security. Proliferating after the Civil War, railroads superimposed on the West a grid of iron rails that was equally useful for moving settlers, troops, and supplies, thereby reducing the army's dependence on cumbersome wagon trains. And whereas rivers were few and froze in the winter, trains ran year-round. Providing supplies no matter what the season, railroads made winter campaigns less difficult.

Finally, the near extinction of the bison doomed much of the Plains nomads' culture. Decades before the Civil War astute observers noticed a decline in bison numbers and predicted that, like the great auk, the shaggy beasts would ultimately disappear. Whites often slaughtered them, but Indians also killed excessive numbers after becoming enmeshed in the emerging market economy, exchanging buffalo robes and hides for European goods. Before robe traders arrived in the early nineteenth century Native Americans rarely killed more bison than necessary to sustain life. But as they became increasingly dependent on Euro-American goods they harvested more and more to trade for manufactured items and alcohol. The carnage put pressure on bison herds that were already under environmental stress from droughts, blizzards, fires, natural predation, and competition with millions of horses for grass and water.

The situation worsened after midcentury. Cattle and sheep introduced new bovine diseases and competed with bison for forage. By 1870 government officials embraced an unwritten policy of exterminating the bison to force Plains Indians onto reservations, a policy that coincided with two other developments: the discovery of a tanning process that turned buffalo hides into an elastic leather that was ideal for industrial belts, and the railroads' extension onto the Plains, which made it easy to transport hundreds of thousands of hides annually. Armed with high-powered rifles and encouraged by the government and the army, hundreds of hide hunters combined with continued overkilling by Indians to perpetrate a slaughter of staggering proportions. By 1883 only a few hundred bison, once numbering perhaps thirty million, were still alive.

Eradicating the bison eliminated the Plains Indians' primary resource, leaving them no alternative but the reservation. "A cold wind blew across the prairie when the last buffalo fell," lamented Sitting Bull, ". . . a death-wind for my people."[25]

The war's ending may have initially seemed definitive, but it actually resulted in a messy future as the relationship between the conquerors and the conquered remained unresolved. True, whites achieved their primary objective of dispossessing the Indians. Aside from the parcels reserved for Native Americans, primarily in regions where agriculture was difficult, the territory encompassing the lower forty-eight states was open for exploitation. With the "Indian problem" resolved and a resource-rich continent at its disposal, the United States attained Great Power status in terms of geographic expanse, population, and industrial productivity even before much of the public was aware of it.

Yet the army remained virtually unchanged. The 300-Years War sustained the aggressive fighting spirit inherited from the Mexican and Civil Wars, but for what? With the army's primary mission of policing the Indian frontier completed, what was its purpose? Garrisoning the expanding network of coastal fortifications the Endicott Board recommended? Serving as a national police force to quell labor strife? Preparing for foreign war? The army's consolidation into fewer posts—in 1870 it garrisoned ninety-two in the West, but by 1895 only thirty-eight—encouraged a few minimal preparations for a larger war, but it was hard to see who the enemy would be. The army's authorized strength, set at 27,442 in 1876, hardly varied until the Spanish-American War began twenty-two years later.

And when the army fought an unconventional foe in the Philippine-American War at the turn of the century it still had no appropriate doctrine, because the 300-Years War inspired no systematic study of guerrilla warfare. After all, the perception that Native Americans represented a transient nuisance, not a long-term threat, proved correct. Since the army would never fight Indians again, why bother studying that war? Who wanted to devote energy to such a nasty, unromantic affair, one that involved incessant hunting and chasing, burning lodges, killing noncombatants, and slaughtering ponies? Why study a war devoid of glorious titanic battles that decided the fate of nations? True, the late nineteenth-century army bubbled with intellectual ferment, but the reformers' goal was to better prepare the land forces for conventional warfare. When officers fought guerrillas in "Indian country" in the Philippines, most of them learned the same way officers learned about fighting Native Americans: through experience, conversations with fellow soldiers, and, in the best cases, a large dose of common sense.

For those other Americans, the Native Americans who lost the war, the changes were cataclysmic, even for those who sided with the United States. Two Leggings was a minor Crow leader who strove (unsuccessfully) to acquire a glowing military reputation, especially by fighting his tribe's Indian foes. "We helped the white man so we could own our land in peace. Our blood is mixed in the ground with the blood of white soldiers," he said bitterly. "We did not know they were going to take our land. That is what they gave us for our friendship." After being penned up on a reservation he wrote, "We just lived. There were no more war parties, no capturing horses from the Piegans and the Sioux, no buffalo to hunt. There is nothing more to tell."[26] Two Leggings lived another forty years, yet to him life ended when reservation life began. But he was wrong. There was more to tell. Much more.

And he was not alone in being wrong. Those who prophesied that Indians would vanish from the earth were wrong. Although some small tribes did in fact disappear, census figures reveal that the Indian population increased from 248,253 in 1890 to 1,365,676 in 1980. Two Leggings should have told of Indian population growth.

He also should have told of endurance and resilience and the continuing difficulty of determining exactly how Native Americans related to the nation that vanquished them. Paternalistic reformers who hoped to "save" the Indians through assimilation were wrong. Whites tried to destroy tribal culture, assuming that as Natives lost their Indianness they would dissolve as identifiable groups and merge into the broader society as individuals. Convinced they knew what was best for Indians, the do-gooders had no compunction about dictating new lifeways. Native Americans must farm rather than hunt, eat beef rather than buffalo, learn English, cease their religious practices such as the Sun Dance, organize their day by the hands on a clock instead of the sun's movements, wear drab, ill-fitting clothing rather than beautifully embroidered robes and moccasins, cut off their long braids, send their children to boarding schools where "civilized" values could replace tribal heritage.

In the face of this concerted effort to compel them to live a life they did not want, Indians struggled to continue not just living, but living *as Indians*. Despite defeat, demoralization, and hardship they converted reservations from jail-like enclaves into micro-homelands where Native children learned the old ways; communal lifestyles and tribal affiliations survived; Indian religions, for decades practiced illegally, survived; many Indian languages survived; reverence for the land survived; efforts to live meaningful lives on their own terms survived. "But we will never be white men," Olney Runs After insisted. "We can talk and work and go to school like the white people, but we're still Indians."[27]

SUGGESTED READING

The works of three scholars provide an indispensable starting point. In addition to their writings cited in the endnotes, see Colin G. Calloway, *One Vast Winter Count: The Native American West before Lewis and Clark* (Lincoln: University of Nebraska Press, 2003) and *New Worlds for All: Indians, Europeans, and the Remaking of Early America* (Baltimore: Johns Hopkins University Press, 1997); Francis Paul Prucha's *The Great Father: The United States Government and the American Indians,* 2 vols. (Lincoln: University of Nebraska Press, 1984); and Robert M. Utley, *Frontiersmen in Blue: The United States Army and the Indian, 1848–1865* (New York: Macmillan, 1967) and *Frontier Regulars: The United States Army and the Indian, 1866–1891* (New York: Macmillan, 1973). For the violence from colonial America into the early nineteenth century, consult Patrick M. Malone, *The Skulking Way of War: Technology and Tactics among the New England Indians* (Lanham, MD: Madison Books, 1991); Alfred A. Cave, *The Pequot War* (Amherst: University of Massachusetts Press, 1996); John Grenier, *The First Way of War: American War Making on the Frontier, 1607–1814* (Cambridge: Cambridge University Press, 2005). Books about specific tribes and campaigns include Gregory Michno, *The Deadliest Indian War in the West: The Snake Conflict, 1864–1868* (Caldwell, ID: Caxton Press, 2007); Frederick E. Hoxie, *Parading through History: The Making of the Crow Nation in America, 1805–1935* (Cambridge: Cambridge University Press, 1995); Pekka Hämäläinen, *The Comanche Empire* (New Haven: Yale University Press, 2009); Jeffrey Ostler, *The Plains Sioux and U.S. Colonialism from Lewis and Clark to Wounded Knee* (Cambridge: Cambridge University Press, 2004); John S. Gray, *Centennial Campaign: The Sioux War of 1876* (n.p.: The Old Army Press, 1976).

BRIAN MCALLISTER LINN

Batangas:
Ending the Philippines War

At an impromptu social call on December 1, 1901, newly arrived brigade commander J. Franklin Bell outlined his operational plan to "to put an end to insurrection and re-establish peace in the shortest time practicable" in Batangas province. Bell had been in the Philippines for more than three years, excelling in a multitude of assignments, including district commander and provost marshal of Manila. He supported the army's "benevolent and conciliatory policy," but he also recognized that pacification required soldiers to sever the links between guerrillas in the boondocks and the "amigos" in the army-occupied towns. Breaking these connections would be even more important in southeastern Luzon, home of the Tagalog tribe, where the "insurrection [had] been more vigorously and numerously sustained" by the socioeconomic elites (or *principales*)— the landowners, merchants, and civic officials.[1] The only solution was to "make life so miserable for the supporters of the Insurrection, that they will themselves bring about peace."[2] To achieve this, Bell intended a series of measures: food deprivation, imprisonment, destroying shelters and crops, and, most controversial, to "reconcentrate" the populations in some areas into "protected zones" outside of which any Filipino would be considered a combatant. By the time Miguel Malvar, Batangas's military *jefe,* and his few dispirited followers surrendered on April 16, Bell's soldiers had indeed made life miserable, not only for the guerrillas and their allies, but for most of the Batangueno population. The campaign

155

would be held up by its supporters as a "model of counterguerrilla warfare" and by its detractors as one of the most harsh and cruel campaigns in American history.

How did a war that began in 1898 to aid a subject people fighting against foreign domination in Cuba become a war to impose American domination on another subject people nearly 10,000 miles from there? The origins of the U.S. military intervention in the Philippines are controversial and confused. From an Olympian perspective, the rush to empire may appear to be the inevitable result of Manifest Destiny, imperialist cabals, the demand for new economic markets, Great Power rivalries, or Alfred Thayer Mahan's sea power theories. From a narrower viewpoint, the Philippine intervention was the result of war's unplanned outcomes. It was due in large measure to American military and political leaders focusing on winning the battle and ignoring the consequences. Once the enemy's military forces had been defeated, the nation's political leadership had to improvise a mission, an objective, and an end state, all the while reacting to rapidly shifting conditions. It was a messy process, and it directly contributed to a very messy unanticipated war.

In the early 1890s, as part of their service's war planning in a conflict with Spain over Cuban independence, a handful of U.S. Navy strategists proposed an attack on the Spanish squadron in Manila Bay. Fixated on tactics and operations, they gave little thought to how this might achieve the nation's strategic objectives or what might be the long-term results. They assumed that once at war, the United States should strike its enemy everywhere and anywhere. This target-of-opportunity rationale became integrated into naval planning without serious discussion with political leaders. As tensions with Spain over Cuba approached a climax, navy planners, including Assistant Secretary of the Navy Theodore Roosevelt, moved to implement the Philippine option. The result exceeded their expectations. Six days after the U.S. declaration of war on April 25, 1898, Cmd. George Dewey shattered the Spanish in a stunningly one-sided victory at Manila Bay. But even as he reported his triumph, Dewey raised the question that the planners had failed to address: What now?

The only person who could answer that question, President William McKinley, was unable to do so. He had far greater problems than deciding the fate of an obscure archipelago somewhere in the Pacific. Many of these problems were of his own doing. Bowing to political pressure, the president had authorized a tenfold expansion of the army, sending thousands of enthusiastic but untrained citizen soldiers into uniform. This deluge almost immediately triggered the virtual collapse of the army's antiquated administrative and logistics organizations. Compounding McKinley's troubles were an insubordinate commanding general, an incompetent secretary of war, a sensationalist press, and a public demanding immediate action.

McKinley temporized. Claiming that Dewey's victory had transferred sovereignty of the Philippines to the United States, he ordered an army expedition to Manila with the vague directive to complete the defeat of the Spanish forces and establish order and security. But he did not reveal whether this mission would be temporary or permanent. Indeed, he did not even tell the expedition's commander whether his objective was to protect Dewey's squadron, capture Manila, or occupy the entire archipelago. Overwhelmed by other, more pressing political and military priorities, McKinley may have rationalized that he had little to gain, politically or militarily, by committing himself and the nation to a definite policy on the Philippines. The expedition would demonstrate his commitment to supporting the hero of the hour, Dewey, and might lead to some other, as yet unforeseen benefits. And if upon arrival in Manila Bay the Americans found the situation too hostile or the American public rejected any overseas adventures, McKinley had left himself free to withdraw the troops with no great loss of national or personal prestige. Ironically, despite his determination to keep all his options open, McKinley would soon conclude that he had none: he could not return the Philippines to Spain; he could not turn them over to some other Great Power; and he could not leave them to the Filipinos and invite civil war and foreign intervention. Ultimately he became convinced that having broken Spanish rule and, in the process, touched off an archipelago-wide uprising, it was the responsibility of the United States to fix the Philippines.

The first army troopships arrived at Manila Bay on June 30, to be followed by two other flotillas totaling some 14,000 troops. Although they captured Manila on August 13, the Americans soon found that the Spanish were less dangerous opponents than those fighting for an independent Philippines. Led by local elites, Filipinos soon isolated the Spanish in a few cities and assumed control of towns and provinces. Emilio Aguinaldo, who had led an abortive rebellion in 1896, returned from exile to his power base in the Tagalog-speaking areas of Luzon, particularly the provinces south of Manila: Cavite, Batangas, Laguna, and Tayabas. Aguinaldo claimed to be president of an independent Philippine republic and announced a constitutional convention to create a national government, but he restricted the franchise to the small minority of wealthy and influential Filipinos. In any case his personal authority was confined to the Tagalog regions, and even there he governed by the sufferance of regional military-political jefes. In other islands, such as Panay and Negros, Filipino patriots declared their own independent republics.

Throughout the archipelago the resistance to Spanish and American rule was elite-based and intensely local. Both those taking up arms against Spain (and later the United States) and those who supported accommodation sought the local political and economic power to which they believed their wealth, experience, and position entitled them. Virtually none wanted to extend the benefits of the revolution to the peasantry, the vast majority of the populace. Beyond their shared class interests the revolutionaries had little in common, and divisions between Aguinaldo's supporters and the regional governments were deep, and sometimes violent. The only thing that could unite the independence movement was a common enemy, and the Americans soon provided this.

By the close of 1898, McKinley recognized that the consequences of Dewey's victory, and his own reactive decisions, could no longer be avoided. But the president's position was much stronger than it had been in May. Occasionally cooperating, the U.S. armed forces and the Cuban rebels had forced Spain to seek an armistice in August. That war was won. And even though many Americans rejected imperial aggrandizement, McKinley recognized that many more already viewed the Philippines as part of the national patrimony. In December, having demanded that Spain cede the archipelago as part of the peace settlement, McKinley declared that the United States would govern for the benefit of the Filipino populace and that the American armed forces would be the first agents of this "benevolent assimilation."

McKinley's declaration that the Philippines were now a U.S. possession, when coupled with Aguinaldo's nearly simultaneous declaration of an independent Philippine Republic, rapidly increased tensions in Manila. Fighting broke out on the night of February 4, 1899, and for three weeks the armies clashed in a series of battles around the city. The legal status of this conflict was unclear. Only after the treaty with Spain came into force on April 11 could the McKinley administration claim that U.S. military forces were suppressing an "insurrection" in the Philippines. But if the legality of the fighting was obscure, the results of the Battle of Manila were both clear and decisive. Aguinaldo's army suffered a crushing defeat. He lost any chance of driving the Americans out of the archipelago. From then on, Aguinaldo was fighting on the defensive, seeking to buy time in hopes that either the U.S. Army would collapse from disease and fatigue or the American public would tire of the war and recall its troops.

Throughout 1899, U.S. forces conducted a series of campaigns north of Manila, scattering the last of Aguinaldo's conventional forces in December. As his army disintegrated, Aguinaldo declared guerrilla war and escaped to the mountains with a few followers, maintaining a symbolic leadership of the resistance on Luzon but losing any control over operations in the field. In the early months of 1900, U.S. forces pushed into southern Luzon and the Visayas Islands. Maj. Gen. Elwell S. Otis, the U.S. Army's commander, reorganized his tactical units into occupation forces and spread them throughout the archipelago; ultimately soldiers garrisoned more than 500 posts.

Throughout McKinley's tenure as commander in chief, his understanding of the situation confronting his military subordinates in the Philippines was often unrealistic, in large part due to misinformation from those military subordinates. But he showed considerable prescience in his long-term strategic goals. The president assumed that Aguinaldo and his followers were a minority who represented neither a Philippine state nor the Filipino people. In his view, the resistance to the U.S. occupation was essentially a rebellion by one "tribe," the Tagalogs, supported by various brigands, military chieftains, religious fanatics, and some profoundly ignorant and misled peasants. As McKinley explained to Congress, "obeying no concerted plan of strategic action" some "dissatisfied Tagals" had violently resisted American authority. America's responsibility was "moral as well as material": "[Troops should treat Filipinos] so that our flag may be no less beloved in the mountains of Luzon and the fertile zones of Mindanao and Negros than it is at home, there as here it shall be the revered symbol of liberty, enlightenment, and progress in every avenue of development."[3] Having stumbled into a war because of a tactical plan that had no strategic objective, McKinley was now determined to keep the strategic objective at the forefront. Unfortunately, he grossly underestimated the tactical problems in achieving this end state.

McKinley's insistence that the military focus on the benevolent aspects of colonial government—schools, roads, an honest judiciary, economic prosperity, and so forth—was not simple idealism but an attempt to remove the sources of Filipino resistance. He maintained, and Congress agreed, that the Philippines were not a territory (they were later termed an "insular possession"), and therefore the commander in chief and his agency, the War Department, held legislative, executive, and judicial powers. From August 14, 1898, until July 1901 the Philippines were under a military governor who also served as the commanding general, and all officers down to the lowest lieutenant were expected to serve both civil and military duties. Those provinces that were too unruly or that were identified as Muslim remained under military rule, while those deemed pacified were transferred to the authority of the civilian Philippine Commission. Thus, from the beginning, the army was expected to both conquer and govern.

Some army veterans soon recognized that conflict on the new Pacific frontier had more than a passing similarity to the Indian wars. As in the West, in many cases the U.S. Army faced, not a unified foe, but a number of tribes and chiefs as much at war with each other as with American soldiers. The intrusion of U.S. troops into Philippine regions already torn by economic, social, and political strife, and in some cases ravaged by disease and natural disasters, often sparked resistance with little direct connection to Aguinaldo or the concept of statehood he espoused. In some areas this resistance was minimal; most Filipino Muslims, or Moros, were neutral, and planters and merchants on Negros even helped U.S. troops hunt down peasant rebels. But in other areas military chieftains mobilized their followers to ambush U.S. patrols, attack supply lines and communications, and punish any Filipinos who assisted the Americans. Between February 1899 and July 1902 the army counted some 3,000 engagements between insurgents and American soldiers. The majority of these were long-range skirmishes in which there were few casualties, but some were bloody indeed.

The leaders of most of the anti-American resistance were local merchants, landowners, and businessmen who had benefited from the overthrow of Spanish authority. Often stigmatized by Americans as brigands, terrorists, or malcontents, many were sincere patriots who fought for an independent Philippines. But it is important to note that their vision of independence rarely was that of the Tagalog-dominated republic of Aguinaldo. Indeed, on many islands there was such tension between Aguinaldo's appointees and the local leaders that only the mutual conflict with the Americans prevented a civil war. For the most part the guerrilla organization was decentralized, usually based at the level of the municipality and its outlying villages and barrios. Indigenous military-political jefes commanded or cajoled subordinates who, like them, were drawn from the local elites and often tied by family or business connections. They in turn led bands of peasant guerrillas drawn from their tenants and clients, most of whom lived in the barrios and towns and assembled occasionally. A clandestine network of tax collectors, informants, porters, recruiters, and enforcers sustained the guerrillas and prevented collaboration. In many cases the guerrillas and their supporters lived in municipalities garrisoned by American troops.

McKinley directed the armed forces to convince the Filipino people of America's benevolence, to rectify the injustices of Spanish colonialism, and to suppress oppression and disorder. But he also required Filipinos to accept U.S. sovereignty; no armed resistance was tolerated. Thus, while officers built schools, roads, clinics, markets, and courtrooms, they also scoured the boondocks for guerrillas, brigands, and other rebels. Villages and provinces that accepted pacification received better roads, access to waterborne trade, schools, markets, and a number of other benefits. Those who collaborated, especially the elite, found the Americans willing to give them most of the powers they had sought as insurgents. A number of former guerrillas became governors of provinces or important figures in the national assembly; one, Manuel Quezon, become president of the Philippine Commonwealth.

Although such conciliatory practices gained crucial support in some areas and between some tribal and religious groups, military commanders in roughly half the provinces also had to conduct counterinsurgency operations. Like their opponents, American soldiers adapted and innovated according to local conditions. Many regiments raised mounted scout units; others became expert at riverine operations. The U.S. Navy imposed a draconian blockade on all waterborne commerce, excepting only those vessels that traded from approved ports. New roads and improved logistics meant that whereas in 1899 it had been impossible to sustain large troop movements, by 1901 the Americans could send hundreds of troops on sustained cordon-and-sweep operations into areas that had previously been inaccessible. In some areas soldiers burned buildings and fields to deny sustenance to the rebels or in retaliation for attacks, imposed rigorous food controls, restricted travel, or pursued other policies that adversely affected the population.

Both the American commanders and their various opponents recognized the importance of population and resource control. But many officers did not appreciate that the American occupation governments were often superimposed over an existing revolutionary administration. As Lt. William T. Johnston discovered in his province, "each and every pueblo had its designated detachment of armed insurrectos, completely armed and officered, for which it furnished quarters and subsistence and not a little pay. The provincial and town officials and prominent people generally were aiding the insurrection almost openly."[4] Johnston's revelation of the close relations between the towns and the guerrillas was quickly passed up the chain of command, from province to district to department, influencing counterinsurgency methods at all these levels. His district commander ordered Johnston to investigate the surrounding towns and authorized his recruitment of Filipino auxiliaries to identify guerrillas. Within a few months Johnston's superiors had implemented a number of new policies, including a thorough purge of the civil administration, restrictions on food and individual travel, and harsher penalties for those found supporting the guerrillas.

Johnston's report confirmed the views of Otis's successor as Philippine commander, Maj. Gen. Arthur MacArthur. In December 1900, MacArthur promulgated the Union Army's Civil War code of conduct for military occupation, General Order 100. Though endorsing benevolence and conciliation, he directed his subordinates to pursue all measures within the laws of war to sever the connections between the guerrillas and the towns. Post commanders received far greater authority to arrest, fine, and deport suspects, to burn houses and fields, and to purge and punish any official who was found to have supported the insurgents. Through both coercion and conciliation many prominent Filipinos were required to visibly demonstrate their loyalty to the United States or risk imprisonment, fines, and confiscation of their property. Once so publicly committed they faced the threat of kidnapping and assassination by the remaining insurgents, and thus had every incentive to secure peace.

One of the most significant demonstrations of the army's new policies was Bell's January–February 1901 campaign in Abra province in northeastern Luzon. Bell isolated Abra from all outside commerce, imposed rigorous food control in the towns, condoned the burning of houses and crops, and forcibly relocated the residents of some outlying villages into protected zones, after which all males outside these protected zones were treated as guerrillas. He also employed a variety of Filipino auxiliaries, including both army-authorized scout units and unauthorized paramilitaries that included the followers of a religious sect. Harsh and destructive as Bell's measures were, they worked.

With the April 1900 arrival of the civilian Philippine Commission, led by William Howard Taft, the benefits of collaboration became even stronger. The Commission gradually took over many of the army's functions in the pacified provinces. It held elections for municipal and provincial offices, took over the educational system and civil service, and raised its own law enforcement agency, the Philippine Constabulary. The Commission, and Taft in particular, proved adept at winning over many Filipinos who had been alienated by the authoritarian manners of army officers. Equally important, it created alternatives to military resistance. Although the Commission did seek to raise the general populace through education and some civil rights, it was guided by cooperative regional elites, even appointing the leader of Abra's guerrillas that province's lieutenant governor. Taft also was crucial in the December 1900 formation of the Federal Party by prominent politicians, landowners, and professionals. Not only was the Federal Party an important signal of the Americans' intent to allow Filipino participation in the colonial government, but it had an immediate practical impact as well. The party sent emissaries into the boondocks who convinced many guerrilla leaders, who were in many cases relatives or friends, to surrender.

The Commission's success in conciliating Filipino elites was enhanced by increased military coercion. American soldiers, moving on new roads and coordinated by telegraphed orders, pushed into previously inaccessible jungles and mountains, burning supply depots and shelters, and reducing guerrilla bands to a handful of weary, hungry, and demoralized refugees. MacArthur belatedly authorized the recruitment of more Filipino scout units and loosened restrictions on raising police, guides, and local defense forces. Thousands of local paramilitaries joined the soldiers. They were encouraged both by threats of punishment and by large rewards for captured insurgent leaders and rifles—and in many cases by tribal, town, or personal rivalries—and eager to end the war.

Under this combined Filipino and American pressure, the majority of insurgent leaders surrendered, and those who did not were hunted down and killed. Most of Luzon north of Manila was pacified by March 1901. Manuel Trias, the supreme commander for southern Luzon and head of the resistance in Aguinaldo's own province of Cavite, surrendered in April. Aguinaldo was captured shortly afterward and in May ordered his remaining supporters to surrender. Nationalist resistance collapsed in all but a few areas. By July, McKinley judged the archipelago peaceful enough to transfer political authority from MacArthur to Taft, leaving only the Muslim region and a handful of provinces under military rule. The worst of these recalcitrant provinces was Batangas.

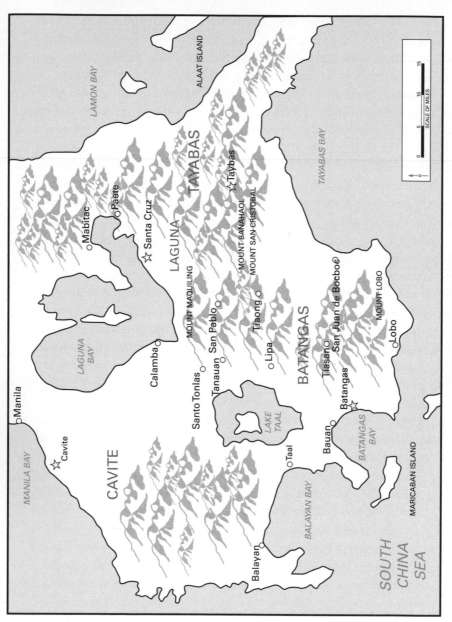

THE PHILIPPINES
BATANGAS REGION

The southwestern Luzon provinces of Batangas, Laguna, and Tayabas cover roughly 4,200 square miles and in 1900 had a population of more than half a million. The region was agriculturally productive and in some areas densely settled, usually with a central municipality surrounded by a number of smaller villages and hamlets, termed *barrios*. The historian Glenn A. May's description of Batangas as "an almost ideal setting for the waging of unconventional warfare" was true of all three provinces.[5] The hills and mountains and nearly impenetrable vegetation could hide camps and storehouses, and the populace provided food, information, and recruits. Although there were class and local divisions, the population was more homogeneous than in other areas, preventing army commanders from exploiting ethnic divisions as they did in much of the rest of the archipelago.

U.S. troops first entered southeastern Luzon in force in January 1900 and quickly brushed aside the provincial defense forces in a few sanguinary battles. They seized the main towns, broke up the regiments into company- and battalion-size garrisons, and set to work on "benevolent assimilation." When the Americans reorganized from tactical to administrative commands in April, Batangas, Laguna, and Tayabas became the Second District Department of Southern Luzon; neighboring Cavite province was the First District. Combined, the two districts were held by some 8,000 troops. For several months the occupation appeared to be a resounding success, with little overt resistance. In reality the insurgents were regrouping to wage a protracted struggle against the American military government.

Although anti-American resistance in Batangas was as diffuse and localized as in other regions, it had an unusually competent and popular political-military chieftain. Miguel Malvar, born in 1865, was a prosperous businessman with close social and financial ties to prominent families in the Batangas-Laguna-Tayabas area. Like many local elites, Malvar had deeply resented the Spanish authorities, both political and religious, who denied Filipinos the right to direct their own municipal affairs. He took a prominent part in the 1896 revolt and joined Aguinaldo in exile, returning in 1898 to rally Batangas's elites, first against Spain and then against the United States.

In his instructions to his guerrillas Malvar stressed organization, logistics, and the importance of close cooperation between irregular military units and the population that supported them. Each of Batangas's towns was to support a guerrilla column, with members divided into small sections, so that "each company may have its own barrios, and obtain recruits and supplies or rice and money."[6] Malvar himself traveled through southeastern Batangas and the Tiaong area, accompanied by only a few trusted aides, never sleeping in the same place two nights in a row, and using drop-offs and intermediaries to hide his location. To American eyes he was indistinguishable from any other middle-aged peasant, and American efforts to catch him—such as orders to "arrest every fat Filipino of about forty years and hold until identification is proven"—were unsuccessful.[7] Throughout 1900, Malvar and his partisans stalemated American efforts to pacify Batangas and impose colonial government.

The capitulations of Trias and Aguinaldo and the collapse of most of the resistance north of Manila by spring 1901 left Malvar little chance of success. But his years as a guerrilla had given him a concept of Philippine independence different from Aguinaldo's limited elite-based political movement. Assuming supreme command over all revolutionary forces in April, he proclaimed himself the servant of the people, declaring, "The lowest laborers . . . are the ones who act with the greater honesty of intentions and are more sincere in their aspirations."[8] All who fought for independence, regardless of social class, would share in its benefits. Malvar extended the revolution's benefits, and he also extended its obligations by conscripting soldiers, levying taxes, and requisitioning supplies. He outlined tactics for a prolonged war of attrition: all fighting was to be done from ambush and only under the most favorable conditions; if necessary the insurgents should be ready to continue to resist for a decade. He emphasized that it was crucial to retain control of rifles and ammunition, to maintain close connections between the guerrillas and the populace, to suppress collaboration, and to make Batangas ungovernable by the American colonial authorities. Malvar insisted that his guerrillas were not only the protectors of the population against American imperialism; they were the guardians of public order and morality. Even as they fought the invaders and executed traitors, they would punish brigands, bigamists, and those who abused women.

Malvar's decision to continue fighting coincided with a decline in American military effectiveness that both directly and indirectly affected operations in Batangas. Thousands of soldiers who had enlisted for service in 1898 and 1899 were due for discharge, leaving many regiments far below their authorized strength. The veterans' replacements were mostly new recruits who required extensive training for and acclimatization to Philippine conditions. The transition from military to civilian rule in much of the archipelago required shutting down hundreds of small posts, moving equipment and personnel, and turning over municipal accounts to civilian authorities. In Batangas these problems were exacerbated by MacArthur's inexplicable decision to turn the province over to the Philippine Commission in May. In less than two months the army was back in control, but with little apparent effect. The summer monsoon sent sick lists soaring and frustrated efforts to hunt down the guerrillas. The province was impoverished by years of war, fever and cholera were ravaging the population, and business and agriculture were devastated, but Malvar showed every indication of being able to sustain the war indefinitely.

MacArthur's successor as Philippine commander, Maj. Gen. Adna R. Chaffee, confessed in early November, "We are practically at a standstill in Batangas. Troops are continually scouting but find no one. The damned insurrectos are now resting in the barrios—doubtless laughing heartily at the efforts the troops are making to find them in the brush."[9] He later reported, "The inhabitants of the province of Batangas were largely insurrectionary. . . . A considerable number of armed and unarmed men living in [U.S.-occupied towns] actively served the cause of the insurrection, either as soldiers in the field as occasion required, or as agents in the towns and barrios supplying food, clothing, and information. Such a state of affairs might have continued to exist for months, if not for years."[10] Chaffee recognized the urgency of ending armed resistance in the Philippines, which by now threatened to derail Secretary of War Elihu Root's entire reform agenda. There could be no reorganization into tactical units, no professional education system, no large unit training—and perhaps no congressional support for further reforms—until the army could disengage itself from its costly, debilitating, and increasingly unpopular pacification duties in the Philippines.

On December 1, Chaffee assigned Bell to command the Third Separate Brigade and directed him to secure the pacification of Batangas. Bell had several advantages over his predecessors, including virtual carte blanche from both his military and civilian superiors to pacify the region as rapidly as possible. They now were willing to accept measures that were previously forbidden, including the forcible relocation of the population, the closing of the ports to trade, and the burning of crops. With the surrounding provinces pacified and the gunboats blockading lake and ocean ingress, Bell could isolate southern Luzon more effectively than had previously been possible. Drawing troops from pacified provinces, Chaffee authorized a "surge," giving Batangas alone almost as many American soldiers as had been assigned to all of southeastern Luzon in 1900 and 1901. Chaffee also assigned Bell 700 Native scouts, soldiers who had proven invaluable at identifying insurgents, gathering information, and guiding expeditions into the boondocks.

Bell was the beneficiary of the cumulative adaptations and improvements in two areas. The first were those the army had implemented in three years of campaigning in the Philippines, including a far more efficient supply system in Manila, miles of telegraph wire, and a system of roads that allowed large concentrations of troops to conduct sustained operations. Second, Bell could call on a reorganized intelligence network that embraced a number of important collection and analytical procedures, including the distribution of photographs of and information on insurgent leaders and suspected agents. In September 1901, the army belatedly moved to close the gap between local and central intelligence when it ordered each post commander to designate an intelligence officer whose first task was to conduct a full survey of everything from the area's water supply to the loyalty of the local officials. These surveys not only provided crucial information to local military commanders, but were analyzed by the army's Division of Military Information in Manila, allowing for a much better strategic assessment of conditions in both individual provinces and the entire archipelago. The cumulative effects of the army's improved intelligence procedures were manifested in the field. Whereas in 1900 it had taken months to translate captured documents, by late 1901 they were being returned to combatant commanders within a week, along with updated descriptions of prominent insurgent leaders and their supporters.

Equally valuable were the innovations and adaptations made by local commanders in Batangas. In many towns, enterprising post commanders had recruited spies, identified insurgent sympathizers, and mapped the surrounding territory. In some the commander's ingenuity or resentment of insurgent terrorism had caused the population to rally to the United States. Nor should the cumulative effects of army benevolence—schools, roads, markets, honest governments, protection from criminal attacks, generous surrender terms, and so on—be discounted. As a result, and perhaps to his surprise, Bell would be able to employ hundreds of paramilitary volunteers, including former guerrillas familiar with hiding places and caches, so that his own Filipino contingents far outnumbered Malvar's guerrillas. In short, Bell was able to conduct a campaign that would have been impossible even a year earlier, and to his credit he exploited every advantage.

Bell's first and foremost priority was to deny Malvar's guerrillas all food, information, recruits, and shelter from the towns. On December 6, he ordered commanding officers to delineate a zone around their towns sufficient to supervise and protect, then to require the population in the surrounding area to move all their food to that zone within twenty days. After this deadline all food found outside the zone would be confiscated, and all adult males would be captured or killed. Then and now, soldiers and civilians compared this policy with the "reconcentration" campaign Spain had applied in Cuba that killed thousands of civilians. In practice, Bell recognized that many areas were already pacified, and he gave his post officers considerable leeway. Much of eastern Batangas was exempt, as were towns whose citizens had shown their loyalty to the Americans. But at Malvar's hometown of Santo Tomas, some 8,000 Filipinos were quartered in a two-square-mile area surrounded by a "dead zone," which no one could cross without a pass. Each barrio was assigned a section of a street, and people moved their houses, livestock, and rice into it. Every morning the men would search the countryside for caches of food outside the zone, escorted by soldiers to protect them from insurgents and brigands.

The zones were one means of severing connections between the guerrillas and the population. Another was an elite corps of six provost marshals assigned to investigate towns known to harbor insurgent sympathizers. The recently promoted Captain Johnston, a veteran of Bell's Abra campaign, was one of the most effective. In February 1902 he arrived at Tiaong in Tayabas province. Tiaong, near the Laguna-Batangas border, served as a supply depot, recruiting area, and sanctuary for Malvar's guerrillas, including the jefe himself. The town's *vice-presidente* (deputy mayor) collected taxes on everything from gambling houses to the supplies sold to the U.S. garrison. Even the priest donated fees from religious ceremonies. A guerrilla chieftain took control of the police force; the constables' primary duties were to spy on and misinform American troops and collect taxes for the insurgents, including half their own salaries. Several hundred guerrillas residing in the surrounding barrios visited the town at will. Any collaboration with the Americans was ruthlessly dealt with; the police sergeant knew personally of *Americanistas* who had been murdered.

Johnston, applying methods he had developed over almost two years of similar work, patiently interviewed hundreds of people, compared their stories, exposed contradictions, and sent out troops to track down new information and suspects. He employed a troop of Filipino volunteers recruited, under some compulsion, from another town to scout the surrounding area for storehouses and guerrilla camps. Suspected guerrillas were imprisoned and interrogated, and their information led to more arrests. Gradually, by meticulously cross-indexing names, residences, and eventually the guerrillas and their weapons, Johnston built up a picture of Tiaong's finances, kinship and interest groups, and the local guerrilla organization. Tiaong became a counterinsurgency clinic, and Bell sent officers to learn Johnston's methods. Within a month, most of the guerrilla leaders had surrendered or been captured, their civilian collaborators arrested, and the area pacified. Bell promptly dispatched Johnston to break up the insurgent infrastructure in Malvar's hometown of Santo Tomas.

While isolating the towns' populations in the protected zones and deciphering the insurgents' clandestine information and logistic systems, Bell unleashed a series of forays into the countryside to destroy supply caches and camps and kill, capture, or scatter the guerrillas. He drew on a 2,500-troop mobile force, broken into fifty-man columns, for four cordon-and-sweep operations into the mountain ranges, first striking south into the Loboo range, then east to Lake Taal, and finally into the northwest region along the Batangas-Laguna-Tayabas borders. The soldiers, aided by hundreds of Filipinos, systematically moved through the jungles, ravines, and mountains, confiscating or destroying crops and livestock and burning thousands of houses. The soldiers also detained any civilians found in the countryside. Although Bell personally disapproved of burning and issued numerous orders emphasizing the importance of bringing supplies back to the towns, his subordinates were far less scrupulous. The result was immense devastation and hardship.

When he initiated the campaign in December, Bell confidently predicted that he would break insurgent resistance by late February. By mid-January the surrender of Col. Anastacio Marasigan, his staff, a known insurgent priest, and 245 soldiers with 233 rifles at Taal essentially pacified the western third of Batangas province. Chaffee reported at the end of the month that the guerrillas had "ceased to fight" and that American soldiers were moving unchallenged through the south and east of the province, securing rifles "in batches."[11] Hunted by American troops and Filipino militia and increasingly fearful of betrayal from their former supporters, some guerrillas turned on each other or simply threw away their weapons. Those who returned to the towns were arrested and imprisoned, and only by surrendering weapons or informing on their comrades could they secure their release. Malvar himself was harried and pursued, his family either captured or sick. Finally, after negotiating with Bell, he capitulated on April 16, effectively ending resistance in the Batangas-Laguna-Tayabas region.

Malvar's surrender occurred almost simultaneously with that of the last few holdouts on Samar, bringing an end to military operations against Filipino nationalists. On July 4, 1902, President Theodore Roosevelt declared the insurrection over, thanked the army for its exemplary service, and terminated the office of military governor. Roosevelt maintained that the army had fulfilled McKinley's instructions and achieved American war aims. His proclamation stated that whereas since 1896 many Filipinos had been in a state of violent insurrection, they were now in a state of peace under the authority of the United States. The army's governing responsibilities were now limited to the Muslim provinces of Mindanao and the Jolo archipelago. Its primary mission would be to assist the civil government in maintaining law and order. Reflecting both its diminished obligations and other commitments, between 1902 and 1904 the number of American troops in the Philippines shrank from 29,000 to fewer than 18,000; within a few years it was 12,000.

The end of the war occurred amid a series of charges and counter-charges on the conduct of American troops in the Philippines. The anti-imperialists had been thrashed in the 1900 presidential election and pilloried as defeatists, and they now seized on sensationalist accounts of torture and indiscriminate killing. Virtually all of the press departed at the end of conventional operations in early 1900, with the result that both pro- and anti-annexation newspapers engaged in a great deal of creative journalism. Many of the most graphic incidents were inventive "war stories" lifted from soldiers' letters to their families or concocted from hasty interviews, some of which were later recanted. Yet even amid much smoke there was evidence that some Americans had been guilty of war crimes. The Samar campaign, with its revelations that the commanding general had ordered a subordinate to "kill and burn" and to treat all male Filipinos over ten as hostile, inflamed this controversy. So too did a letter from Governor Cornelius Gardener of Tayabas accusing Bell's forces of brutality, destruction, indiscriminate killing, and the "water cure" torture. An army inquiry determined that Gardener had misrepresented conditions in Tayabas (and had himself countenanced some of the brutal methods he deplored), but an independent investigator found seventeen instances of torture during Bell's campaign. To his credit, Bell forbade "unauthorized methods of exacting information," writing, "We want to accomplish our purpose without resorting to any methods that are liable to demoralize our men and that always do more harm than good."[12] But it is clear that far too many officers violated these restrictions.

Between January and June 1902, a Senate committee investigated the conduct of American troops in the Philippines. Some of the findings spawned sensationalist news reports, but they had little discernible impact on the American people, who were glad the war was over and showed no desire to prosecute its victors. But the atrocity controversy refused to die. Scholars, or more accurately, authors with an agenda, dug through the anti-imperialist literature and the Senate hearings and selected incidents that put American troops in the worst light, often overlooking contradictory testimony. This material was often incorporated into textbooks and popular histories, blackening soldiers' reputations and contributing to the perception that the army had engaged in a genocidal slaughter of defenseless Filipinos.

It is vital to realize that in the larger context of guerrilla resistance and counterinsurgency in the Philippines, Batangas was more typical than atypical. The Philippine War was above all a regional struggle for control over villages and provinces, in which American officers had to innovate and adjust to the unique and distinct conditions in their areas. Yet for a variety of reasons the Batangas campaign became *the* example of successful counterinsurgency within the army. Bell's telegraphic circulars were incorporated into the Senate investigation, and the Third Brigade's chief of staff published a compilation for his fellow officers. Later authors portrayed the Batangas campaign as the epitome of army counterinsurgency in the Philippine War, the successful climax of a long process of adaptation and innovation against irregular units that stretched back to the colonial era. There is some support for this interpretation. Bell clearly drew on counterinsurgency lessons he had learned in earlier campaigns. He exploited the army's improved intelligence, sanitation and medicine, communications, roads, and logistics; the methods he employed and the control he was able to exercise over his scattered forces, as well as their ability to sustain themselves in the boondocks, would have been impossible a year earlier. Bell was also the beneficiary of the usually overlooked efforts of his predecessors, who, by the time he arrived, had largely pacified Cavite, Laguna, and Tayabas and reduced the resistance to a few hundred guerrillas under Malvar.

Between 1899 and 1902, roughly 125,000 American soldiers were deployed to the Philippines, with troop strength averaging about 40,000 a year. The army's records are contradictory, but a 1922 summary counted 1,004 combat fatalities, 2,572 dead of disease, 589 other deaths, and 2,911 wounded.[13] The number of veterans who were permanently affected by disease, injuries, and psychological problems is unknown, but the limited evidence suggests it was very high.

The cost of the American invasion to the Philippines was catastrophic in people, resources, and morale. Filipino casualties are a matter of much controversy but little reputable evidence. The army concluded that it was impossible even to guess at Filipino combat fatalities; most of the fighting was at long ranges and in difficult terrain, American soldiers consistently overestimated their body count, and Filipinos usually carried away their wounded and dead. Estimates of the number of Filipino civilian casualties during the war are even more problematic, and the commonly cited figure of 200,000 is purely speculative. Clearly, U.S. military operations contributed greatly to civilian casualties, but critics often ignore the fact that many ecological and epidemiological problems predated the Americans' arrival. Indeed, since the existing records do not reveal—within about a million people—how many Filipinos were alive in 1898, it is virtually impossible to determine how many were either direct or indirect casualties of the war. The war certainly created thousands of refugees, destroyed agriculture and livestock, and left much of the population malnourished and susceptible to disease. As many as 40,000 Batanguenos, or 13 percent of the population, may have perished between 1902 and 1904 from cholera alone.

Roosevelt's termination of the insurrection did not end army involvement in pacification. Three days after his proclamation, the War Department issued General Order 152, which placed the islands' military forces at the call of the civil government. Governor Taft and his successors were quick to take advantage, appropriating the army's 5,000-man Philippine scout organization with such regularity that by 1905 it was essentially an adjunct of the civil government. Although the near simultaneous surrenders of Malvar and Samar's insurgent leadership ended the last of the original nationalist resistance, violence continued to roil the archipelago. Brigand gangs and religious devotees, sometimes in mobs of hundreds of armed men, raided villages, kidnapping and murdering from northern Luzon to Mindanao. On Samar the Pulahan sect virtually controlled the mountains and inflicted bloody defeats on the civil government's constabulary. Bandits and militant religious cults terrorized Negros, Cebu, and Leyte.

The devastation committed by Bell's troops, cholera, the death of livestock, drought, and exploitation of the peasantry by the American-supported elites all contributed to an outbreak of brigandage in southern Luzon. A former insurgent officer, Macario Sakay, claimed he would fulfill Malvar's social revolution as the "Supreme President of the Tagalog Isles." By 1904, Sakay's followers encompassed millenarian sects, brigands, displaced farmers, and former insurgents, and they defeated the civil government's constabulary in several skirmishes. In January 1905, these rebels occupied two towns, looted the treasuries, and kidnapped the family of Cavite's governor. The civil government declared martial law, creating a "provisional district" under the command of a constabulary colonel (and Philippine War veteran), David Baker. Baker followed many of Bell's methods. He revamped the intelligence services, forcibly relocated much of the population into protected zones, threatened and punished the rich and powerful until they collaborated, and sent combined army, constabulary, and militia task forces to burn fields and houses and hunt down brigands.

As with Bell's campaign the 1905 Cavite Incident sparked complaints of abuse, including torture and summary execution. Also like Bell's campaign, Baker's methods achieved short-term success. Sakay surrendered, and most of his lieutenants were soon captured or killed. The long-term consequences were less favorable for the Americans. Outrage over the government's harsh methods in southern Luzon, Negros, and other regions fueled nationalist sentiment and threatened Filipino collaboration with the civil government. Baker and the head of the constabulary were replaced; the Filipino legislature emerged as coequal with the American administration, and the elites were largely confirmed in their political and economic power, which they hold to this day.

In the Muslim Moro provinces in the southern Philippines, the army was the primary agent of imperial government until 1913. A general served as the area's governor and administered a colonial civil service largely composed of fellow officers. As they had during the Philippine War, post commanders had extensive political and administrative duties: they built roads and telegraph lines, regulated sanitation and health codes, established marketplaces, encouraged local trade, and in numerous other ways provided law and stability. This last mission often drew them into mediating intra-Moro quarrels and, occasionally, into leading punitive expeditions against tribes or leaders judged to be a menace. Leonard Wood's tenure as governor was marred by a bloody and probably unnecessary campaign on Jolo in March 1906 that resulted in the deaths of hundreds of Moros, many of them women and children, and reignited many of the charges of army brutality from the Philippine War.

The Moro Wars evoked numerous comparisons with earlier campaigns against Native Americans. In many ways the problems were similar: to maintain order between mutually antagonistic tribes, avoid a religious war, and foster economic growth, education, and law. But it is important to recognize that many of these parallels—such as Frank McCoy's 1903 declaration the "the military problem is not a hard one [and] the methods employed are very much the same as handling the Indians of the plains"—were made by officers who had virtually no experience fighting on the western frontier.[14] Like the Indian conflicts, the Moro struggles were viewed as a distraction in both the local government and Washington. Increasingly for both military and political leaders, the army's purpose in the Philippines was not to enforce internal security, but to protect the Islands from foreign attack. This was no easy task, with a garrison of roughly 12,000 Americans and 5,000 Filipino scouts. Military planners initially envisioned a Dewey-like small-scale naval raid by a European power that would try to seize Manila and then, as McKinley had, assert sovereignty over the entire Philippines. The American solution—a complex of fortifications at the mouth of Manila Bay, a powerful naval squadron, and a small mobile land force—appeared to cover this eventuality.

The Russo-Japanese War of 1905 revealed a Far Eastern opponent with the ability to destroy the defender's maritime defenses and land tens of thousands of veteran troops in a few weeks. In 1907, tensions between Japan and the United States prompted the army's newly created General Staff, headed by Bell, to draw up the first of several war plans for the defense of the Pacific. They concluded that the only solution was for the American military forces to abandon the entire archipelago, including Manila, fall back to Subic Bay, and hold out until the navy's battle fleet arrived in three to six months. Roosevelt, who had previously supported Philippine acquisition, now saw it as America's Achilles' heel.

The vulnerability of the "insular possession" became a major concern for both military and political leaders and greatly influenced U.S. foreign policy in the Far East. American diplomats traded concessions, maritime bases, and China's territorial integrity to secure Japanese recognition of U.S. sovereignty in the Philippines. The problems of defending the Philippines contributed to the American willingness to forgo naval supremacy at the Washington Naval Treaties of 1921 and were perhaps the most important factor in the decision to grant the Philippines independence. Indeed, it is not too much of an overstatement to say that from the moment of Roosevelt's declaration of victory, Pacific defense remained a continuing conundrum for American strategists, a source of civil-military tension and bitter debates both between and within the services. The ultimate consequence was the humiliating surrender to an outnumbered Japanese invading army in 1942.

The immediate and long-term consequences for the army were immense. The war in the Philippines destroyed what remained of the "Old Army" of the Civil War and the western frontier: by 1902 two-thirds of the officer corps were men commissioned after 1898. The war accelerated the army's reform efforts, providing Elihu Root with a rationale for modernizing and professionalizing the force. But the demand for harbor defenses and mobile garrisons to protect Hawaii, the Philippines, and the Canal Zone delayed the implementation of the reformers' agenda. Economic prosperity discouraged enlistments, and congressional parsimony—and some fear of future imperial adventures—kept the army at between 60 and 80 percent of its authorized postwar strength of 100,000. American soldiers shuttled back and forth with such regularity that in some years almost half the army was overseas. Assignments to schools, staffs, or colonial administration left some regiments with barely half their authorized officers. Not until 1912 did the army create distinct continental and colonial organizations. The price of this stability was that the overseas garrisons had only a fraction of the number of troops required to hold them against foreign invasion.

The lessons of the Philippine War are as contested today as they were a century ago. Anti-imperialists like Mark Twain charged that acquiring a far-distant colony marked a radical shift in U.S. foreign policy from peaceful neutrality to belligerent interventionism. Later polemicists found a clear historical parallel between the Philippines and Vietnam and, more recently, with Iraq and Afghanistan. As some historians became more fixated on social, cultural, and racial explanations, they portrayed the war as another manifestation of American racism and cultural oppression. Others argued that the Philippine intervention marked the beginning of American efforts to dominate Far Eastern trade and ensure dependent economies in the underdeveloped world. Postindependence Philippine treatments of the war were heavily influenced by Marxist class warfare analysis, and even more by nationalist mythology, portraying it as a "revolt of the masses" betrayed by the elites. More current research has highlighted the social, economic, and regional differences within the Philippine polity and criticized Aguinaldo and other nationalists for their failures. In short, the termination of the war has spawned a large and vituperative historiography but little agreement.

Until quite recently the U.S. Army's response to the Philippine War was largely to ignore it. The War Department ordered Bell to write a summary of his counterinsurgency experiences, but the general persistently delayed, arguing that it would do little good and might do much harm. Instead he devoted his efforts to teaching officers the complexities of modern conventional warfare at the newly reorganized school at Fort Leavenworth. Under his direction the army published its first combined-arms operational doctrine in 1905, a manual based almost entirely on German practice. Bell's chief of staff published Bell's telegraphic orders for the Batangas campaign in a pamphlet and circulated it among his colleagues, but a hundred years passed before the army's Combat Studies Institute gave it official distribution. Taft suppressed publication of Capt. John R. M. Taylor's "official" history, and not until 1939 did an officer publish a narrative of the conflict. Officers in the post–World War II military studied British and French counterinsurgency and Maoist revolutionary war but generally ignored their own service's experiences in the Far East. Indeed the previous decade may have seen more institutional effort to extract the lessons of the Philippine War than the entire preceding century. Unfortunately, much of this analysis remains focused on the tactics and methods of counterinsurgency, and not on the burdens of empire that fell upon the army as a consequence of its victory in 1902.

SELECTED READING

The Batangas campaign is well documented, compared to the rest of the Philippine War. Essential readings are John M. Gates, *Schoolbooks and Krags: The United States Army in the Philippines, 1898–1902* (Westport, CT: Greenwood Press, 1973); Brian McAllister Linn, *The U.S. Army and Counterinsurgency in the Philippine War, 1899–1902* (Chapel Hill: University of North Carolina Press, 1989); Glenn A. May, *Battle for Batangas: A Philippine Province at War* (New Haven: Yale University Press, 1991); Robert D. Ramsey III, *A Masterpiece of Counterguerrilla Warfare: BG J. Franklin Bell in the Philippines* (Fort Leavenworth, KS: Combat Studies Institute Press, 2007). For military histories of the conflict and its aftermath, see James Bradford, ed., *Crucible of Empire: The Spanish-*

American War and Its Aftermath (Annapolis, MD: Naval Institute Press, 1993); Robert A. Fulton, *Moroland, 1899–1906* (Bend, OR: Tumalo Creek Press); Brian McAllister Linn, *The Philippine War, 1899–1902* (Lawrence: University Press of Kansas, 2000); William T. Sexton, *Soldiers in the Sun: An Adventure in Imperialism* (Harrisburg, PA: Military Service Publishing, 1939); John R. M. Taylor, *The Philippine Insurrection against the United States, 1898–1903: A Compilation of Documents and Introduction,* 5 vols. (1906; Pasay City, P.I.: Eugenio Lopez Foundation, 1971); Marion Wilcox, ed., *Harper's History of the War in the Philippines* (New York: Harper Bros., 1900). On the domestic impact of the war and U.S.-Philippine relations, see H. W. Brands, *Bound to Empire: The United States and the Philippines* (New York: Oxford University Press, 1992); Richard E. Welch, *Response to Imperialism: The United States and the Philippine-American War, 1899–1902* (Chapel Hill: University of North Carolina Press, 1979). For treatments of postwar operations and Pacific defense, see William Reynolds Braisted, *The United States Navy in the Pacific, 1897–1909* (Austin: University of Texas Press, 1958) and *The United States Navy in the Pacific, 1909–1922* (Austin: University of Texas Press, 1971); Brian McAllister Linn, *Guardians of Empire: The U.S. Army and the Pacific, 1902–1940* (Chapel Hill: University of North Carolina Press, 1997); Alfred W. McCoy, *Policing America's Empire: The United States, the Philippines, and the Rise of the Surveillance State* (Madison: University of Wisconsin Press, 2009). For overviews of U.S. counterinsurgency and the impact of the Philippines, see Andrew J. Birtle, *U.S. Army Counterinsurgency and Contingency Operations Doctrine, 1860–1941* (Washington: Center of Military History, 1998); Mark Moyar, *A Question of Command: Counterinsurgency from the Civil War to Iraq* (New Haven: Yale University Press, 2009).

EDWARD M. COFFMAN

The Meuse-Argonne Offensive:
The Final Battle of World War I?

The United States entered the Great War in April 1917 after the French and British had battled the Germans for almost three years. It was clear the Allies needed massive reinforcements. Although the war also raged on far-flung fronts in Eastern Europe, Africa, and the Middle East, the Americans concentrated their major effort on the Western Front, which stretched more than 400 miles from the English Channel to Switzerland. When the United States went to war its army comprised some 200,000 troops, two-thirds of whom were regulars, the rest national guard veterans of service on the Mexican border. By the end of the war nineteen months later, volunteers and draftees had increased the army to four million, half of whom were in France. During the last month and a half, in the Meuse-Argonne offensive, a million-man American field army played a significant role in defeating the Germans. The German commander, Field Marshal Paul von Hindenburg, made this point clear in his postwar comment: "The American infantry in the Argonne won the war."[1]

The American service medal called it "the Great War for Civilization." Yet in its aftermath, despite worldwide war weariness and hopes for a lasting peace, the treaty to end the war fell prey to the same human failings that had caused it. The peace negotiations and the American debate that followed dashed high expectations of a new era in history. The Great War could not end all wars. Indeed, the ramifications of the war and the peace that followed led to an even greater global conflict two decades later, in which the United States played a decisive role.

I

National ambitions and rivalries laid the foundation for the European war in 1914. Germany's militaristic, ambitious emperor, Wilhelm II, commanded a large, impressive army and a vast colonial empire and had begun to build a navy to compete with Britain's fleet. His closest ally, Austria-Hungary, was concerned about the rise of pan-Slavism in the Balkans. Germany's archenemy, France, seethed with desire for revenge over its 1870 defeat by the Germans and their seizure of Alsace and Lorraine. Russia, allied with France, promoted pan-Slavism, thereby incurring the enmity of the Austrians. The Germans thus understood that if they went to war with France a huge Russian army would open a dangerous second front. Meanwhile the British, whose only formal ally was Japan, reached an understanding with France because of their concern about the Germans' colonial expansion and navy.

Recognizing the strategic ramifications of this diplomatic tangle a decade earlier, Count Alfred von Schlieffen, chief of the German general staff, had completed a mobilization plan for a two-front war. Because the French would be ready to fight before the Russians could mobilize, the Schlieffen Plan aimed to launch a massive surprise offensive to envelop and rout the French before the Russians entered the war. However, the plan called for a march through Belgium, ignoring long-standing British guarantees of its neutrality, almost ensuring that Great Britain would enter the war.

On June 28, 1914, a Slav terrorist murdered Archduke Franz Ferdinand, heir to the throne of Austria-Hungary. Austrian leaders seized this opportunity to crush Serbia, the major Slavic power in the Balkans. Even though the Serbs acceded to most of the demands in the Austrian ultimatum, Austria went to war with German support. In early August the nations of Europe declared war according to the dictates of their alliances, and the Germans commenced their offensive through Belgium into France.

By 1914 Schlieffen's successors had weakened his plan enough that the French Army was able to survive the onslaught. As the Germans should have expected, the British supported the Belgians and the French, and within months the belligerents had dug in and the war on the Western

Front became a stalemate. All of the powers had assumed it would be a short war, but huge trained armies with new and deadly weapons and backed by large industrial and railway systems made hopes of a quick victory obsolete. Over the next two years the Germans and Austrians fought on the Eastern Front and in the Balkans. Turkey's entry as a German ally led to fighting in the Middle East and repelling the British invasion at Gallipoli, and Italy went to war against Austria. On the Western Front the belligerents waged offensives that resulted in enormous casualties. Two battles in 1916 illustrate the great losses: Verdun (February 21–December 15) cost an estimated 162,000 French and 142,000 German dead and missing. From July 1 to November 18 in the Somme there were 419,654 British, 204,253 French, and an estimated 450,000 to 600,000 German casualties.

II

Most Americans and their president, Woodrow Wilson, were determined to continue the nation's traditional neutrality. As the war progressed, however, the Germans attempted to counter the British naval blockade by sending out submarines to sink British shipping. In May 1915 a submarine sank a large passenger liner, the *Lusitania,* killing almost 1,200 civilians, including 128 Americans. This attack outraged the American public, and Wilson pressed the Germans to give up unrestricted submarine warfare. They initially refused but, as Wilson's pressure increased, acquiesced with the promise that in the future their submarines would surface, warn the targeted ships, and permit them to put passengers on lifeboats. In effect this accession ended submarine warfare, allowing Wilson to run for a second term in 1916 on the slogan "He kept us out of war."

Wilson had come to the presidency with domestic reforms in mind. Yet turbulence in Mexico had compelled him to send brief expeditions there in 1914 and 1916. As the war in Europe continued he made some futile efforts to induce the belligerents to make peace. Increasingly, however, he became aware of the possibility of being pulled into war and the need to strengthen the navy and army. He pushed the necessary legislation through Congress in 1916. However, Wilson was generally uninterested in and naïve about military matters. In 1915 he became furious when he read in a newspaper that the general staff was working on a plan for a possible war with Germany. He ordered the acting secretary of war to investigate and, if the report were true, to relieve the officers involved and send them out of Washington. When a senior general staff officer explained that the staff was expected to make plans and had prepared them in case of war with not only Germany but also England, Japan, and other possible enemies, the president backed down.

In a speech before the Senate on January 22, 1917, Wilson called upon the belligerents to make "peace without victory." Within ten days, Germany responded by resuming submarine warfare. This provocation, together with their effort to entice the Mexicans to go to war against the Americans by promising them return of the territory they lost in the Mexican War, led Wilson to ask Congress on April 2 to declare war on Germany. He was willing to take this momentous step because of his basic war aim of a nonpunitive peace and new world order. Later, in January 1918, he spelled out his altruistic war aims in his Fourteen Points, which included open covenants, removal of economic barriers, freedom of the seas, disarmament, adjustment of colonial claims, appropriate territorial adjustments, and an international association to guarantee the independence and integrity of all nations.

During the war, Wilson continued to concentrate on those aims and delegated military matters to the secretaries of war and the navy. A wartime confidant, the affable Sir William Wiseman, Chief of British Intelligence in the United States, recalled, "He wasn't interested in the conduct of the war. It was only a means to the aftermath. He was interested in his Points and the League of Nations." Nor was he interested in professional soldiers or sailors. "He did not think he would like to talk with them."[2] Although he had a grand strategy for the peace to follow the war, he did not seek advice from his military leaders about his plans.

Secretary of War Newton D. Baker consulted with the president before he named Maj. Gen. John J. Pershing, who led the Punitive Expedition in Mexico in 1916–17, to command the American Expeditionary Forces. In late May, before he left for France, Pershing visited Wilson and Baker at the White House. The general was surprised that Wilson, rather than giving any instructions or advice, simply offered Pershing his full support. Just before he sailed, Pershing did receive a letter from Secretary Baker with instructions from Wilson, which included the crucial point that he should maintain the AEF as a national force separate from the European armies.

Pershing arrived in France on June 13, 1917, followed by advance elements of the 1st Division two weeks later. By that time he had already decided, with the tentative agreement of the French army commander, Gen. Henri Pétain, that the AEF would occupy a sector in Lorraine, where it could eliminate the German salient at St. Mihiel and strike a decisive blow against the rail center at Metz.

At first, American forces were slow to deploy. Over the winter only three other divisions arrived in France. After visiting the front and conferring with French and British generals, Pershing cabled the War Department that he needed a million men within the year. Meanwhile the nation mobilized, began conscription, built temporary camps, and developed plans to supply and train the huge force.

Although the American entry in 1917 was a boon to the Allies, a series of four disasters marred that year: a failed French offensive that resulted in mutinies in the spring, a costly British offensive in Passchendaele that lasted from late summer into November, an Austro-German break-through against the Italians at Caporetto in the fall, and the impending collapse of the Eastern Front as the Bolsheviks came into power in Russia in November. These great blows made the British and the French realize that they needed all the men the United States could provide. In November the Allies formed a Supreme War Council consisting of the heads of the governments in Britain, France, Italy, and the United States, their civilian assistants, and military advisors in order to facilitate the unity of their efforts. President Wilson, who wanted to maintain his independence as a peacemaker, insisted that his nation was an associated power rather than an ally and sent his close advisor, Edward M. House, to represent him at the meetings.

During the winter of 1917–18 the British and French increasingly pressed Pershing to send men to serve as individual replacements in Allied ranks, rather than taking the time and resources to train and build an independent force. The Allied manpower pool was virtually exhausted, and they assumed that the closure of the Eastern Front would enable the Germans to redeploy forces for a major offensive in the West. When Prime Minister David Lloyd George tried to get Wilson's support to send companies or battalions to serve in British units, the president backed Pershing in refusing, but added a caveat that this position was secondary to the demands of a critical situation. Unfortunately for Pershing this message leaked to Allied leaders, who put even greater pressure on him at a Supreme War Council meeting. Ultimately he agreed to send seventy-two battalions to train with the British and assigned four black regiments to serve with the French. In exchange the British furnished increased shipping capacity to the Americans, allowing the AEF to grow by 1.7 million troops from April to November 1918.

As British and French leaders feared, the Germans launched a series of offensives in late March, leading the Allies to make Gen. Ferdinand Foch their supreme commander to coordinate efforts on the Western Front. The Germans continued with four more offensives in April, May, June, and July against the British, French, and Americans. In early May, at another Supreme War Council meeting, Lloyd George, Premier Georges Clemenceau, and their military leaders hammered at Pershing to send them more infantry and machine-gun units to help make up for their losses. He reluctantly agreed to permit 120,000 combat troops, brought over by British ships in May, to serve temporarily with the British and tentatively promised another 120,000 in June, but he insisted that the Supreme War Council endorse the principle of an independent American army.

Throughout this period, when disaster seemed imminent, both Lloyd George and Clemenceau were appalled that Wilson had left such a crucial decision up to his military commander. Neither would have permitted their military leaders such license. It was Clemenceau who made the oft-quoted statement "War is too important to be left to generals."[3]

In late May 1918, the AEF began to play a role in the war by making a successful regimental assault with French help at Cantigny. Less than a month later the marine brigade of the 2nd Division drove the Germans out of Belleau Wood while the 3rd Division fought at Chateau Thierry. The major American debut, however, came after the quick collapse of the last German offensive in mid-July, when the 1st and 2nd Divisions led a counteroffensive at Soissons. From late July to early September five American divisions took part in the Aisne-Marne offensive. The Germans and the French agreed in their critiques of the AEF that its leadership was faulty but American soldiers' morale was high. These factors, combined with Pershing's open-warfare doctrine emphasizing the infantry's reliance on rifles and bayonets rather than artillery and machine-guns, resulted in a high percentage of casualties.

The growing strength of the AEF demanded periodic reorganization and the creation of additional commands. On August 10, Pershing established the First Army, but retained himself in command of it. Commanding the field army and the AEF meant that he dealt not only with AEF logistics and field army operations, but also with the secretary of war, the French premier and president, the supreme commander, Marshal Foch, the French army commander, General Pétain, and the British and Italian army commanders. Pershing and his staffs found themselves stretched thin to meet all these demands.

In mid-August, Foch approved Pershing's plan to attack the St. Mihiel salient in September. A few days later he changed his mind when the British commander, Field Marshal Sir Douglas Haig, approached him with a plan to stage a huge pincer offensive against the Germans with the British, French, and Americans. Foch then asked Pershing to provide four divisions to serve under the French in the Meuse-Argonne sector and to have the First Army take a position on the other side of the French Second Army. He also recommended that a French general supervise the First Army's staff work. Although Pershing understood the strategic possibilities of the great pincer movement, he did not like the idea of turning over four American divisions to the French or of letting them plan and direct the First Army's battle. Nevertheless, he agreed to take over the Meuse-Argonne sector providing that he would still carry out the St. Mihiel attack and the First Army's staff would conduct the staff work. Foch agreed, even though it meant that the untried First Army would have to execute two major operations 30 miles apart within two weeks. The Americans began planning their attack in the Meuse-Argonne as well as moving men and supplies to that area before the attack on St. Mihiel. Within two days (September 12–13) eleven American and four French divisions drove the weakened Germans out of the St. Mihiel salient. The First Army's first operation was successful, but the second proved to be more difficult.

The strategic importance of the Meuse-Argonne sector was that the German front there was closer (32 miles) than anywhere else to the railroad, which was the Germans' main supply line for the Western Front. The sector, which had been quiet for most of four years, stretched some 20 miles from the unfordable Meuse River through the large Argonne Forest. Most of the front was rolling countryside with occasional hills and forests, but deep ravines scarred the densely wooded Argonne. Five understrength German divisions defended the sector in three belts—trenches, strong points, and machine-gun positions all reinforced with barbed-wire entanglements—of which the Hindenburg Line was the most formidable. A fourth line was planned but incomplete.

The First Army staff drew up an ambitious attack plan that crammed nine divisions (each with 25,000 troops, twice as large as a full-strength German division) into the front with the expectation that their great

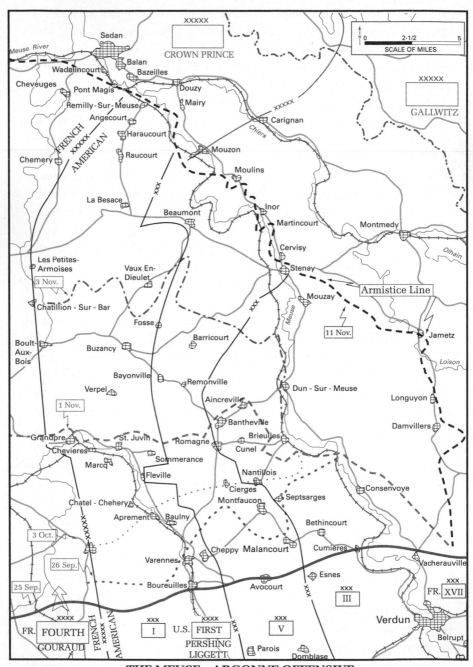

Sedan

CROWN PRINCE

XXXXX

GALLWITZ

SCALE OF MILES

0   2-1/2   5

Meuse River

Balan
Wadelincourt
Bazeilles
Cheveuges
Pont Magis
Douzy
Remilly-Sur-Meuse
Mairy
Angecourt
Carignan
Chiers
Haraucourt
Mouzon
Chemery
Raucourt
Moulins
La Besace
Inor
Beaumont
Martincourt
Montmedy
Cervisy
Olhain
Les Petites-Armoises
Vaux En-Dieulet
Stenay
3 Nov.
Armistice Line
Chatillion - Sur - Bar
Mouzay
Fosse
11 Nov.
Meuse
Jametz
Barricourt
Boult-Aux-Bois
Buzancy
Loison
Bayonville
Remonville
Dun - Sur - Meuse
Longuyon
Verpel
Aincreville
1 Nov.
Bantheville
Damvillers
Grandpre
St. Juvin
Brieulles
Chevieres
Romagne
Cunel
Marcq
Sommerance
Nantillois
Fleville
Consenvoye
Cierges
Chatel - Cheheryl
Montfaucon
Septsarges
Aprement
Baulny
Bethincourt
3 Oct.
Cheppy Malancourt
Cumieres
26 Sep.
Varennes
Esnes
Vacherauville
25 Sep.
Boureuilles
Avocourt
XXX
FR. XVII
XXX
III
Verdun
FR. FOURTH
XXX I
U.S. FIRST
XXX V
Belrupt
GOURAUD
PERSHING
LIGGETT
Parois
Domblase
FRENCH
AMERICAN
XXXXX

THE MEUSE - ARGONNE OFFENSIVE
SEDAN - VERDUN AND VICINITY
September - October 1918

advantage in strength would enable them to overwhelm the defenders in the first two lines and reach the Hindenburg Line, nine miles from their line of departure, by the end of the first day, September 26. It was asking a great deal from these troops. General Pétain thought the Americans would be lucky to advance a third of that distance before winter.

Pétain had a point: the challenge was daunting. Five of the attack divisions had never seen combat, and many more troops were not well trained. Shortly before the battle, one of the experienced divisions received 4,000 replacements who had been drafted only six weeks earlier. Moreover the logistical requirements would have challenged a thoroughly experienced army. Using only three roads mostly at night, 600,000 Americans in fifteen divisions had just two weeks to relieve 220,000 Frenchmen holding the Meuse-Argonne lines. The staff officer who planned and supervised moving 400,000 American troops and supplies from the St. Mihiel sector was Col. George C. Marshall.

The operational movement to the Meuse-Argonne worked, but the American assault plan unraveled on the first day, September 26. Rather than advancing nine miles to the Hindenburg Line, the two divisions in the Argonne Forest gained only a mile. Three others in more open terrain advanced three miles and penetrated the second line. The Germans, however, held the key high ground at Montfaucon until the next day. On that day the British launched their offensive on the western end of the salient. Within the next two days, the British, French, and Belgians commenced two more offensives so that the entire pincer movement was hammering the Germans. The two predominantly British attacking forces (including the 27th and 30th American divisions) engaged the largest number of Germans, and in one attack quickly penetrated the Hindenburg Line in their area. The Germans were able to reinforce their troops facing the Americans, but they had to maintain sufficient troops to combat the Allied offensives.

Pershing later wrote, "The battle from October 1st to the 11th involved the heaviest strain on the army and on me."[4] In twelve days of fighting early in October, the 1st Division, most veteran in the AEF, drove a wedge into the German defense that enabled three other divisions to clear the Argonne Forest. Their effort cost the 1st Division 8,200 casualties, the heaviest losses of any American division in the battle. All told, the AEF required three weeks of enervating combat to penetrate the Hindenburg Line. Hard fighting against experienced leaders and determined troops in good defensive positions produced heavy casualties and severe stresses on the Americans. Then there was the difficulty of sustaining the attack with troops, artillery, and supplies along only three roads into the sector. Cold, rainy weather, constant combat, and scant food and water combined to lower morale. Junior officers and noncommissioned officers, many of whom had been in uniform less than a year, lacked the leadership skills to control their men in such conditions. The First Army suffered as many as 100,000 stragglers by mid-October.

Pershing was aware of these problems, but he had little patience with allies who expressed their doubts about American fighting abilities. On October 1, Marshal Foch sent his chief of staff to meet with Pershing and suggest that he turn over much of his army to the French. Not surprisingly Pershing was enraged, and Foch withdrew the suggestion. A week later Pétain tried unsuccessfully to persuade Pershing to dissolve the First Army and turn over some of its divisions to the French. Meanwhile Prime Minister Lloyd George told the British ambassador to the United States that the AEF had been ineffective in battle and that Wilson should be informed of his commander's problems. Premier Clemenceau was even more adamant. He had been caught in a traffic jam when he visited St. Mihiel sector and again in late September when he tried to get to the Meuse-Argonne. In late October he wrote Foch that the British and French armies were making progress but the AEF was merely marking time. Clemenceau thought Wilson should be informed so that, presumably, he would relieve Pershing. By then, however, the situation had changed, and Foch defended the American commander.

During this battle Pershing relieved a corps commander, three division and four brigade commanders, and himself. In mid-October he turned over command of the First Army to his most able corps commander, Hunter Liggett, and created the Second Army under the command of Robert L. Bullard. He also promoted his two best division commanders, John L. Hines and Charles P. Summerall, to command III Corps and V Corps. Liggett's greatest asset was his ability to recognize what was important. He realized that the First Army needed a respite to regroup after weeks of constant fighting. He also understood that he had to disregard the prewar American army doctrine, which Pershing had put into effect, of depending primarily on the infantryman, his rifle, and his bayonet while downplaying the value of artillery and machine-guns. To his credit Pershing had made some modifications before the Meuse-Argonne battle, but Liggett made a more concerted effort. As the First Army staff drew up plans for an offensive beginning on November 1, Liggett made sure that they incorporated greater use of supporting weapons. His combined-arms approach included not only more artillery but also gas, which the AEF had used rarely to that point, and aircraft in strafing missions. Summerall's V Corps had the most support, a dream come true for this artillery officer, who had greatly irritated Pershing's staff early in the war by advocating a large increase of field artillery in the divisions. (Incidentally, almost all of the artillery guns and ammunition were French-made and on loan to the Americans.) In addition to Liggett's reforms and increased support, commanders and staffs at every level had learned from the bitter fighting, so that they were more prepared for this last stage of the great battle.

On November 1, seven divisions in three corps began the attack. The III and V Corps made great advances the first day as their supporting weapons knocked out machine-gun positions similar to those that had given infantry so much trouble in the first three weeks of the battle. The I Corps was held up, however, by the difficulty of overcoming the enemy defenses in a wooded area. Liggett solved that problem by firing a heavy gas barrage into the woods, which allowed the attackers to walk through those woods the next day. In five days Liggett's attack advanced farther than the First Army had moved from September 26 to October 15.

Despite their army's desperate defense, Germany was on the verge of collapse. The British naval blockade combined with heavy casualties to sap the German public's morale. The German chancellor, who was ready to negotiate on the basis of the Fourteen Points and hoped that the Allies were also, appealed directly to Wilson to make peace. The president responded that the Germans must give up the territory they had conquered and asked if the chancellor represented the will of his people. The French, British, and Italian prime ministers promptly asked for harsh armistice terms. As before, Wilson dispatched House to represent him at the Supreme War Council. Before House reached France, Pershing, Haig, Pétain, and Foch met to discuss armistice terms. At this meeting Pershing pressed for sterner demands than the others. He wanted to crush the German army and demand unconditional surrender. Pershing cabled his proposal to Secretary of War Baker, who then showed it to the president, but Wilson made it clear that he did not want to humiliate the Germans. The AEF commander ignored his commander in chief's implication that he should leave peace terms to the civilian leadership. Without consulting House, who was now in Paris, Pershing sent a message to the Supreme War Council advocating unconditional surrender rather than armistice. After he informed Baker of his action, the secretary met with the president and Chief of Staff Peyton C. March and flatly stated that Pershing was now on record for terms far harsher than Wilson's. Baker drafted a letter of reprimand, but the president ordered him not to send it because Pershing had by then discussed the situation with House and acknowledged his blunder.

During the first week of November the German situation worsened as elements of its navy mutinied, revolution broke out in Bavaria, and Austria-Hungary left the war. American troops kept advancing, but the end was at hand. In the early morning of November 11, a German delegation signed an armistice agreement in Foch's private train car. Only French and British representatives were present, although by then the AEF had more troops in France and occupied a longer section of the front than did the British. Later, Gen. Max von Gallwitz, German commander in the Meuse-Argonne sector, wrote his account of the battle. He pointed out the lack of experience and training of the AEF's officers and men, but lauded their bravery and concluded, "We were surprised at the vastness and vigour of America's military expansion. . . . After all, it was the astonishing display of American strength which definitely decided the war against us."[5]

III

Less than a month before the Armistice, the American military representative on the Supreme War Council, Gen. Tasker H. Bliss, wrote March a prophetic letter predicting that the Allies would "attempt to minimize the American effort as much as possible."[6] The French and British had been fighting for four years and the Italians for three and a half. The battle deaths of the three major European Allies reflected the terrible price they had paid: France, 1,385,300; Great Britain, 900,000; Italy, 364,000. Of the American total of 50,300, more than half (26,277) had occurred in the Meuse-Argonne.

Woodrow Wilson went to Paris to represent his nation at the peace conference. In mid-December he landed in Brest and passed through triumphal flower arches and cheering crowds. The next day, Parisians gave him a similarly enthusiastic welcome. On a cold and wet Christmas Day, he squeezed in a quick visit to Pershing and the AEF, where he characteristically showed little interest in his troops. The general wanted to meet him at Montfaucon, where he could see the battlefield, but the president preferred to visit Pershing's headquarters in Chaumont. Then Pershing escorted him to a nearby training area where he reviewed 12,000 troops who then stood in the mud as the president made a brief speech. Afterward he lunched with Pershing and a few of his generals. Pershing briefed Wilson on occupation plans and the redeployment of troops to the United States, after which the president hastened back to Paris. He went to England and then Italy, where he received the same adulation he had enjoyed in France.

These enthusiastic welcomes heartened Wilson as he prepared to negotiate peace terms with Allied leaders. He had suffered a major political defeat at home when the American people ignored his strong partisan appeal in the November congressional election, returning Republican majorities to both the House and the Senate. As a result, one of Wilson's greatest enemies, Senator Henry Cabot Lodge of Massachusetts, would become chairman of the Foreign Relations Committee. Lodge promptly wrote the British foreign minister, Lord Balfour, that Congress would support neither Wilson's league of nations plan nor his desire for lenient treatment of Germany. Another bitter foe, Theodore Roosevelt, made the same points in letters to Lloyd George, Clemenceau, and Balfour.

Before the conference formally opened in mid-January, Wilson began meeting with Allied leaders. He also attended Supreme War Council meetings. Except for his initial dependence on his close friend House, Wilson played a lone hand in Paris. When he returned to Washington for a brief visit in February, he named House as his surrogate in dealing with the Allied leaders during his absence. Upon his return in mid-March, he came to believe that House had been too conciliatory with the Allies and, in particular, did not push the league of nations proposal strongly enough. The resulting estrangement with his closest advisor meant that Wilson had to carry the burden of his crusade alone in the many long meetings with the Allies, who wanted to mete out harsh terms to the Germans and to obtain the goals promised in their secret treaty agreements. Clemenceau commented to House that discussing issues with Wilson made him feel as if he were "talking to Jesus Christ."[7]

The stress of these meetings, sometimes fifteen-hour days of argument, began to affect Wilson's health. In early April, he had to leave a meeting because of intense pain. His doctor found that he had a high fever and confined him to bed for several days.

Earlier, in March, the "Big Four"—Wilson, Lloyd George, Clemenceau, and Prime Minister Vittorio Orlando of Italy—began meeting without other Allied leaders. In this smaller group the French and the Italians were more adamant in their demands than the British. The French wanted to permanently occupy part of Germany, exact large war reparations, and drastically reduce German military and economic capacity. Lloyd George joined Wilson in gaining some concessions from France by promising support in case of another war with Germany. Lloyd George, however, was on Clemenceau's side when it came to reparations and severely limiting the German military not only in strength but in weapons. Wilson was able to limit the reparations demands somewhat, but he gave in on drastic cuts in the German military as well as agreeing to a clause that declared Germany guilty of bringing on the war. Italy was determined to grab as much of old Austria-Hungary and Turkey as possible, and left dissatisfied with the smaller area the other Big Four nations permitted. A particularly difficult problem for Wilson was a Japanese demand for China's Shantung peninsula, which they had seized from the Germans during the war. Acceding to this request would be a gross violation of one of the Fourteen Points, which specified that the interests of the inhabitants of any colony should be given equal value in deciding its future. After much agonizing, Wilson conceded when the Japanese flatly said that if they were refused, they would neither sign the treaty nor join the League of Nations. The League was Wilson's major hope for a future devoid of war.

On June 28, 1919, the Germans and the Allies signed the treaty in the palace at Versailles. Wilson sailed for home to face an even tougher fight. He spent much of his first eight weeks back in Washington arguing for the treaty's ratification. The opposition ranged from those who would support the treaty under no circumstances to those with reservations. In an unprecedented presidential move, Wilson met for three hours with the Senate Foreign Relations Committee, gave his view on the reservations, and answered the senators' questions—but to no avail. In early September, he embarked on a train tour from Ohio to California, delivering forty speeches in three weeks. The stress of travel, the heat of the western plains, the rarified atmosphere of the Rockies, and the demands of public speaking sapped his already weakened health. Despite a bad headache, he gave a speech in Pueblo, Colorado, on September 25. That night, the pain worsened and his doctor told him he would have to return to Washington. Back in the White House, he suffered severe headaches and stayed in seclusion. On October 2, he suffered a stroke that left him partially paralyzed. In March 1920, he refused to accept the Senate's treaty reservations. Despite his herculean efforts, the United States failed to ratify the Versailles Treaty and rejected membership in the League of Nations.

The treaty terms dissipated public elation in the days following the

Armistice, when hopes that Allied victory in "the war to end all wars" would result in eternal peace. In the new nations in Europe, ethnic minorities protested vehemently when they found their dreams of self-determination dashed on the rocks of Great Power politics. Elsewhere, colonial peoples who had trusted the Fourteen Points to gain them nation-hood found that the Allies had annexed German possessions and maintained their own. Even though the Germans did establish a short-lived democracy, they were bitter at the harsh terms of the Armistice. Many Germans refused to recognize their defeat; after all, the war had ended not with a surrender, but an armistice. The army marched back under their colors from foreign battlefields to find their cities and countryside intact. As the years passed, most of the German public began to believe that rather than being defeated in battle they had lost the war because of Jews, Communists, and weak political leaders. Revenge, which had motivated the French for four and a half decades, now stirred the German populace. When Marshal Foch heard of the harsh terms, he lamented, "This is not Peace. It is an Armistice for twenty years."[8]

IV

At the end of the war, the United States had the world's strongest economy and was arguably the world's greatest power. Yet disillusionment began to set in soon after the Armistice. Wilson's inspiring rhetoric and the efforts of his wartime propaganda agency, the Committee on Public Information, had set very high stakes. Yet as he failed to achieve his aims at the peace conference, the arguments of his opponents began to sound more realistic. Americans also resented the sometimes heavy-handed efforts of Allies to obtain the goals of their secret agreements. As the years passed, more Americans began to believe that their nation had been duped into the war by the Allies and the machinations of the so-called merchants of death: American bankers and munitions makers who profited from the war. It did not help that the Allies began to renege on their war debts, arguing that those loans, rather than the gallant efforts of the AEF, had been America's major contribution to the war.

The United States hosted an international gathering in 1921–22 to reduce armaments and to improve relations between key nations. The Washington Conference resulted in a series of treaties that limited the number of the five major powers' battleships and the use of submarines and restored the Shantung peninsula to the Chinese. In 1928, the United

States cosponsored the Kellogg-Briand Treaty, in which more than sixty nations ambitiously and altruistically agreed to outlaw war. American involvement in world affairs lessened during the Great Depression as the government coped with the desperate economic situation. Meanwhile, the League of Nations demonstrated that it was unable to deal with imperialistic Japan's invasion of Manchuria and, later, its war against China or with Italy's invasion of Ethiopia.

In the 1930s, Congress enacted two neutrality bills intended to keep the United States out of war. A peace movement in the United States grew to the point that a 1937 poll revealed that 95 percent of Americans were against fighting in any future war. During that year, antiwar protesters rallied in 2,000 cities. Even the unwarranted attack and sinking by the Japanese of the U.S. gunboat *Panay* on the Yangtze River, which wounded or killed several sailors, did not deter the peace movement. As late as 1940 a pacifist advertisement featured a drawing of a World War I veteran in a wheelchair with the caption "Hello Sucker."[9]

When Winston Churchill wrote of the 1930s, he summed up the Allies' problem thus: "The malice of the wicked was reinforced by the weakness of the virtuous."[10] Tepid efforts by the League of Nations and outright appeasement by France and Britain could not stem the rise of fascism. Hitler ignored treaty restrictions, built up German armed forces, and then marched them into Austria and Czechoslovakia. Mussolini exercised Italy's fascist muscle in the conquest of Ethiopia. Japan blatantly built an Asian and Pacific empire. On the other side, France had maintained a large army and constructed the Maginot Line, but hoped that reason would prevail. After agreeing at Munich to Hitler's seizure of part of Czechoslovakia, the British believed that they had preserved peace in our time. Meanwhile, Franklin D. Roosevelt let the Europeans know that the United States had no political involvements in Europe.

There was little that the United States could have contributed at that time to the defense of Britain and France. In 1938, the U.S. Army's strength was 185,488 troops, the largest it had been since 1921, yet it ranked just eighteenth among the world's armies. In 1923, the secretary of war pointed out in his annual report that Americans "spend six times as much for soda and confections as we spend for military purposes." It was a time of understrength units, slow promotion, and low budgets. Anthony C. McAuliffe spent fifteen years as a lieutenant in the 1920s and 1930s, and later commanded the 101st Airborne Division at the 1944 siege of Bastogne. In his recollection of those interwar years, he commented, "The Army seemed to have a feeling that they had been forgotten." A World War II corps commander and later army chief of staff, J. Lawton Collins, remembered that during those lean years:, "It was our schools that saved the Army."[11] Most of the instructors and many of the students at the Command and General Staff School and the Army War College were World War I veterans. At the former they studied the Meuse-Argonne campaign and learned, from Pershing's reliefs of commanders, the obvious lessons of the need for competent leadership and, from Liggett's last offensive, the efficacy of massive firepower and combined arms. Many veterans regretted that the Allies had granted an armistice to the Germans instead of forcing their surrender, thereby making their defeat clear not only to the soldiers, but to the German people. Throughout the 1930s, the possibility of another war became increasingly real to professional officers, and on September 1, 1939, Germany invaded Poland and began World War II.

V

As Hindenburg and Gallwitz later testified, the huge American reinforcement of the Allies and the demonstration of its effect in the Meuse-Argonne campaign ended World War I. Yet within eight months the Treaty of Versailles had set the scene for World War II. In the twenty-three years before World War II the French, the British, and the German Nazis all denigrated the American effort in the Great War. The Allies' motivation stemmed from postwar disputes over war debts and from their losses of millions of lives in four years of war, contrasted with tens of thousands of American casualties in their nineteen months in the war. Increasingly the Germans denied that they had lost the war, arguing that a chance at victory had been stolen from them, thereby giving rise to a racist nationalist named Adolf Hitler, who had no respect for the American military. In the United States, postwar disillusionment, lost hope for the Treaty of Versailles, and economic malaise combined to foster a broad and popular peace movement that belittled and even ignored the great American effort and the significant victory in the Meuse-Argonne. Many Americans in the 1930s came to embrace isolationism and reflexive pacifism.

The Japanese attack on Pearl Harbor brought the United States into a war that eventually eclipsed the memory of the Great War. In November 1943, as the American Fifth Army battled the Germans in Italy, *Time* magazine commemorated the twenty-fifth anniversary of the Armistice with a cover portrait of General Pershing, then living at Walter Reed Hospital. In the background were doughboys pouring out of a transport, marching to battle, and the railroad car where the Armistice was signed at Compiègne. The accompanying article quoted Pershing's comment from 1918: "The complete victory can only be obtained by continuing the war until we force unconditional surrender."[12] Earlier that year, at Casablanca, President Franklin D. Roosevelt and Prime Minister Winston S. Churchill declared that victory meant the unconditional surrender of Germany, Japan, and Italy.

SUGGESTED READING

Michael S. Neiberg, *Fighting the Great War: A Global History* (2005) is a good summary of World War I. The best books on the Meuse-Argonne campaign are Robert Ferrell, *America's Deadliest Battle: Meuse-Argonne, 1918* (2007) and Edward G. Lengel, *To Conquer Hell: The Meuse-Argonne, 1918* (2008). Mark E. Grotelueschen, *The AEF Way of War: The American Army and Combat in World War I* (2007) is a thoughtful analysis of the doctrinal change in tactics that contributed much to Liggett's last attack. Donald Smythe, *Pershing, General of the Armies* (1986) is the best book on Pershing during the war. David F. Trask, *The AEF and Coalition Warmaking, 1917–1918* (1993) ably explains that aspect of the war. Edward M. Coffman, *The War to End All Wars: The American Military Experience in World War I* (1968, reprinted in 1986 and 1998) covers America's contribution. One of the best reference books is Leonard P. Ayres, *The War with Germany: A Statistical Summary* (1919). The American Battle Monuments Commission, *American Armies and Battlefields in Europe* (originally published by the American Battle Monuments Commission in 1938 and reprinted in 1992 by the Army Center of Military History) includes the best maps as well as a history and guidebook of the American war. John Milton Cooper Jr., *Woodrow Wilson: A Biography* (2009) has excellent coverage of Wilson's role in the war, in the treaty negotiations and in the fight for its ratification. George C. Herring's monumental *From Colony to Superpower: U.S. Foreign Relations Since 1778* (2008) has an excellent account of the treaty-making process and the postwar ramifications in American foreign policy in the 1920s and 1930s.

THEODORE A. WILSON

Götterdämmerung:
War's End in Europe, 1945

I

In a message to the Combined Chiefs of Staff on November 20, 1944, the commanding general of the Supreme Headquarters Allied Expeditionary Force (SHAEF), Dwight D. Eisenhower, acknowledged, "German morale on this front shows no sign of cracking at present. . . . Successful Nazi propaganda . . . is convincing every German that unconditional surrender means the complete devastation of Germany and her elimination as a nation."[1] Prime Minister Winston S. Churchill agreed and seized on Eisenhower's message as an opportunity to dispel the false confidence about the imminent collapse of German resistance apparently held by President Roosevelt and the British and American peoples. "I feel that the time has come for me to place before you the serious and disappointing war situation which faces us at the close of this year," Churchill stressed in a follow-up message on December 6. Although the Allies had achieved "many fine tactical victories" on the Western Front and although he agreed that Metz and Strasbourg were "trophies," he pointed out that the strategic objective of crossing the Rhine in strength had not been achieved: "We shall have to continue the great battle for many weeks before we can hope to reach the Rhine and establish our bridgeheads."[2] Further, German military strength elsewhere was still impressive. In Italy some twenty-six German divisions still opposed the Allied armies.

The situation in the East, Churchill admitted, offered happier prospects. In recent weeks Soviet forces had undertaken operations to consolidate the great summer and fall offensives that had battered the way into Poland and had knocked Rumania and Bulgaria out of the war. Stalin had promised a winter campaign, presumably to begin in January, and the German position was so strained that any heavy penetration might trigger partial, perhaps total collapse. But Hitler's generals were successfully extricating some twelve divisions from Greece and the Balkans for possible use against the Russians or in the West.

Churchill acknowledged that these grim realities clashed sharply "with the rosy expectations of our peoples" and asked rhetorically, "What are we going to do about it?" His answer was an urgent plea for an immediate meeting with FDR and his advisors or, failing that, of the British and American chiefs of staff. British civilians suffering under rocket attacks would have agreed with the prime minister's sentiments. Though the V-2 threat was rapidly diminishing by year's end, V-1 and V-2 attacks in December 1944 brought more than 700 deaths and 1,500 casualties. Roosevelt declined a bilateral meeting, having decided that all future summit conferences must involve all three Allied leaders, and he dismissed the British leader's gloomy assessment as a visit by "Winnie's black dog," Churchill's periodic struggle with depression. After all, the war was all but won. German forces, although resisting stubbornly, were in retreat everywhere. On December 1, the Germans evacuated Suda Bay, Canea, and Maleme, bases on Crete they had occupied for more than three years. The last Nazi forces in the eastern Mediterranean were now gone. U.S. troops, having overrun and bypassed portions of the Siegfried Line, were grinding forward into Germany along a 30-mile front. On December 6, the British Eighth Army crossed the Lamone, another of the Italian river barriers to the broad plains before the Po River and final destruction of Field Marshal Albert Kesselring's armies.

German morale, already weakened by the massive shocks of 1944 in the East and West and by constant Allied bombing, now confronted the reality that the sacred German Reich was a battleground. Enraged, Hitler relieved his First Army commander for permitting the Americans to penetrate the Siegfried Line. On the Eastern Front, signs pointed to a massing of Red Army forces (225 divisions and twenty-two armored corps along a front from the Baltic to the Carpathians) and a deluge of steel within days. The Reich's erstwhile allies continued to drop away. On December 9 the Red Army launched a drive to expel German forces from Hungary and quickly encircled Budapest. Everywhere Nazi leaders looked, their sway was disintegrating.

Despite gloomy warnings by a few political and military leaders who knew how overextended were Allied ground forces in the West, anticipation of Nazi Germany's collapse and the certainty of triumph in the Pacific War spread rapidly. Optimism had some negative manifestations. Americans clamored for the abolition of rationing and other wartime restrictions. Adm. Sir James Somerville, visiting the United States, was amazed by a festive crowd of 70,000 at the Army-Navy game on December 2. His host, Adm. Ernest J. King, chief of naval operations, admitted that the war "was not much occupying the attention of people in America."[3] Not surprisingly, veteran British and American troops fighting in the Low Countries and Alsace-Lorraine began to exhibit an excess of caution. No one wanted to be the last casualty in Europe.

Ironically, over the next six months uncounted numbers of soldiers and civilians on all sides were lost in the war. Why and how was the optimistic timetable of Anglo-American planners in mid-1944 not achieved? What unanticipated consequences flowed from prolonging military conflict in Europe for nearly a year beyond its projected termination? Any assessment of U.S. actions leading to war's end in Europe must acknowledge the long-term consequences of often hasty decisions taken to resolve a particular problem. The circumstances attending America's entry into World War II powerfully influenced its logistical, strategic, and political aims and processes. In turn, wartime decisions determined America's approach to defining both postwar strategic missions and force structure. The touchstone of American military thought and experience from 1945 to the end of the Cold War was the experience of World War II. That conflict's lessons shaped the outlook of those who determined such questions as the configuration of forces to meet potential threats, manpower and mobilization policies, and the civilian and military components of national security planning, force structure, and assignment of missions to the various services over much of the Cold War.

The answers to these questions begin with the assumptions and events that brought the United States into World War II. As war in Europe erupted in 1939, the United States was still mired in depression. Although a majority of Americans were cheering for Allied victory, most saw no purpose in being drawn again into Europe's bloody quarrels. America's unilateral approach stemmed from a presumption of self-sufficiency, apathy toward world affairs reinforced by two decades of drastically restricted immigration, and, perhaps most important, backlash from the causes of U.S. entry into World War I and the attendant frustrations over dashed hopes for a world made safe for democracy. Throughout the 1930s, headlines had shrieked about "merchants of death," British machinations, and the greed of banking interests.

From Europe's descent into war in September 1939 to Japan's surprise attack on Pearl Harbor, the United States gradually expanded its understanding of its interests and how best to achieve the nation's security. Yet the road to America's acceptance of a leading role in a global military coalition was complicated and meandering.

The gradual shift of administration and public attitudes accelerated after Germany's stunning victories in the West in spring 1940. Following the fall of France, FDR obtained authorization for massive expansion of America's armed forces. Once Churchill took power, FDR increased support to Britain as the first line of defense against Hitler through the Destroyer-Bases Deal (which traded some fifty World War I–era destroyers for long-term U.S. leases to British territories near North America), expanded production of war matériel, held secret discussions leading to a "Europe First" strategy, and, most notably, signed the Lend-Lease Act to underwrite the financing of weapons and essential supplies to nations resisting Nazi Germany. While British leaders and many Americans were convinced that FDR was determined to lead Congress and the public to accept full U.S. participation, the next eight months witnessed a commitment to "all aid short of war," frustrating interventionists at home and erstwhile allies abroad. Even the "Victory Program," produced in summer 1941 at the behest of the U.S. Army's chief of staff, George C. Marshall, which presented a projection of the forces required to defeat Nazi Germany were the United States to wage war alone, reinforced doubts about the Roosevelt administration's acceptance of the brutal calculus that only unconditional American involvement offered any possibility of Allied victory.

Debate continues over the wellsprings of American foreign and national security policies during Roosevelt's presidency. Historians citing declassified records and with new perspectives have raised a multitude of issues, including the struggle for control over foreign policy between FDR and Congress, strategic planning and military mobilization, the so-called special relationship between Churchill and FDR, and the course of Russian-American relations. Was Roosevelt an internationally minded leader, or did he operate chiefly from practical political motives? Did he drag the

United States into war unnecessarily? Or did his refusal to act boldly jeopardize American interests and possibly the nation's very survival?

II

World War II was the largest and most deadly armed conflict in human history. A protracted conflict, deserving in certain ways the label *total war,* it produced a global struggle between two powerful coalitions. For six years the war unleashed destruction on a scale unprecedented in human history, including sixty million dead and the systematic murder of six million Jews. Germany's megalomaniacal leader, Adolf Hitler, dictated its war aims: achieve revenge for Germany's defeat in World War I, establish a new European order under Germany's leadership, and undertake the building of a "Thousand Year Reich" by expansion to the east and the brutal eradication of Jews and subjugation of other peoples. Mussolini's Italy mirrored its more powerful ally in desiring to revive the glories of the Roman Empire in the eastern Mediterranean and Africa.

The war aims of the Allies, initially Britain and France and later including the United States and the USSR, began with the goal of restoring the political structures that had been established by the Treaty of Versailles. The guiding assumption of leaders in Paris and London was the belief that Nazi Germany was unable to sustain a war of any duration. But after the stunning German victories of spring and summer 1940, Britain found itself in a struggle for survival and relied initially upon the empire and ultimately, in Churchill's words, upon "the New World, with all its power and might, step[ping] forth to the rescue and the liberation of the old."[4] American leaders gradually saw the need for some sort of cooperation with Britain and possibly U.S. leadership in a global economic and political order. The Atlantic Charter embodied a world in which, "after the final destruction of the Nazi tyranny, [the United States and Britain] hope to see established a peace which will afford to all nations the means of dwelling in safety within their own boundaries, and which will afford assurance that all the men in all the lands may live out their lives in freedom from fear and want."[5] These goals for the postwar world were to be achieved by an Anglo-American consortium working through a nascent international organization, the United Nations.

For the Axis the goal was total victory. For the Allies through 1942, however, the goal was survival. Thereafter, those positions reversed. By 1943, Allied successes led to a focus by many on the nature of the postwar world. The U.S. aim remained total victory: destruction of the Axis regimes. FDR proclaimed a goal of "unconditional surrender" at Casablanca in January 1943, affirming his antipathy toward all things German and also a blithe disregard for the complications of planning and implementing a military occupation. Some have argued that the Allied insistence on unconditional surrender in combination with plans for a retributive occupation ruled out any possibility of a negotiated settlement. But as the historian Gerhard Weinberg has written, "When seen as a whole, the plans the Allies were developing for Germany were quite harsh, but given German behavior, hardly surprising. Putting them in front of the Germans instead of simply calling for unconditional surrender was not likely to make ending the war on Allied terms particularly attractive."[6] In fact the pronouncement reflected the belief that a military *Götterdämmerung* was inevitable and essential, given Hitler's unspeakable crimes. The latter conviction in turn has produced a long-held view that the struggle against the Axis powers was a religious crusade that stood outside of history—and historical patterns of war termination.

Beginning in spring 1943, three U.S. government agencies began planning for the occupation of Germany. Although they agreed on the concept of occupation zones, their proposals regarding prospective administration of a defeated Germany differed significantly. The Department of State advocated establishing a framework for restoring German democratic self-government within a broader program of rehabilitating Europe. As the invasion of Germany would be in "enemy territory" and under the "unconditional surrender principle," the "administration should be definitely military in character."[7] State Department planners expected the army to implement an ambitious program of denazification, demilitarization, and democratization, and they assumed that the occupation would last no more than two years. Proponents of a harsh peace, led by Secretary of the Treasury Henry Morgenthau, urged dividing Germany into smaller states and banning industry so as to preclude the recurrence of "Teutonic" militarism. FDR and Churchill briefly endorsed the Morgenthau Plan at the Quebec Conference in September 1944, but backed away quickly when the implications of creating an economic and political vacuum in central Europe were made clear. The U.S. Army's principal concern was to limit its involvement in the daily administration of an occupied Germany, an approach that led planners to accept rosy predictions about material conditions there after surrender. The War Department belatedly undertook planning for a military occupation in 1943.

The resulting plan, JCS 1067, limited the army's responsibility to preventing outbreaks of "disease and unrest" within the German population. Unavoidably these disparate goals and assumptions guaranteed confusion about the purposes, shape, and duration of any occupation.

III

To the private soldier the grandiose schemes of generals and politicians, which move him and his comrades around the world and across the battlefield like pawns in a gigantic chess match, often appear irrelevant to the day-to-day struggle for survival. [An updated epigram captured the World War II soldier's dislike of armchair strategy: "The mimeograph machine is mightier than the machine-gun."] Nevertheless, the elaborate planning and arcane code words so much caricatured during World War II were essential, probably more so in this conflict because of its complexity and global reach. Operation Torch, Operation Overlord, and the other major operations of the war were products of agreements at the highest levels: decisions about the distribution of war production, about the allocation of manpower between services, and about the relative priorities to be accorded the various theaters of war. It is often said that World War II was preeminently a competition of production and resources, but there was never enough production and never enough manpower to do everything everywhere and at the same time. Though American leaders only gradually understood that fact, they did in the end confront the limits on their freedom of action. When they did so, they began to practice the art of grand strategy and global politics.

The origins of wartime strategic planning predate U.S. entry into the war. American and British representatives held secret strategy discussions in Washington in early 1941. The general policies established at "ABC-1," especially the decision to give first priority to the defeat of Nazi Germany, influenced Anglo-American strategy throughout World War II. But numerous vital issues remained undecided, and the potential for conflict between the two English-speaking allies was huge. In August 1941, as FDR and Churchill were hammering out the Atlantic Charter aboard HMS *Prince of Wales,* anchored off Newfoundland, the U.S. Army's War Plans Division was calculating the forces required to win the war. The Victory Plan assumed that by 1943 the Allies would have been vanquished and the United States would stand alone against Hitler's legions. A gigantic force (some 215 divisions, including sixty-one armored divisions) would be needed to defeat Nazi Germany. Neither the army's sister services nor the British accepted this scenario. An ongoing debate about allocation of manpower and resources prevented agreement on an overall strategy until at least late 1943. Britain won the argument for Mediterranean operations in 1942–43. Thereafter the United States dominated Anglo-American planning. A pivotal constraint during the first two years of the war was shipping. By spring 1943 the casual assumption that manpower would suffice to meet the needs of uncontrolled expansion of America's armed forces and the commitment to become the "arsenal of democracy" had been proved false. In mid-1943, cutbacks on estimates of American manpower available for military service led to a drastic reduction in the size of the U.S. Army. Plans for an enormous ground force were progressively modified, in part because the "tooth to tail ratio," the proportion of the army assigned to supply and combat support roles, increased dramatically. Ultimately the U.S. Army fielded eighty-nine divisions. By mid-1943 it was clear that American and British strategists were relying heavily on Russian military manpower to contain the German Army.

Churchill personified Britain's historic "indirect approach" to strategy in his commitment to the defense of a sprawling empire, his recognition of his country's limited manpower and resources, and his desperate desire to avoid the catastrophes visited by the trench warfare of World War I. Roosevelt, an ardent sea-power enthusiast and follower of the theories of Alfred Thayer Mahan, and recent convert to strategic airpower, found a strategy of indirection and limited war appealing. Yet his military advisors resisted, terming Britain's indirect approach militarily unsound (flouting the basic principle that wars are won by destroying the enemy's armed forces) and politically motivated. Undergirding their opposition was the U.S. military tradition that emphasized overwhelming advantages in manpower and matériel, a direct approach, and campaigns of annihilation rather than attrition.

Outcomes of the British efforts to dictate overall strategic pressure were the self-protective attempts at interservice cooperation that resulted in the creation of the U.S. Joint Chiefs of Staff and the principal continuing mechanism for British-American wartime coordination, the Combined Chiefs of Staff (CCS) organization. At the Arcadia Conference in December 1941 through January 1942, momentous decisions regarding grand strategy were taken. Europe first was affirmed. Arcadia also witnessed a battle over the military direction of the war, how to supervise those regional unified commands being set up. When apprised of a British scheme to have representatives of the British Chiefs of Staff in Washington and their American opposite numbers in London, FDR was decidedly unenthusiastic. The president proposed to locate the CCS in Washington and to have theater commanders route all queries to Washington for transmission to signatories to the United Nations declaration. The British at first balked. One reason was chauvinism, for "requiring theater commanders to report only to Washington meant that on a daily basis the war would be run there."[8] Churchill acceded only after having persuaded the president of the difficulties of controlling affairs within an interallied council including, at the very least, British, American, Soviet, and Chinese representatives. Thus the CCS would be an Anglo-American club.

Strategic bombing was a point of disagreement between the British and U.S. Chiefs of Staff (and also between various American leaders) and, in particular, the policy of attacking German population centers to weaken civilian morale. The British argued that area bombing was effective and, in light of indiscriminate German bombing of British cities, justifiable. In fact, bombing represented the only significant means by which an impoverished Britain could carry the fight to the enemy, and after its arrival in Britain, the U.S. Eighth Air Force tacitly embraced that approach. Such other matters as the priority to be given the Mediterranean versus an attack across the English Channel as soon as was practicable remained unresolved. As General Marshall later admitted, it proved impossible to produce a "coherent strategic plan for defeating the Axis" until summer 1943.[9]

With the possible exception of Operation Torch (the Allied invasion of North Africa), the 1942 successes represented isolated national victories rather than the precisely coordinated, combined operations that would be required to crush still powerful adversaries. Furthermore, the exertions needed to win these struggles had depleted Allied reserves and dispersed their forces. U.S. and British forces were now committed to two secondary theaters, ruling out taking full advantage of the great Soviet victory at Stalingrad. Concentrating sufficient forces for a cross-channel invasion in 1943 would be exceedingly difficult, and the absence of any strategic consensus suggested that further "alarums and excursions" would arise.

Cases in point would be the misunderstandings and failures of communication at Symbol, the January 1943 meeting of Roosevelt and Churchill, over postponement of a Second Front, the question of who had promised how much shipping to alleviate Britain's imports crisis, and the vituperative exchanges over landing craft allocations. Symbol revealed the limits of existing arrangements for bilateral cooperation and, even at the bilateral level, the narrowly circumscribed appreciation Americans and British had of each other's needs.

Symbol displayed both the strengths and the limits of these arrangements. In Warren Kimball's apt imagery, Stalin was the "ghost in the attic" at Casablanca, the sought-after guest who had declined to attend the party.[10] Whether his presence would have produced an ironclad commitment to invade northwest Europe instead of Sicily in 1943 remains an intriguing possibility. The British, determined to limit ground operations to the Mediterranean, overwhelmed an ill-prepared, poorly supported U.S. delegation. "We came, we listened, and we were conquered," acknowledged an American participant.[11] When the dust settled, the CCS had assigned first priority to defeating the German U-boat menace and ensuring that supplies reached the USSR. Second came clearance of Axis forces from North Africa, the invasion of Sicily (Operation Husky), and the combined bombing campaign (Operation Pointblank) against Germany. FDR and Churchill approved a modified Allied buildup in Britain (Operation Bolero) and organization of a combined planning staff for a 1943 cross-channel attack, but Marshall stated flatly that Husky made any such operation "difficult if not impossible." The conferees agreed to tell Premier Stalin that Russia's allies would cross the Channel "as soon as practicable."[12] The Kremlin correctly called this promise meaningless.

In November 1943, Roosevelt, Churchill, and Stalin conferred for the first time at Tehran. The high point of coalition decision making, their meeting resulted in agreements on critical issues related to conduct of the war. Policies that were to dominate international affairs after the war—creation of the United Nations, political arrangements in Eastern Europe, the treatment of Germany—germinated at Tehran. However, Tehran was foremost a conference dealing with grand strategy, and its central focus was the Second Front: when, where, and how much relief, if any, the Anglo-American assault on northwest Europe would offer the Soviet Union. Recent scholarship has suggested that, by Tehran, given the turning tide of war on the Eastern Front, the Second Front might have lost its urgency for Stalin. The final year of the war featured substantial coordination between the USSR and its western allies as the Red Army ground west toward Berlin and the western Allies closed the ring in Italy and northwest Europe. At the same time, political differences, long papered over by military necessities, now reappeared and began to shape strategic priorities.

IV

The final campaign to destroy Hitler's Third Reich and clear the last German forces from northern Italy played out very differently than had been anticipated when the United States first gave serious consideration to how to achieve victory over the Axis. In contrast to optimistic predictions prior to D-Day and during the period of breakout and pursuit, the final months of the ground campaign in the West proved to be a slog, reminiscent in painful ways of 1914–18. American soldiers would have cause to remember such previously unknown places as Huertgen Forest, Schmidt, and Metz. Ironically, the German Ardennes counteroffensive opened the gates for Allied victory.

The Battle of the Bulge confirmed the strong links between the Allies. Facing inexorable pressure from east and west, Hitler made a desperate gamble, ordering the concentration of thirty divisions, some 600,000 men—the bulk of the Wehrmacht's reserves—in a counterattack through the Ardennes to retake Antwerp and crush the British 21st Army Group and the U.S. First and Ninth Armies. Trusting that overcast skies would neutralize Allied air superiority and allow a stunning breakthrough, Hitler convinced himself that the Anglo-American coalition would collapse in mutual recriminations. Most German commanders believed that the operation was reckless in the extreme, but they kept silent.

The Germans launched the Ardennes offensive on December 16, 1944. Despite the initial success of an elaborate deception plan and rapid advances against a lightly defended front, Hitler's bold stroke only briefly halted the Allied march to the Rhine. Shrugging aside irritation among senior British and U.S. commanders following the ill-fated thrust into the Netherlands (Operation Market Garden) and Field Marshal Bernard Montgomery's vocal criticism of the broad-front strategy, Eisenhower placed U.S. forces north of the German breakthrough under Montgomery's command. Nearly all U.S. units caught in the maelstrom fought stubbornly. Aided by improving weather for Anglo-American tactical air forces and the opening of a gigantic Soviet offensive all along the central sector of the Eastern Front, the British and the U.S. First Army from the north and Patton's Third Army from the south eliminated the Ardennes salient. The butcher's bill was high: some 78,000 casual-

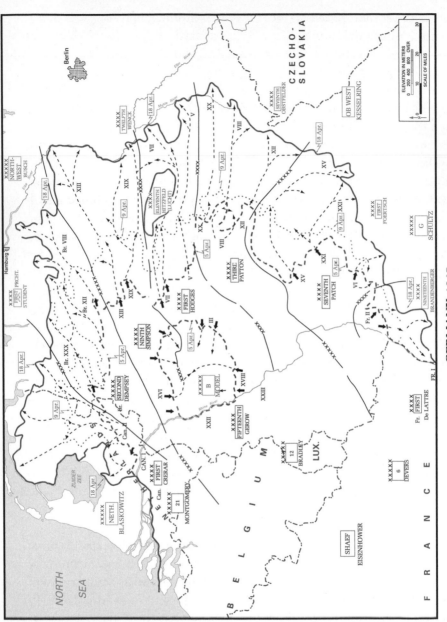

GERMANY, 1945

REDUCTION OF THE RUHR POCKET AND
ADVANCE TO THE ELBE AND MULDE RIVERS

Operations, 5 - 18 April 1945

ties and another 56,000 nonbattle losses (from trench foot and, ominously, substantial numbers of neuropsychiatric cases). The Wehrmacht lost more than 100,000 killed or wounded, and nearly double that number missing or suffering nonbattle injuries. U.S. forces reclaimed all the ground lost by late January 1945. On January 1, Germany launched a final attack (Operation Nordwind) against the Seventh Army facing the Colmar Pocket, a salient on the southern flank of the Bulge. The Nazi aim was to cut behind and encircle two newly arrived U.S. divisions and retake Strasbourg. But the Germans found tough going in deep snow and subzero temperatures against the inexperienced but hard-fighting Americans. Nordwind quickly blew itself out. Soon thereafter, a U.S.-led attack eliminated the Colmar Pocket.

The Allies were readying the final campaign to destroy the Wehrmacht and compel a German surrender. On February 1, 1945, U.S. Army forces in the European Theater of Operations comprised 2,329,042 soldiers spread across Europe and another 605,882 in Britain (mostly service forces and individual replacements). U.S. Army ground forces totaled 1,585,242 assigned to divisions and myriad combat and combat support units. British and Canadian combined strengths were approximately 1,090,000. In all, the Allies pushing east would soon field eighty-five divisions, including five to eight newly organized French divisions being trained and the eight French divisions currently deployed. Eisenhower's intelligence staff estimated that some eighty understrength divisions opposed them, assuming that no large-scale withdrawal from northern Italy had occurred. The Allied armies possessed a number of advantages: control of the skies, the experience gained at all levels from six months of unremitting combat, far greater stores of weapons and other matériel, and—that pearl beyond price—the challenges posed to an enemy having to defend on two fronts.

Nonetheless, SHAEF planners faced a daunting task. German defenses were substantial, especially along the Rhine. Allied numerical superiority was less impressive when the post-Overlord manpower crisis was factored in. By late 1944, the U.S. Army claimed only eighty-nine divisions, no strategic reserve, a dearth of combat replacements, and concerns about growing numbers of combat exhaustion cases among units long on the front lines.

Eisenhower returned to a broad-front advance, a more cautious strategy than many desired. Montgomery demanded to be permitted to dash for Berlin. Bradley and Patton complained about favoritism to the British. But Eisenhower wanted to avoid any further German surprises like the Ardennes counteroffensive, and he was concerned about rumors of Nazi fanatics, so-called Werewolf terrorists holing up in a Bavarian redoubt plotting a postwar guerrilla campaign against the Allied occupation. Gen. Troy Middleton's VIII Corps of Patton's Third Army pushed forward first, smashing through the West Wall along the Schnee Eifel, a rugged ridgeline between Belgium and Germany. Then, just 40 miles from the Rhine, the Third Army ran out of gasoline and ammunition.

The focus shifted to Montgomery, who controlled twenty-five divisions: eight British, five Canadian, one Polish, and the eleven divisions comprising Gen. William Simpson's Ninth Army. Montgomery's plan, Operation Veritable, called for two converging attacks, one by British and Canadian forces southeast toward Wesel, the second by Simpson's Ninth Army northeast toward the Rhine. A massive Royal Air Force carpet-bombing mission and the most intensive British artillery barrage since 1918 kicked off the British attack. Unfortunately, Simpson failed to follow up. Blocked by discharge from the Roer River dams, his forces were unable to cross the river, leaving British XXX Corps vulnerable to a German counterattack. Once the floodwaters subsided, Simpson's divisions drove into the German rear and shattered its main strength, inflicting substantial casualties and taking more than 30,000 prisoners. Only a directive from Montgomery stopped the 2nd Armored Division from seizing a Rhine bridgehead south of Düsseldorf.

A central thrust, launched on February 26 and led by Gen. Courtney Hodge's First Army, now again assigned to Bradley's 12th Army Group, pushed toward Cologne and Bonn. After seizing these objectives the First Army's aim was to link up with Patton's Third Army, also closing on the Rhine. Cologne fell to soldiers of Gen. Lawton Collins's VII Corps on March 5, allowing the 9th Armored Division to seize the Remagen railroad bridge two days later, the first Allied bridgehead across the Rhine.

Rearmed and refueled, an armored spearhead of Patton's Third Army roared along the Moselle, reaching the Rhine in just three days, then turned south to link up with Seventh Army units driving northward through the Saar industrial region. On March 25, all organized German resistance west of the Rhine ended. Hitler's "defend at all costs" policy had yielded another military disaster and the loss of more than 300,000 German soldiers. Both the Wehrmacht and the German populace showed signs of exhaustion.

Exploitation of the Remagen bridgehead quickly followed. Ironically the rapid progress of the U.S. Army overshadowed the intended main effort—a massive assault by the British Second and Ninth Armies across the Rhine north of the Ruhr. Having gathered some twenty-five divisions and ordered a pounding by some 3,000 artillery pieces and repeated bombing attacks, Montgomery ordered his troops to attack the Rhine barrier on March 23. The five defending German divisions were overwhelmed within a few days. By the end of March, seven Allied armies were east of the Rhine. It was clear to everyone except Hitler and his most fanatical supporters that the Nazi situation was hopeless.

The stunning push across the Rhine affirmed the coming of age of the U.S. Army. From a hastily formed organization built on a foundation laid down at Fort Leavenworth and isolated posts across the nation, this army of citizen soldiers had become over the course of three years a formidable fighting force. There had been many fits and starts; learning to apply the prewar combined-arms doctrine took time. In part the army's struggles derived from mistaken assumptions that the war in Europe would follow a blitzkrieg paradigm, emphasizing motorized and mechanized movement, rapid maneuver, and concentrated fires. Deeply flawed personnel assignment policies made worse the effects of these errors. One GI bitterly noted that the rifle had been pushed aside in favor of the typewriter and the tank.[13] Yet instead of a blitzkrieg, by mid-fall 1944, the U.S. Army was in a war of attrition reminiscent of the Western Front in 1916. Combat infantrymen carried the brunt of the fighting and suffered by far the highest rate of casualties.

Fortunately, American commanders at every level had learned on the job to apply existing doctrine with flexibility as circumstances permitted and their judgment and experience dictated. They solved manifold problems of communications, tank-infantry coordination, battlefield treatment of combat exhaustion cases, and the integration of individual replacements. They invented new techniques for weapons employment and learned to combine tactical air and artillery support to infantry units. While German officers scorned the quality of their weapons, they expressed awe at the skill with which the U.S. Army employed those weapons in coordination.

The final weeks of the battle for Germany gave Americans a chance to display their hard-won skill. With multiple Allied bridgeheads across the Rhine, Germany had no natural barriers and only outnumbered and demoralized forces to defend the homeland. General Eisenhower now controlled ninety full-strength divisions, including twenty-five armored and five airborne, one of the most powerful military forces ever arrayed for battle. SHAEF's next major objective was the Ruhr, the heart of German industry. The operational plan called for a double envelopment, sending the Ninth Army to the north of the Ruhr industrial complex and the First Army to the south. On April 1 the two wings converged at Lippstadt, trapping Field Marshal Model's Army Group B and much of Army Group H, the principal German forces remaining in northern Germany. Although a raving Hitler demanded a defense to the last man and last bullet, the survivors, 325,000 German soldiers, surrendered on April 19.

Allied forces now raced forward on all sides. The Canadian First Army liberated nearly all of the Netherlands. The British Second Army occupied Bremen and Hamburg by late April. In Bavaria the U.S. Seventh Army took Nuremberg on April 20 and turned south to clear Munich. Patton's Third Army penetrated deep into eastern Germany, reached the Czech border on April 25, and then, having been denied permission by Eisenhower to take Prague, consolidated its gains.

An enduring controversy has smoldered about Eisenhower's "go slow" policy toward seizing Berlin and other areas within the projected Soviet occupation zone. Montgomery's forces were poised for a dash across the north German plain to Berlin, and elements of the Ninth Army had secured a bridgehead across the Elbe River only 50 miles from the city. Yet Eisenhower, who famously said that Berlin no longer had any military significance, remained concerned about the persistent rumors of a "national redoubt" in Bavaria. The bastion proved a myth, but Eisenhower could not safely discount the possibility that diehard Nazis could continue resistance for years. Furthermore, the U.S. Army had other pressing demands: the appalling discovery of the death camps, huge numbers of German POWs, and an exodus of refugees fleeing the Soviet advance to the east.

As the end neared, operational interaction with the Russians became extensive. From the west, American, British, and Canadian armies were approaching their designated stop lines. From the east, the First Byelorussian, First Ukrainian, Second Byelorussian, and Third and Fourth Ukrainian Fronts were driving on Berlin. The approaching linkup led to bilateral exchanges between Eisenhower and Montgomery and their Soviet counterpart, Marshal Georgi K. Zhukov. A series of personal meetings and radio communications between operational commanders dealt with boundaries, signals protocols, and arrangements for artillery and air attacks. While these communications triggered a bureaucratic firestorm in Washington, the ad hoc arrangements sufficed until the historic linkup of American and Soviet forces at Torgau on the Elbe River.

V

As Red Army soldiers advanced through Berlin's rubble, Adolf Hitler was hiding in a bunker deep below the Reichs Chancellery. He devoted his last days to raging against all those who had betrayed him. When news arrived that Heinrich Himmler had attempted to open peace negotiations with British forces in northern Germany, Hitler drafted a political testament appointing Adm. Karl Dönitz commander in chief of the German armed forces, then shot himself. The end of the war followed quickly. On May 2 remaining German forces surrendered in northern Italy. That same day Dönitz proposed surrendering all German forces facing the Allied armies in the west, although resistance against the Red Army would continue. Eisenhower summarily rejected that proposal. Only unconditional surrender would suffice. Germany surrendered to joint representatives of the entire Allied coalition at Rheims. Eisenhower's communiqué laconically pronounced the end of the greatest war in European history: "The mission of this Allied force was fulfilled at 0241 local time, May 7, 1945."[14]

Wild celebrations erupted around the Allied world. Nowhere was the jubilation greater than in Britain, where, as one GI commented in a letter home, "The feeling was infectious. The strain had lifted. Years of control, black out, bombardment, sacrifice and hardship were over. . . . I wish I had been in New York to celebrate it with you. If at last the dawn of the long night is breaking, and if we could only march together and feel together as we did last night, the people of all nations should have no fear of the future."[15] That utopia was not to be, for the euphoria of V-E Day quickly dissipated into the challenges of managing an occupation that was poorly planned and for which the U.S. Army was hardly prepared. Moreover, the United States now faced enormous geopolitical challenges as the wartime alliance evolved into a global postwar confrontation.

VI

American planners had expected the war in Europe to end by fall 1944 and assumed that final victory against Japan would not occur before late 1946 or early 1947. The guiding assumption was that U.S. forces would be shifted from Europe to the Pacific or demobilized quickly. The war's end in Europe provides a powerful illustration of the concept of unanticipated consequences. To the surprise of the planners, assumptions about the situation that occupying forces would find when taking control of Germany—that the infrastructure would be largely intact, that technocrats not connected with Nazi Party would step forward to make certain that the lights stayed on—proved mistaken. The conflict's extension into late spring 1945, and especially the Allied bombing campaign after September 1944 (during which more tonnage was dropped than in the previous four years), resulted in a physically and psychologically devastated Germany at war's end.

In a Memorial Day speech on May 30, 1945, Congressman Christian Herter observed, "We know what we are going to do to Germany now that she is in allied hands, but we are of a dozen minds as to what we shall do with Germany in the years to come."[16] The confusion associated with three different occupation policies—the State Department's ambitious plans for the U.S. Army, the Morgenthau Plan, and JCS 1067's commitment to a "disease and unrest" formula—led to effective paralysis as the occupation began. The zonal division of Germany (with the belated addition of France) posed huge practical and policy issues. Despite the still current myth of Germany as the model for military occupations, the accommodation between victors and vanquished was not easy or straightforward.

The U.S. armed forces in Europe rapidly demobilized. Six months after V-E Day the U.S. Army was but a shadow of the powerful force that had overwhelmed the Wehrmacht. By mid-1946, U.S. occupation forces, composed mainly of new draftees, were being called the "ice cream army." Those soldiers faced a significant security problem, for despite the enduring mythology about Germany as the model of a perfect occupation, the mood of a disillusioned and desperate civilian population toward the victors was one of passive hostility and, in some instances, violence. A map captioned "Civil and Internal Security Incidents," issued in January 1946 by the Counter Intelligence Branch, G-1, to reflect incidents in the U.S. sector of occupied Germany for the previous three months, listed thirteen categories of attacks. The map documented ten incidents of "sabotage," thirty-one incidents of "underground activities," sixty-nine "attacks on personnel," 140 incidents of "looting," eighty-three "wire cuts" of military communications, and one "riot." The chart could easily be confused with a U.S. Central Command map of Iraq in 2006 indicating "insurgency" activity rather than Germany sixty years earlier. One historian has estimated the number killed by Werewolf action—both Allied personnel and German citizens killed because of perceived traitorous behavior—at between 3,000 and 5,000 during the months after war's end. Americans paid little attention to these concerns back home, where the focus was demobilization, fears of inflation, and the start of the baseball season. The original war aim enunciated by FDR, calling for the "final destruction of Nazi tyranny," had been achieved. But what of those other aims featured in the Atlantic Charter and the Declaration of the United Nations?

VII

For many Americans, World War II ended when Germany surrendered. Even while the war in the Pacific continued, the public clamored for the benefits of peace. The nation engaged in an outburst of triumphalism, taking for granted both the central contribution of the United States in winning the war and the preeminent role it would play, politically and economically, in shaping the peace to come. Once again there were wide-spread assumptions about the postwar world: that the wartime alliance would hold firm and supervise the establishment of a stable world order, that following a short period of rehabilitation and reconstruction of those nations devastated by war there would ensue a tidal wave of prosperity and higher living standards everywhere, and that once the international institutions to undergird this new world order were in place Americans could return, if not to isolation, then to a focus on domestic concerns. The realities facing the United States in the weeks and months after V-E Day differed sharply from wartime imaginings.

A first shock was the dissolution of the alliance between the Soviet Union and the West. Shortly after V-E Day, Eisenhower spoke about the likelihood of continued cooperation with the USSR. He commented that Anglo-American–Soviet relations were "at the same stage of arms-length dealing that marked the early Anglo-American contacts in 1940." How-ever, just as British and Americans had become "allies in spirit as well as on paper," Ike believed that a determined effort to maintain and strengthen contacts with the Russians, relying on "blunt and forthright" communi-cation, would produce similar results.[17] It was not to be. Writing about the Napoleonic Era but also, perhaps, with an eye toward the demise of the World War II Allied coalition, Henry A. Kissinger observed, "As long as the enemy is more powerful than any single member of the coalition, the need for unity outweighs all considerations of individual gain. Then the powers of repose can insist on the definition of war aims which, in all conditions, represent limitations. But when the enemy has been so weakened that each ally has the power to achieve its ends alone, a coalition is at the mercy of its most determined member."[18] Russian actions in Eastern Europe and intransigence regarding such issues as representation in the UN, withdrawal from Iran, and German occupation policies led the administration of President Harry S. Truman to respond forcefully. By 1947 what was to be labeled the "Cold War" was a reality, leading to such actions by the United States as the Truman Doctrine, the Marshall Plan, and the creation of NATO. Rather than settling down to enjoy the benefits of peace, Americans were called upon to provide political, economic, and military leadership to meet a global threat to the nation's security—and one that threatened to endure for generations.

To deal with America's vastly expanded responsibilities in the aftermath of World War II, there took place a further expansion of the wartime powers exercised by FDR's administration. With passage of the National Security Act of 1947, the Truman administration significantly expanded the authority of the executive branch. This act established the National Security Council to advise the president and coordinate activities relating to military and foreign policies. Also in 1947, building on the wartime Joint Chiefs of Staff as a mechanism for interservice cooperation, a single Department of Defense, responsible for overseeing all activities of the armed forces and reporting directly to the White House, was established. The National Security Act of 1947 also authorized formation of a unitary intelligence-gathering organization, the Central Intelligence Agency. The newly formed national security establishment confronted immediate challenges. Of greatest concern was the vulnerability of Western Europe to Soviet invasion, especially dire as the Marshall Plan triggered economic recovery. Making use of the lessons learned from participating in the so-called Grand Alliance, the United States undertook to convert the North Atlantic Treaty, a pledge by its signatories to the principle of collective security, into a functioning military coalition. Over the next fifty years NATO, whatever its limitations, demonstrated how much Americans had learned about what was required to keep together members with disparate cultural traditions, doctrinal practices, and political goals.

The postwar years also witnessed lasting changes in civil-military relationships. Along with the expansion of the federal government's role in the economy an equally significant expansion of communication and cooperation occurred between those in the professional military and civilian leaders. Compelled to work together, they discovered much in common and much that they could learn from each other. The "military-industrial-educational complex" that was to be one of World War II's important legacies was in essence the development of habits of interchange grounded in mutual interest. It is at least arguable that the strains exerted upon the armed forces by radical shifts in priorities and policies would have generated far more serious opposition to the creation of a national defense establishment and the primacy of the newly born U.S. Air Force than were shown by the "revolt of the admirals" and grumbling among senior army officers.

For the U.S. Army the immediate postwar years posed difficult challenges. With almost no forethought there occurred a global expansion of American power. By war's end the United States oversaw an enormous system of bases, some 30,000 installations and 2,000 sites stretching through both hemispheres, north to the Arctic, and south to Antarctica. The U.S. Army occupied many of these bases with a force that had shrunk dramatically. Plans for an orderly demobilization and for the creation of a ground army of approximately one million men had been superseded by budgetary pressures and the failure of the campaign for universal military service. By June 30, 1947, the army was a volunteer body of 684,000 ground troops and, soon to be issued nice blue uniforms, 306,000 airmen. The guiding presumption was that Anglo-American naval supremacy and some number of B-29 groups equipped with atomic bombs would suffice to meet any threat. Only a few prescient planners argued for retention in Europe of substantial ground forces to counter the Red Army.

Throughout demobilization about half the army's diminishing strength remained overseas, the bulk involved in the occupation of Germany and Japan. Another large force was in liberated Korea. American manpower policies were in total disarray. Precisely what missions the U.S. Army would tackle in the event of another war were uncertain, and the force structure with which to accomplish any of numerous potential scenarios had been skewed by the dual effects of wartime personnel policies and the postwar drawdown.

Ironically, what became the central component of America's Cold War defense posture, denial of Central Europe to the Soviet Union, was largely the result of inadvertent actions. The army yearned to shed the fiscal and other costs of the German occupation and was acutely aware that the poor state of training and readiness of U.S. ground forces in Europe made them vulnerable to a Soviet challenge. Not coincidentally, Congress passed a new Selective Service Act in June 1948 and approved a military budget that severely limited the army's size. The army mustered 591,000 men and ten divisions in 1950. Of the ten divisions, four infantry divisions were part of the Far East Command on occupation duty in Japan. One infantry division was stationed in Germany. Some lessons, it appears, had not been learned.

SUGGESTED READING

How the war in Europe was waged begins with the encyclopedic history of World War II by Gerhard Weinberg, *A World at Arms* (New York: Cambridge University Press, 1994). The drift of the United States toward belligerency is explored in Warren F. Kimball, *Forged in War: Roosevelt, Churchill, and the Second World War* (New York: William Morrow, 1997) and Theodore A. Wilson, *The First Summit: Roosevelt and Churchill at Placentia Bay, 1941,* rev. ed. (Lawrence: University Press of Kansas, 1991). Convolutions of Allied wartime strategy are traced in Kent Roberts Greenfield's *American Strategy in World War II: A Reconsideration* (New York: Greenwood, 1979) and Mark Stoler's magisterial study, *Allies and Adversaries: The Joint Chiefs of Staff, the Grand Alliance, and U.S. Strategy in World War II* (Chapel Hill: University of North Carolina Press, 2000).

For the war's final phase, see Forrest C. Pogue, *The Supreme Command* (Washington: U.S. Government Printing Office, 1978); Charles B. Macdonald, *The Last Offensive: Rhineland and Central Germany* (Washington: U.S. Government Printing Office, 1973); Robert W. Coakley and Richard M. Leighton, *Global Logistics and Strategy, 1943–1945* (Washington: U.S. Government Printing Office, 1968); Dwight D. Eisenhower, *Crusade in Europe: A Personal Account of World War II* (New York: Doubleday, 1948); Omar N. Bradley and Clay Blair, *A General's Life: An Autobiography of General of the Army Omar N. Bradley* (New York: Simon and Schuster, 1983); Forrest C. Pogue, *George C. Marshall: Organizer of Victory, 1943–1945* (New York: Viking Press, 1973); Carlos D'Este, *Patton: A Genius for War* (New York: HarperCollins, 1995); Raymond Callahan, *Churchill and His Generals* (Lawrence: University Press of Kansas, 2007). Among recent studies are Edward Miller, *A Dark and Bloody Ground: The Huertgen Forest and the Roer Dams, 1944–1945* (College

Station: Texas A&M University Press, 2003); Derek Zumbro, *Battle for the Ruhr: The German Army's Final Defeat in the West* (Lawrence: University Press of Kansas, 2006); Perry Biddiscombe, *Werewolf: The History of the National Socialist Guerrilla Movement, 1944–1946* (Toronto: University of Toronto Press, 1998); Stephen G. Fritz, *Endkampf: Soldiers, Civilians, and the Death of the Third Reich* (Lexington: University Press of Kentucky, 2004).

Relevant works on the transition from war to troubled peace in Europe and the origins of the Cold War include Theodore A. Wilson, ed., *Victory in Europe, 1945: From World War to Cold War* (Lawrence: University Press of Kansas, 2000); Melvyn Leffler, *A Preponderance of Power: National Security, the Truman Administration, and the Cold War* (Palo Alto, CA: Stanford University Press, 1992); James McAllister, *No Exit: America and the German Problem* (Ithaca, NY: Cornell University Press, 2002); Earl Ziemke, *The U.S. Army and the Occupation of Germany, 1944–1946* (Washington: U.S. Government Printing Office, 1975).

GERHARD L. WEINBERG

The End of the Pacific War
in World War II

The battle for Okinawa, the largest of the islands in the Ryukyu chain
southwest of the home islands of Japan, had been designed by both
sides as a preliminary to the climactic campaigns of the war in the Pacific:
the American landing on the Japanese home island of Kyushu in November 1945 (Operation Olympic) and the Allied landing in Tokyo Bay in the
spring of 1946 (Operation Coronet). By its very nature, however, it would
become the final battle of the war between Japan and the United States.

The Japanese attack on the United States, Great Britain, and the Netherlands in December 1941 had been designed to supplement the earlier
Japanese campaign in China, the occupation of French Indo-China, and
the effective control of Thailand by a series of rapid thrusts that would
bring Japan control of all of East, Southeast, and South Asia, the Dutch
East Indies, all the islands of the Southwest Pacific, Australia, New Zealand, Hawaii, Alaska, and parts of Canada, the state of Washington, Central America, the islands of the Caribbean, and the northwest portion of
South America. The halting of the Japanese advance in the summer of
1942 by American and Australian forces at the Battles of the Coral Sea
and Midway and on the island of New Guinea in the South and West as
well as by British Indian forces on the border of India in the East, and
the clearly successful resistance of the Soviet Union to the German invasion, contributed to a complete and quite drastic change of aims by the
Japanese government.

From the summer of 1942 on, the aim of Japan was first to hold as much conquered territory as possible but, in any case, to make the war so costly for the Americans and their allies in lives and treasure that they would settle for a negotiated peace that would leave Japan, if without her conquests, at least unoccupied, not disarmed, and without any trials of war criminals. As American casualties increased in the fighting for the Philippines starting in October 1944, on Iwo Jima in February 1945, and on Okinawa in April, May, and June of that year, the Japanese prepared to make the landings on the home islands—which they correctly anticipated as to both location and timing—so costly for the Americans that there was hope in Tokyo that these latter aims could still be attained.

The aim of the United States beginning in December 1941 was the unconditional surrender of Japan, evacuation by the Japanese of all territories occupied during hostilities and especially any portion of pre-1894 China, a complete occupation of Japan by the Allies, and, after an imposed domestic reconstruction, Japan's return to the more moderate and democratic policies it had followed in the 1920s. Although not publicly announced until January 1943, these aims were held by President Franklin D. Roosevelt from December 1941 on and remained in effect until 1945. The British government adhered to them and insisted on the inclusion of Italy in the 1943 public demand for the unconditional surrender of the powers of the Tripartite Pact. The expectation was that unconditional surrender followed by the occupation of any portions of the Axis powers not already occupied during the fighting would discourage any thought of trying to fight the Allies again. The experience of having granted Germany an armistice in 1918 only to have that country warring again two decades later was very much on the minds of Allied leaders as they looked to the future in which they hoped not to find themselves again in the situation they currently found themselves.

The Japanese strategy to attain its aims after the summer of 1942 was to fight for every bit of territory. In 1945 a minimal but important tactical flexibility was introduced into the implementation of this strategy. As a series of Japanese defeats showed them that American landings could not be defeated on the beaches of islands conquered earlier, local Japanese commanders shifted to making their main stand not at the beaches but inland, at places of their choosing. This procedure proved effective for the Japanese and costly for the Americans on Iwo Jima and Okinawa, but the basic strategy remained that of making every American advance as costly as possible. The Japanese expected that what they considered the inherently spoiled and weak Americans would never expend the blood and treasure to retake places of which they had never heard so that these places could then be returned to colonial masters of whom the Americans disapproved.

The U.S. strategy to bring about Japan's surrender looked to approaches to the home islands of Japan on three axes of advance, hopefully assisted by a fourth. From the Southwest Pacific, American forces, assisted by substantial Australian and some New Zealand forces, would head for the Philippines and then to Japan itself. In the Central Pacific, American naval and marine forces would head across the Pacific to the Japanese home islands, possibly also participating in a return to the Philippines and to Formosa (Taiwan) on the way. A third thrust would be based on Nationalist China, assisted by American air force units based on Chinese soil, on the shortest route to Japan itself. There was hope that the Soviet Union would provide a fourth thrust that would both tie down Japanese forces on the mainland of Asia and also strike the home islands from the North. The crushing defeat of the Chinese Nationalists by the Japanese Ichigo offensive in the summer of 1944 eliminated the third thrust, made an assault on Formosa less useful, and greatly increased American interest in the fourth, that of the Soviet Union. The division of the American advance into two thrusts under separate commanders was influenced by the rivalry between the army and the navy. Not only did the two thrusts assist each other by forcing the Japanese to confront two offensives simultaneously, but it also appears doubtful that a single commander and staff could have directed a theater ranging from Alaska to New Guinea.

The American thrust from the Southwest Pacific began with the landing on Guadalcanal in the Solomon Islands in August 1942 and the fighting in October 1942 to eliminate the Japanese force at Buna and Gona on the north shore of New Guinea, where they had landed earlier in the hope of seizing Port Moresby on the south coast as a base for the attack on Australia. The Central Pacific thrust began with landings on Tarawa and Makin in the Gilbert Islands in November 1943. From these beginnings the two thrusts moved along the north coast of New Guinea and from island to island until they in effect met in the landing on Leyte in the Philippines in October 1944. The struggle there took longer than anticipated, and, in spite of what should have been known from the earlier American presence on the island, the terrain proved to be unsuitable for the large number of airfields needed to support the attack on Luzon.

A landing on Mindoro had to follow, and the planned landing on Luzon had to be postponed until January 1945. There followed a bitter and bloody struggle on Luzon and for the capital, Manila, with substantial Japanese forces holding out in the northeast corner of Luzon until September. While that fighting continued, American forces on the liberated portions of the island began building up men and supplies for the operations that were to follow.

Once successfully established in the Philippines, the Americans landed on Iwo Jima in the Bonin Islands in February 1945 to deny the Japanese the airfields on the island and instead utilize them for support of the air attacks and eventual landing on Japan itself. The struggle for this island was lengthy and bitter. It showed that the American forces could indeed overcome the most resilient Japanese units, but it also demonstrated two important factors that would influence the next major operation. The Japanese tactical change from trying to stop a landing to choosing the interior ground on which to fight had contributed to the desperate nature of the fighting. The inability of Allied naval gunfire and bombing to penetrate the volcanic terrain sufficiently to reach the deeply dug-in Japanese provided the Japanese with an incentive to repeat the tactic utilized on Iwo and showed the Americans that even the heaviest bombardment from the sea and control of the air could not be counted on to preclude fierce Japanese resistance that had to be overcome by strenuous—and costly—combat for every inch of land.

Operation Iceberg, the landing on the west coast of Okinawa, was designed to seize the largest of the Ryukyu Islands as a major staging base for the invasion of Kyushu. A new Tenth Army was organized under Lt. Gen. Simon Bolivar Buckner Jr.; it landed on the west coast on April 1, 1945. The plan was to seize the airfields in the central portion of the island and then move both north and south to clear the whole island. A preliminary landing on the nearby small Kerama islands gave the Americans a nearby base and the opportunity to destroy 300 suicide boats that the Japanese held there for defense against the expected American landing on Okinawa. This proved to be a significant blow to the Japanese expectation of sinking many of the troopships and other vessels essential to the American effort.

The Japanese commander, Gen. Ushijima Mitsuru, had decided to let the Americans land, rely on kamikaze fliers and suicide ships to damage as much as possible of the American and British warships, troop transports, and supply ships, and concentrate his defenders in prepared posi-

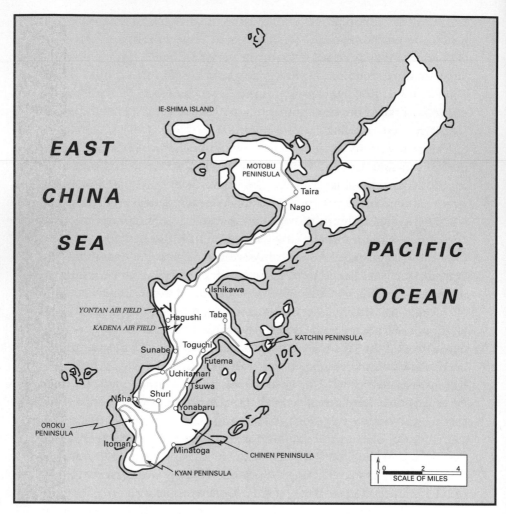

OKINAWA, RYUKYU ISLANDS, 1945

tions in the southern portion of the island. To their pleasant surprise, the Americans landed essentially unopposed. They were able to seize the airfields on the first day and reach the east coast the next day. The Japanese had recently deliberately wrecked the airfields they had earlier toiled to build, but this was a problem that the American engineers and Seabees were prepared to cope with. The Marine Corps units sent to take the northern portion of the island ran into relatively little resistance, except on the westward-projecting Motobu peninsula, and were able to complete that assignment by April 20. The major struggle on and near Okinawa was, however, just beginning. As was true almost invariably in the Southwest Pacific campaign, Gen. Douglas MacArthur's intelligence had drastically underestimated the Japanese forces on Okinawa at 65,000 instead of a more realistic figure in excess of 100,000.

As the marines moved north and the army divisions headed south, the Japanese Air Force launched a massive series of kamikaze attacks on the American and British naval task forces off the coast of Okinawa. Some planes dove directly into the ships; smaller planes dropped from larger ones to crash into ships. The attack quickly became the bloodiest battle of the Pacific War for the U.S. Navy. Many of these attacks concentrated on the destroyers stationed at a distance as pickets but did not succeed in breaking the supply system of the American forces on the island. They did, however, inflict heavy losses; twenty ships were sunk and 150 damaged. At the same time, the kamikaze attacks cost the Japanese more than 1,800 planes. The related effort by the huge Japanese battleship *Yamato*, by contrast, proved useless for the Japanese, as it was sunk along with an accompanying cruiser and four destroyers by American bombs and torpedoes before getting close enough to the supporting ships off Okinawa to inflict any damage.

It was the fighting for the southern portion of Okinawa that proved slow and deadly. Two army divisions initiated the offensive out of the bridgehead on April 4. They would subsequently be reinforced by the units that had cleared the northern portion of the island. This reinforcement was very much needed as the Americans ground their way forward yard by yard in a manner that resembled the fighting on the Western Front of World War I. The Japanese soldiers and guns were dug in so deep that neither naval nor air bombardment made much of an impact and did not provide as much assistance to the American troops on the ground as had been expected. Furthermore, the Japanese had more infantry and artillery equipment available to them than usual because much that had originally been destined for the Philippines had remained on Okinawa when the Americans interrupted the supply route to that prior campaign. Strategists canvassed the possibility of landing additional American troops in the rear of the Japanese main defense line to break what was beginning to look like a bloody stalemate, but General Buckner turned down such a project.

Officers in the headquarters of the Japanese Thirty-second Army were divided on the key question of whether to launch a major counteroffensive against the Americans or to remain on the defensive. Orders from Tokyo were to attack, and this operation, launched in the night of April 12–13, proved disastrous for the Japanese. Heavy losses for essentially no gain left the remaining defenders greatly weakened. An American effort on April 19 to break the first Japanese defensive line also failed, but was the prelude to a substantial push forward. The Americans were able to move south between 100 and 150 yards per day, but suffered heavy casualties and substantial losses of tanks. The Japanese decided on another counteroffensive, which was launched on May 4. This time there was not only a breach to be made through the American front by a division that had not been badly affected by earlier fighting, but there were also to be small landings by special units behind the American lines on both shores of the island. This Japanese effort was again rebuffed with massive losses. The subsequent American push brought the capture of the capital of Naha and forced Japanese Army headquarters to a new decision. After some debate they decided to retreat to the Kyan peninsula in the southwest part of Okinawa and to fight to the death there.

The bad weather hindered American air support of the troops and simultaneously turned what roads there were into mud, thus substantially slowing their advance. The Japanese also had serious difficulties in reorganizing their units in the withdrawal; of the 50,000 men facing the Americans, only about 30,000 reached the Kyan line. The American attack on that line began on June 8, a month after the repulse of the previous Japanese thrust. This time the American forces broke through, leading to the dissolution of the remaining Japanese units. Those units continued to fight desperately but were crushed in detail during the following weeks. General Buckner was killed by Japanese artillery on June 18; General Ushijima committed suicide three days later. Fighting ended on July 2, and for the second time in the war (after Iwo Jima) total American casualties in a campaign exceeded the number of Japanese dead. This time some Japanese soldiers and a substantial number of conscripted Okinawans surrendered, but as the fighting moved closer to Japan the cost to the American armed forces was clearly growing.

Even as the fighting on Okinawa raged, both the Allies and the Japanese continued to look toward the next steps in the war. While the commanders in the theater prepared for the next operations, with the Americans and Australians looking toward the southern Philippines and Java and the British to finishing the retaking of Burma and landing on the coast of Malaya, their headquarters in the capitals and the Combined Chiefs of Staff concentrated on plans for the invasion of the Japanese home islands. At their January 1945 conference on Malta the CCS hoped that the war in the Pacific could be ended a year and a half after the war in Europe, then clearly winding down, had ended. Germany surrendered in early May; this meant that the Allies hoped for an end in the Pacific in the winter of 1946–47.

The American Sixth Army was to land on Kyushu in November 1945, and the American First and Eighth Armies on Honshu in March 1946, followed by units from the British Commonwealth and the French. The Soviet Union had promised to enter the war against Japan three months after the end of the war in Europe. The Americans assumed that the Red Army would strike in Manchuria and then move south, thus making it impossible for the Japanese to transfer units from the mainland to the home islands. After seizing the Kurile Islands and southern Sakhalin the Soviets were expected to land on the northern home island of Hokkaido. A major concern was the large Japanese forces on the Asian mainland and islands in the Indian Ocean and Pacific that would be left after the occupation of the home islands: Would they surrender, or would the Allies have to fight them to the death, as had been happening in all the fighting in the Pacific and Southeast Asian theaters up to that time? Referred to as "post-Coronet" operations, the possibility of extended fighting subsequent to the occupation of the home islands constituted a dark shadow in the background of Allied deliberations.

The United States expected to bear the major share of the fighting in the last stage of the Pacific War, though it anticipated contributions from its allies in land and sea forces and minimal support in long-range bombers from the British. Estimates of casualties ranged from half a million to a million and a half, and there was great concern about morale issues as units were redeployed from Europe to the Pacific and medical and other provisions had to be made for what, on the basis of the Okinawa experience, were likely to be long and bitter battles. In mid-June the new president, Harry S. Truman, ordered the project for the landing on Kyushu to go forward. At the Potsdam Conference in July he was delighted to hear Joseph Stalin repeat his promise to enter the war against Japan. Informed of Soviet espionage into the atomic bomb project, Truman mentioned the success of the project to Stalin, who encouraged him to use the weapon against Japan. Both before and after that conference there was discussion within the U.S. government about ways to encourage the Japanese to surrender without the need for an invasion; some suggested offering reassurances that the imperial system would endure, but without substantively modifying the demand for unconditional surrender. Plans were also under way and beginning to be implemented for a large artificial harbor to be towed across the Pacific on the model of the "Mulberries" that had been provided for the Normandy invasion of June 1944.

American intelligence in the spring and summer of 1945 was bringing Washington two types of important information, primarily on the basis of intercepted and decoded Japanese messages. On the one hand, these messages revealed a steady increase in Japanese forces assigned to the defense of Kyushu. It began to look as if the defending army would be larger than the planned landing force, and for the first time in the war, Army Chief of Staff Gen. George Marshall asked the designated commander for the operation, Gen. Douglas MacArthur, whether it was wise to proceed. He answered that it was the best option. On the other hand, the intercepts also revealed two things that pointed in a different direction. They showed that all Japanese efforts to persuade the Soviet Union to help them find a negotiated end to the war or even to switch sides by joining them were falling on deaf ears in Moscow. The Soviet Union was adhering to its commitments to its allies. The intercepts also showed that Japanese diplomats in Europe, especially Sato Naotake, the ambassador in Moscow, were urging the authorities in Tokyo not to follow the German example of fighting to the bitter end, but rather to accept the demand for surrender as repeated publicly by the Allies from their Potsdam Conference. The response from Tokyo, read in Washington, was that they thanked Sato for his advice but after discussion had unanimously rejected it.

Perhaps some severe shocks could lead to further discussion in Tokyo with hopefully a different outcome. It was in this context that the decision was made by Truman, Marshall, and Secretary of War Henry Stimson to drop one and if necessary two atomic bombs on Japan in the hope of shocking the Japanese government into surrender. If Japan did not surrender then, additional atomic bombs becoming available were to be saved up to support the landing on Kyushu. It was a concept that intersected with the Japanese plans for the continuation of the war after it had become obvious that the campaign on Okinawa was going to be another American victory.

Japanese planning for the next campaign after Okinawa was relatively simple. An American invasion of Kyushu in the fall of 1945 followed by an invasion of Honshu in the spring of 1946 looked to the leaders in Tokyo like the most likely next step, as it did to the Americans. Given the terrain of these two home islands and what the Japanese had learned from prior American operational procedures, it was fairly obvious where the Americans were likely to land, and preparations to crush such landings were made accordingly. Additional troops were raised in Japan, much of the civilian population was prepared for participation in the defense of the islands, and some units were returned home from the Asian mainland. Thousands of planes had been carefully hidden and a secret fuel reserve established; they were ready to attack the troopships and supply ships when the Americans were landing. In the summer of 1945, when American and British naval task forces cruised off the Japanese coast, these planes were deliberately not committed in operations, thus deluding the Allies as to the size of the remaining Japanese Air Force as well as its fuel situation. The Japanese believed that strong resistance on land and massive strikes from the air would crush the American invaders, or at least inflict such tremendous casualties as to discourage the Americans and bring about a tolerable settlement. Tokyo anticipated that the Japanese military and civilians would suffer twenty million casualties in the coming fighting in the home islands, but this was considered an acceptable price.

Emperor Hirohito had accepted the planning of the military leaders both for Okinawa and for the home islands, but with defeat on Okinawa looming, he became doubtful. The Americans were clearly not being stopped by the human and material costs, Okinawa was being lost, and the Soviets were not about to switch sides. Furthermore, and this clearly had considerable influence on Hirohito, some of his advisors were beginning to stress that the tremendous suffering being imposed on the population at home by the casualties at the front and the increasing and devastating American air raids on Japan itself opened up the real possibility of a domestic upheaval that could endanger the imperial institution. It was under these circumstances that the dropping of the atomic bombs brought about a new decision in Tokyo.

Japan's ruling council of six was equally divided between those in favor of continuing the war and those who advocated ending it by surrender. The supporters of continuing the war believed in the prospects of the Japanese military plans for the defense of Kyushu. Ironically, they interpreted Truman's early May public statement that surrender did not mean the end of Japan's existence as a sign that America was weakening in the face of rising casualties. They took the position that those killed by the new type of weapon were no more dead than those killed by the types of bombs and incendiaries that the Americans had been dropping on Japanese cities for months. The basic strategy that Japan had been following, they argued, was the proper one; it offered the hope of a decent negotiated end to the war and should be adhered to. Those who supported surrender saw the second atomic bomb as an indication that the Americans either had or would soon have many more such bombs. They could simply kill off the whole Japanese population without ever having to stage a landing and without ever having to face the Japanese defense that had been so carefully planned. Furthermore, they saw hope in the formula offered by the Allies that the Japanese could have an emperor if they wished to, but that he would be under the authority of the Allied supreme commander. Like the Americans, those advocating surrender assumed that the Japanese people very much wanted to maintain the emperor system. In the face of this deadlock, the advocates of surrender brought the emperor himself into the deliberations.

In prior years, when confronted with an essentially unanimous government, Hirohito had agreed to whatever was proposed to him. But faced with an evenly divided council the emperor ordered that the surrender terms be accepted. Those opposed to this course tried to stage a coup, and they asked War Minister Anami Korechika to join them. Anami had repeatedly expressed his support of continued fighting, but in the conflict between his belief in the proper course for the country and his having personally heard the emperor order surrender, Anami committed suicide, and the coup failed.

Japan surrendered, and with the emperor and members of his family playing a significant role in bringing the surrender message to all Japanese-controlled areas, essentially all Japanese forces obeyed the order to lay down their arms. There followed the famous surrender ceremony on the battleship *Missouri* and the occupation of the home islands of Japan without military resistance and practically without incident. Of great importance to the Americans, British, and Dutch was the fact that the

surrender stopped the Japanese from killing all the numerous Allied prisoners of war whom they still held and had planned to kill if there was a
chance of their being liberated. The Allies knew that orders to this effect
had been issued and that they had been implemented in two instances, on
Wake Island in October 1943 and on Palawan Island in December 1944.
Even before such murder commands could be implemented, more than
a quarter of Allied POWs had been killed or had died from mistreatment
in the preceding years, and most who survived were in terrible condition.
But they were not murdered at the last minute and could return home.

The possibility of lengthy post-Coronet operations in the face of likely
flagging home support was also averted by the surrender. The tiny number of Japanese soldiers who hid and held out into the 1970s presented
no real threat to anyone except nearby villages that they might raid for
supplies. In retrospect the worry over post-Coronet has disappeared from
the picture most have of the Pacific War, but no one should underesti-
mate its importance at the time.

There was another element in the surrender related to the reasoning
behind the demand for unconditional surrender in the first place. In
many ways Japan in 1945 was in a situation that resembled that of Germany in 1918, with much of its military still in the field and occupying
substantial territories taken during hostilities. Under these circumstances
the requirement that there be a formal surrender in anticipation of a
total occupation of the country could not leave anyone in Japan with the
notion, so widely held after 1918 in Germany, that the country had really
not been defeated at the front.

After considerable debate the Allies agreed on the formula for surrender that the Americans presented to the Japanese. All had seen the wisdom of allowing the Japanese to keep their imperial system, and at the
urging of the British government they had also agreed that Japanese military and diplomatic representatives could sign the instrument of surrender without the emperor having to do so in person. Although the Soviet
military continued operations for some days, there were no further significant military clashes involving American or British forces. Because there
had not been invasions of the home islands, the country was not divided
into occupation zones the way Germany was. Most of the country was
under American military occupation. Although the Soviets, in addition
to occupying the Kurile Islands, seized some small islands off the north
coast of Hokkaido—an issue that has prevented a Japanese-Russian peace
treaty until now—Truman stopped their attempts to have Hokkaido

allocated to the Red Army as an occupation zone. The country retained an administration of its own that was centrally directed by the Suprme Commander of the Allied Powers (SCAP), Gen. MacArthur. A British Commonwealth Occupation Force was stationed in western Honshu and took a minor symbolic part in guarding the imperial palace in Tokyo, but there was no British occupation zone. Japan had its national govern-ment and administrative apparatus—purged and reformed, to be sure—but without the division into zones and sectors that would be a part of Austria's heritage until 1955, Germany's until 1989, and Berlin's until 1994. Furthermore, there was none of the additional massive destruction in Japan that would certainly have been produced by lengthy campaigns in the home islands, to say nothing of the millions of Japanese casual-ties that such a struggle would have entailed. Although the Soviets kept many captured Japanese soldiers in Manchuria for years, far fewer Japa-nese than German soldiers had lost their lives in the war in part because of the early surrender, and the vast majority of those who did surrender in 1945 returned home within a few years and could play a role in the social and economic recovery of their country. The postwar development of Japan cannot be understood without reference to the fact that in spite of its substantially larger population than Germany, it had suffered far fewer military and civilian casualties as well as much less physical dam-age to its towns, farms, and infrastructure than its major European ally.

The Japanese surrender and occupation meant that America's key aim had been attained. The surrender and occupation eliminated any doubt that the country had been defeated in war and simultaneously opened the way for its internal political restructuring along peaceful and democratic lines. Furthermore, the hope that Japan could be returned to the civilized world was far easier to realize under circumstances in which the country, however damaged by the war, remained a unit. The fact that an American was supreme commander and through his staff could provide direction to the country as a whole enormously simplified a process that would not be hampered by any need for unanimity—or more likely conflicting plans and intentions—of several occupying powers. There was an Allied Coun-cil that met regularly in Tokyo and included Soviet, British, and Chinese representatives, but it operated in practice as an advisory, not an executive or administrative body. The recasting of Japan would take some time, and major problems in that country's facing up to its own past remain, but a peace treaty was signed after a conference in 1951.

In view of the upheavals in East Asia that followed the war, including independence efforts in French Indo-China and the Dutch East Indies as well as a civil war in China, the fact that the United States effectively occupied Japan and the Ryukyu Islands meant that the U.S. strategic position was safe. As the Philippines continued the move toward independence that had been interrupted by the war, the abandonment of bases there left the United States adequately supplied with other bases. In opposition to his civilian and military advisors, President Roosevelt had refused to contemplate the annexation of the former Japanese mandated islands in the Pacific but had instead insisted on their having trusteeship status on their road to independence. This aspect of his anticolonial policy was upheld by President Truman at the end of the Pacific War but in no way precluded experimental nuclear detonations or the establishment of American bases on some of the islands either then or subsequently.

The significance of this continuation of American bases on the western portion of the Pacific Ocean became clear when President Truman decided that the Soviet-authorized invasion of South Korea by North Korea in June 1950 required a military response by the United States and whatever other countries were prepared to take part. It was from the bases acquired as a result of the prior victory over Japan that American troops, warships, and planes engaged the North Korean and later Chinese forces that threatened to take over South Korea. Ironically, it was under the American commander of the occupation of Japan, General MacArthur, that the initial stages of the Korean War were fought by the United Nations. Similarly, with the Communists in control of China at the end of the civil war there, the bases on Japanese territory provided the United States with a position to contain the new regime in Beijing and to assure some level of protection to Taiwan, where the remnants of the Chinese Nationalist government and army had established themselves. It was also from these bases that the United States could observe the Sino-Soviet ideological split and their occasional military hostilities, until the dissolution of the Soviet Union altered the situation in East Asia. Even after the withdrawal of the last American troops from Vietnam and the triumph of the Communist regime there, the position that the United States had acquired continued, as it continues today, to provide a means of retaining a direct influence on developments in a critical part of the world.

For the American military the fighting itself had ended but a new era had begun. The nature of warfare between major powers had changed. The American monopoly on atomic weapons would provide an unusual margin of safety for a time, but at some point that monopoly would end.

This meant that for years to come the means of delivering atomic bombs, whether by airplanes from land bases or from aircraft carriers or out of silos in the West, would become a central concern of the U.S. military. Whatever the details and whatever the arguments over them, the relative significance of the different arms of the military services would be affected by this new weapon. The relationship between the new weapon and the conventional ones that had carried the burden of fighting in the war just ended was likely to be not only controversial but also of major influence on peacetime appropriations. The marines and the army had learned a great deal about amphibious operations in the preceding years and had shown their proficiency at this task. As knowledge of the nature of radioactive fallout became available, however, such projects as the intended landing on Kyushu through an area that had been affected by the dropping of atomic bombs now looked very different from the time when those plans were originally drawn up. The balance between nuclear and conventional weapons and whether the United States or other countries would employ them were certain to become dominant issues after 1945. And whatever answers the leaders might give to these puzzles, there would surely be major arguments about them into the indefinite future. If the Pacific War demonstrated the enormous importance of aircraft carriers and the absolutely essential nature of a large fleet train if the United States were to project power across the vast reaches of the Pacific, it had at its ending brought about a very dramatic change in the way a country could fight.

Although not yet seen at the time, except perhaps dimly by a few, there would eventually be a junction between the new technologies that had come to the fore in the war's last stages. The combination of the ballistic missile, a weapon introduced by the Germans, and nuclear weapons would lead to the intercontinental ballistic missile with one or more nuclear warheads. Nuclear technology would be combined with the new type of submarine the Germans had brought into service in the last days of the war, creating submarines that could stay submerged for extended periods and move enormous distances. Similarly the new technology would be combined with the fleet carriers that had played such an important role in the American drive toward Japan. The Germans had taken some steps to share their technological innovations in weapons with their Japanese ally, and it was from Japanese reports that the Allies learned many details about what might lie ahead if the war were not ended quickly. However, none of those innovations made any impact on the war in the Pacific by the time the battle for Okinawa had eventuated in an end of the fighting between the Allies and Japan.

SUGGESTED READING

The U.S. Army's official history is Roy E. Appleman et al., *Okinawa: The Last Battle* (Washington: U.S. Government Printing Office, 1948); the Navy's is Samuel Eliot Morison, *Victory in the Pacific 1945* (Boston: Little Brown, 1990); the Army Air Force's is Wesley F. Craven and James L. Cate, *Matterhorn to Nagasaki, June 1944 to August 1945* (Washington: Office of Air Force History, 1953); the Marine Corps' is Bemis M. Frank and Henry I. Shaw, *Victory and Occupation* (Washington: U.S. Marine Corps Historical Branch, 1968). Very helpful is Thomas H. Huber, *Japan's Battle of Okinawa, April–June 1945* (Fort Leavenworth, KS: Combat Studies Institute, 1990). On the kamikaze, see Mordecai G. Sheftall, *Blossoms in the Wind: Human Legacies of the Kamikaze* (New York: Penguin, 2005).

For the final stage of the war in the Pacific, see Max Hastings, *Retribution: The Battle for Japan, 1944–45* (New York: Knopf, 2008); John Ray Skates, *The Invasion of Japan: Alternative to the Bomb* (Columbia: University of South Carolina Press, 1994); and two thoughtful analyses, Thomas B. Allen and Norman Polmar, *Codename Downfall: The Secret Plan to Invade Japan—And Why Truman Dropped the Bomb* (New York: Simon and Schuster, 1995), and Richard B. Frank, *Downfall: The End of the Imperial Japanese Empire* (New York: Random House, 1999).

Helpful for understanding American and Japanese planning is D. M. Giangreco, *Hell to Pay: Operation Downfall and the Invasion of Japan, 1945–1947* (Annapolis, MD: Naval Institute Press, 2009). On the involvement of the Allies, see Nicholas Evan Sarantakes, *Allies against the Rising Sun: The United States, the British Nations and the Defeat of Imperial Japan* (Lawrence: University Press of Kansas, 2009). Although published many years ago, Robert J. C. Butow, *Japan's Decision to Surrender* (Stanford: Stanford University Press, 1954) remains important. For many significant aspects of the fighting, consult Edward J. Drea, *In the Service of the Emperor: Essays on the Imperial Japanese Army* (Lincoln: University of Nebraska Press, 1998). On the upheavals all over East and Southeast Asia immediately after the war, see Ronald H. Spector, *In the Ruins of Empire: The Japanese Surrender and the Battle for Postwar Asia* (New York: Random House, 2007).

None of the books listed supports the various interpretations that relate the dropping of atomic bombs on Japan to racial factors, threats to the Soviet Union, and other far-fetched fairy tales popular in some quarters. This author has never seen any evidence to substantiate any of them.

CONRAD C. CRANE

Exerting Air Pressure
and Globalizing Containment:
War Termination in Korea

On the afternoon of June 23, 1952, workers at the massive Suiho Dam complex along the Yalu River continued to pump hydroelectric power into China and North Korea. The fourth-largest dam in the world was located close to MiG-15 fighter bases in Manchuria, and because many considered the dam a nonmilitary target it had not been attacked by United Nations airpower. That was about to change. The aerial assault that day was a model joint operation. It began with thirty-five U.S. Navy F9F Panther jets sweeping in to suppress enemy air defenses. Following them were the same number of lumbering Skyraiders, who dumped their 5,000-pound bomb loads on the penstocks, transformers, and power distribution facilities around the dam. All had been launched from Task Force 77's fast aircraft carriers. Ten minutes later, 124 F-84 Thunderjet fighter-bombers from the Fifth Air Force joined the assault. The whole operation was protected by 84 F-86 Sabrejets swarming overhead.

This assault was just the beginning of an organized attack on the entire hydroelectric industry. Within four days 546 navy sorties along with 730 by U.S. Fifth Air Force fighter-bombers had destroyed 90 percent of North Korea's electric power potential.

The attacks had many repercussions besides a reduction in the production of Manchurian industry. The impact on North Korea was apparent to American prisoners of war, who never got to see the end of any of the propaganda films they were exposed to that summer because the electricity always failed. But the most obvious effect of the new bombing program was not in Pyongyang, Moscow, or Beijing, but in London. The British Labour Party denounced the bombings in Parliament as a provocation that could lead to World War III, and only Prime Minister Winston Churchill's announcement that he was appointing a British deputy for the UN Command in Korea mollified them. U.S. Secretary of Defense Robert Lovett publicly endorsed the addition to Gen. Mark Clark's staff, while also providing the misleading explanation to the press that the Joint Chiefs of Staff had given special permission to allow the raids on the hydroelectric plants based only on military considerations. American newspapers were not fooled; they speculated that the attacks that had darkened much of North Korea and a good part of Manchuria were the start of a tougher policy to break the stalemate over POW repatriation at the peace talks at Panmunjom. Some congressmen even questioned why the plants had not been bombed earlier. Both Churchill and Lovett denied that the attacks signified any change in UN policies.

But the attacks did indeed herald a significant change in both policy and strategy. Although its beginning was inauspicious, the air campaign aimed to coerce a satisfactory negotiated conclusion to a war that had been dragging on for two years, an unprecedented reliance on airpower to achieve a strategic objective. Not until the Kosovo campaign of 1999 would the United States depend so heavily on airpower as the primary military arm to terminate a conflict. In World War II, strategic air campaigns were key elements of American strategy, and the fire raids on Japanese cities and the deployment of atomic bombs were key components of the series of blows that produced Japanese surrender, but so were extensive ground campaigns in Manchuria and Okinawa, as well as an extremely effective submarine blockade. Airpower set the stage for the ground campaign in Operation Desert Storm and policed Iraq afterward, but an extensive land campaign was still essential to liberate Kuwait and achieve the objectives of the war. Once both sides dug in across Korea in mid-1951, no one was willing to pay the price it would have taken to achieve decisive results on the ground, and America turned to its asymmetric advantage in the air.

I

The Korean War had not always been typified by military stalemate and diplomatic frustration. Its first year featured dramatic advances, desperate retreats, and ambitious objectives. Both sides were guilty of overextending their supply lines and their war aims.

In many ways the preconditions for the conflict were the result of a botched American occupation at the end of World War II. While U.S. military preparations for governing Germany, Italy, Japan, and the Philippines had begun as early as 1942, Korea was neglected along with most other remnants of the Japanese Empire. When Japan capitulated, the Americans and Soviets agreed to split the Korean peninsula to accept the surrender of forces there. A couple of U.S. Army colonels looking at a map in Washington selected the 38th Parallel as the dividing line between the areas of national responsibility. That soon became an international border between two very different states. While the Soviets nurtured a new Communist Democratic People's Republic of Korea and strengthened its army with T-34 tanks, an American military governor struggled to unite divergent South Korean factions enough to allow a speedy withdrawal of his troops. With the creation of the Republic of Korea in 1948 the United States began to pull out its forces, by mid-1949 leaving behind just a small advisory group for an army kept purposefully weak so it would not be tempted to try to conquer the North. The ROK Army was equipped primarily to suppress Communist rebels in the new country's interior. When the main American forces departed, they left behind a weak South Korean government rent by factional strife and fighting a growing insurgency. The fledgling state was a tempting target for an aggressive neighbor.

The Korean War began because the North Korean leader Kim Il Sung saw an opportunity to reunify the peninsula under his rule and persuaded his sponsors in the Soviet Union and China to back him. The conflict ensued along five rough phases. The first began on June 25, 1950, when the North Korean People's Army overwhelmed poorly prepared Republic of Korea forces and swarmed southward over the 38th Parallel. American leaders believed that the Soviets had to be the main perpetrators of the attack and were fearful that this operation was just the opening gambit of a wider war. Reinforcements rushed to Europe as well as the Far East. The United States and its UN allies rallied to South Korea's defense, with an initial war objective of stopping the aggression and preserving the non-

Communist nation. But overconfident American units deployed from Japan were driven back, and United Nations forces were soon bottled up in a perimeter behind the Naktong River, defending the key port of Pusan. However, the NKPA had suffered tremendous attrition from constant combat, and its lines of communication were overextended, leaving it vulnerable to counterattack.

The war's second phase began on September 15, when Gen. Douglas MacArthur landed a strong force at Inchon in the enemy rear, and the besieged U.S. Eighth Army broke out of the Pusan Perimeter along with South Korean forces. The NKPA collapsed. The quick turn of events forced both sides to make strategic decisions of great import on short notice. Now American and UN military objectives expanded to include conquering the whole peninsula, while the Soviets and Chinese were faced with increasing their active involvement to preserve a suddenly beleaguered ally. American leaders gave MacArthur permission to cross the 38th Parallel and reunite the two Koreas, and as UN forces headed for the Yalu it was their turn to become vulnerable and overextended.

The war turned again as a massive Chinese intervention in late November caught the American Eighth Army and X Corps with their allies in North Korea by surprise, and they were lucky to escape without even heavier losses. The Chinese armies rolled over the 38th Parallel and retook the South Korean capital, Seoul, and for a while Mao Zedong envisioned permanently removing American influence from the peninsula. However, because of long supply lines, harsh weather, and growing UN resistance, Communist forces reached their culminating point in early 1951. Then the Eighth Army, rejuvenated by the dynamic leadership of Matthew Ridgway, spearheaded a counteroffensive that could not be stopped by massive Chinese attacks or even President Truman's relief of MacArthur in April for insubordination. By June, UN forces and firepower had recaptured Seoul and restored the battle line to roughly the 38th Parallel.

When the Chinese intervened in force, the Truman administration and the UN scaled back their war objectives to restore the status quo. Ridgway's combination of controlled offensives and firepower rolled inexorably northward, prodding the Soviets to ask the UN for a cease-fire and armistice. It appeared that both sides now agreed on how the conflict should end, but for the next two years the war settled down to a stalemate in the mountainous Korean terrain and at the peace table.

As Ridgway feared, Communist forces used the respite gained from the cease-fire to create defensive lines resembling the Western Front in

World War I. With neither side willing to pay the high price of trying to gain military victory on this new fortified battlefield, both focused on achieving some sort of success in negotiations. Americans used to negotiating from a position of strength with a defeated enemy found these discussions very different and difficult. After much sparring and posturing, a suspension of the discussions at Kaesong in August 1951, and a limited UN ground offensive in September, talks resumed in October at Panmunjom. While agreement was achieved fairly quickly on items such as fixing a military demarcation line and a supervisory organization for the armistice, some issues were more intractable. The rotation and replenishment of military forces after the armistice remained a sticking point, but the major disagreement that would prolong the war well into 1953 involved repatriation of prisoners of war.

Of the tens of thousands of prisoners herded into UN POW camps after the collapse of the NKPA offensive, many were South Koreans who had been impressed into service to replace NKPA losses on their drive down the peninsula. Among the Chinese prisoners were many who claimed to be Nationalists forced to serve under the Reds. Neither group wanted to return to their former military masters. Not only did many UN leaders see forced repatriation of these soldiers as immoral, but the propaganda value of so many refusing to return to Communist rule was apparent to both sides. Hence the Communists insisted that all their prisoners had to be returned to them, and the talks bogged down. China and the Soviet Union also had other motives to let the war continue. Mao Zedong could train his army in battle against a Western army while receiving bountiful military assistance from the USSR. Stalin thought he could use Korea to bleed American lives and dollars while distracting it from Europe. And the Soviet armed forces used Korean battlefields as a laboratory to perfect their air defenses against the formidable U.S. Air Force. All the Communist belligerents also hoped that extending the war might cause the contentious American–South Korean alliance to self-destruct.

II

By mid-1952 both sides were looking for some way to break the deadlock by forcing concessions from their opponent. While most of this essay deals with the U.S. and UN airpower approach to influence negotiations, it is worth mentioning the alternatives exploited by the Communists.

Along with continuing attrition at the fortified front to wear down UN will, these primarily involved influencing international perceptions through adroit information campaigns. In February and March 1952, North Korean and Chinese leaders accused the United States of carrying on biological warfare against them. In May they released confessions coerced from American airmen who admitted they had dropped "germ bombs" as part of an extensive biological warfare campaign against China and Korea. Eventually as many as thirty-eight fliers confessed to such attacks. Besides the obvious propaganda value of the accusations, they also were designed to discredit American airpower that was punishing Communist forces and facilities. While the United States investigated the confessions and actively worked to counter the charges, they had the ironic effect of spurring American efforts to develop the means to actually carry out such biological attacks. Leaders wanted a retaliatory capability because they feared that the Communists were making the accusations in order to provide an excuse to launch their own biological operations. However, the Americans were not able to develop a viable biological warfare system before the war ended, and when the post-Stalin government in Moscow found evidence that the Chinese and North Koreans were fabricating biowar claims in the spring of 1953, the Soviets got the accusations to cease.

Another information campaign was aimed more directly at the POW issue. The Communists carefully trained selected officers as provocateurs and had them surrender. They took advantage of overcrowded conditions in prison camps on the island of Koje-Do to organize resistance there. In May 1952 the prisoners actually lured the American commander, Brig. Gen. Francis Dodd, into the compound and captured him, and then forced Brig. Gen. Charles Colson to sign a pledge to stop a list of alleged atrocities against the prisoners in order to get Dodd out of their clutches. This acquiescence appeared to be an admission of guilt, and it was echoed throughout the world press. The Communists hoped that embarrassment over abuses at Koje-Do could break the UN position on POWs at the peace talks. The camps threatened to get out of control, until Brig. Gen. Haydon "Bull" Boatner and a few battalions of combat infantry restored order and broke up the Communist cells in June. After that, the UN kept better control of their POW facilities and effectively countered any more accusations of abuse.

Shortly after Boatner ended one Communist campaign to coerce concessions at Panmunjom, American and UN airmen started their own. As the conflict and truce talks continued through 1952 the stalemate on the ground and ineffectiveness of air interdiction inspired Brig. Gen. Jacob Smart, the Far East Air Forces (FEAF) deputy commander for operations, to look for a better way to apply his resources. He directed two members of his staff, Col. R. L. Randolph and Lt. Col. B. I. Mayo, "to devise ways and means of exerting maximum pressure on the Communist Forces in North Korea through optimum application of FEAF effort." Smart was frustrated by the United Nations' lack of progress in ending the war, and his subordinates' mission was "truly a search for new ideas." Randolph and Mayo began with an examination of the course and results of the interdiction campaign, which had been focused on enemy railroads since August 1951. The campaign's objective had been to cut rail lines at selected points and force the enemy to use roads as the primary channel of supply. Planners had hoped that Fifth Air Force aircraft could cause enough attrition of enemy trucks so that frontline armies could not be supplied, thus subjecting them to "unbearable pressure, despite the lack of offensive ground action." The plan had failed, despite more than 15,000 rail cuts and at least partial destruction of 199 bridges. Enemy repair efforts, night movement, and MiG-15 jet fighter attacks had foiled FEAF efforts to close transportation routes. Randolph and Mayo also pointed out that the enemy's daily mortar shell requirement could be carried by only one truck or 100 coolies with A-frames, and it would be virtually impossible for interdiction to stop all such traffic. In addition FEAF losses had been heavy. The campaign had thus far cost 243 aircraft destroyed and 290 heavily damaged, while only 131 replacements had been received. The two staff officers looked for a way to reapply American airpower to bring real pressure on the Communists to conclude an armistice.[1]

Their staff study, completed on April 12, 1952, recommended that any air resources beyond those required to maintain air superiority "be employed toward accomplishing the maximum amount of selected destruction, thus making the Korean conflict as costly as possible to the enemy in terms of equipment, supplies, and personnel." Randolph and Mayo prioritized targets based on the effect their destruction would have on the enemy, their vulnerability to available weapons, and the probable cost to FEAF of attacking them. Suggested objectives included hydroelectric plants (if they were cleared for attack by the Joint Chiefs of Staff), locomotives and vehicles, stored supplies, and even buildings in cities and villages, especially in areas "active in support of enemy forces." Based on the study, Smart planned to de-emphasize interdiction to concentrate on the new target systems: "[The aim is to] bring about defeat of the enemy as expeditiously as possible [rather than] allowing him to languish in comparative quiescence while we expand our efforts beating up supply routes." He knew the well dug-in enemy was under no real pressure on the front line and needed very few supplies anyway to sustain operations during the stalemate. Smart also believed attacks should be scheduled "against targets of military significance so situated that their destruction will have a deleterious effect upon the morale of the civilian population actively engaged in the logistic support of the enemy forces." He knew that the selection of proper targets to influence enemy decision makers would be difficult, not only for operational reasons, but because of uncertainty about just who those key decision makers were and how their minds worked.[2]

After MacArthur's relief, Ridgway had become United Nations forces commander and U.S. Far East commander. His initial determination to influence negotiations with airpower had been tempered by his disappointment in the results of the aerial interdiction campaign and early battles with the Joint Chiefs of Staff (JCS) about bombing North Korean ports and the capital of Pyongyang. He also appeared hesitant to risk anything that might cause the Communists to break off the peace talks. They had already used air attacks on the negotiating site as an excuse to do that twice, once with apparently faked evidence and another time because of an actual UN bombing error. After Ridgway left to take command of forces in Europe in May 1952, his successor, Gen. Mark Clark, was not as skeptical about the efficacy of airpower or as reluctant to confront the JCS, who were also increasingly frustrated by the seemingly interminable armistice discussions. Clark's previous experience bargaining with the Soviets as American high commissioner for Austria had taught him that in negotiations they respected only the threat of force. The new commander might also have been more realistic in his expectations about interdiction. Ridgway had commanded a division and corps in northwest Europe in the final drive against the Germans in World War II and had seen the obvious effects of Allied airpower on enemy fuel and transportation in speeding final victory. Clark had commanded an army in Italy, where Operation Strangle had caused the Germans great logistical difficulty and produced some battlefield success but had failed to bring swift victory in another deadly struggle in mountainous terrain. When FEAF commander Lt. Gen. O. P. Weyland and Smart approached their new boss about their air pressure strategy, they were pleasantly surprised to find a willing and supportive listener.

The FEAF directive outlining the policies of the new Air Attack Program was published in the second week of July. It was shaped by three major factors. The first was that the Communists had massed "considerable airpower" in the Far East that could be used offensively against UN forces at any time. The second was that the enemy's major source of supply was off-limits to air attack and transportation routes from sanctuaries to the front lines for small enemy supply requirements were relatively short. The third key factor was that with a stabilized front, friendly ground forces needed only minimal close air support. The first priority for FEAF air action remained air superiority, followed by "maximum selected destruction," and then direct support of ground forces. Specific targets within the second category were prioritized as follows:

1. Aircraft
2. Serviceable airfields
3. Electric power facilities
4. Radar equipment
5. Manufacturing facilities
6. Communication centers
7. Military headquarters
8. Rail repair facilities
9. Vehicle repair facilities
10. Locomotives
11. Supplies, ordnance, petroleum, lubricants
12. Rail cars
13. Vehicles
14. Military personnel
15. Rail bridges and tunnels
16. Marshaling yards
17. Road bridges

The new directive still required that sufficient attacks be maintained against the rail system to prevent it from being able to support "extensive sustained enemy ground operations."[3]

The first major operation for the escalated air campaign would be the attack on North Korean hydroelectric plants described earlier. In March 1952, Ridgway had rebuffed a request for a similar raid from the Fifth Air Force and FEAF by stating that intelligence did not justify destroying targets whose primary use was for the civilian economy, and that their destruction would not hasten Communist agreement to UN armistice terms. He would sanction attacks only if negotiations were hopelessly deadlocked or were broken off. To prepare for April discussions with the JCS, U.S. Air Force Headquarters in Washington queried FEAF about the feasibility and desirability of attacking the installations, also as a possible response to a breakdown or continued deadlock in armistice talks. In preparing a response, FEAF asked its Bomber Command what it would take to destroy the targets; they received a rather gloomy reply that discussed the problems of conducting night bombing so far from navigation beacons, and predicted anywhere from nine to twenty-nine days to achieve 50 percent destruction of each facility. Fifth Air Force was more optimistic, and FEAF told USAF Headquarters that they could accomplish the mission in two or three days, relying heavily on fighter-bombers. A May message from the JCS, probably intended to goad Ridgway into action, reminded him that their most recent directives specifically prohibited attacking only Suiho Dam on the Yalu, and the other power facilities were outside restricted areas. On June 11, 1952, Weyland sent Clark a plan to bomb all complexes except Suiho. In the meantime USAF Chief of Staff Gen. Hoyt Vandenberg was shepherding through the JCS removal of all restrictions on attacks against Yalu River hydroelectric installations. Far East Command received notification of this order in time to add Suiho to the target list, and Clark approved the attack for June 23 or 24, days that navy carriers were available to hit eastern objectives.

The addition of Suiho presented a number of difficulties to FEAF planners beyond just its location on the Yalu in "MiG Alley." It was a massive structure, the fourth-largest dam in the world, and beyond the capabilities of FEAF to destroy. Even the smaller dams turned out to present similar difficulties. Smart reviewed techniques used by RAF dam-busters in World War II, but discovered that the USAF could not emulate them. As a result, penstocks, transformers, and power distribution facilities were targeted at Suiho and the other hydroelectric sites, instead of the dams themselves. The difficulty of completely destroying those diverse objectives limited the long-term effects of the eventual attack to some extent. However, a successful strike against the Suiho complex was seen as critical to applying effective pressure on Communist decision makers. Whereas most of the other hydroelectric facilities were for North Korean use, planners knew that much of Suiho's output went to China.

The next sign of increased air pressure after the hydroelectric attacks was an all-out assault on Pyongyang, which the JCS cleared for attack in early July. Operation Pressure Pump on July 11 involved 1,254 sorties from Fifth Air Force and Marine, naval, Korean, Australian, South African, and British aircraft by day and fifty-four B-29s at night. Psychological warfare leaflets warning civilians to leave the city were dropped before the strike as part of Psychological Operation Blast, designed to demonstrate the omnipotence of UN airpower and to disrupt industrial activity in the city. Radio Pyongyang was knocked off the air for two days; when it came back on, it announced that the "brutal" attacks had destroyed 1,500 buildings and inflicted thousands of civilian casualties. Intelligence sources reported that one extra benefit from this attack was a direct hit by an errant B-29 on an air raid shelter used by high-ranking officials that resulted in 400 to 500 casualties. The effort was repeated on August 29 in an operation called All United Nations Air Effort, which involved more than 1,400 sorties and had a special purpose: "to achieve psychological benefit from our ability to punish the enemy through airpower" during the Moscow Conference between the Chinese and Russians. Smart also scheduled additional attacks on targets in the far northwest of the peninsula to further "display the effect of our air power" to the attendees.[4]

The way these raids were perceived in different parts of the world reveals much about views on the efficacy of American airpower. The British press emphasized the multinational composition of the strike force and gave equal coverage to North Korean accusations of nonmilitary damage, while also noting the irony that antiaircraft guns surrounding the "undefended city" claimed to have downed ten UN aircraft. The *Times* of London observed, with some optimism and surprise, "The signs are that, in spite of the bombing, the enemy has become more eager for a ceasefire." An Asian delegate to the UN summed up the fears of his regional representatives there: "It seems to me to be a dangerous business, this policy of mass air attacks while the truce talks are going on. Knowing the Chinese, I think it likely that they would regard the signing of an armistice under such military pressure as a loss of face." Chinese representatives in Delhi characterized the air attacks as "19th-century gunboat tactics" and assured Indian diplomats that the operations would have no effect on Communist forces or negotiators. American press coverage played up the mass nature of the raids along with the fires and explosions they caused among stockpiled Communist supplies. It also highlighted the heavy defenses of the "peaceful city" and pointed out that civilians had received ample warning about the bombing. News-reels portrayed "a relentless attack on the city's rich military targets" by UN fighter-bombers of five nations, utilizing film footage provided by the Department of Defense. As with the hydroelectric complex attacks, American newspapers perceived the air activity as part of "a new initiative intended to demonstrate to the Communists that they have nothing to gain and much to lose by prolonging the present deadlock."[5]

Pyongyang was not the only North Korean city or town attacked during the air pressure campaign. A FEAF Operational Policy Directive, dated July 10, 1952, outlined the new Air Attack Program to all subordinate units, and they moved swiftly to comply. Task Force 77 also participated. More than thirty joint "maximum effort air strikes" against key industrial objectives were conducted by Navy and FEAF aircraft in the second half of 1952. Targets included supply, power, manufacturing, mining, oil, and rail centers. On July 20, Fifth Air Force B-26s began night attacks on enemy communications centers using incendiary and demolition bombs as part of Operations Plan 72–52, designed to destroy "supply concentration points, vehicle repair areas and military installations in towns where damaged buildings were being utilized." To increase the effect of the air attacks, beginning on July 13, Psychological Operation Strike dropped leaflets on seventy-eight towns warning civilians to get away from military targets. Illustrations depicted North Korean transportation routes and support facilities. The text announced that the UN Command knew where all military targets were and wanted to protect innocent civilians. They were advised to leave immediately with their families and friends and to stay away from the danger area for days because of delayed-action bombs. In addition to the 1.8 million psywar leaflets dropped by Fifth Air Force between July 13 and 26, Radio Seoul broadcast a series of warnings before each night attack advising civilians in the specific target area to seek shelter. Newsreels called the bombing operation a "warn 'em, sock 'em campaign." A press release issued on August 5 from Lt. Gen. Glen Barcus, commander of the Fifth Air Force, announced the widespread attacks and explained that the radio notices and leaflet campaign were a "concerted humanitarian effort at reducing civilian population casualties." The release brought protests from the State Department, which feared that the warnings and bombing operations might be exploited by enemy propaganda and would harm the UN position in world opinion. Weyland, who believed that few useful targets remained in North Korean cities and towns anyway, relayed Washington's and General Clark's concerns about the release to the embarrassed Barcus, who said he got the idea from Weyland's own public information officer![6]

The press releases stopped and the mass Strike warnings were curtailed, though occasionally civilians were still given advance notice of some raids. But the bombing of North Korean towns and cities continued unabated. Even the B-29 Superfortresses of Bomber Command joined in the attacks on communication centers. By early 1953, Bomber Command considered small cities and towns the last vulnerable link in the supply system for the Communist armies. Intelligence reported them all taken over as supply and troop centers, and they were too heavily defended for daylight attacks by lighter bombers. Contrail problems and bright moonlight that helped night interceptors limited operations along the Yalu to one week a month, so the medium-range bombers spent most of their time hitting airfields and communication targets in the rest of North Korea.

III

General Clark was very pleased with the strikes against the hydroelectric plants and Pyongyang and was anxious to continue the air pressure campaign. Weyland gave him a detailed briefing on FEAF target selection in late July 1952 and explained that they did not expect to find any targets in North Korea comparable in importance to the power facilities. The key military installations in most towns and cities had already been hit, and "incidental to the destruction of those military objectives," in Weyland's estimation, "the destruction of the towns and cities ranged from forty to ninety per cent." He said he could wipe out the rest of the urban areas, but he was loath to do so because they were "primarily residential." Clark agreed; "he did not himself want to recommend the complete destruction of these towns." Weyland then covered the remaining target possibilities: previously off-limits cities near the Soviet border and some metallurgy plants and installations. Clark offered to check into remaining JCS restrictions about the port of Rashin and also accepted a Weyland memorandum that asked the JCS to give him authority to conduct preemptive strikes against Manchurian airfields "if it became evident that the Communists were about to launch a major attack against our installations." Weyland did not expect Clark to submit the request, nor for the JCS to grant it, but Clark did authorize photographic reconnaissance missions by an RF-80 and two RF-86s over Manchurian airfields that were executed on August 1.[7]

Some members of the FEAF staff remained skeptical about the shift from interdiction to destruction, most notably Brig. Gen. Charles Banfill, Weyland's deputy for intelligence. In late August he sent Smart a detailed memorandum, claiming, "Factors restricting the successful application of this program are of such a nature as to make results commensurate with the cost extremely doubtful." Banfill outlined the flaws in the program: the enemy had moved most industrial facilities into a "safety zone" in the northeast that was heavily defended and out of range for Fifth Air Force fighter bombers and radar navigation stations; other, smaller targets had been moved underground, and the principal sources of supply and most important strategic targets were outside Korea's borders. Banfill lamented, "We are somewhat in the position of trying to starve a beggar by raiding his pantry when we know he gets his meals from his rich relatives up the street." He was concerned that while FEAF aircraft searched for the few lucrative targets to destroy, unrestricted enemy transportation was allowing Communist forces to increase their artillery fire by a factor of ten, thereby tripling UN casualties. He concluded, "Although rail interdiction may not prove decisive, statistical evidence indicates that immediate resumption of the rail interdiction program is warranted [to limit enemy resources at the front]."[8]

Smart sent back an equally detailed reply explaining his rationale for the new program. While conceding that "the majority of medium bombardment targets remaining throughout North Korea appear[ed] to be of marginal value," he argued that attacking them was still more useful than interdiction. Political and military restrictions combined with a static battle front to make an effective program of interdiction "almost impossible of execution." The new policy had elicited "a more telling response from the enemy," as evidenced by "references to [American] 'savagery' by even the Communist armistice delegation." He interpreted the increase in enemy artillery fire as "a retributive reaction to our present pattern of air action, rather than the expenditure of a handy surplus accumulated since the curtailment of our interdiction program." If that was true, goading the enemy into action would increase supply requirements and generate some "truly remunerative air targets." He concluded, "I feel that the purpose of any air action is to bring about defeat of the enemy as expeditiously as possible, not merely to complicate his maintenance of a position in which demonstrably he not only can support but actually can replenish himself, despite our efforts to prevent his doing so." However, interdiction was only de-emphasized, not prohibited, while air pressure was applied "against an expanded target spectrum."[9]

Once in a while throughout 1952, FEAF did manage to find some lucrative industrial targets to hit. They attacked mining facilities and struck remnants of North Korean industry that were mostly concentrated along the Soviet and Manchurian frontier. As Banfill had pointed out, many of these targets were out of range of Fifth Air Force jets. When Bomber Command conducted its last great daylight raid against the Kowon marshaling yard in October, Banshees from navy carriers had to serve as escorts. Usually, however, naval aircraft acted alone to hit such objectives. The largest carrier strike of the war occurred in September when 142 planes from three carriers destroyed the Aoji oil refinery and attacked other industrial areas at Munsan and Ch'ongjin. These targets were in an area less than five miles from Manchuria and eleven from the USSR, and the raids caught enemy fighters and flak defense completely by surprise. This time the British were notified a few days before the attacks, and they agreed the objectives were valid military targets.

In his messages to the JCS in late 1952, General Clark continued to emphasize "firmness in negotiations to be supported militarily by continued heavy bombing attacks." The JCS agreed: "The principal factor favorable to the [UN Command] in the present military situation on Korea is the air superiority which the UNC forces hold over North Korea." It deprived the Communists of the ability to support larger forces, enabled outnumbered UN ground forces to hold their positions, and constituted the most potent means to pressure the enemy into agreeing to acceptable armistice terms. At one time JCS Chairman Gen. Omar Bradley and Air Force Chief of Staff Gen. Hoyt Vandenberg even proposed to try to intimidate China with a mass B-29 raid aimed at Shanghai. The formation would come close enough to get picked up on radar and then "veer off about fifteen miles away and fly down the coast." The State Department discouraged the gambit, however, fearing that such a "show of force might boomerang" with Allies and world opinion. At the same time agencies in Washington and the Far East continued to worry about a Communist air buildup that threatened UN air superiority. The Central Intelligence Agency noted an increase in aircraft based in Manchuria and declared, "Soviet participation in enemy air operations is so extensive that a *de facto* air war exists over North Korea between the UN and USSR." Ironically, by mid-1952 coordination between the Communist Chinese Air Force and their Soviet mentors had almost completely broken down, but Department of Defense concerns that the Russians were really running the Communist air war became great enough that the secretaries of the air force and army tried to persuade the State Department to allow more publicity about Soviet personnel fighting directly against American forces. Planning also continued on actions to be conducted in case negotiations broke down or the war escalated. Far East Command and the JCS considered air options, including attacks on the USSR, the use of atomic or chemical weapons, and bombing of Chinese airdromes and communication centers.[10]

In the meantime they also remained alert for any signs that the air pressure campaign might be working. In September, Clark transmitted an intelligence report to the JCS that bombing was breaking down civilian morale in North Korea. Cities and towns that had been subjected to UN air attacks were bordering on panic. Civilians who had joined labor battalions because of job and food shortages or conscription were now deserting to return to their homes. They believed that air attacks were really the prelude to a UN general offensive to end the war. The report also noted that the North Korean government was afraid air attacks would motivate many civilians to join UN guerrillas. Further information provided to the FEAF Target Committee added that the Communist government had to send special agents to help control the unrest in those cities hardest hit by UN air blows. Clark's optimistic assessment was seconded by the ambassador to Japan, but one old report was not enough to persuade the State Department or JCS that an armistice was imminent. They continued to look for other signs that air pressure was producing results. Initial optimism waned as peace talks dragged on through 1952 and into 1953, and the search continued for some way to apply more effective airpower to produce an acceptable armistice.

Clark and his subordinates continued to grapple with how best to execute this new concept of "employing air forces as the single strategic offensive in a war." The JCS supported their efforts and, except for delaying an attack on a major supply complex at Yangsi because of a nearby prisoner exchange, approved all of Clark's target requests, including more attacks on hydroelectric plants. However, the JCS prohibited any public statements announcing the intent of such operations to pressure the Communists into an agreement, fearing that if Communist prestige became "seriously engaged" they would find it difficult to accept any armistice. High-level statements had to treat the air attacks as routine operations "based upon solely military grounds." Ironically, the more the raids aimed to achieve a political settlement, the less this could be admitted publicly as their justification.[11]

Destroying the last major target system in North Korea would be hard to justify as "solely military." In March 1953, the FEAF Formal Target Committee began to study the irrigation system for 422,000 acres of rice in the main agricultural complexes of South Pyongan and Hwanghae. The deployment of North Korean security units to protect key reservoirs from guerrillas during the growing season indicated the importance of those targets to Banfill. His staff estimated that destroying the rice crop would cause a food shortage, tie up transportation routes importing rice from China, and require the diversion of troops for security and repair efforts. Clark advised the JCS that in case of a prolonged recess in the peace talks, he planned to breach twenty dams to inundate the two areas and destroy an estimated 250,000 tons of rice, "thereby curtailing the enemy's ability to live off the land and aggravating a reported Chinese rice shortage and logistic problem."[12]

That was not the only proposal to escalate the air war. Weyland held back a Bomber Command attack that "would effectively [have] obliterated what remains of the city of Pyongyang" for possible later use, as another means to ratchet up pressure if necessary. He also appears to have doubted the military utility of the attack, just as he was "skeptical of the feasibility and desirability" of the attacks on the rice irrigation system. However, his planners convinced him to authorize attacks on three dams near important railways to wash away the lines as part of the interdiction program, even though among themselves they considered that rationale a "mode of deception" to deceive the enemy about the true objective of destroying the rice crop. Fifth Air Force fighter-bombers hit the Toksan and Chasan Dams in mid-May, one of the most vulnerable times for newly planted rice, followed by Bomber Command night missions against Kuwonga Dam. Clark informed Washington that these missions had been "as effective as weeks of rail interdiction."[13]

The JCS quickly approved the bombing of two more dams by fighter-bombers to inundate jet airfields at Namsi and Taechon. The draft armistice agreement provided that the number of combat aircraft allowed within Korea for each side could not exceed the number in place on the effective date of the armistice, and Clark worried that the Communists intended to sneak high-performance aircraft into North Korea just prior to that day, possibly taking advantage of marginal weather during the rainy season. His intelligence had noted an increased pace of airfield construction and intensive repair efforts after raids. Smart suspected that the airfields were just decoys to distract UN bombers from more valuable targets, but Bomber Command hammered them at night and fighter-bombers hit them by day. Clark knew that further dam attacks risked a negative reaction from the Allies and might affect the armistice negotiations, but he and Weyland believed the missions had to be conducted to eliminate the airfields.

Contrary to Clark's expectations, the dam attacks attracted very little notice in the world press. American newspapers were preoccupied with the exploits of the jet aces, and each MiG that was downed received more coverage than any bombing raid. The biggest war story in May was whether Capt. Joseph McConnell or Capt. Manuel Fernandez would hold the record for air-to-air victories. Ironically, many of those MiG kills were happening over China, in contravention of official policy and unknown to the press but another sign of possible escalation of the war for Communist observers. FEAF press releases dutifully reported attacks by F-84s on the earthen dams and mentioned that the Kuwonga Dam hit by B-29s was close to key rail and road bridges. North Korea decried what they considered barbarous attacks on peaceful water reservoirs that were not military objectives, but no one seemed to notice. Perhaps like the boy who cried "Wolf," the Communist complaints about UN air atrocities just were not being taken seriously anymore. Or perhaps since no mention was made of targeting rice crops, reservoirs did not seem to merit any consideration in the press as particularly promising or questionable objectives.

The last few FEAF Formal Target Committee meetings were dominated by discussion about how best to exploit dam attacks. New ideas included proposals to use delayed-action bombs to deter repair efforts and to drop leaflets blaming the continuing air attacks and the loss of water for irrigation on the Chinese Communists. Weyland was adamant that the dam attacks were for interdiction purposes; he vetoed a proposal by Smart for a psychological warfare campaign warning farmers and populations below all the dams in North Korea of their imminent destruction.

Although Weyland and Clark justified the dam attacks as interdiction raids, neither their planners nor the Communists perceived them that way. The Toksan and Chasan attacks flooded two key rail lines and many roads, but they also inundated nearby villages and rice fields. The flash flood from Toksan scoured 27 miles of river valley, and both raids sent water into the streets of Pyongyang. Bomber Command delayed its attack long enough so that the North Koreans were able to develop countermeasures, and by lowering the level of water in the reservoir they were able to avoid the catastrophic results of the first two raids. This tactic also worked for the last two dams. The Communists put more than 4,000 laborers to work repairing the Toksan Dam and emplaced antiaircraft defenses around it.

Weyland was amazed at the speed of enemy recovery operations. Only thirteen days after the strike they had completed a temporary dam and all rail repairs. When Clark queried him as to what targets were left to exert more pressure for an armistice, the all-out blow on Pyongyang was all that came to mind. Clark had Weyland prepare a message to solicit JCS approval for the raid, but it was never sent.

The UN's resorting to such extreme measures as the dam attacks might have alarmed the enemy enough to influence their negotiating position to some degree. The war was a significant issue in the 1952 U.S. presidential campaign. Candidate Dwight Eisenhower had boldly, but vaguely, declared in October that he "would go to Korea," and as president-elect he did visit in December. He had a clear mandate from the electorate to end the war honorably, and eventually he decided, as did Clark, that the Communists had to be coerced with the threat, or application, of more force. Eisenhower was prepared to lift restrictions on nuclear weapons in Korea, but there is no evidence that U.S. diplomats successfully transmitted that intent or that such warnings ever reached Soviet or Chinese leaders. Yet there were plenty of obvious signs that American patience was wearing thin and that the war might expand if it continued. Rumors about Eisenhower's threat to escalate military operations absent a ceasefire were rampant throughout Korea and would have been picked up by the Communists from spies or POWs. But many other factors also pressed the Communists to sign the armistice and give up their demand for forced repatriation of all POWs. Stalin's death and the continuing instability within the Kremlin combined with riots in Czechoslovakia and East Germany to give the Soviet Union plenty of incentive to disengage from Korea. Mao had another war to support in Indochina and was under pressure at home to direct more resources to economic development and liberating Formosa. Late gains on the ground against ROK troops allowed the Communists to save face while making concessions for the armistice.

Further delays might also have had other repercussions, including allowing South Korea's unpredictable Syngman Rhee to further disrupt peace efforts. Steadfastly against the armistice, the cantankerous president had threatened to detach the ROK Army from UN Command and continue the war, and in June he ordered ROK guards to free NKPA prisoners who did not want to be repatriated; 25,000 escaped, and the UN submitted a formal written apology, which Communist negotiators grudgingly accepted. A longer war would also have led to even heavier Communist casualties from the bombardment of UN artillery and aircraft. All these other factors probably influenced enemy decision makers more than threats of escalation, though the archival sources to make that determination adequately remain undiscovered or closed to researchers.

Instead of influencing armistice talks with any specific bombing operation, airpower's major contribution probably resulted from the accumulative massive punishment it delivered to Chinese armies and North Korean towns during the course of the war. Eighteen of twenty-two major cities were half-obliterated by bombs, and most villages were reduced to mounds of ashes. That is what the North Koreans remember most about American airpower, and their programs to develop missiles and weapons of mass destruction have been motivated to a large extent by the desire to deter any future applications of American air pressure.

Indeed, the biggest losers of the conflict were the two Koreas, both devastated by the war that raged over them and left frustrated by unfulfilled hopes for reunification on their terms. No formal peace treaty has ever been signed, so technically the war has not ended. Hundreds of Koreans and scores of Americans have died from border clashes and North Korean infiltration since 1953. Kim Il Sung pursued a low-intensity conflict across the Demilitarized Zone well into the 1970s and continued to seek support from his Communist allies for another invasion during that period. The Soviet Union also has to be classified as a loser, as it was widely perceived to have failed in its proxy war to expand Communist territory, while the seeds of the Sino-Soviet split were planted. Communist China perhaps gained most from the war, as it emerged as a powerful new player on the world stage that had stood up to the United States. The United Nations played a critical role in defending South Korea while avoiding World War III, but its reputation was not really enhanced by the effort, and it would never again act in an official capacity to defend a state from aggression during the Cold War.

The impact of the Korean War and the perceptions about its conclusion on the United States were profound. Truman's commitment of forces to a "police action" and his conduct of the conflict strengthened the power of the presidency, a common result of most American wars. The successful effort to preserve South Korea reinforced the logic of containment poli-cies, especially the military aspects, which were now globalized to cover parts of the world not considered in initial concepts. The war speeded the rearmament and development of NATO, along with a major shift in strategy to halt the Soviets in Europe with the rearmament of Germany and permanent stationing of major American forces there. This was part of a burgeoning Free World system of collective, forward defense that drew the United States into mutual security agreements with many Asian nations as well, including Japan, and increased support for the French war in Indochina. A decade later American military forces would be engaged in another war in Asia to limit yet another attempt to expand Commu-nist influence. After all previous American wars, the armed forces had been quickly and sharply reduced, but there was no massive drawdown in 1953. Cold war military expenditures continued to rise, and force levels remained relatively high until after the collapse of the Soviet Union and the conclusion of Operation Desert Storm. Americans learned to accept the existence of a permanently strong security establishment.

Eisenhower eventually became convinced that his nuclear threats were the main reason the Communists finally signed the armistice agreement.[14] That belief reinforced his emphasis on such weapons for his "New Look." The armed services also scrambled to increase atomic capacities. Strategic Air Command dominated the air force, and even its Tactical Air Com-mand came to focus primarily on delivering nuclear weapons with its fighter-bombers. The navy fought for its own piece of the atomic pie, with larger aircraft carriers and nuclear submarines. Even the army succumbed to the trend, pursuing atomic cannons and the pentomic division. When American advisors began to work with a new ally in Vietnam, they would use the ROK Army as their model, developing a force designed to resist a conventional invasion with firepower on a linear battlefield.

In the end, as with all wars, the results of the Korean conflict were mixed and muddied and far different from initial expectations on either side. South Korea was preserved to begin its meteoric rise to prosperity, while its battered northern counterpart became a pariah. The apparently monolithic Communist bloc began to splinter with the emergence of an assertive China. The perceived lessons of the war and its conclusion reinforced and expanded American containment policies and increased the resources and influence of the security establishment, but in such ways as to lead the nation into another Asian war with the wrong tools to fight it.

SUGGESTED READING

The standard work on American air operations in Korea is Robert F. Futrell's *The United States Air Force in Korea, 1950–1953* (Washington: U.S. Government Printing Office, 1983). This story has been updated with new scholarship and the best account of the air pressure campaign by Conrad Crane in *American Airpower Strategy in Korea, 1950–1953* (Lawrence: University Press of Kansas, 2000). The most thorough and up-to-date work on the Korean War as a whole has been done by Allan Millett in the first two volumes of his trilogy, *The War for Korea, 1945–1950: A House Burning* (Lawrence: University Press of Kansas, 2005) and *The War for Korea, 1950–1951: They Came from the North* (Lawrence: University Press of Kansas, 2010). Until his third volume is written, the best account of the war's final ground operations remains Walter G. Hermes's official U.S. Army history, *Truce Tent and Fighting Front* (Washington: U.S. Government Printing Office, 1966). That book also describes the complex negotiations at Panmunjom, as does William Stueck's *The Korean War: An International History* (Princeton: Princeton University Press, 1995), which presents a comprehensive view of the complex conclusion of the war and its international implications. For a description of how the Korean War affected the broader course of American security policies, see Allan Millett and Peter Maslowski, *For the Common Defense: A Military History of the United States of America*, revised and expanded ed. (New York: Free Press, 1994).

GIAN P. GENTILE

Vietnam: Ending the Lost War

In his first night in the White House, President Richard M. Nixon barely slept. He arose early, showered, and shaved. As he dragged the razor across his famously dark stubble, Nixon thought of a safe hidden in a room near the oval office that Lyndon B. Johnson had told him about during a postelection visit the previous November. Later that morning Nixon opened the safe and found a solitary, slender folder. It contained the president's daily "Vietnam Situation Report," which noted that during Johnson's last week in office 185 Americans had been killed and 1,257 had been wounded. As he replaced the folder, Nixon decided to keep it in the safe "until the war was over, a constant reminder of its tragic cost."[1]

During the first five months of his presidency, Nixon thought that he could win the war against North Vietnam militarily. He believed that if he created the perception of unpredictability—his "madman theory," bluffs and threats of massive force, possibly even of nuclear weapons—the North Vietnamese would end the war and withdraw from South Vietnam. But like everything else the United States tried in Vietnam, Nixon's ploy confronted the enemy's strident will. Over time, Nixon realized that threats would not be enough to bring American troops home. He needed something more. "Vietnamization," which Nixon announced as his new policy in June 1969, called for a buildup and training of South Vietnamese military forces so that they could take over the war as American soldiers withdrew.

Several weeks after his announcement Nixon traveled to Asia to welcome home the Apollo 11 astronauts as they splashed down in the Pacific.

On the island of Guam he delivered another foreign policy statement, an extension of the first. He declared that America's Asian allies would thereafter be responsible for their own internal defense against Communist aggression, adding, "Except for the threat of a major power involving nuclear weapons, . . . the U.S. is going to encourage and has a right to expect that this problem will be increasingly handled by and the responsibility for it taken by, the Asian nations themselves."[2] This new policy soon came to be known as the Nixon Doctrine and expanded beyond Asia to other regions of the globe. The United States would continue to provide support and assistance to its allies in Asia and elsewhere, Nixon promised. However, that support would be limited to economic and material assistance and military advisors, but would not extend to direct deployment of American combat troops as in Vietnam. It was an admission that Americans were no longer willing, in the words of Nixon's old adversary, John F. Kennedy, "to pay any price, bear any burden" to sustain the freedom of its allies in the face of Communist aggression.

The Vietnam War is the only unmitigated failure in American military history. Because it detracted from vital national interests both foreign and domestic, it was a war that should never have been fought. With no critical interest at stake the United States injected troops piecemeal into the war, reflecting a failure to formulate an effective strategic balance of ends, ways, and means. Its allies, the government of South Vietnam and the Army of the Republic of Vietnam (ARVN), suffered from poor leadership and rampant corruption that crippled their capacity to develop a skilled military force. By contrast, the North Vietnamese and their South Vietnamese allies, often referred to as the Viet Cong, exhibited a deep moral commitment to their war aims that made them formidable and finally invincible. With no sound policy or strategic logic the United States never matched that commitment. Setbacks, frustration, losses, and ultimately disillusionment with the South Vietnamese government and its military compelled an agonizing, costly withdrawal that took far too long. For years vain hopes of ending the war with the nation's honor intact, either through a miraculous military victory or an acceptable interval between American departure and South Vietnamese collapse, kept the United States from withdrawing unilaterally. After the fateful Tet Offensive of 1968 the United States failed to discern that the war was lost and to terminate it as quickly as possible.

In the end the war claimed some 58,000 American lives, 20,000 after the declaration of Vietnamization and the Nixon Doctrine, as well as millions of Vietnamese from both sides. The war's greatest legacy has been the recurrence of a persistent question every time the government contemplates sending military forces into harm's way: Will this be another Vietnam?

I

The path to American involvement in Vietnam began at the end of World War II. After that war France attempted to reestablish control over its former Indochinese possessions of Cochin China, Annam, and Tonkin, as well as Cambodia and Laos. However, between 1946 and 1954, Vietnamese nationalists under Ho Chi Minh resisted recolonization and fought to expel the French. Because the Vietnamese resistance, the Viet Minh, was led by Communists, the United States saw in them further proof of a worldwide Soviet effort to take over the "free countries of Asia." The logic of the Cold War strategy of containment demanded American action to oppose Soviet expansion. By 1947, the United States had begun to read into Soviet actions and rhetoric a global strategy to chip away at "free world" countries in search of worldwide dominance. A leftist insurgency in Greece, Mao Zedong's 1949 Revolution in China, and then the North Korean invasion of South Korea in 1950 all seemed to confirm American suspicions.

The United States provided about 75 percent of the funds and material for the French effort in Indochina. Yet by the spring of 1954 the French Army, surrounded and besieged by the Viet Minh at Dien Bien Phu, urgently asked the United States for firepower support, including nuclear weapons, to stave off defeat. Unwilling to commit American combat power to preserve a colonial empire, President Dwight D. Eisenhower refused. The French were defeated and, under Eisenhower's prodding, agreed to sign a peace treaty with the Viet Minh in 1954. The Geneva Accords split the country in two, leaving Ho Chi Minh and the Viet Minh in control north of the 17th Parallel and a U.S.-allied, nationalist government south of it. This division was meant to be temporary, pending national elections to be held in 1956. Even the physical separation was untidy as the partition left a substantial number of Viet Minh in South Vietnam, who came to be known as the Viet Cong. When President Ngo Dinh Diem of South Vietnam balked at holding the promised elections, the Viet Minh launched an insurgency against the government in Saigon.

In 1955, the United States began providing military advice and assistance to Vietnam, becoming a fourth major party in the conflict. Ostensibly the political aims of the four warring sides remained constant throughout the war. The North Vietnamese wanted to produce a social revolution in the South and reunify all of Vietnam under Ho Chi Minh's regime. The Viet Cong, also called the National Liberation Front (NLF), sought to foment revolution in the South, overthrow the Saigon regime, unify the country under a Communist government, and, when the United States entered the war, expel U.S. forces from Vietnam. The North Vietnamese and Viet Cong, allies throughout the long and costly war, generally agreed on the overarching goal of unifying Vietnam, but often disagreed sharply on the ways and means to achieve it. South Vietnam's main political aim was to maintain the sovereignty of its government and to expel its North Vietnamese and Viet Cong enemies. The fourth side, the United States, aimed to maintain a viable, effective, and non-Communist South Vietnamese government. Richard Nixon, the American president during the final years of the war, publicly held to the aim of maintaining the existence of the South Vietnamese government, but privately his thinking changed to the point that he was willing to accept a reasonable period between the time of American withdrawal—a "decent interval"—and the certain collapse of the South Vietnamese regime.

From 1954 to the beginning of substantial American commitment of conventional ground and air forces in 1965, the American role in Vietnam was largely to advise and support the South Vietnamese government and military. From 1956 to 1958, Diem aggressively pursued the NLF and nearly defeated them. But in 1959, North Vietnam authorized the insurgents to resume armed struggle against Diem's regime and provided them considerable material support. Meanwhile, Diem's regime came under increasing pressure from elements in the South seeking major societal and governmental reforms. That pressure, combined with revived Viet Cong activity, produced a series of tactical defeats for the ARVN. In November 1963 a group of ARVN generals (with tacit American approval) launched a coup that killed President Diem. The coup only exacerbated government instability and allowed the Viet Cong to make further gains. In late 1964 the North Vietnamese Army (NVA) began to reinforce the Viet Cong in large numbers. By the end of the year, the South Vietnamese regime was on the brink of collapse.

II

In August 1964, the Johnson administration alleged that on two occasions North Vietnamese naval vessels had launched unprovoked attacks on American ships in the Tonkin Gulf. However, the first was not unprovoked and the second never occurred. President Johnson used the alleged incident to ask Congress for authorization to take military action against the North Vietnamese. The Gulf of Tonkin Resolution, authorizing "all necessary measures to repel armed attacks," passed by near unanimous margins within days, freeing Johnson to prosecute the war with little congressional oversight or public scrutiny. Johnson coasted to election victory a few months later, having repeatedly insisted during the campaign, "We seek no wider war." Yet in February 1965 the United States began a three-year bombing campaign against North Vietnam called Rolling Thunder. A few weeks later Gen. William C. Westmoreland, U.S. commander of Military Advisory Command—Vietnam (MACV), requested deployment of marines to protect the bombers' bases. With little fanfare and no acknowledgment that the introduction of ground forces constituted a major policy shift, Johnson ordered a major deployment into the theater. Two battalions of U.S. Marines arrived in early March to defend airfields but gradually began offensive operations. In July, the United States initiated a major buildup of combat forces.

With this escalation Johnson and Secretary of Defense Robert McNamara sought to pressure North Vietnam to end its military operations in South Vietnam and its support of the Viet Cong. Over the next three years, Westmoreland repeatedly requested more troops and airpower. Johnson temporized, usually ordering escalations, but never as much as Westmoreland wanted. Nevertheless, the American commitment incrementally grew, reaching a peak of 550,000 troops in early 1969. That commitment weakened U.S. forces in Europe and placed ever greater demands on the home front for volunteers and conscripts. The draft and the war kindled a peace movement, which grew apace with Westmoreland's command in Vietnam.

Johnson often referred to Vietnam as "that bitch of a war." He would have preferred not to fight it, but felt bound by Cold War logic and a potential threat from the political right not to "lose" Vietnam, as Truman was said to have "lost" China. Johnson's greater "love," as he sometimes quipped, was his domestic reform agenda, called the Great Society.[3]

But the lives of the harlot and his sweetheart were inextricably intertwined. Domestic political pressures stemming from Cold War sensibilities demanded that Johnson stand firm against Communist expansion in order to gain the political support necessary to carry out his domestic reforms. He was unable to make hard decisions—to mobilize the reserves, to force the South Vietnamese government to reform, to commit fully to the war, or to explain his policy clearly to the American people. Instead he dithered and agonized.

Between Johnson's escalation in 1965 and the Tet Offensive in 1968, the United States and its South Vietnamese allies fought three simultaneous wars. One was an aerial campaign against North Vietnam and the infiltration routes along the Ho Chi Minh Trail through Laos. Another was a war of attrition by the U.S. Army and Marines against the North Vietnamese and Viet Cong armies in South Vietnam. U.S. forces conducted massive sweeps of areas thought to contain North Vietnamese Army and Viet Cong units. If they found their quarry, American commanders would employ devastating combinations of artillery and aerial bombing to destroy the enemy. Using these "search and destroy" tactics, Westmoreland hoped to achieve a "crossover" point, a sustained level of combat losses that the North Vietnamese would find impossible to replace. Yet the North Vietnamese never seemed to run out of men. Moreover, Johnson forbade a geographic broadening of the ground war into Cambodia, Laos, or North Vietnam. With good reason he feared Soviet or Chinese retaliation and a broader Cold War confrontation if the war expanded farther into Indochina. Both the USSR and China provided political and material support to North Vietnam, and the Chinese had proven in Korea that they would intervene if war came too close to their borders. Therefore, Westmoreland had to restrict his ground operations to South Vietnam proper and could not attack enemy bases across the border, in effect ceding the enemy a sanctuary for threatened forces and relatively secure lines to bring in supplies and reinforcements. The third war was a pacification campaign, at first conducted mostly by the government of South Vietnam with U.S. support, which aimed to wrest the loyalty of the countryside from the Viet Cong. Success was a dubious prospect because of the political alienation of most of the rural populace from the corrupt and incompetent government of South Vietnam.

By the end of 1967 the war had reached a deadlock. The United States had committed enough military power to keep the South Vietnamese government from collapsing, but not enough to force North Vietnamese withdrawal. Neither could the Americans pacify major portions of the countryside. To tilt the balance, the North Vietnamese and Viet Cong launched a major offensive on January 31, 1968, the Vietnamese New Year's Day commonly referred to as Tet. Their objectives were to weaken the South Vietnamese government and inspire a popular uprising in the South. They also hoped to force the United States to negotiate, halt bombing in the North, and perhaps abandon the war. Viet Cong units, assisted by the NVA in certain areas, attacked provincial and district capitals, major cities, and other key government facilities. Although initially caught off guard, the Americans and South Vietnamese responded quickly and defeated the assaulting forces, inflicting heavy losses over the next few weeks and months.

Tet was the terminal campaign of the Vietnam War. The North Vietnamese and Viet Cong lost the Tet Offensive: no popular uprising occurred and the Viet Cong would take years to recover from its horrendous losses. Yet the strategic and political setbacks for the United States were far more profound. Popular American dissent against the war had begun in earnest in 1967. Tet breathed new life into the protest movement and caused a broad segment of the populace to question whether the war was winnable. Doubt quickly hardened to conviction, and a vocal American plurality no longer supported the war. The CBS News anchorman Walter Cronkite, sometimes called the most trusted man in America, broadcast a rare editorial in which he told his viewers, "We are mired in stalemate [in Vietnam]." Senators Eugene McCarthy and Robert F. Kennedy, vying to lead a growing antiwar movement, challenged President Johnson for the 1968 Democratic presidential nomination. Johnson stunned the nation by announcing that he was withdrawing from the race in order to focus on the war effort. Republican Richard Nixon won the election partly on the strength of a "secret plan" to end the war. By the time he took office it became politically imperative to begin to withdraw American forces from Vietnam.

After Tet the United States faced a strategic dilemma. As long as it sustained the South Vietnamese government militarily it could not lose the war, but neither could it win at the moral and material price it was willing to pay. A stalemate existed, but not in a parity of will between the warring sides. American faith in the war effort was seriously eroding. The same was not true of the enemy. In the summer of 1969 the North Vietnamese government reaffirmed its consistent war aim: to obtain the "objectives of the Revolution in the South, namely independence [and] the unification of [the] country." Reflecting this commitment, a Viet Cong fighter in the Mekong Delta noted that despite the "artillery and big sweeps" by the Americans and ARVN the "cadres [were] able to stick it out." He believed that the Americans and the South Vietnamese government were unable to establish lasting political bonds with the people because they pacified by "force" and had not "won the hearts and minds of the people." A former South Vietnamese army officer, Hoang Ngoc Lung, later explained that the NVA and NLF did not win the war through superior tactics and operations, but by a "coherent, long-term, immutable devotion to a strategy that assumed, without question, that victory would come eventually to their side." The enemy fought a total war that the South Vietnamese and Americans "could not match . . . with any theory of war that they were prepared or willing to follow."[4]

III

Nineteen sixty-eight was a year of Cold War drama and American tragedy. Just a few days before the start of the Tet Offensive the North Koreans seized a U.S. spy ship, the *Pueblo,* which had been patrolling off their coast, causing a yearlong diplomatic wrangle. In August the Soviet Union invaded Czechoslovakia and brutally quashed an incipient democratic movement while the United States and its Western European allies floundered for an appropriate response. Combined with the Tet Offensive, Americans began to feel powerless in the face of a string of setbacks. At home they reeled from the assassinations of two beloved leaders, the civil rights champion Martin Luther King Jr. and presidential candidate Senator Robert F. Kennedy, brother of the slain president. Washington, Los Angeles, and Chicago convulsed in race riots. Popular demonstrations involving students and many others rallied against the war. And in August the Democratic National Convention descended into chaos on the convention floor and in the streets of Chicago. The country seemed on the edge of collapse.

Compared to the Viet Cong, U.S. and ARVN forces were militarily strong in the beginning of 1969. The American military reached its peak strength early in the year, and the ARVN had gained confidence as a result of Tet. The South Vietnamese government renewed pacification programs in the countryside and rapidly spread their territorial forces into small outposts in hamlets and villages. But the North Vietnamese and Viet Cong adjusted effectively, withdrawing most main force units into secure base areas along the Cambodian and Laotian borders to begin the long process of rebuilding.

The American reaction to Tet was to turn the war over to the South Vietnamese. LBJ quietly began the policy change, denying requests for substantial troop increases and recalling Westmoreland from Vietnam. Shortly after Nixon took office he announced a policy of "Vietnamization," wherein the United States would focus on training, equipping, and strengthening the Republic of Vietnam Armed Forces (RVNAF) and gradually turn prosecution of the war over to them as American forces withdrew. In June 1969, Nixon announced the redeployment of 25,000 troops from Vietnam, the first of several incremental withdrawals that took place over the next four years. Vietnamization was not a campaign, but a process to modernize and improve the RVNAF's capabilities to combat its enemies without American assistance. American aerial and artillery firepower held the process of Vietnamization together and allowed it to proceed against the enemy. Without that firepower the RVNAF proved to be a house of cards. Meanwhile pacification, the final campaign of the war, failed.

Pacification had begun in earnest in 1967. The United States consolidated its advisory effort under a newly formed agency called Civilian Operations and Revolutionary Development Support (CORDS). Before then, pacification had been a poorly coordinated affair conducted mainly by the South Vietnamese government. Westmoreland's strategy of attrition had placed the main U.S. effort on finding and fighting the NVA and the Viet Cong main force units. Pacification was a lesser but important priority, wherein American forces supported the government of South Vietnam and its military. It was a program for armed nation building.

Pacification presented a daunting challenge because the Viet Cong controlled most hamlets and villages in 1967. However, the Viet Cong's heavy casualties during Tet and its operational withdrawal thereafter left a political vacuum in the countryside for the government of South Vietnam to exploit. Gen. Creighton W. Abrams, who succeeded Westmoreland as MACV commander in June 1968, pushed the South Vietnamese to launch the Accelerated Pacification Campaign. Begun in November 1968, the intensive, three-month effort aimed to establish security in as many hamlets and villages as possible, as well as creating local governments loyal to Saigon. The beginning of the Paris peace talks added urgency to the project, as the South Vietnamese hurried to sustain their claim of sovereignty over the countryside. Shortly after the campaign, a study concluded that of 1,317 targeted hamlets only about 15 percent remained under Viet Cong control.[5] Encouraged by apparent success, Abrams and his newly appointed CORDS director, William Colby, persuaded President Nguyen Van Thieu of South Vietnam to continue pacification programs for the next three years.

The perception of success was a chimera. Although the Viet Cong was weaker, the Saigon government had not won over the people. A military advisor in Hau Nghia province, Maj. Stuart Herrington, noted that pacification efforts were "building schools and clinics and the like, but the government still was viewed with basic cynicism." Herrington blamed "corruption at all levels [that] generally had the effect of angering the people." Moreover, military operations forced civilians from contested zones into "safe areas," skewing the results of pacification surveys. When engaged by Viet Cong forces, U.S. or ARVN commanders would respond with overwhelming firepower, often destroying homes and hamlets in the process. As Herrington observed, the only way for rural folk to protect themselves was to move to a "district capital" or "strategic hamlet." Thus the perception of pacification rested on the mass migration of civilians into camps policed and guarded by the government. A 1972 report indicated that 90 percent of the provinces had become "pacified," but the next year a CORDS history of the war noted that over the course of the war "seven million Vietnamese [were] forced to leave their homes due to military activities." The United States Agency for International Development concluded that in the cities of Da Nang, Qui Nhon, and Cam Ranh over 60 percent of the population were refugees who had entered between 1962 and 1972.[6]

Nonetheless, the combination of Viet Cong withdrawal to border sanctuaries and depopulation of the interior left Viet Cong units isolated. Viet Cong cadres lost access to large segments of the rural population. ARVN and American military operations, along with liberal applications of artillery and aerial bombing, took their toll on Viet Cong military strength. Thus the Viet Cong were significantly weaker by the time the U.S. military finally withdrew from Vietnam in February 1973.

Yet the Viet Cong were not defeated, and a critical core element remained, ready to emerge when conditions allowed. Pacification had failed to connect the rural South Vietnamese populace to their government in a moral and meaningful way.[7] American military leaders had no clear sense of Viet Cong resilience, its potential to reconnect with people in the countryside, or its capacity to assist their allies in North Vietnam. Unable to see the reality that the war was already lost, they came to believe in the chimera, a façade of victory through pacification behind which Vietnamization and American withdrawal continued.

In March 1970, Henry Kissinger, an American national security advisor and special negotiator, met with North Vietnamese representatives in a small, dingy apartment in Paris for secret talks to negotiate an end to the war. Le Duc Tho, Kissinger's North Vietnamese opposite number, summed up the bankruptcy of the American strategic position in Vietnam. Tho told Kissinger that the Vietnamese people had endured many hardships in years of war with the United States. Kissinger, nodding along, was caught off guard when Tho abruptly stated that North Vietnam had "won the war." Tho reiterated to an incredulous Kissinger, "We have won the war [and] you have failed." The American public, Tho noted, was demanding an end to the war and of U.S. policy "to withdraw from Vietnam while building up the South Vietnamese military to operate on its own." He added, "[Before the Tet Offensive] there were over a million U.S. and puppet troops, and you failed. How can you succeed when you let the puppet troops do the fighting? . . . How can you win?"[8]

The ancient Chinese philosopher of war, Sun Tzu, said, "Strategy without tactics is the slow road to victory, [but] tactics without strategy is the noise before defeat." The tactical application of American firepower supported the policy of Vietnamization and the campaigns of pacification, but the strategy that brought the three together was irrelevant in the face of a war that the United States had already lost. Gen. William Peers, commander in one of the four regions in South Vietnam, lamented that he was not sure whether to concentrate his efforts on pacification, Vietnamization, or fighting the NVA and Viet Cong. Peers summarized the bankruptcy of American strategy when he called for the military and Washington to "come up with a more structured plan, outlining concrete military objectives, matching them with political goals, and suggesting specific methods to achieve both."[9] Pacification was a chimera. Vietnamization was a policy of withdrawal, not a strategy for victory. The fact of that withdrawal, which had steadily been reducing American combat power since 1969, crippled MACV's capacity to fight the enemy. The tripartite approach was no strategy at all; it was gloss on a program intended to give the appearance of progress but that blinded its authors to the realization that the war was already lost. The noise of a bankrupt strategy grew deafening.

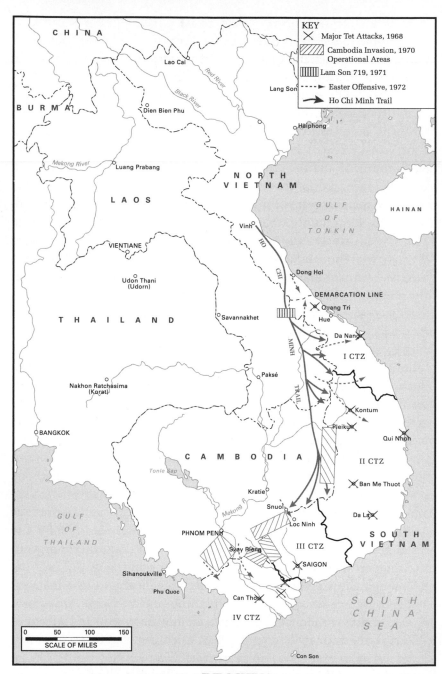

INDOCHINA

Map based on Richard W. Stewart, ed., *American Military History*, Vol. II,
The United States in a Global Era, 1917 - 2003 (Washington, D.C.:
Center of Military History, 2005)

IV

The Nixon administration and General Abrams held differing views of American objectives. By the end of 1969, having given up on the possibility of military victory, Nixon and Kissinger sought a negotiated end to the war. They saw firepower as a means to force the North Vietnamese to the peace table. Committed to an inchoate notion of "peace with honor," they privately hoped for a "decent interval" between America's final withdrawal and the likely capitulation of the Saigon regime. Kissinger acknowledged in a discussion with Le Duc Tho in July 1971 that the United States required a "transition period between the military withdrawal and the political evolution." He added, "Not so that we can reenter, but so that we can let the people of Vietnam . . . determine their own fate."[10] Abrams and his advisors viewed firepower as a means to help the South Vietnamese military defeat the enemy. The difference between those goals—winning or withdrawing—was profound evidence of civilian-military miscommunication of the first order. Over the final two years of American involvement in Vietnam that chasm between policy and strategy manifested itself in a series of major operations.

The first test of Vietnamization came with an American and South Vietnamese invasion of Cambodia in the spring of 1970. A new Cambodian government under Lon Nol was friendly to the United States and South Vietnam. With his acquiescence, the offensive aimed to destroy North Vietnamese supply lines and command posts just inside Cambodia's eastern border. The campaign plan called for a pincer movement, with American troops in the north and the ARVN in the south. The ARVN fought fairly well in the southern thrust against North Vietnamese Army units who stood and fought, but eventually withdrew to the northeast. Yet typically, American artillery and airstrikes proved to be crucial to success, often stiffening ARVN commanders' resolve or compensating for their lack of tactical skill.

Although the Cambodian invasion was a military success in terms of destroying enemy sanctuaries and disrupting supply lines, it was a political disaster in the United States. The invasion provoked mass protests across the country on many college campuses, demonstrations that turned deadly in May 1970, when National Guard troops shot and killed four students at Ohio's Kent State University. Public outcry over the Kent State shootings and the Cambodian invasion itself was dramatic. If Nixon had gained military space for Vietnamization by reducing NVA supplies, he only heightened the American public's desire to withdraw from Vietnam as quickly as possible. In June the U.S. Senate voted in angry defiance to revoke the Gulf of Tonkin Resolution of 1964.

About a year after the Cambodian invasion ARVN forces again attempted to disrupt NVA supply lines, this time without direct U.S. advisory help. The operation, Lam Son 719, targeted the Ho Chi Minh Trail in the Laotian panhandle. Hesitant and lethargic Vietnamese commanders allowed the offensive to grind to a halt almost as soon as it began. Without U.S. advisors coordinating American firepower, the offensive failed. The NVA reacted strongly, maneuvering regiments and divisions into positions on high ground that dominated the ARVN approach. After about six weeks President Thieu ordered a hasty and embarrassing withdrawal.

Nixon and Kissinger were angry, concerned that the failed operation had weakened their negotiating position. Abrams, acknowledging that the offensive had been a rocky affair, nonetheless deemed it a success because it showed that the Vietnamese could conduct a major maneuver operation on their own. He even went so far as to call Lam Son 719 "the only decisive battle of the war."[11] Even though he was managing the American withdrawal from Saigon, he was still hoping that American firepower could help the RVNAF win the war. Nixon and Kissinger wanted punishing applications of American firepower to gain an acceptable peace and a decent interval.

A few months after Lam Son 719, Nixon told Kissinger that as long as he had the U.S. Air Force he would employ it ruthlessly against North Vietnam. Pounding his fist on a desk, Nixon shouted, "We're gonna take out the dikes, we're gonna take out the power plants, we're gonna take out Haiphong, we're gonna level that goddamn country." Later, Nixon vented his frustration over North Vietnamese resistance to American conditions for ending the war. The president railed that if Hanoi did not give him the cease-fire agreement he wanted he would "bomb those bastards so that they lack the capability to take over South Vietnam."[12]

On March 31, 1972, the North had launched the Easter Offensive, a massive and multipronged invasion of South Vietnam that lasted three months. By that point the American military had drawn down to about 30,000 troops, mostly support personnel and advisors to the RVNAF. North Vietnam's goal was to split South Vietnam through the Central Highlands while launching assaults to capture important cities like Hue and Saigon. Although it made significant gains, the offensive ultimately failed in the face of American firepower delivered by air force and navy aircraft and adroitly coordinated by U.S. advisors.

The split between the Nixon administration and Abrams became acute during the Easter Offensive over the use of American B-52 bombers. Abrams, thinking in traditional, war-winning terms, employed B-52s to provide close air support to the ARVN and attack NVA lines of communication. Kissinger described Abrams as a senior military officer stuck in the "routine" of conventional warfare. He later opined that campaign objectives often became "obsessions" for commanders, suggesting that they were too immersed in operational processes to see the strategic picture. Nixon was especially critical, calling the military "timid." He wanted a bold stroke, demanding that the B-52s strike Hanoi and Haiphong Harbor with a vengeance in order to get better concessions at the negotiating table and to ensure a reasonable interval after U.S. departure. Nixon demanded that his generals get off their "backside and give [him] some recommendations as to how" to end the war through negotiated settlement and allow for American withdrawal. In the summer of 1972 he ordered a naval blockade of the North, the mining of Haiphong Harbor, and a merciless bombing of Hanoi.[13]

Shortly after the Easter Offensive a group of White House analysts sent to Vietnam asked the MACV staff critical questions about American strategy: How important was the role of firepower in defeating the North Vietnamese during the offensive? What would be the implication in future battles if that firepower were no longer available? The White House team was alarmed by the absence of "any long-range military planning" for the war after American forces had redeployed.[14] No one had given much thought to the RVNAF's capacity to survive without American firepower. American strategy looked no further than withdrawal, while planners gave lip service to the policy of Vietnamization that was to ensure an American "peace with honor."

By the end of 1972, North Vietnamese and American goals had begun to converge: both sides desired an American withdrawal from South Vietnam. North Vietnam hoped thereby to gain a military advantage that would allow it to overthrow the South Vietnamese regime. To be sure, unrelenting U.S. bombing in the North had devastating effects and weakened their will to continue the war. More important, however, was the North Vietnamese government's keen understanding of American political distress and desire to end the war as quickly as possible. Tho expertly employed that knowledge at the Paris talks.

Firepower halted the Easter Offensive, producing a stasis that induced each side to make concessions leading eventually to a peace settlement in January 1973. The United States agreed to withdraw from South Vietnam, and the North Vietnamese promised to return American prisoners of war. Parts of the North Vietnamese Army, some 150,000 men, remained in the South. With American withdrawal they had achieved a favorable balance of military forces. The treaty also recognized the National Liberation Front (which became known in 1969 as the Provisional Revolutionary Government) as a legitimate political entity in South Vietnam. And the North Vietnamese withdrew their long-standing demand for President Thieu's removal. But Thieu and his South Vietnamese government felt abandoned by the United States and questioned whether American firepower would be available if the NVA decided to attack again. The last American troops departed South Vietnam in March 1973.

The final North Vietnamese offensive began in March 1975. The collapse of the South Vietnamese government and military arrived with stunning speed. Between January 1973 and the 1975 offensives the NVA and Viet Cong forces cooperated effectively to harass the RVNAF and defeat them with decisive coordinated thrusts. Although there were instances of RVNAF valor, the superior NVA deftly outmaneuvered and overpowered them. The iconic image of U.S. helicopters lifting American and South Vietnamese people off a Saigon rooftop dramatized the fragility and ultimate bankruptcy of the Saigon regime in the absence of American support. On August 9, 1974, Richard Nixon had resigned in disgrace in the wake of the Watergate scandal. His successor, Gerald Ford, found it politically impossible to come to the aid of the South Vietnamese government. Congress had enacted several laws to prevent the president from sending matériel to the South. As commander in chief, however, President Ford chose not to employ American air and naval support to the RVNAF. Instead he arranged to place the immediate blame for Saigon's collapse on Congress by requesting aid he knew it would disapprove. Army Chief of Staff Gen. Frederick C. Weyand, observing in South Vietnam during the final months, reported that the only hope of halting the NVA offensive lay in the massive and unrestrained application of U.S. firepower.[15] Absent U.S. material or air support, the government of South Vietnam fell. The Vietnam war was over.

V

The United States and South Vietnam lost the war. NVA tanks rolling down the streets of Saigon refuted any other interpretation. The collapse of the South Vietnamese regime was a humiliating loss for America. The effects of that loss in the United States were profound and wide-ranging.

The United States failed politically and strategically in Vietnam. Large-scale engagement in a protracted Southeast Asian land war was never in America's vital interests. Indeed, it distracted the United States from the Cold War in Europe and caused concern among allies there about the strength of American commitment to NATO. The war sapped American strategic resources for the greater Cold War struggle. Lyndon Johnson placed prudent political constraints on the conduct of the war, given the possibility of a wider war with the Chinese or the Soviets. But those restrictions hamstrung military strategy by giving the enemy secure base areas and lines of communications in Laos and Cambodia. As a result, and because of the indomitable will of the North Vietnamese people and their Viet Cong allies, the war was not winnable at a material and moral cost that the United States was willing to pay. Given that the war was not in the national interest and that it was unwinnable, no strategy would have availed. The only sensible policy, then, was to end the war as quickly as possible with the smallest possible loss in blood and treasure. The painful truth for the United States was that the war was simply not worth the cost.

North Vietnam and the Viet Cong indisputably won the war. They maintained clear political objectives and adjusted strategy and operations appropriately, attacking when they were strong, retrenching when they were weak. They made mistakes, principally in the Tet Offensive of 1968 and the Easter Offensive of 1972, but their enemies could not profit from their errors. Throughout, the Viet Cong retained a measure of support in the countryside of South Vietnam. The corrupt South Vietnamese government was unable to break that hold on popular allegiance. Mostly the South Vietnamese insurgency and North Vietnam won because of their unwavering will to succeed and willingness to persevere through years of struggle.

The American armed forces had lost their first war. By the time they withdrew from South Vietnam they were weakened and the army was broken. The army's officer corps faced a crisis in morale and had lost confidence in its generals. Its noncommissioned officer corps had lost many of its senior leaders and was filled with rapidly promoted veterans. Drug abuse and indiscipline roiled the enlisted ranks. The army's material and organizational structure had atrophied from years of combat. Fundamentally the army had lost the ability to fight. By the early 1980s, however, the army was putting itself back together. It rewrote its operational doctrine, reorganized itself around new tanks, helicopters, and infantry fighting vehicles, and created a training program to prepare troops to fight and win the first battles of the next war. The U.S. Army demonstrated its recovery in Panama in 1989 and Iraq in 1991.

A controlling metaphor of the containment doctrine that drove U.S. entry into Vietnam was the "domino theory." Its logic held that if the United States allowed South Vietnam to fall to the Communists, other Southeast Asian nations would follow like a column of dominoes. They did not. After the war, apologists for America's loss in Vietnam argued that by fighting the war for so many years the United States had in fact buttressed other non-Communist nations in Southeast Asia, thereby preventing their fall. This argument rested on some very dubious reasoning. The first was the faulty premise that the USSR and China had the desire and the wherewithal to pursue military expeditions in other Southeast Asian countries, which they never manifested. A second assumption was that without U.S. intervention, Vietnam and China would have remained close allies in expanding Communism in the region, when in fact their competing national interests ultimately led to war in 1979. A third fallacy was the notion that the "domino" states of Southeast Asia were prone to fall to Communism, as if they had no say in the matter and their fate turned on American action. The argument was American hubris run amok.

The Vietnam War produced lasting, divisive effects on American society. In 1973, Congress passed the War Powers Resolution in reaction to what it saw as excessive presidential control of foreign policy, intending to rein in executive power to commit the American military to future wars. The law had negligible effect, but it heightened tensions over foreign policy for years thereafter. The drumbeat of misleading policy pronouncements and rosy progress reports by the Johnson and Nixon administrations and a series of senior military leaders fostered within the citizenry a profound distrust of government that resonates today. The war produced deep social rifts, beginning with the apparent radicalization of the peace movement, then with a conservative reaction that polarized American political culture. Nixon's "silent majority," which had purportedly remained quietly supportive of the war in the face of radical protests, now formed the nucleus of a conservative political movement that came to fruition in the 1980s.

During the war the question of who served and who fought became a key moral issue. Although in theory the conscription of Americans should have been blind to race and class, in practice, college deferments allowed young middle-class men to avoid military service, forcing a disproportionate number of men from lower-class and ethnic groups into the army to do the fighting. Some Americans chose to avoid military service by moving to Canada, while others found alternatives to serving in Vietnam by entering the Reserves or National Guard. The rift between those who served in Vietnam and those who did not exacerbated the political polarization of the following decades. Vietnam helped to bring about the end of the draft in 1973. Following that, the American military moved to an all-volunteer force that would be severely tested in the post-9/11 wars of Iraq and Afghanistan.

The Vietnam War also had a profound influence on America's role in the world. The *Washington Post* columnist David Broder noted on the eve of Saigon's collapse in March 1975, "Vietnam has left a rancid aftertaste that clings to almost every mention of direct military intervention."[16] Broder's "aftertaste" developed into a mentality of concrete avoidance of foreign military entanglements that became known as "the Vietnam syndrome." The lingering fear that any American military deployment would produce another Vietnam "quagmire" hung over the heads of policymakers and strategists. The syndrome influenced actions and reactions in American military operations in the 1980s in Grenada, Central America, and Panama and into the 1990s with the First Gulf War and subsequent interventions in Somalia and the Balkans. During the tactically successful 1991 Gulf War, American political and military leaders were often quoted as gleefully stating that the United States had "kicked" the Vietnam syndrome, meaning that America was again confident in its ability to apply military force in the world. Subsequent interventions would test whether those celebrations were premature.

One response to the Vietnam syndrome came in the form of a cohort of apologists and revisionists who became more vocal after the second American invasion of Iraq, in 2003. This school looked back to Vietnam and developed arguments that the war might have been won if only the army had had better generals and had been more adept at counterinsurgency tactics and operations. A "better war" narrative suggested that the war could have been won following a different approach, but that the U.S. government and the army chose not to pursue it and therefore lost the war. The argument placed primacy on the idea that in Vietnam good tactics could have rescued failed strategy and policy. Many in the defense and policy establishments applied that reasoning to the wars in Iraq and Afghanistan, implicitly arguing that those wars could be won by better tactics.

In the years since 9/11 the United States seems to have disregarded the object lessons of failed policy and strategy. American political and military leaders have argued that the country is in the middle of a "long war against terrorism," which is a policy that offers no end state and a strategy in search of an enemy. In the "long war" formulation there is no alternative to the persistence of conflict and endless deployments of American military power to the world's trouble spots.

Eight years after the fall of Saigon, Secretary of Defense Caspar Weinberger outlined a set of "tests" for the United States to apply when considering the use of military force. Weinberger's tests were also an implicit call to avoid another Vietnam "quagmire." The Weinberger Doctrine, as it came to be known, crystallized thinking around a national consensus to avoid another unwinnable war, although the consensus did not extend to his prescription. He insisted that, first, the United States should commit military forces only when vital national interests were at stake. Second, if the United States decided to commit, it should do so with overwhelming force and the "intention of winning." The third test was to always have "clearly defined political and military objectives." Fourth, the nation should continually assess the relationship between the size, composition, and disposition of the force committed and the assigned objectives. Fifth, there should always be a "reasonable assurance" that the American people would support the commitment of military force. Sixth, the United States should commit military forces as a "last resort."

But the Weinberger Doctrine was not a call to avoid the use of military force in the world. Instead it sought to create a framework for clear strategic thinking about where, when, and how to apply the American military in pursuit of national interests and policy goals. In that sense it still resonates today and can be seen as a conceptual approach to U.S. foreign policy that appreciates the limits of American power, while still acknowledging the key role that America has played and must continue to play in the world.

The history of the Vietnam War suggests that there are limits to what

American military power can accomplish. Some wars are not in the national interest. Some wars are not worth the cost, and when they are fought often become unwinnable based on the moral and material price to be paid. The Vietnam War, never in the national interest, quickly reached the point of being lost. Unfortunately, U.S. political and military strategists failed to perceive the reality and continued to apply an irrelevant strategy years beyond that point. The process of war termination, badly handled, can be every bit as damaging as the war itself, or more so. The miscalculations that got the United States into the Vietnam War persisted throughout, even intensifying, and poisoned the process of war termination and the peace that followed. The United States is still living with the ravages of the Vietnam War, as are Cambodia, Laos, and Vietnam. Indeed, the miscalculations that led to the Vietnam War and America's botched and bloody process for ending it look eerily familiar today.

The essential insight from Vietnam is that the crucial elements in war are not smarter tactics, better generals, or more malleable popular support, but clear-headed thinking about policy and strategy that aligns ways, means, and ends relative to our national interests and the potential of our enemies. In Vietnam, the United States failed that test.

SUGGESTED READING

Vietnam continues to generate vigorous scholarly debate. The best diplomatic-military history is still George C. Herring's *America's Longest War: The United States and Vietnam 1950–1975*, 4th ed. (New York: McGraw-Hill, 2001). For various interpretations of the war, see Gary R. Hess's *Vietnam: Explaining America's Longest War* (New York: Wiley-Blackwell, 2008).

For the final years of the war, see Jeffrey Kimball's excellent *Nixon's Vietnam War* (Lawrence: University Press of Kansas, 1998) and his *The Vietnam War Files: Uncovering the Secret History of the Nixon-Era Strategy* (Lawrence: University Press of Kansas, 2004); Jeffrey J. Clarke, *Advice and Support: The Final Years* (Washington: U.S. Army Center of Military History, 1988); James H. Willbanks, *Abandoning Vietnam: How America Left and South Vietnam Lost Its War* (Lawrence: University Press of Kansas, 2004); Gregory A. Daddis, *No Sure Victory: Measuring U.S. Army Effectiveness and Progress in the Vietnam War* (New York: Oxford University Press, 2011).

For the Vietnamese side of the war, see Robert K. Brigham, *ARVN: Life and Death in the South Vietnamese Army* (Lawrence: University Press of Kansas, 2006) and David W. P. Elliot's groundbreaking *The Vietnam War: Social Change in the Mekong Delta, 1930–1975,* 2 vols. (London: M. E. Sharpe, 2003).

On pacification and its failure, see Richard A. Hunt, *Pacification: The American Struggle for Vietnam's Hearts and Minds* (Boulder, CO: Westview Press, 1995); Eric M. Bergerud, *The Dynamics of Defeat: The Vietnam War in Hau Nghia Province* (Boulder, CO: Westview Press, 1991); Thomas L. Ahern Jr., *Vietnam Declassified: The CIA and Counterinsurgency* (Lexington: University Press of Kentucky, 2010). For a worthwhile study at the province level, see James Walker Trullinger Jr. *Village at War: An Account of Revolution in Vietnam* (New York: Longman, 1980).

Lewis Sorley advanced the "better war" thesis in *A Better War: The Unexamined Victories and Final Tragedy of America's Last Years in Vietnam* (New York: Harcourt Brace, 1999). Andrew J. Birtle effectively challenged Sorley in "PROVN, Westmoreland, and the Historians: A Reappraisal," *Journal of Military History,* October 2008.

On the Weinberger Doctrine, see Gail E. S. Yoshitani, *National Power and Military Force: The Origins of the Weinberger Doctrine, 1980–1984* (College Station: Texas A&M University Press, forthcoming).

GEORGE C. HERRING

The Cold War:
Ending by Inadvertence

Over the weekend of December 1–3, 1989, U.S. President George H. W. Bush and Soviet General Secretary Mikhail Gorbachev met in Marsaxlokk Bay, Malta, for the first Soviet-American summit at sea. The political climate was uncertain. In recent months, one-by-one, the USSR's Eastern European satellites had given way to reformist governments. That most conspicuous of Cold War symbols, the Berlin Wall, had been torn down, and the specter of a reunited Germany loomed over a nervous Europe. Bush's ascent to office in January had created what Soviet officials called a troublesome hiatus in Soviet-American relations, each leader uneasy about the firmness of the other's commitment to accommodation. The violent storms that struck Malta that weekend seemed to symbolize the dangers. Twenty-foot waves and gale-force winds compelled cancellation of meetings aboard the Soviet cruiser *Slava;* instead they were held on the elegantly refurbished cruise liner *Maxim Gorky,* safely docked in Valletta Harbor. Bush's life was actually in jeopardy on one occasion, when the launch taking him from the *Gorky* to his quarters aboard the USS *Belknap* was tossed about in perilous seas.

The appearance of sunlight as the dignitaries departed Malta hailed the significance of what happened there. The two leaders sparred over sensitive issues. Bush protested Cuban involvement in Central America. Gorbachev complained that the United States, while condemning the intervention of other nations, reserved for itself the right to intervene where it chose and claimed to be the sole arbiter of universal human rights. On the other hand, through promises of aid and trade, Bush offered tangible support for Gorbachev's *perestroika* reforms, leading one Soviet official to hail the end of economic warfare. Gorbachev insisted that the United States must remain in Europe, a stark contrast to the traditional Soviet position. As personal relationships warmed, the rhetoric of peace escalated. Gorbachev averred, "We don't consider you an enemy any more" and vowed that the Soviet Union "under no circumstances" would "start a war against the United States." At an unprecedented joint press conference the two men spoke of a new era of peace and cooperation, a "historic watershed." Although no agreements were reached, the so-called seasick summit proved a significant milestone. "[The] way of the Cold War has been defeated," Gorbachev concluded. "[The] world leaves one epoch . . . and enters another epoch."[1]

I

The term *Cold War* was coined by the American journalist Walter Lippmann in 1947 to describe the condition of neither war nor peace that characterized Soviet-American relations after the Second World War. This new kind of war resembled traditional power struggles between nation-states. But it was also a clash of ideas, and its ideological dimensions and global scope gave it a measure of distinction. It was unique in that the major combatants, in time each possessing nuclear weapons of enormous destructive force, chose to wage their struggle through propaganda, threats of force, diplomacy, and client states rather than by going to war with each other.

The Cold War stemmed directly from World War II. That epic conflict shattered the international system beyond recognition, leaving across the globe a broad swath of destruction and human misery, as many as sixty million people dead, cities in ruin, factories demolished or idle, roads and bridges destroyed, and fields untended. The war produced a sweeping redistribution of power. Germany and Japan lay devastated; Britain and France were exhausted financially and emotionally and reduced to second-rate powers. It also spurred powerful currents of nationalism that challenged the colonial empires that had been a standard feature of world politics for centuries. It left economic and political chaos throughout much of the world. At the same time technology, especially the advent of jet aircraft, dramatically shrank distances, making the globe a more intimate—and more dangerous—place. The production of new weapons of incredible destructive capacity aroused fears for humankind's survival.

Only the United States and the Soviet Union emerged from the war with the ability to exert influence beyond their borders (although the power of the former vastly exceeded that of the latter), and these nations were deeply divided by ideology. Communist dogma preached undying hostility to capitalism and fear of capitalist encirclement. Such suspicions seemed validated to Soviet leaders by Western intervention in Russia at the end of World War I, the diplomatic isolation of the Soviet Union in the postwar years, and the 1938 Munich Agreement, which left the USSR exposed to Hitler. Dictator Joseph Stalin's government had little option but to turn to the West after being invaded by Germany in June 1941, but it remained wary of its allies. Western leaders were equally suspicious. Americans despised Communism for its economic doctrines and its hostility to religion, which assailed vital parts of their own national character. Certain that the depression and World War II had been caused by failed economic doctrines, Americans believed that the postwar world must be rebuilt along liberal capitalist lines. Ideology was less important than national security concerns in causing the Cold War, but it influenced the way both powers looked at themselves, each other, and the world.

Not surprisingly, given the new international system and their conflicting ideologies, the two nations clashed over major postwar issues. Lacking natural boundaries, Russia throughout its history had been repeatedly invaded by external enemies. During both world wars Germany had inflicted horrendous destruction and loss of life. Stalin thus insisted that his nation should have "friendly" governments in Eastern and Central Europe to form a buffer against yet another German invasion. He also demanded that Germany be disarmed, de-industrialized, and even dismembered. U.S. President Franklin Roosevelt acknowledged Soviet security needs and increasingly recognized that the USSR would wield preeminent power in postwar Eastern Europe. But American leaders continued to insist that nations in the Soviet sphere must hold free elections and be open to trade with other countries. The United States and Great Britain also believed that German economic recovery was essential to rebuilding Western Europe. These questions could not be resolved during the war and formed the core issues over which the Cold War began.

Through a cyclical process that has been called "the security dilemma" each side's moves in Europe between 1946 and 1949 aroused fears that provoked countermoves by the other. The Soviet Union's takeover of Eastern Europe, its slow withdrawal from Iran, and its threats against Turkey stirred U.S. fears that Stalin sought further expansion, even perhaps into Western Europe. An economic crisis in that region and the possibility of Communist Party victories in elections in France and Italy prompted a strong response from Washington. The United States in 1947 began to implement a policy of containing Soviet expansion, first through the Truman Doctrine, which provided economic aid to Greece and Turkey, and then through the Marshall Plan, a major foreign aid program designed to rebuild Western Europe economically and stabilize it politically. Alarmed by Western initiatives and even fearing a possible assault on his Eastern European buffer zone, Stalin tightened his grip on Eastern Europe, placing loyal henchmen in power and brutally suppressing dissent. Through aid and trade programs Moscow bound the Eastern European economies tightly to its own. Most alarming to the West was a coup in Czechoslovakia in early 1948 that replaced a government desperately seeking to retain ties with both East and West with a hard-core Communist regime obeisant to Moscow.

For a moment in 1948 the Cold War adversaries seemed on the verge of hot war. Concerned about the prospect of a re-industrialized Germany under Western control, Stalin launched a risky gamble in July to drive the West from its Berlin enclave, sealing off access to the city by highway, rail, and water. Some U.S. officials spoke of war, but the Harry S. Truman administration took a more cautious course, supplying embattled West Berlin with an airlift of heroic proportions. A murderous tyrant at home, Stalin tended toward realism in foreign policy, and after months of acute tension he backed off. The most significant consequence of the Berlin blockade was the formation in 1949 of the North Atlantic Treaty Organization (NATO), a military alliance binding its members, the United States included, to come to each other's aid in the event of an attack. Soon after, the Soviet Union created the Warsaw Pact. Europe was divided into two hostile power blocs.

During the next four years the Cold War was globalized and increasingly militarized. The fall of China to Mao Zedong's Communists in the summer of 1949 stunned Americans, who had long seen that nation as a protégé and budding democracy. Revelations of Soviet espionage in the United States aroused additional fears, and the Soviet explosion of an atomic bomb suddenly eliminated America's atomic monopoly. A threat seemingly limited to Europe extended to East Asia. The global balance appeared to be shifting against the Western allies.

The outbreak of war in Korea in June 1950 had global ramifications. Mistakenly believing that the United States would not intervene, Stalin endorsed North Korean leader Kim Il Sung's proposal to invade South Korea. Misperceiving the invasion as a sign of Moscow's global ambitions, the United States quickly dispatched troops to South Korea. Briefly gaining the upper hand in the fall of 1950 and eager for a Cold War victory, Washington sent U.S. and South Korean troops to the Yalu River, provoking Chinese intervention in the war. By early 1951 the conflict had settled into a bloody slugfest back and forth across the 38th Parallel, the line dividing the two Koreas. Its consequences extended far beyond the Korean peninsula. By positioning the U.S. Seventh Fleet in the Taiwan Straits and sending military assistance to the French fighting a Communist-led nationalist revolution in Vietnam, the United States extended the containment policy to East and Southeast Asia. National Security Council Document 68 (NSC 68), approved in 1950, set forth the concept of a world irrevocably divided into two hostile power blocs, a precarious global balance of power, and a zero-sum game in which any gain for Communism was automatically deemed a loss for what was now called the Free World. It also provided for a massive military buildup with the aim of eventually winning the Cold War by forcing the detachment of Eastern Europe from the Soviet bloc and indeed changes in the Russian government itself. The Truman administration beefed up NATO forces in Europe and negotiated a peace treaty that tied Japan closely to the United States. Stalin's miscalculations in Berlin and Korea produced his worst nightmare: all-out U.S. mobilization for the Cold War, the buildup of European defenses, and the first steps toward German rearmament.

The Cold War took new directions in the 1950s. Gen. Dwight Eisenhower assumed the U.S. presidency in January 1953. Stalin's death shortly after produced a new collective leadership, from which Nikita Khrushchev eventually emerged preeminent. A tenuous Korean settlement was arranged. The United States and the USSR agreed to neutralize and withdraw troops from Austria. But an overall European settlement continued to elude them, and a divided Germany and especially Berlin remained the most explosive Cold War hot spots. The arms race assumed increasingly ominous proportions, each side developing nuclear weapons with frightful destructive capacity and sophisticated delivery systems, including long-range bombers, missiles, and submarines capable of firing nuclear warheads. Deadlocked in Europe, the major Cold War combatants increasingly focused on the Third World, the scores of new nations emerging from colonial control and seeking to consolidate their independence. Using propaganda, covert operations, and economic and military assistance, the great powers sought to win over the new nations to their side and indeed to their way of life. By doing so they brought the Cold War to the Third World.

The Cuban missile crisis of October 1962—the most dangerous of Cold War confrontations—highlighted the perils of competition in the Third World. Exploiting the opportunity presented by the revolutionary Fidel Castro's break with the United States, Khrushchev first provided economic and military assistance to Cuba. After a failed U.S.-sponsored invasion by Cuban exiles at the Bay of Pigs in April 1961, he took the boldest gamble of the Cold War by placing medium-range missiles in Cuba. This reckless intrusion into the U.S. sphere affirmed Soviet support for Castro and helped close the USSR's growing missile gap with the United States. It also posed a challenge that U.S. President John F. Kennedy could not ignore. Rejecting proposals for an invasion of Cuba, JFK instituted a blockade of Cuba euphemistically called a "quarantine." For almost two weeks the world teetered on the brink of nuclear war. Accepting secret pledges from Kennedy not to invade Cuba and to remove U.S. missiles positioned in Turkey, Khrushchev eventually agreed to dismantle the weapons and launching sites in Cuba. The sheer terror of the experience prompted Kennedy and Khrushchev to improve communications between their nations in times of crisis and in 1963 to conclude a nuclear test ban agreement. The missile crisis also loosened the bipolarity that had marked the first phase of the Cold War, bringing into the open long-simmering conflict between the Soviet Union and China and opening rifts between the United States and its European allies.

Over the next ten years the Cold War was marked by two seemingly contradictory trends. Soviet-American competition persisted, and proxy conflicts escalated. The United States eventually sent more than a half-million troops and a vast panoply of weapons to help embattled South Vietnam fend off an internal insurgency backed by Communist North Vietnam. The North Vietnamese exploited the Sino-Soviet conflict to secure aid from each. The two superpowers also competed in Africa and the Middle East, leading to crises in 1967 and 1973. They went to great lengths to avoid a repetition of the missile crisis, and the United States took measures to keep China from intervening in Vietnam, as it had in Korea. At the same time concern on both sides about the costs and dangers of the nuclear arms race led to discussions of limiting the number of nuclear weapons. The United States and the Soviet Union also looked to each other for trade to help address worsening economic problems. Soviet conflict with China that brought the two nations to the point of war in 1969 increased the Kremlin's need to ease tensions with the United States. For U.S. President Richard M. Nixon the possibility of rapprochement with China seemed to offer the United States some leverage with the USSR. In moves that shook to their foundations long-standing Cold War verities, Nixon began normalizing relations with China in 1972 through a much publicized summit in Beijing, and in Moscow later that year he concluded major agreements with the Soviet Union on nuclear arms limits and trade, the first step in what was envisioned as a widening process of détente.

In truth, détente was doomed from the start. In both countries ideological zealots, hard-liners, and military-industrial groups with vested interests in conflict questioned its value. Nixon's ability to sustain the policy was severely compromised by domestic scandals that eventually forced his resignation. American supporters of Israel linked the trade agreements negotiated in Moscow to freedom for Jews to emigrate from the Soviet Union, effectively thwarting their approval. After the fall of South Vietnam in the spring of 1975, a huge psychological blow to the United States, congressional blocs from both left and right mounted full-scale rebellions against the efforts of Presidents Gerald Ford and Jimmy Carter to expand détente. Détente was also a victim of its own expectations. U.S. officials believed the Soviets would be content with the Great Power status accorded them in the Moscow agreements, but the Kremlin saw no contradiction between détente and support for revolutionary groups abroad. Exploiting U.S. weakness after the fall of Vietnam, Moscow mounted a full-scale offensive in Angola, Ethiopia, and the Horn of Africa, arousing loud protest among disillusioned Americans. Subsequent negotiations produced little of substance. By 1979, détente was all but dead.

II

The "final campaign" of the Cold War began that same year, although there was no inkling among Soviet and U.S. leaders that their actions might have that kind of significance. Typical of the larger conflict, this phase was waged mostly through client states, with no shots fired between the two major powers. As before, the crisis of 1979 and after resulted from gross misperceptions by each power of what the other was doing.

The Soviet invasion of Afghanistan in December 1979 triggered this climactic stage of the Cold War. The Islamic revolution in Iran favored the Kremlin by forcing the United States out of that oil-rich nation, but it also aroused grave concern about religious upheaval elsewhere in Southwest Asia, especially in those Soviet republics with large Muslim populations. The outbreak of religious rebellion in neighboring Afghanistan and the chronic instability of the pro-Soviet government in Kabul stoked Kremlin concern. When the Islamic revolt in Afghanistan gained ground, the USSR increased military and economic aid to the government. But the murder of a pro-Soviet leader by a rival who spoke of closer ties with the United States increased pressure to do something. Those officials who pressed for military intervention warned ominously of U.S. missile bases and intelligence listening posts on Afghan soil. The KGB and the Defense Ministry pushed hardest for intervention and eventually sold it to an aging, increasingly sclerotic Politburo by raising the specter of Afghanistan as a U.S. outpost. The leadership finally acquiesced, convincing themselves, as so often in such situations, that Red Army troops could quickly stabilize Afghanistan and return home.

The U.S. response stunned a Kremlin that had acted for essentially defensive reasons and as a last resort. Carter and his top advisors misread the Soviet move as an aggressive action aimed at taking over the entire Persian Gulf region. Under fire from conservatives for being "soft" on national security and facing a tough reelection campaign, Carter responded with uncharacteristic decisiveness. In an alarmist speech on January 4, 1980, he labeled Soviet aggression the greatest threat to peace since World War II. Subsequently he enunciated the Carter Doctrine, pledging that the United States would respond forcibly to any Soviet attempt to gain control of Persian Gulf oil fields. He scrapped strategic arms limitation negotiations that had been under way since the Nixon presidency. In slapdash fashion he imposed a range of sanctions, including a boycott of the 1980 Olympic Games to be held in Moscow. He mounted an arms buildup worthy of Truman's NSC 68 and approved a new nuclear doctrine calling for the United States to develop the capacity to fight—and win—a nuclear war. Having only recently reestablished full diplomatic relations with China, the United States took steps such as the sharing of intelligence and military assistance that put the two nations into a virtual alliance. Eager to make Afghanistan the USSR's Vietnam and without much thought to long-term implications, the Carter administration also drastically stepped up military aid for the

Islamist Mujahideen rebels. Soviet-American tensions returned to early Cold War levels.

Carter's successor, a former movie actor and governor of California, Ronald Reagan, had built his political career on Americanism and hardcore anti-Communism. During his first years in office he unleashed a torrent of invective against the Soviet Union, labeling it the "evil empire" and the "focus of evil in the modern world." He expanded on Carter's military buildup in both nuclear and conventional weapons, boosting the defense budget by 12 percent in 1981 and 15 percent the following year. In time the Pentagon was spending an incredible $28 million per hour. Some U.S. officials hoped to spend the Soviet Union into bankruptcy; Reagan sought to establish a position of strength from which to negotiate. In nuclear arms negotiations his administration took a hard line, seeking to reduce weapons systems rather than limit them and developing proposals that were impossible for the Kremlin even to consider. The administration blamed a new wave of revolutionary activism in the Third World, even in nearby Central America, on Soviet adventurism and responded with the Reagan Doctrine, which sought to undermine leftist governments already in power and thus roll back Communism.

The Kremlin responded in kind. During the first years of the Reagan administration the Soviet leadership was in disarray. Aging General Secretary Leonid Brezhnev died in November 1982. His successor, the former KGB boss Yuri Andropov, was a capable administrator and entertained thoughts of reform, but he too fell ill, died in February 1984, and was succeeded by Konstantin Cherenko, who lasted just over two years. "How am I supposed to get anyplace with the Russians if they keep dying on me?" Reagan quipped.[2] The faltering Soviet economy lagged far behind the West's. Popular discontent mounted. Few decisions were made, fewer actions taken. Soviet officials protested that Reagan's hostile rhetoric exceeded the usual bounds of Cold War propriety and complained that the atmosphere in Soviet-American relations was "white hot." (Such was the level of misunderstanding that Americans could not fathom why Soviet leaders were angry.) The Kremlin cracked down on internal dissent and beefed up its military defenses.

The Cold War thus reescalated sharply during Reagan's first years. Central America became a major new battleground. The United States provided aid and advisors to the embattled government of tiny El Salvador, trying to hold off leftist rebels supported by Cuba and Nicaragua. In Nicaragua itself the United States helped create and lavishly funded through legal and illegal means a group of counterrevolutionaries seeking to overthrow the leftist Sandinista government backed by Cuba and to some extent the USSR. The United States also stepped up aid to the Afghan Mujahideen, eventually sending such sophisticated equipment as handheld Stinger missiles capable of bringing down Soviet helicopters. When the Soviets shot down a Korean Air Lines passenger plane in September 1983, killing 269 people, a product of nervous and inept air defenses, Americans were outraged. Reagan's stunning proposal in March 1983 of a Strategic Defense Initiative (SDI), a system of lasers deployed from space-based platforms that would supposedly create an impregnable shield against a nuclear attack (promptly labeled "Star Wars" by critics who doubted its efficacy), sent Soviet leaders into hysterics. Arms talks were terminated in late 1983. Fear of nuclear war gripped both sides. On November 11, 1983, millions of Americans (Reagan included) watched a television film, *The Day After*, a chilling account of the effects of a nuclear attack on Lawrence, Kansas. Just days before, and unknown to Americans, a NATO exercise code-named Able Archer was launched; designed to test the firing capabilities of alliance weapons systems in wartime and also to test Soviet missile defenses, it provoked the Soviet Defense Ministry, fearing that a nuclear attack might be imminent, to go on full defense alert. The final campaign had produced a full-fledged war scare.

III

Through a truly remarkable process, the final campaign, culminating in the crisis of 1983, created the conditions that brought the Cold War to an end. It is difficult to find a comparable case of a long-standing international conflict ending without a shot being fired or a third power ascending to drive former rivals together. Those who implemented the policies that led to this result had no sense of the ultimate consequences of their actions. They saw themselves as easing or stabilizing a conflict that had gone on for nearly a half-century. Instead, inadvertently, they ended it. The road they followed was not always smooth, but in time the process took on a life of its own. The end came suddenly and produced changes of a magnitude no one foresaw.

Growing stability in the international system helped make possible the diplomatic revolution of 1988–90. The bipolarity of the early Cold War had given way by the 1980s to a multipolar system. The Western European nations and Japan were increasingly independent of the United

States. The Europeans had pioneered détente in the 1960s, and twenty years later Germany's Helmut Kohl and France's François Mitterrand also worked to promote Great Power accommodation. A strong European peace movement pressed the Cold War combatants to contain the arms race. In Soviet-dominated Eastern Europe there was rising ferment for internal reform. China had long since taken an independent path, and in the 1980s shifted to a market economy, with huge long-term ramifications. The era of decolonization was ending. After years of internal struggle and conflict tied to the Cold War, the Third World was disappearing as a distinct entity. Cold war conflict in the Third World had been costly for both superpowers and had sharply increased the friction between them, prompting them to contemplate disengagement. Greater pluralism made it more difficult for them to control events. The crisis of 1983 highlighted the pitfalls of nuclear deterrence and spurred thinking about other means to preserve the peace.

Conditions inside both nations also provided an impetus to go in new directions and the freedom to do so. The Soviet economy was in shambles by the mid-1980s, provoking rising demands for reform. Frustration with foreign interventions, especially the increasingly costly war in Afghanistan, produced calls for redirecting resources to pressing domestic needs. Reagan's massive defense buildup and his sunny talk of "morning in America" lifted his nation's spirits from the malaise of the late 1970s and provided a secure environment in which to make foreign policy changes. His huge reelection victory in 1984 gave him political security. Perhaps alone among U.S. politicians his staunch anti-Communism rendered him invulnerable to charges of appeasement. Rising domestic opposition to U.S. involvement in Central America produced pressures from the political left that made it expedient for Reagan to seek negotiations with the USSR.

To an extent unusual in history, personalities played a crucial role in ending the Cold War. Mikhail Gorbachev, who took power in March 1985, was a new kind of Soviet leader. Unlike his predecessors, he had traveled widely, even in the West. He had seen firsthand the extent to which the USSR lagged behind other industrial nations, and he recognized the desperate need for domestic reform. Self-confident and hard-driving, Gorbachev was a risk taker and innovator, open to new ideas and willing to experiment, even to challenge long-standing ideological verities. He was also a shrewd, tough politician capable of implementing radical change in the face of formidable opposition. "[He has a] nice smile," a colleague remarked, "but he's got iron teeth."[3] Once in power Gorbachev moved so rapidly and in such revolutionary ways that his U.S. counterparts often failed to grasp what he was doing. More than any other individual he was responsible for ending the Cold War.

Reagan played an indispensable supporting role. His hatred of Communism never wavered, but he welcomed peaceful competition with the USSR, and he differed from many of his advisors in viewing the defense buildup as a prerequisite to negotiations. His powerful antinuclearism also influenced his willingness to negotiate. He despised nuclear weapons, viewed the concept of deterrence as dangerous folly, and dismissed as "crazy" those of his advisors who believed that any nation could win a nuclear war. *The Day After* left him depressed. He took a keen interest in Russian history and gradually sensed what perhaps should have been obvious: that Russians, like Americans, feared for their security. Some Americans continue to insist that Reagan's tough talk and massive defense buildup forced a Soviet surrender. In fact it was his willingness to negotiate that set loose forces leading to the end of the Cold War.

Gorbachev and Reagan also established a close personal relationship. After difficult early encounters they grew comfortable with each other and in time even developed what the president called a "kind of chemistry."[4] They spoke frankly to each other and built a strong mutual trust. Their camaraderie extended to lower levels. Secretary of State George Shultz strongly advocated negotiating with the Soviet Union and helped sway Reagan in that direction. A skilled bureaucratic infighter, he also fended off hard-liners among the president's key advisors. Shultz established especially close ties with his Soviet counterpart, Eduard Shevardnadze. They discussed difficult issues with a candor unusual in diplomatic interchange.

Within a year after taking office, Gorbachev began to enact fundamental changes. Part of a new generation of reform-minded officials, the one-time farm worker and aspiring actor broke sharply with his predecessors. Finding the economy in desperate shape, he set out to save the Soviet system by restructuring, what he called *perestroika,* and *glasnost,* greater openness in decision making. He came to see that if domestic reforms were to be implemented, the USSR could no longer sustain an aggressive, expansionist foreign policy. His "new thinking" thus boldly and radically challenged long-standing ideology, abandoning the Marxist dogma of an inevitable conflict with capitalism and in time speaking of an "interdependent and integral world." Influenced by European defense theorists and transnational peace activists, he embraced new ideas of non-offensive defense and alternative security that led to redefinition of the Warsaw Pact as exclusively a defensive alliance and to drastic cutbacks in conventional forces in Eastern Europe. Seeking to reduce the economic burden and threat of war caused by the arms race, he declared himself willing to negotiate with the United States. Perceiving that Third World interventionism had brought great costs and few gains, he sought to end them, especially the "bleeding wound" of Afghanistan.

Reagan's change of heart evolved slowly and from a mix of motives. As early as January 1984 he conspicuously toned down his anti-Communist rhetoric, spoke hopefully of peace, and publicly declared, "The fact that neither of us likes the other's system is no reason to refuse to talk." In one of his more memorable speeches he wondered aloud what might happen if ordinary Russians and Americans could sit down and talk with each other. By the beginning of his second term he was increasingly sensitive to his place in history. He was confident that the United States had achieved the position of strength necessary for productive negotiations.

Despite the growing commitment of the two heads of state, the path was strewn with obstacles. Even after they established bonds of trust, Reagan and Gorbachev continued to spar over the contentious issues of human rights, Central America, Afghanistan, and especially SDI. Conditioned by years of Cold War thinking, Americans were often slow to grasp the impact of what Gorbachev was doing. The Soviet leader faced stubborn opposition from his military advisors and hard-line civilians who attacked his "capitulationist line" toward the United States. It took time for him to replace old-timers like the diplomat Andrei Gromyko with his own people. He could not build a solid consensus around his domestic and foreign policy reforms and repeatedly had to outmaneuver his foes. The deep divisions within the Reagan administration, especially on nuclear issues, complicated the formulation of agreed-upon positions. Hard-liners fought bitterly with Shultz and other pragmatists. Differences between the two nations remained sharp even if no longer generally beyond resolution. Especially on SDI, which Gorbachev was determined to eliminate and Reagan to implement, the conflict proved insurmountable.

Through a series of summits the two leaders eventually achieved major results. At Geneva in November 1985, according to Reagan's wife, Nancy, they began to establish a certain warmth, and they vaguely agreed to seek 50 percent reductions in nuclear weapons. At a hastily called October 1986 summit in Reykjavik, Iceland, only SDI appeared to block truly astounding achievements. Before the meeting, Reagan had proposed to eliminate all intermediate-range weapons in Europe. Gorbachev countered with stunning proposals for huge across-the-board cuts and the elimination of all nuclear weapons by the year 2000. During a surreal weekend in a bleak, seaside house reputed to be haunted, the Soviet leader advanced the deadline by five years. The idea appealed to Reagan's antinuclearism, and the leaders' apparent agreement pushed the negotiations into new areas. After an extended late-night session the technical experts appeared to agree on terms, but Gorbachev's insistence that SDI be limited to the laboratory ended the talks amid great frustration and disappointment. It was the angriest day of his presidency, Reagan later recalled. At the next summit, in Washington in December 1987, however, the two sides agreed to substantial cuts in their nuclear arsenals. Even more shocking, Gorbachev consented to the kind of on-site inspections that would have been instantly rebuffed by his predecessors.

The two leaders fared less well on Third World issues. Reagan had pushed Gorbachev mercilessly to stop interfering in Central America and Africa and to get out of Afghanistan, provoking the Soviet leader to complain of blackmail. In fact Gorbachev realized that the Soviet Union could no longer afford foreign interventions, but extrication posed major difficulties. Thanks to the Reagan administration's entanglement in the Iran-contra scandal, by which arms sold illegally to Iran had been used to illegally fund the Nicaraguan contras, and to Gorbachev's late 1987 rejection of yet another Nicaraguan request for aid, the two powers began awkwardly to disengage from Central America. For the USSR, Afghanistan proved the most formidable challenge. Brezhnev's presumed quick fix had become a quagmire, drawing in Islamic "freedom fighters" from across the world, generously supported by the United States, Pakistan, China, and Saudi Arabia. Gorbachev knew that the war must be ended, but he could not figure out how to do it without causing the fall of the Soviet client government and loss of face for the USSR. He appealed to Reagan repeatedly—and to no avail—to cooperate in ending the war. U.S. officials, the president apparently included, seemed happy to prolong it, thereby weakening the Soviet Union and further embarrassing it internationally. Yet by doing so the United States *delayed* Soviet withdrawal from Afghanistan. In early 1988, largely to further his domestic aims, Gorbachev decided to withdraw Soviet troops. The war continued, however, with the USSR sending aid to the Afghan government and the United States violating an earlier agreement by continuing to assist the rebels.

Despite these obstacles, improvement in superpower relations proceeded apace. The two nations conspicuously cooperated in the United Nations by calling for a cease-fire in the Iran-Iraq War. Cultural exchanges expanded well beyond the heyday of détente in the 1970s. "Gorby fever" infected Washington, D.C., during the general secretary's visit in December 1987. At a May 1988 summit in Moscow, while strolling through Red Square with Gorbachev, Reagan told reporters that his 1983 "evil empire" statement had been about "another time, another era."[5] The Moscow summit represented for all practical purposes a normalization of Soviet-American relations. There was even talk of ending the Cold War. In a truly radical speech at the UN on December 7, 1988, Gorbachev conceded that Moscow had no monopoly on the truth, seemed to forswear the use of force, and announced the reduction of Soviet conventional forces by half and the withdrawal of 50,000 troops and 5,000 tanks from Warsaw Pact countries. Most shocking and significant, he opened the way for self-determination in Eastern Europe by proclaiming, "[The] principle of freedom of choice is mandatory." With this statement, Gorbachev publicly scrapped the notorious Brezhnev Doctrine, by which the Kremlin had assumed for itself the right to intervene in Eastern Europe whenever it chose. He replaced it with what one Soviet official called the "Sinatra Doctrine" (named for the crooner's song "My Way"), which enabled Eastern Europeans to do as they pleased. This effectively removed the central issue around which the Cold War had begun, a "Fulton in reverse," Gorbachev called it, referring to Winston Churchill's famous February 1946 speech declaring the existence of an Iron Curtain across Central Europe.[6]

Growing Soviet-American concord helped spur the resolution of other conflicts, leading to what was called "a season of peace." Iran and Iraq agreed to a cease-fire in their seemingly interminable war. South Africa and Angola moved to end their fifteen-year conflict. Vietnam set out to eliminate its ten-year occupation of Cambodia. And through a strange set of circumstances, in which the United States played at best a peripheral part, peace finally came to embattled Central America.

A series of revolutions in Eastern Europe during the *annus mirabilis* of 1989 posed the ultimate test for Gorbachev's New Thinking. Fittingly the upheaval started in Poland, where Cold War conflict had begun. It then spread to Hungary and Czechoslovakia. Even more shocking, in early November the Berlin Wall was torn down by ordinary Germans, eliminating one of the most conspicuous and despised symbols of East-

West conflict. In 1956 and 1968, Soviet leaders had brutally suppressed revolutions in Hungary and Czechoslovakia. This time the Kremlin did nothing. Soviet officials insisted that their security was not threatened by freedom in Eastern Europe. They no longer feared capitalist encirclement. From Gorbachev down they recognized that any effort to suppress the revolutions would do enormous damage to the Soviet image in Europe. In any event, by this time Moscow was most concerned with rising nationalist protest in its own far-flung republics. "This is the end of Yalta [and] the Stalinist legacy," one official tellingly observed.[7] The Kremlin insisted only that Germany must remain divided.

The George H. W. Bush administration handled the great transformation of 1989 with considerable skill. The new president and his advisors came into office unpersuaded of Gorbachev's commitment to Great Power cooperation and even suspicious that an aging, gullible Reagan may have been seduced by the Soviet leader's charms. Their watchwords were "caution" and "strength." Like people across the world, U.S. officials watched the events in Eastern Europe with shock and private satisfaction, but they avoided anything that might have made it more difficult for Gorbachev. They did not "dance on the wall," as Bush put it. Soviet refusal to intervene finally persuaded Bush that Gorbachev was sincere. "If the Soviets are going to let the communists fall in East Germany," he mused, "they've got to be . . . more serious than I thought."[8] At Malta the president began to establish a good working relationship with his Soviet counterpart. The most difficult issue was German unification, which struck fear not only in Moscow but throughout much of Europe. The United States was firmly committed to a united Germany in NATO, which especially concerned Soviet leaders. The Bush administration eventually achieved its goal in ways that made it possible for Gorbachev to acquiesce. A German settlement that provided for U.S. troops to remain in Europe formalized what had already become clear: the Cold War was over.

IV

Among the first and major consequences of the end of the Cold War was the collapse of the Soviet Union in August 1991, an event as momentous in its ramifications as it was anticlimactic. Gorbachev had dreamed of a reformed and revivified USSR, but the changes he implemented loosened the cement that held an unwieldy empire together. Following the revolutions in Eastern Europe, the Soviet republics declared themselves independent, beginning, ironically, with the Russian Republic. Seeking to restore the Communist Party and what was left of the Soviet state, a group of hard-liners in a badly bungled coup attempt placed Gorbachev under house arrest at his vacation spot in the Crimea and sought to take over the government. Anticoup forces instead seized power and eventually replaced Gorbachev. In December, Russia, Ukraine, and Belarus formed a short-lived Confederation of Independent States, subsequently replaced by the Russian Republic. "Never before," the philosopher Isaiah Berlin declared, "has there been a case of an empire that caved in without a war, revolution, or an invasion."[9]

The demise of the USSR left the United States the world's lone superpower, and for many Americans their Cold War victory brought a sense of enormous pride, even a triumphalist spirit. The nation's success was trumpeted as a validation of its ideals. Some commentators even proclaimed "the end of history," the defeat of fascism and Communism and the victory of free market capitalism and democracy, foreshadowing the eventual universalization of liberal democracy.

As is always the case with war, America's victory did not come without cost. The Cold War had been a way of life for Americans, and its impact spread across all segments of society. Massive military spending was a hallmark of the nation's post–World War II budgetary landscape, leaving the United States by the 1980s a debtor nation for the first time since World War I. A swollen federal government, a national security state, and what Eisenhower called a military-industrial complex were also legacies of the forty-four-year conflict. The so-called imperial presidency took form during the Cold War, and in the name of national security Presidents Nixon and Reagan committed flagrant abuses of power. The United States experienced nothing like the horrors of Stalin's gulags or Mao Zedong's Red Guards, but especially during the 1950s the Cold War produced a rampant assault on civil liberties. A byproduct of the larger conflict, the Vietnam War provoked bitter internal divisions that morphed into so-called culture wars that persisted into the next century. Four decades of absorption with external conflict deflected attention from urgent domestic needs, such as infrastructure and education.

The impact of the Cold War in the Third World was enormous. Each superpower had sought to remake its client states in its own image, enabling them to secure much-needed economic assistance but also subjecting them to external interference and costly military interventions.

Even though the Great Powers professed to be pursuing anticolonial visions, often with the assistance of local elites they imposed neocolonial designs on Third World nations. In some cases they put them in a "state of semipermanent civil war"; the conflict in Vietnam, for example, lasted thirty years and resulted in huge human losses, devastation of the land, and aborted economic development.[10] The negative effects still linger in many areas.

The post–Cold War international system manifested conflicting trends. The United States, the European nations, and Japan developed a security system of like-minded countries among whom the possibility of war with each other was unthinkable, a major boost to international peace. The onrushing process of globalization—loosely defined as world-wide networks of interdependence—served as a major propellant of inte-gration. Virtually unnoticed amid the final stages of the Cold War, an information revolution shattered old ways of thinking and doing things. The development of computers and the Internet, cable television, satellite technology, and new high-speed jet aircraft created global networks that brought people worldwide closer together. These innovations made it difficult if not impossible for governments to control information. They empowered individuals and groups, sometimes at the expense of nations, enhancing the influence of nonstate actors in international politics and economics. They permitted the proliferation of multinational corpora-tions and the expansion of trade in ways previously unimaginable.

Coexisting uneasily with this process of integration were older and potentially much more disruptive forces: nationalism, religion, ethnic rivalries, and tribal hatreds. The end of the Cold War unleashed fierce conflicts with centuries-old roots. Most prominent in the 1990s were the brutal wars between Serbs, Croats, and Muslims in the former Yugo-slavia, and conflicts between Sunni and Shia Muslims and Kurds in the Middle East. Pundits also warned of conflict between the industrialized North and the developing South, the haves and the have-nots, and even of a clash of civilizations between the modernist West and the world of radical Islam, which looked backward in terms of its ideals but could use modern instruments of communication and possibly even weapons of mass destruction to advance its cause. Among the most significant unforeseen and unintended consequences of the Cold War was the emer-gence in the 1990s of militant Islamic fundamentalism, first evidenced in revolutionary Iran and then, ironically with sizable U.S. support, gaining strength in the anti-Soviet war in Afghanistan. Islamic fundamentalism would provide a major challenge for U.S. foreign policy in the twenty-first century.

For the world's lone superpower the post–Cold War world presented no compelling traditional threats in the form of nation-states like Nazi Germany or the Soviet Union. But to many analysts the vague and elusive dangers of the new era seemed no less menacing. The Cold War left in its wake huge arsenals of nuclear weapons, far more than two former enemies needed to defend themselves. The technological revolution left the United States vulnerable to terrorists who, armed with biological, chemical, or even nuclear weapons, could wreak havoc. Skilled cyberterrorists might paralyze defense establishments and economic systems driven by computers. In a broader sense, globalization was viewed as vital to American prosperity, and military power was therefore deemed essential to protect oil resources and other critical raw materials, keep trade routes open, maintain world order, and actively promote the nation's interests by projecting its power globally. Abetted by the World War II Munich analogy that called for firm resistance to aggression, the Cold War enshrined toughness as a technique for dealing with other nations and equated negotiation with appeasement. Some national security experts learned the wrong lessons from the outcome of the Cold War, insisting that Reagan's belligerence and U.S. military superiority rather than diplomacy had been responsible for America's "victory." In their triumphalist frame of mind they concluded that the nation must maintain a defense capability that would enable it to defend against any potential threat and prevail against any competing power or combination of powers. "Full spectrum dominance," the Pentagon called it.

The U.S. military establishment was thus not significantly reconfigured to meet the different challenges of a new era. Some politicians hoped for a peace dividend from the end of the Cold War. Some defense experts argued that a military designed mainly to wage conventional warfare against the Soviet Union on the plains of Central Europe was not well suited to meet the diverse challenges of a new era. Throughout the 1990s there were numerous proposals for reform, but the individual services staunchly resisted any change that threatened to reduce their size or alter their mission. They were often backed by powerful forces in Congress and corporate interests with a stake in the status quo. Retaining a Cold War mind-set, politicians continued to try to score points by accusing opponents of being weak on national defense. Although the size of U.S. forces was reduced by roughly one-third, in terms of its organization, command systems, and weapons the military of 2000 did not look much different from that of the 1950s. Reflecting traditional Cold War missions, the United States retained sizable forces in Western Europe and East Asia.

The Cold War ended not with the clash of armies on fields of battle or navies at sea, but as it had been fought: through threats and counterthreats, proxy wars waged through client states, and diplomatic maneuvers. It ended mainly because of the extraordinary efforts of two exceptional individuals who came to recognize the astronomical costs of the conflict for both sides and the frightful prospects of a war no one could truly win. After forty-four years of struggle, the United States achieved its essential war aims precisely as they had been formulated— the liberation of Eastern Europe and the demise of the Soviet Union—a success as complete as any in the history of warfare. Even then the costs were high, and the unintended and unanticipated consequences would provide some of the major security challenges of the post–Cold War era.

SUGGESTED READING

Not surprisingly, given its long duration and global scope, the Cold War produced a substantial scholarly literature. The best up-to-date surveys are John Lewis Gaddis, *The Cold War: A New History* (New York, 2005), and Walter LaFeber, *America, Russia, and the Cold War, 1945–2005*, 10th ed. (New York, 2008), which approach the subject from strikingly divergent perspectives. Vladislav Zubok, *A Failed Empire: The Soviet Union in the Cold War from Stalin to Gorbachev* (Chapel Hill, NC, 2007) provides important insight into Soviet personalities and policies. Odd Arne Westad, *The Global Cold War: Third World Interventions and the Making of Our Times* (New York, 2005) is excellent on the way the Third World affected the Cold War, and the Cold War the Third World. Melvyn P. Leffler, *For the Soul of Mankind: The United States, the Soviet Union, and the Cold War* (New York, 2007) skillfully analyzes episodes and personalities from Truman and Stalin to Reagan and Gorbachev, seeking to explain why the conflict lasted as long as it did and ended when it did. Vladislav Zubok and Constantine Pleshakov, *Inside the Kremlin's Cold War: From Stalin to Khrushchev* (Cambridge, MA, 1996) is an early effort to use newly available Soviet archival sources to analyze a side of the struggle often neglected in early U.S. studies. William Taubman, *Khrushchev: The Man and His Era* (London, 2003) and Aleksandr Fursenko, *Khrushchev's Cold War: The Inside Story of an American Adversary* (New York, 2006) are excellent for the middle years of the Cold War.

The origins of the Cold War by itself produced an enormous literature. Among the standard works are Thomas G. Paterson, *On Every Front: The Making and Unmaking of the Cold War,* revised ed. (New York, 1992) and John Lewis Gaddis, *The United States and the Origins of the Cold War* (New York, 1971), which offer quite different interpretations.

For détente, the final campaign, and the beginning of the end of the Cold War, the massive and magisterial Raymond Garthoff, *Detente and Confrontation: American-Soviet Relations from Nixon to Reagan* (Washington, 1985) is indispensable. Garthoff's sequel, *The Great Transition: American-Soviet Relations and the End of the Cold War* (Washington, 1994) is also useful. The best survey of the end of the Cold War is Don Oberdorfer, *From the Cold War to a New Era: The United States and the Soviet Union, 1983–1991,* revised ed. (Baltimore, 1998). William C. Wohlforth, ed., *Witnesses to the End of the Cold War* (Baltimore, 1996) contains valuable oral histories of key participants as well as excellent analytical essays by scholars. Matthew Evangelista, *Unarmed Forces: The Transnational Movement to End the Cold War* (Ithaca, NY, 1999) establishes the influence of nonstate actors, especially on Gorbachev. Anatoly S. Chernyaev, *My Years with Gorbachev,* trans. Robert D. English and Elizabeth Tucker (University Park, PA, 2000) provides an inside look at Gorbachev's actions. Lou Cannon's *President Reagan: The Role of a Lifetime,* revised ed. (New York, 2000) is a balanced account emphasizing Reagan's pragmatism. Also valuable is James Mann, *The Rebellion of Ronald Reagan: A History of the End of the Cold War* (New York, 2009). Andrew J. Bacevich, *American Empire* (Cambridge, MA, 2002) provides a searching critique of U.S. post–Cold War defense policy.

ANDREW J. BACEVICH

The United States in Iraq:
Terminating an Interminable War

I

The senior U.S. field commander knew it was over before it was over. The forces under his command had accomplished what they had been sent to do. The imperative was now to wind down the war, promptly and neatly. Avoiding unnecessary bloodshed had become a priority. So too was upholding the warrior's code of honor, demonstrating that the troops under his command were not only brave but also humane. Given all that had been accomplished on the battlefield, the task of bringing Operation Desert Storm to an end did not appear to be particularly difficult. The heavy lifting was done.

So when Gen. H. Norman Schwarzkopf, commanding U.S. Central Command (CENTCOM) and all the coalition forces assembled to liberate Iraqi-occupied Kuwait, appeared before the press on February 27, 1991, in Riyadh, Saudi Arabia, his mood was ebullient. In assessing the situation that evening (early afternoon Washington time) Schwarzkopf turned in a boffo performance.[1] Quickly enshrined as "the mother of all briefings," it completed the gruff general's transformation into Stormin' Norman and vaulted him, however briefly, into the uppermost ranks of global celebrity.

Yet Schwarzkopf's purpose was less to offer a progress report than to seize the historical initiative. In effect he aimed to do in the course of an hour-long televised presentation what Winston Churchill had accomplished over the course of his six-volume memoir of the Second World War: to lay down an authoritative firsthand account with the intention of establishing an interpretive framework to which others thereafter would adhere.

The overarching theme of Churchill's work had been one of tragedy: out of a war that foresight and resolve might have averted came not enduring peace but continuing and potentially even more dangerous conflict. The overarching theme of Schwarzkopf's hastily prepared presentation differed; simply put, he used the occasion to declare victory.[2]

Against tall odds, the outnumbered U.S. forces, assisted by loyal allies, had executed an epic feat of arms. Outgeneraled and outfought, the Iraqi army had all but ceased to exist. What Schwarzkopf described as a "classic tank battle" had left 3,700 of the enemy's 4,000 tanks hors de combat. Over the course of a mere four days the troops under his command had "almost completely destroyed the offensive capability of the Iraqi forces in the Kuwait theater of operations." The surviving remnant, pursued on the ground and pummeled from the air, was doomed. There was no escape. "The gates are closed."[3] For the coalition, the road to Baghdad lay open. Yet Schwarzkopf evinced neither the intention nor the desire to march on the Iraqi capital. Although fighting continued, he considered his task complete. "We've accomplished our mission," he concluded, "and when the decision makers come to the decision that there should be a cease-fire, nobody will be happier than me."[4]

The views expressed by the field commander in Riyadh meshed with and reinforced those gaining currency back in Washington. In the desert, things had gone much better than expected. Senior U.S. officials, civilian and military alike, felt little inclination to press their luck. Better to stop now and cash in their winnings, which promised to be considerable. Besides, to continue clobbering an already beaten foe might give the wrong impression. Concern for appearances and reputations was eclipsing serious strategic analysis.[5]

A call to CENTCOM headquarters earlier that same day from Gen. Colin Powell, chairman of the Joint Chiefs of Staff and an officer of acute political sensitivity, signaled which way the winds were blowing at home. "The doves are starting to complain about all the damage you're doing," Powell told Schwarzkopf. Images of mangled Iraqi trucks and burning armored vehicles piled up on the main road leading from Kuwait City back toward Iraq, dubbed by the press "the Highway of Death," were causing unease. "The reports make it look like wanton killing."[6] Perhaps, Powell suggested, it was time to bring things to a halt.

Schwarzkopf's initial inclination was to continue the pursuit for another day. "[I want to] drive to the sea, and totally destroy everything in our path. That's the way I wrote the plan," he told the JCS chairman, "and in one more day we'll be done."[7]

Yet when pressed by Powell, Schwarzkopf quickly gave way. With Kuwait liberated and the Iraqi army no longer an effective fighting force, the time had come to think about the history books. When it came to winning a decisive victory, the Israeli Six-Day War of 1967 represented the reigning gold standard. By ending the fight on February 28, U.S. forces could outdo the Israelis by a day, Operation Desert Storm becoming the Five-Day War. Both Powell and Schwarzkopf (ignoring the several weeks of bombing that had preceded the launch of ground operations) found this an appealing prospect.[8]

A short time later in the Oval Office the JCS chairman duly relayed Schwarzkopf's assessment to the commander in chief. "Mr. President, it's going much better than we expected. The Iraqi army is broken. All they're trying to do now is get out," he said, adding, "By sometime tomorrow the job will be done."[9]

"If that's the case," President George H. W. Bush wondered aloud, "why not end it today?" Caught off guard by the president's suggestion, Powell said he needed once more to consult the field commander. Ducking into the president's study, he placed another call to Riyadh. Schwarzkopf needed little persuading. "I don't have any problem," he replied when briefed on the president's inclination to end the fighting forthwith. "Our objective was to drive 'em out and we've done it."[10] Although Schwarzkopf wanted to check with his own chief subordinates, he fully expected them to concur.

Schwarzkopf's views proved decisive. At 6:00 p.m. Washington time, after a final round of discussion with his advisors, Bush rendered his decision. In a 9:00 p.m. televised address from the Oval Office he would announce a cessation of hostilities. There was just one wrinkle: rather than declaring an immediate termination of combat operations, the president would designate 12:01 a.m. as the endpoint of Operation Desert Storm. White House Chief of Staff John Sununu had suggested that "the One Hundred Hour War" had a nice ring to it. Midnight marked exactly 100 hours since ground operations had commenced. Once again playing to the history books nudged other considerations aside.

"Kuwait is liberated," President Bush told the nation and the world that evening in his televised presentation. "Iraq's army is defeated. Our military objectives are met." The president and his administration were ready to move on. "This war is now behind us."[11]

That judgment proved premature. Even as Operation Desert Storm wound down, complications were beginning to emerge. Expectations of overwhelmingly superior U.S. military power producing a decisive outcome soon proved to be illusory. President Bush himself was among the first to suspect that something might be amiss. "Still no feeling of euphoria," his diary entry for that night reads. "It hasn't been a clean end—there is no battleship *Missouri* surrender. This is what's missing to make this akin to World War II, to separate Kuwait from Korea and Vietnam."[12]

At the time, few Americans shared Bush's sense of unease. Most had bought into his administration's depiction of the Persian Gulf crisis as a morality tale, replaying the events of Europe from 1939 to 1945. The crisis had ostensibly sprung out of the blue on August 1, 1990, when the Hitler-like figure of Saddam Hussein had invaded an innocent, unassuming neighbor. In defeating Saddam's legions and liberating Kuwait, U.S. troops (with a bit of allied assistance) had now put things right. End of story.

This reassuring narrative was deeply misleading, however. It failed in at least three respects. First, rather than embodying the problem facing the United States, Saddam merely represented a prominent symptom. Second, rather than suddenly appearing in August 1990, the actual problem—pent-up resentment throughout much of the Islamic world finding expression in anti-Western violence—had been festering for decades. Third, rather than offering an antidote to that problem, the employment of U.S. military might would only serve to make matters worse.

A World War II–style outcome was not in the cards if only because the enterprise in which the United States was engaged in no way resembled World War II. Since the promulgation of the Carter Doctrine in 1980, its declaratory purpose being to prevent a hostile nation from gaining control of the Persian Gulf, Washington had sought to achieve a commanding position in the Gulf and its environs. Power and presence promised to ensure access and stability; whatever the author of the Carter Doctrine may have intended, within a decade this had emerged as the doctrine's underlying rationale.

At a superficial level Operation Desert Storm seemed to validate this strategy while creating fresh opportunities to exert U.S. influence across the region. Beneath the surface, however, the American-led intervention and its aftermath only served to affirm suspicions that the United States had become simply the latest in a long list of Western powers seeking to impose its will on the Islamic world. Viewed from this perspective, American power and presence, which the Persian Gulf War of 1991 had vividly displayed, served as a rallying cry for jihad.

President Bush's declaration of an end to hostilities on February 28, 1991, terminated one small war while paving the way for a much larger one. Operation Desert Storm settled nothing of importance. Instead, the One Hundred Hour War served as a precursor and catalyst for what a decade later became known as the Long War.

II

Why did victory over Saddam yield such perverse results? Why did Operation Desert Storm, briefly celebrated as an epic feat of arms, so quickly lose its luster? Existing answers to these questions reflect two distinctive schools of thought.

According to the first, Operation Desert Storm was a brilliantly conceived and executed military campaign, botched at the very end and thereby leaving unfortunate loose ends. The failures were military in nature, reflecting the errors and inadequacies of very senior military officers.

According to the second school of thought, Operation Desert Storm was a brilliantly conceived and executed military campaign launched in pursuit of the wrong mission. In essence the United States had erroneously planted the goalposts well short of the end zone. From this perspective the failures were political in nature, with the fault laid to very senior civilian officials.

Adherents of the first school spread the blame among three U.S. Army generals, including in their indictment, along with Powell and Schwarzkopf, Lt. Gen. Frederick M. Franks, commander of VII Corps. The charge against Franks—within the officer corps a widely revered figure— is an especially severe one. It amounts to this: he failed to accomplish his assigned mission. As conceived by planners working for Schwarzkopf, the coalition ground offensive was to consist of two essential elements. First, a supporting attack from south to north toward Kuwait City would fix Iraqi forces in place. Second, a wide flanking attack from west to east would envelop the enemy and ensure his defeat in detail. VII Corps—50,000 vehicles and 146,000 soldiers strong—was to execute that flanking attack. More specifically, the war plan assigned Franks the task of destroying the Iraqi Republican Guard, the best-equipped, best-trained, and most formidable element of Saddam Hussein's otherwise raggedy army.

In the end, the Republican Guard, although badly damaged and put to flight, evaded destruction, major elements fleeing back toward Baghdad.[13] The hit on Franks, one that Schwarzkopf in particular endorsed, was that in a situation calling for dash, the VII Corps commander had exhibited caution. Determined to minimize coalition casualties—the avoidance of fratricide competed with destruction of the enemy as a priority—Franks attacked methodically and deliberately, allowing his quarry to escape.[14] At one point, in response to a reported friendly-fire incident, he ordered a cease-fire throughout the entire corps, a tribute to the general's humanity but not a decision likely to have found favor with W. T. Sherman or George S. Patton.[15]

In the immediate wake of Operation Desert Storm, with dissident Iraqi Shiites and Kurds (encouraged by President Bush) rising up to overthrow Saddam, the Republican Guard provided the Iraqi dictator with the wherewithal to crush internal opposition to his regime and retain his hold on power. Saddam survived, creating an abiding problem for the United States, a direct result, according to some, of VII Corps having come up short.

The charge against the CENTCOM commander is broader. Simply put, over the four days during which the ground offensive unfolded, Schwarzkopf's temperament, volcanic in the best of circumstances, became a major source of dysfunction that eventually permeated the senior levels of his command. In a job that required cool, he ran piping hot, cultivating a style of leadership that emphasized bluster, intimidation, and threats of relief.

Whether due to fatigue, pressure, or sheer orneriness, Schwarzkopf erred repeatedly on issues of primary importance, a tendency that became especially evident as Operation Desert Storm wound down. Having overestimated the expected level of enemy resistance, he adjusted only belatedly to evidence that the Iraqis were far weaker than advertised.[16] Overstating the losses his forces had inflicted on the enemy, he concluded prematurely that his work was finished. By declaring publicly, with hostilities still under way, that his forces were not going to Baghdad, he made a great gift to Saddam Hussein offering authoritative insight into the coalition's ultimate intentions.

When the White House, with public relations uppermost in mind, proposed to slip the cessation of hostilities by three hours, Schwarzkopf meekly assented, heedless of the implications of this change—trivial as Washington saw things, massive from the perspective of the various troop units scattered across Kuwait and southern Iraq. Furious at discovering that operations were coming to a halt three hours earlier than Washington had announced, he demanded that his commanders resume an all-out offensive for this brief interval. In the field this stop—go—stop again sequence of orders from on high simply generated confusion. Schwarzkopf was acting more like a squad leader than the overall commander of a massive air, ground, and naval coalition.[17] The campaign's very last act served to showcase Schwarzkopf's shortcomings. Charged by the White House with negotiating a formal cease-fire, the CENTCOM commander paid more attention to appearance and atmospherics than to substance, with fateful results.

As the site for this event Schwarzkopf selected Safwan, an obscure crossroads in southern Iraq. While President Bush was lamenting the absence of a World War II–style surrender ceremony, his field commander intended to preside over a reasonable facsimile, Safwan standing in for the battleship *Missouri,* Schwarzkopf casting himself in the role of Douglas MacArthur.

After notifying Washington that he had designated Safwan as the chosen venue, however, Schwarzkopf learned that the Iraqi army still occupied the place; a garbled report had erroneously put it under the control of U.S. forces. This glitch proved too much for Schwarzkopf. By his own account he now "came completely unglued," with General Franks the specific target of his wrath. "I felt as if I'd been lied to. All of my accumulated frustration and rage with VII Corps came boiling out."[18]

Moving the cease-fire talks to a different location was out of the question: doing so might cast doubt on Schwarzkopf's omniscience and stain a campaign that all concerned were eager to portray as flawless. So for the next twenty-four hours nudging the Iraqis out of Safwan without instigating a major bloodletting became CENTCOM priority number one, taking precedence over all other considerations, not least of all any substantive considerations related to war termination.

Schwarzkopf himself had drafted proposed terms of reference for the talks. His own views were quite simple: "Our side had *won,* so we were in a position to dictate terms."[19] After some minor wordsmithing, Washington had approved Schwarzkopf's draft. As he headed toward Safwan on March 3, 1991, the general was in the driver's seat.

His mandate, as he himself understood it, was "confined to military issues," above all securing the release of coalition soldiers taken prisoner. When Schwarzkopf arrived for the talks, a reporter shouted a question: What exactly was going to be negotiated? "This isn't a negotiation," came Schwarzkopf's curt reply. "I don't plan to give them anything. I'm here to tell them exactly what we expect them to do."[20]

As he sat down across from two hitherto obscure Iraqi generals— Schwarzkopf's thoughts were focused on donating the furniture to the Smithsonian Institution "in case they ever wanted to re-create the Safwan negotiation [*sic*] scene"—he wasted little time before straying beyond his mandate and offering his interlocutors generous concessions.[21]

However unwittingly, Schwarzkopf used Safwan as an occasion to convey to Saddam Hussein this essential message: with the status quo ante bellum now restored, the United States (and by extension the coalition as a whole) had no interest in wresting further concessions from Iraq. The job was done and the quarrel largely ended.

The American general assured his interlocutors that the United States and its allies viewed Iraq's boundaries as sacrosanct. U.S. forces were going home forthwith. "We have no intention of leaving our forces permanently in Iraqi territory once the cease-fire is signed," he announced. As the talks proceeded, an atmosphere of stiff formality gave way to a spirit of mutual accommodation. The Iraqis had given Schwarzkopf what he wanted most; he returned the favor. Asked if the Iraqi army might resume use of its helicopters after the cease-fire, Schwarzkopf readily assented. "Given that the Iraqis had agreed to all of our requests, I didn't feel it was unreasonable to grant one of theirs."[22] As if to affirm that the crisis triggered by Iraq's invasion of Kuwait had reached a definitive conclusion, Schwarzkopf concluded his conversation with the Iraqi generals by exchanging salutes and comradely handshakes.

For Saddam Hussein, Schwarzkopf's loquaciousness and magnanimity came as a welcome if wholly unearned gift. The helicopters alone proved invaluable. At the very moment when Saddam's hold on power was most precarious here was another asset employed in his vicious campaign to suppress internal opposition. Yet even more important to the Iraqi dictator was Schwarzkopf's tacit admission that the United States had no interest in interfering in Iraq's internal affairs. Safwan assured Saddam that he need not worry about an externally mounted challenge to his continued rule.

Schwarzkopf may have fancied himself reprising MacArthur's role on

V-J Day. In their penchant for theatricality, the two generals bore more than a passing resemblance to each other. Yet even though Japan in 1945 lay utterly prostrate, MacArthur grasped this essential point: politically, much work remained to be done. After surrender was to come occupation and rehabilitation. In his encounter with the defeated foe on the deck of the *Missouri,* therefore, MacArthur gave away nothing. By comparison, Schwarzkopf at Safwan gave away the farm. In his haste to terminate the war he mistakenly thought he had won decisively, the CENTCOM commander helped ensure the war's de facto continuation.

Finally there is the charge against Powell. Here matters cross fully from the operational realm into the arena of politics. To characterize Powell as a political general is to acknowledge a convergence of the obvious and the essential, much like calling Marilyn Monroe a sex symbol. Yet Powell's political concerns were of a very specific sort. In his hierarchy of aims one priority outranked all others: as the U.S. military's senior serving officer he was absolutely determined that nothing bring into disrepute the institution over which he exercised stewardship. Any policy or action posing a threat to the military's standing in the eyes of the American people—especially anything smacking of another Vietnam—he opposed. Any policy or action that promised to enhance the military's collective reputation—especially anything that might help bury the memory of Vietnam—he favored. When it came to war termination, the JCS chairman, his own agenda complementing Schwarzkopf's, served in effect as the CENTCOM commander's enabler.

When the Persian Gulf crisis erupted in August 1990, Powell supported the deployment of U.S. forces to defend Saudi Arabia but evinced little enthusiasm for liberating Kuwait by force, preferring instead to rely on economic sanctions to pry Saddam Hussein out.[23] Although Powell lost that argument, he remained intent on doing everything possible to preclude U.S. forces from being drawn into anything remotely resembling a quagmire.

The design parameters informing Operation Desert Storm reflected Powell's own preferences for how the United States ought to wage war. Risk avoidance was a priority. The mission therefore was specific, concrete, and narrowly drawn, with Powell's own statement of purpose a model of economy. "Our strategy to go after this army is very, very simple," he announced at a press conference. "First we're going to cut it off, and then we're going to kill it."[24] In pursuit of that aim the United States assembled a broad allied coalition (no going it alone) and deployed a combat force of overwhelming strength (calling up citizen reserves ensured the country's commitment to what was to come). Deliberation rather than daring defined the spirit of the enterprise, as illustrated by the weeks of bombing that preceded the launch of the ground offensive. Once hostilities had commenced, Powell worked hard to guarantee Schwarzkopf complete freedom of action, insulating him from the sort of meddling by high-ranking civilian officials that had ostensibly made such a hash of Vietnam.

Here was the real essence of what came to be called the Powell Doctrine: minimizing uncertainty by employing maximum force and allowing commanders in the field to exercise broad autonomy, and by implication subordinating political considerations to operational ones. In the context of Desert Storm this meant, among other things, calling it quits at the first available moment.

All of these views put Powell in Schwarzkopf's corner when it came to hastening an end to hostilities. Although aware that coalition forces had not in fact "killed" the Iraqi army, the JCS chairman nonetheless urged a prompt and unilateral end to hostilities. "There was no need to fight a battle of annihilation," he argued. Although Powell himself believed "that Saddam would likely survive the war," that was no reason to prolong the fighting.[25] Schwarzkopf had shattered the Iraqi defenses and put Saddam's legions to flight. To give the appearance of piling on was unseemly. "There is," Powell remarked during the course of one Oval Office meeting, "chivalry in war"—an astonishing statement to make at the end of a blood-soaked century devoid of even an approximation of chivalry.[26]

Largely due to Powell's efforts, generals, not politicians, determined the precise terms that concluded the Persian Gulf War of 1990–91. President Bush "had promised the American people that Desert Storm would not become a Persian Gulf Vietnam," Powell wrote in his memoirs, "and he kept his promise."[27] The JCS chairman contributed mightily to ensuring that outcome. For Powell (and for other members of the officer corps) precluding Desert Storm from becoming another Vietnam ranked as a paramount objective. Based on that criterion, he and Schwarzkopf had collaborated to achieve a rousing success.

III

Commanders temperamentally ill-suited for the responsibilities to which they were assigned; fog and friction that in this war no less than others bred confusion, obscured reality, and clouded judgment; a pronounced tendency to subordinate strategy to institutional goals; and (in Schwarz-kopf's case) a penchant for grandstanding: these number among the factors accounting for the errors senior military officers committed in bringing the Gulf War to a conclusion.

In the war's immediate aftermath, however, few of these miscues attracted more than passing attention. If noticed at all, they didn't seem to matter and certainly didn't affect the general view that Desert Storm had ended in a historic victory.

Among the vast majority of Americans the Persian Gulf War elicited a euphoric response that allowed little room for skepticism or second thoughts. A compendium of reporting assembled by the editors of *Time* captured the mood of the moment. *Time* described Operation Desert Storm as "a drama of dazzling display, brutal crispness and amazingly decisive outcome." Out of victory had come "a glow of righteousness." For the United States the brief conflict in the Gulf had produced "a giddy mixture of pride and a renewed sense of the nation's worth." Expelling Iraq from Kuwait signaled "the end of the old American depression called the Vietnam syndrome, the compulsion to look for downside and dooms." It marked "the birth of a new American century—the onset of a unipolar world, with America at the center of it." The brilliance displayed by Schwarzkopf and his warriors heralded "the apotheosis of warmaking as a brilliant American craft."[28]

Setting aside his own initial misgivings, President Bush himself signed on to the proposition that something truly profound had occurred in the desert. Asked at a press conference on March 1, 1991, if Operation Desert Storm presaged a new era of U.S. military interventionism, the president demurred: "I think because of what has happened, we won't have to use U.S. forces around the world. I think when we say something that is objectively correct, like don't take over a neighbor or you're going to bear some responsibility, people are going to listen. . . . So, I look at the opposite. I say that what our troops have done over there will not only enhance the peace but reduce the risk that their successors have to go into battle someplace."[29]

Bush expected Desert Storm to create the foundation for "a new world order": less violent, more law abiding, a spirit of goodwill supplanting old-fashioned power politics. The triumph over Saddam Hussein, enhancing the authority and influence of the United States, especially in the Muslim world, had created opportunities to take on other problems. Head-ing the list, the president believed, was the Arab-Israeli conflict. As never before, the prospects for bringing peace to the Holy Land seemed bright.

In the end, none of this came to pass. As a mechanism to advance the cause of global peace and harmony, the war proved a total bust. Apart from restoring Kuwaiti sovereignty, Operation Desert Storm solved remarkably little. With a defiant Saddam Hussein still hunkering down in Baghdad, even the security of the Gulf itself remained uncertain. By the time Desert Storm's first anniversary had arrived, the journalist Rick Atkinson wrote, the war was well on its way to becoming "a footnote, a conflict as distant as the Boxer Rebellion of 1900." For most Americans a conflict that had briefly seemed to mark a turning point in history was fast becoming "irrelevant."[30]

As if to emphasize the point, the hostilities thought to have ended at Safwan soon resumed. In March 1991, under the guise of keeping Saddam in his "box," the United States and Great Britain launched a program of coercive intimidation intended to ensure that Iraq would remain militarily weak. This campaign of recurring air strikes and demonstrations continued for more than a decade.[31] To support this open-ended quasi-war, beefed-up U.S. military contingents remained in the region, operating out of a network of bases in Saudi Arabia, Kuwait, Turkey, and elsewhere. Viewed in some quarters as occupiers, these U.S. forces became themselves the target of attack. The upshot was this: the event that President Bush's advisors had enthusiastically marketed as the One Hundred Hour War became instead an amorphous conflict that dragged on indefinitely. Instead of reducing the likelihood of U.S. troops going into harm's way, as President Bush had predicted, it produced precisely the opposite effect.

The disappointing results produced by Operation Desert Storm gave rise to this revisionist interpretation; while the troops had done all they were asked to do, the politicians had screwed up. President Bush had assigned Schwarzkopf the wrong task. Whatever mistakes might have occurred in the desert, the really big gaffes were committed back in the Oval Office.

Put simply, the president had failed to adjust U.S. strategy to take into account success being achieved on the battlefield. The ease with which U.S. and allied forces had ousted the Iraqi army from Kuwait (the agreed-upon coalition mission) had created the opportunity to solve the Saddam Hussein problem once and for all. The Bush administration should have seized that opportunity. Whether out of timidity, a lack of imagination, or simply because events were outrunning his administration's decision cycle, President Bush chose instead to stick with the original, and in retrospect too narrowly drawn, mission.

The president had misunderstood the problem, which was not Iraq annexing Kuwait, but Saddam Hussein ruling in Baghdad. As long as the Iraqi dictator remained in power he would menace the entire Middle East. Peace and stability in the region therefore required Saddam's removal. Baghdad rather than Safwan was the proper place to settle things. In failing to grasp this essential fact, Bush and his advisors had erred fundamentally. Viewed from this perspective, Operation Desert Storm represented not a great victory but a squandered opportunity.

No group articulated this revisionist interpretation of Desert Storm with greater fervor and persistence than the very same militarists (mostly but not exclusively Republicans) who in 1991 had cheered President Bush as a courageous and farsighted statesman. Once Bill Clinton gained control of the White House in 1993 and embraced Bush's strategy of containing Iraq, these hawks began agitating for aggressive efforts aimed at eliminating Saddam. Regime change in Baghdad, they believed, was sure to fix things. Jousting in the skies above Iraq wasn't good enough. They hankered for the real thing.

Here, from an essay written in 1998, is Robert Kagan, a prominent militarist, making the case for an outright invasion of Iraq. Likening Saddam to Adolf Hitler—Kagan refers to the Iraqi dictator as "Herr Hussein"—Kagan depicts the existing policy of containment as hardly better than supine appeasement: "The only solution to the problem in Iraq today is to use air power *and* ground power, and not stop until we have finished what President Bush began in 1991. An air campaign is not enough. . . . Only ground forces can remove Saddam and his regime from power and open the way for a new post-Saddam Iraq whose intentions can safely be assumed to be benign." Kagan expresses confidence that victory will come easily and produce a windfall of positive effects. "A successful intervention in Iraq," he breezily predicts, "would revolutionize the strategic situation in the Middle East, in ways both tangible and intangible, and all to the benefit of American interests."[32]

The point of citing this passage is not to suggest that it carried any particular weight in shaping policy. Yet views such as Kagan's illustrate the trend of opinion as Operation Desert Storm lost some of its luster. The victory narrative that briefly vaulted the likes of Schwarzkopf to the status of Great American Hero no longer retained any persuasive authority.

During the 1980s, Washington had quietly collaborated with Saddam Hussein, ignoring his many crimes while supporting Iraq in its war of aggression against the Islamic Republic of Iran. Throughout the 1990s, with the Iran-Iraq War now ended, American policymakers and pundits discovered those crimes and elevated the Iraqi dictator to the status of global bogeyman. Saddam's mere survival now seemed an intolerable insult, and U.S. policy became increasingly personalized as a result. Out of that fixation with Saddam emerged this new consensus, shared by Republicans and Democrats alike: the key to achieving peace and stability in the Middle East was to complete the task that President Bush had foolishly left undone in 1991.[33]

The events of 9/11 found a second President Bush in office and many prominent anti-Saddam militarists occupying positions of influence. Iraq was in no way involved in the terrorist attacks of September 11, 2001, of course. Yet for those who had obsessed about Saddam for so long, this fact proved utterly irrelevant. The "global war on terror" offered a made-to-order opportunity to test what had by now become an article of faith: the only problem with Operation Desert Storm was that it hadn't gone far enough. The new Bush administration now set out to amend this perceived defect. Through regime change in Baghdad the United States would, in Kagan's phrase, "revolutionize the strategic situation" and reap handsome benefits.

Informed by such large ambitions, Operation Iraqi Freedom, launched in March 2003, differed from Operation Desert Storm in important ways. Speed, not deliberation, now became the name of the game. Quagmire? An emphasis on "shock and awe" would preclude any such possibility. As for foot-dragging or hand-wringing generals, they were either marginalized, ignored, or subjected to public humiliation. Senior civilian officials, most prominently Secretary of Defense Donald Rumsfeld, left no doubt about who was calling the shots. The concept that Rumsfeld devised for toppling Saddam aimed to blow through the Iraqi army, get to Baghdad as fast as possible, and have done with it.

U.S. forces did blow through the Iraqi army, occupy Baghdad, and overthrow the Baath Party regime, all in a matter of weeks. To all appearances the younger President Bush had triumphed, thereby outdoing his father: "Mission Accomplished." At first blush, the victory achieved over Iraq in 1991 had *seemed* definitive. Surely this victory actually *was* definitive, marking, President Bush promised on May 1, 2003, "the arrival of a new era."[34]

Appearances proved deceptive, however. Once again, bringing the conflict to a tidy conclusion proved elusive. The Anglo-American invasion of 2003 transformed Iraq from a crumbling dictatorship into a failed state. Soon thereafter an ethnically based civil war engulfed the country, while radical Islamists infiltrated Iraq to wage jihad against occupying infidels. What was intended to be a short conventional war morphed into a protracted, very ugly, and very costly unconventional one. U.S. forces found themselves caught in the middle.

Operation Iraqi Freedom defied the president's insistence that major combat operations had ended. The war lingered on and on, costing the United States thousands of dead and wounded and hundreds of billions of dollars. Worse, rather than solving problems, Saddam's removal saddled Washington with onerous new problems, regime change in Baghdad further emboldening anti-Western forces not only in Iraq but elsewhere in the region.

Colin Powell had given the older President Bush high marks for waging his Persian Gulf War in ways that avoided its becoming another Vietnam. A variant of Vietnam, sans the jungles and rice paddies, now all but consumed the younger Bush's presidency.

What had gone wrong? Secretary Rumsfeld quickly emerged as a favored scapegoat, tagged with having failed to plan adequately for "Phase IV," all the tasks inherent in occupying and rebuilding Iraq after Saddam's removal. The challenges cropping up following the fall of Baghdad had caught American leaders, military no less than civilian, flatfooted. A string of unimpressive American generals—Tommy Franks, John Abizaid, Ricardo Sanchez, and George Casey—spent several painful years struggling to figure out exactly what had hit them.

Yet amid the floundering, those who had planned and orchestrated the first U.S. military encounter with Saddam Hussein could claim a certain vindication: on second thought, their reluctance to march on Baghdad when the opportunity first presented itself back in 1991 may not have been so terribly misguided after all.

IV

As Americans today reflect back on twenty years of war and quasi-war in Iraq, they might think a bit more kindly about the generalship and the statesmanship displayed way back when that conflict was young. Perhaps Generals Franks, Schwarzkopf, and Powell didn't do such a bad job after all. Perhaps George H. W. Bush knew a few things that George W. Bush ought to have absorbed. Certainly any mistakes committed by Bush I and his lieutenants appear almost trivial in comparison to the blunders perpetrated by Bush II and his circle.

Taking this two-decade-long narrative as a whole, Operation Desert Storm may even represent a high point of sorts. For American soldiers serving in the Persian Gulf it has been mostly downhill since. Yet despite all that has ensued since General Schwarzkopf swaggered into Safwan, and despite all that his successors have (presumably) learned since, ringing down the curtain on the U.S. military misadventure in Iraq continues to pose daunting problems. Why has war there proven to be so interminable?

The real explanation lies with this depressing fact: from 1991 to the present, American policymakers, along with the senior U.S. military commanders serving as their agents, have committed the most fundamental of errors. Simply put, in the Persian Gulf and in the so-called Greater Middle East more broadly, they misconstrued the problem. Having done so, they devised inappropriate solutions. The persistent reliance on those solutions exacerbated actual problems to which Washington has remained steadfastly oblivious.

For decades, two assumptions have formed the basis for U.S. policy in the Persian Gulf, the provenance of both those assumptions traceable back to the Carter Doctrine of 1980.[35] According to the first assumption, the key to establishing Persian Gulf stability lies in fostering a balance of power congenial to the United States. Yet in attempting to create such a balance, Washington has sought more than simply an equilibrium among the major Gulf states. It has sought to place the United States itself in a position to manage that balance, with Washington having the final say on matters determining the course of events in the Gulf. Furthermore, U.S. policymakers have sought to change the character of Gulf states, with an eye toward making them less susceptible to irresponsible behavior and more amenable to Washington's coaching or direction.

Always, however, the United States has clung to the view that the region consists of a more or less fixed number of legitimate states governed by more or less legitimate governments—in short that the Persian Gulf (and the Middle East more broadly) does not differ structurally from Europe or Latin America. Implicit in this perspective is a tendency on the part of U.S. policymakers (operating in a largely post-Christian milieu and blind to the history of American imperialism) to undervalue the importance of Islam and to ignore the legacy of Western colonialism and postcolonial meddling in the region.

According to the second assumption, the key to orchestrating and managing a Persian Gulf balance lies in the adroit application of American power, either directly or through proxies. Policymakers have accepted as axiomatic this proposition: that American activism—diplomatic, economic, but above all military—serves to reduce the sources of regional conflict, thereby advancing core American interests. If instability persists in the face of U.S. exertions—as it has—then the antidote is to be found in trying harder, bringing to the task more resources, almost inevitably expressed in terms of an enlarged military presence and agenda.

In essence Washington's concept of balance in the Persian Gulf implied the region's incorporation into the post-1945 Pax Americana. Bluntly, the phrase *balance of power* was a code word for hegemony.

The historical record suggests that these two assumptions are false. Adherence to the Carter Doctrine over the past three decades has vastly enlarged the scope of U.S. commitments to the Persian Gulf (and across the Greater Middle East). It has also resulted in the expenditure of American resources in staggering quantities. Yet these exertions have served not to reduce but to enflame the sources of conflict. The region has become not more stable but less. Proponents of violent anti-Western Islamism have had little difficulty garnering support and even recruiting foot soldiers. Terrorism has become epidemic. U.S. hegemony meanwhile has remained a chimera.

Washington's response to the Gulf crisis of 1990–91 illustrates in microcosm the abiding defects of Washington's preferred approach to policy. Operation Desert Storm and its aftermath help us understand why U.S. efforts time and again produce outcomes radically at odds with professed American intentions, and why wars in that region once begun prove so difficult to end.

Deliberations within the Bush I administration leading up to Desert Storm routinely cited the concept of a regional balance as both source and solution to the Persian Gulf crisis. "The Iraqi invasion of Kuwait was possible because of a collapse of the regional balance of power": such was the analysis offered by a typical National Security Council paper, which then went on to insist that reestablishing a regional balance ranked as "a key security objective."[36] In maintaining any such restored balance the United States would necessarily play an ongoing and pivotal role.

So too would Saddam Hussein's Iraq. With that in mind, the immediate task facing the United States, in ejecting Iraq from Kuwait, was to reduce without entirely destroying Iraqi military power. The Bush I administration wanted to render Iraq incapable of further aggression without leaving a gaping hole in the center of the Persian Gulf. Doing so meant walking a fine line. As one study by the National Security Council put it, in gauging the punishment to be visited upon Iraq, the United States needed to avoid "so weaken[ing] Iraqi military capability as to create a power vacuum in the region."[37]

Even as preparations for Operation Desert Storm proceeded, however, the White House had begun to place the upcoming offensive in a much broader context. Saddam's expulsion from Kuwait would mark not an end point but a new beginning. Up to this time the Persian Gulf had lagged behind Western Europe and East Asia in the hierarchy of U.S. strategic interests. The war was going to change that. With the Cold War now all but ended, from now on the Middle East was likely to rank "first in terms of threats to our interests and the need for the United States to act."[38]

Whether the upcoming fight proved to be tough or easy, the administration saw victory over Iraq as a foregone conclusion. The big question was how the United States should capitalize on the success gained on the battlefield. Within the administration the preferred answer emphasized three components: the creation of new regional security structures, increased emphasis on opening up and modernizing the nations of the Islamic world, and intensified efforts to broker peace between Israel and its Arab neighbors.[39] Common to all three was this feature: each implied a more forceful U.S. role and an enlarged U.S. presence.

Actions undertaken by the Pentagon pursuant to the imperatives of the Carter Doctrine already provided a basis for more robust regional security arrangements. From a U.S. perspective these included "negotiating access agreements, building bases, having highly mobile forces, prepositioning equipment, conducting joint exercises and the like"—the very actions that were even then facilitating the ongoing buildup of U.S. forces in the Gulf.[40] Although administration analysts wanted the U.S. military "to have as low a profile as possible," they also wanted to be sure that forces would be readily available when needed. The idea was to do things with the minimum amount of publicity. "Details about the size of U.S. forces," one State Department memo recommended, referring to postwar arrangements, "should be as vague as possible consistent with U.S. domestic requirements."[41]

The Joint Chiefs of Staff concurred in the need to develop "an enhanced U.S. capability to rapidly reinsert forces," advocating "expanded security guarantees" to friendly nations throughout the region. To keep the door to the Persian Gulf propped open, the JCS called for "bilateral agreements, exercises, and planning teams to establish and maintain visible military-to-military relationships in the region." Adding to the quantities of U.S. military equipment stashed in the region would also be helpful. The JCS was counting on the increased "credibility" accruing to the United States for "defending one Arab state against another" to make the region's various emirs, kings, and presidents amenable to such a program.[42] The bottom line was simply this: for the national security apparatus, Operation Desert Storm promised to open up a vast new array of opportunities for deepening military engagement.

The second element informing administration thinking about the region related to the methods of governance prevailing in and around the Persian Gulf. Within the Arab world "impulses toward political openness and democratic institutions" met with resistance in the form of "regime preoccupation with short-term stability." The result was "unfulfilled basic human needs," which in turn left "little space for political and social fulfillment."[43] In the wake of Desert Storm these matters too were about to become Washington's business.

Administration analysts understood that tampering with Arab political arrangements carried considerable danger. In the near term, promoting political and economic liberalization might actually increase rather than guard against instability. Still, on balance, the promised gains outweighed those risks.

Bolstering the administration's sense of self-confidence was its clear understanding of exactly what had been holding back the peoples of the Middle East. In Washington the antidote to backwardness and stagnation appeared all but self-evident. Arab countries "need to be receptive to new ideas." They had to understand that "to be competitive in an increasingly interdependent world, they have to be able to deal with the free flow of information and technology." The upshot was that the "Middle East should become less insular." To flourish, Arab nations would have to "keep their borders and airwaves open, encourage broad-based participation in political decision-making, and promote free economic choices and reduced government control over economic and trade decisions."[44] It was therefore incumbent upon Arabs to "move toward greater economic integration with the industrialized world."[45] In terms of political economy Arabs had no real alternative but to subscribe to the norms prevailing throughout the Pax Americana. Only then would the peoples of the Middle East "become full beneficiaries of the new world order."[46]

Finally, although the administration did not delude itself into thinking that resolving the Israeli-Palestinian conflict would be easy, renewed support for the so-called peace process constituted the third leg of Washington's planned post–Desert Storm strategy. Administration officials expected the war to transform U.S.-Israeli relations as well as U.S.-Arab relations and therefore to enhance Washington's leverage as mediator. Making progress on this front was an urgent priority for the United States. As long as the United States remained close to Israel, Arab perceptions that Palestinian grievances were being ignored would adversely affect U.S. relations with the entire Islamic world. In that regard, wrote Richard Haass, the National Security Council's senior director for Near East and South Asian affairs, "we may deny linkage as a matter of policy, but we cannot ignore it as a fact of life."[47] Here too victory over Iraq had the potential to be a game changer.

The strategy devised as an adjunct and follow-up to Operation Desert Storm—emphasizing the assertion of military primacy, the export of liberal democratic capitalism, and the mediation of conflicts viewed in Washington as extraneous—was entirely consistent with the post–World War II tradition of American statecraft. Such an approach had worked quite well in Europe and at least passably well in East Asia and Latin America.

What policymakers in 1990 and 1991 could not see or refused to entertain was the possibility that conditions in the Islamic world—Islam itself seldom qualified for mention in the policy papers circulated by the National Security Council—differed, and those differences rendered methods applied elsewhere not only irrelevant but even counterproductive. Rather than inducing acquiescence, continuing efforts to assert U.S. military primacy since Operation Desert Storm—for example, stationing U.S. forces in Saudi Arabia for a decade—have inspired sustained resistance. Efforts to promote liberal values have made little headway. And efforts to impose a solution ending the Israeli-Palestinian conflict have done little except to breed cynicism.

The real failure afflicting Operation Desert Storm, evident both at Safwan and in Washington, was not mishandled war termination. Rather the real failure lay in a grotesque misunderstanding of the context from which the Persian Gulf War had emerged: a persistent refusal on the part of the West to allow the people of the Islamic world to determine their own fate in their own way. And that refusal contributed mightily to the rise of violent anti-Western Islamism.

However inadvertently, Operation Desert Storm advanced the Islamist cause. This became its principal legacy. As a consequence, the partial victory over Saddam in 1991 helped set the stage for what Americans in the wake of 9/11 chose to call their Global War on Terror. That conflict, subsequently redesignated the Long War, continues today with no end in sight, even as the Obama administration clings stubbornly to the conviction that asserting military dominance, exporting liberal values, and advancing the peace process promise a way out. Flawed twenty years ago, that approach to strategy remains no less flawed today. Washington's insistence to the contrary makes prospects of terminating the Long War any time soon nearly nonexistent.

SUGGESTED READING

The most insightful and most richly documented history of Operation Desert Storm during its ground phase is Richard Swain, *Lucky War: Third Army in Desert Storm* (Fort Leavenworth, KS, 1994). Important journalistic accounts include Rick Atkinson, *Crusade: The Untold Story of the Persian Gulf War* (New York, 1993) and Michael R. Gordon and Bernard E. Trainor, *The Generals' War: The Inside Story of the Conflict in the Gulf* (New York, 1994).

Acknowledgments

This project began in July 2009 when General Martin E. Dempsey, commanding general of the U.S. Army Training and Doctrine Command (TRADOC), asked me to lead a project to study war termination in American history. Since then, he has been stalwart in his support of the enterprise. He shares with us a conviction that intellectual inquiry in general and study of this topic in particular are vital to the future of our army and the nation. Despite his enthusiasm for our work, he never attempted to fetter our research or edit our conclusions, preferring to foster the pursuit of honest and serious history. The project would never have begun and could never have been completed without his encouragement.

For the past year we have worked with members of the TRADOC staff to plan a conference of leading military historians to discuss the topic. The leader of this group was Brig. Gen. H. R. McMaster, who lent us his boundless energy and broad historical expertise. Other members of the staff who worked tirelessly on this unusual project included Lieut. Col. Howard Christie, Mr. Burley Gardner, Ms. Crystal Faucett, and Ms. Edna Van Lieu. Chief among them was Col. (ret.) Mike Starry, Gen. McMaster's deputy. Mike championed this effort at every step, coordinating with various headquarters, cutting through red tape, all the while exuding good humor and patience even through the most unforeseen and trying circumstances. Mike Starry's skill and leadership are directly responsible for the success of this enterprise.

In January the contributors assembled at the University of North Carolina at Chapel Hill to prepare for a conference to be held in June. There we discussed the topic in broad terms, explored its theoretical significance, and talked about how each of the pieces contributed to the whole. That meeting was instrumental in setting the conditions for all our subsequent efforts. We owe a tremendous debt of gratitude to our fellow contributors and UNC faculty members Joe Glatthaar and Wayne Lee, and especially to Jackie Gorman at the Curriculum in Peace, War and Defense and LaTissa Davis in the UNC Department of History.

In June 2010 the Training and Doctrine Command and the Department of History of the United States Military Academy hosted a conference at West Point on the subject of ending America's wars. The panel discussions and videotaped interviews of all our participants will be used to develop professional military education curriculum within TRADOC and West Point. The Department of History faculty and staff executed the conference with their typical aplomb, making the impossible seem effortless. We owe special thanks to Col. Lance Betros, Maj. Josh Bradley, Mr. Todd Brewster, Lt. Col. Greg Daddis, Col. Gian Gentile, Ms. Melissa Mills, Maj. John Ringquist, Col. Ty Seidule, Dr. Antonio Thompson, Maj. Jason Warren, and Dr. Jackie Whitt. We are grateful to the Department of History cartographer, Mr. Frank Martini, who ably edited the maps in this volume, continuing the tradition of excellence that has been a hallmark of his office for decades.

We wish to thank the expert and friendly editorial staff at the Free Press, who have continually demonstrated remarkable skill and efficiency. Each of them has been a fan and supporter of this effort. All of them have made it better with their sharp eyes and tireless efforts. They include Hilary Redmon, our editor, and her assistants Sydney Tanigawa and Jonathan Evans. We also want to express our gratitude to Martin Beiser, who was the first person at the Free Press to see the potential in this work, a faith he demonstrated despite the fact that we had yet to write a word of it.

Finally, I wish to say a personal word of thanks to all fifteen contributors. At the outset, many friends warned me about the pitfalls of taking on the editorship of such a project. While it was quite an undertaking, the authors lifted my burden daily with their professionalism, collegiality, and good cheer. I have made several new and cherished friends along the way, which adds deeply to the honor I feel to have been associated with such a distinguished collection of scholars.

—Matthew Moten
West Point, August 2010

About the Contributors

Andrew J. Bacevich is professor of history and international relations at Boston University. A graduate of the U. S. Military Academy, he received his Ph.D. in American diplomatic history from Princeton. He is the author of *The New American Militarism: How Americans Are Seduced by War* (2005), *The Limits of Power: The End of American Exceptionalism* (2008), and *Washington Rules: America's Path to Permanent War* (2010), among other books.

Edward M. Coffman did all of his undergraduate and graduate work at the University of Kentucky and served two years during the Korean War as an infantry officer. He began his teaching career at the University of Memphis, then spent thirty-one years at the University of Wisconsin-Madison where he retired in 1992. During that period, he also served as a visiting professor at Kansas State University, West Point, the Air Force Academy, the Army Command and General Staff College, and the Army War College. He served one term as the OAH representative on the National Publications and Research Commission and two terms (one as chair) on the Department of the Army Historical Advisory Committee. The U.S. Army awarded him the Distinguished Civilian Service Medal, Outstanding Civilian Service Medal, and the Commander's Award for Public Service. He has been a member of the Society for Military History for more than fifty years and served as vice president and president of the organization and received its Distinguished Book Award for *The Regulars* and the Samuel Eliot Morison Prize for Lifetime Contribution to Military History. A Guggenheim Fellow, he has published *The Hilt of the Sword: The Career of Peyton C. March* (1966), *The War To End All Wars: The American Military Experience in World War I* (1968); *The Old*

Army: A Portrait of the American Army in Peacetime, 1784–1898 (1986), and *The Regulars: The American Army, 1898–1941* (2004).

Conrad C. Crane became the Director of the U.S. Army Military History Institute on February 1, 2003. Before accepting that position, Dr. Crane served with the Strategic Studies Institute at the U.S. Army War College from September 2000 to January 2003, where he held the General Douglas MacArthur Chair of Research. He has also held the General Hoyt S. Vandenberg Chair of Aerospace Studies at the War College. He joined SSI after his retirement from active military service, a twenty-six-year military career that concluded with nine years as Professor of History at the U.S. Military Academy. He holds a B.S. from USMA and an M.A. and Ph.D. from Stanford University. He is also a graduate of the U.S. Army Command and General Staff College and the U.S. Army War College. He has authored or edited books and monographs on the Civil War, World War I, World War II, Korea and Vietnam, and has written and lectured widely on airpower and landpower issues. Before leaving SSI he coauthored a prewar study on Reconstructing Iraq that influenced Army planners and has attracted much attention from the media. He was the lead author for the new Army-USMC counterinsurgency manual which was released in December, 2006. For that effort he was named one of *Newsweek*'s people to watch in 2007. He visited Iraq in November 2007 at General Petraeus's request to evaluate the new doctrine in action. In November 2008, he was named the international Archivist of the Year by the Scone Foundation.

Joseph G. Dawson III focuses on U.S. military history in the nineteenth century, with interest in civil-military relations. His books include *Army Generals and Reconstruction: Louisiana, 1862–1877* (LSU Press, 1982) and *Doniphan's Epic March: The 1st Missouri Volunteers in the Mexican War* (Kansas, 1999). He contributed "American Volunteer Colonels Serving in the U.S.-Mexican War" to the journal *American Nineteenth Century History* (2006) and "Zealous for Annexation" on volunteer soldiering and military government in New Mexico to the *Journal of Strategic Studies* (1996). He has also published articles in the *Journal of Military History* on "General Archibald Henderson's Lasting Legacy to the U.S. Marine Corps" (1996) and "Jefferson Davis and the Confederacy's Offensive-Defensive Strategy" (2009). He has written several chapters in edited works, including "The First of the Modern Wars?" in *Themes in the Amer-*

ican Civil War (2000; 2009), edited by Susan-Mary Grant and Brian Holden Reid. He is professor of history at Texas A&M University and earned the Ph.D. from Louisiana State University in 1978.

Colonel Gian P. Gentile received a Bachelor of Arts Degree in history from the University of California, Berkeley, in 1986 and was commissioned through ROTC as second lieutenant of Armor. He has served in command and staff positions in the continental United States, Germany, and Korea, and in Iraq in 2003 and 2006. In 2003 he was a Brigade Combat Team Executive Officer in the 4th Infantry Division in Tikrit. In 2006 he commanded a Cavalry Squadron in the 4th Infantry Division in west Baghdad. He is a graduate of the Army's School of Advanced Military Studies (SAMS) and he holds a doctorate in history from Stanford University. His book *How Effective Is Strategic Bombing? Lessons Learned from World War II to Kosovo,* was published by New York University Press in 2000. He has published articles in the *Pacific Historical Review, Air Power History, Journal of Military History, Joint Forces Quarterly, Parameters,* and *Armed Forces Journal.* He has also published numerous opinion pieces in the *Washington Post, Christian Science Monitor, Washington Times,* and the *International Herald Tribune.* He is a member of the Armor Association, the Veterans of Foreign Wars, and Phi Beta Kappa. He has directed the Military and American History Programs at the United States Military Academy at West Point and is currently a visiting fellow at the Council on Foreign Relations in New York City.

Joseph T. Glatthaar is Stephenson Distinguished Professor of History at the University of North Carolina–Chapel Hill. Glatthaar is the author of numerous award-winning books and articles, including *General Lee's Army: From Victory to Defeat, Partners in Command: Relationships Between Civil War Leaders,* and *Forged in Battle: The Civil War Alliance of Black Soldiers and Their White Officers.* Glatthaar received a Ph.D. from the University of Wisconsin-Madison and has taught at the U.S. Military Academy, the U.S. Army War College, and the U.S. Army Command and General Staff College.

Ira D. Gruber is Harris Masterson, Jr., Professor Emeritus of History, at Rice University, where he taught early American and military history from 1966 to 2009. He has also served as a visiting professor at the United States Army Command and General Staff College and at the

United States Military Academy. His books include *The Howe Brothers and the American Revolution* (New York, 1972); *Warfare in the Western World: Military Operations since 1600* with Robert A. Doughty et al., 2 vols. (Lexington, Mass., 1996); *John Peebles' American War: The Diary of a Scottish Grenadier, 1776–1782,* edited for the Army Records Society (Stroud, Gloucestershire, 1998); and *Books and the British Army in the Age of the American Revolution* (Chapel Hill, 2010).

John W. Hall is the Ambrose-Hesseltine Assistant Professor of U.S. Military History at the University of Wisconsin-Madison. He previously served fifteen years as an officer in the U.S. Army and taught at the U.S. Military Academy at West Point. He is the author of *Uncommon Defense: Indian Allies in the Black Hawk War,* which Harvard University Press published in 2009. He is presently working on a military history of Indian removal (also to be published by Harvard) and several smaller projects. Dr. Hall is a graduate of the U.S. Military Academy and received his Ph.D. from the University of North Carolina–Chapel Hill.

George C. Herring is Alumni Professor of History Emeritus at the University of Kentucky. A native of Virginia, he received the B.A. degree from Roanoke College and earned M.A. and Ph.D. degrees from the University of Virginia. A specialist in the history of U.S. foreign relations, his writing has focused on the Vietnam War and includes most importantly *America's Longest War: The United States and Vietnam, 1950–1975,* now in its fourth edition. His book *From Colony to Superpower: U.S. Foreign Relations Since 1776* was published in Oxford University Press's History of the United States series. He has been a visiting professor at the University of Otago in New Zealand, the U.S. Military Academy, and the University of Richmond.

Wayne E. Lee is an Associate Professor of History at the University of North Carolina, and currently the chair of the Curriculum in Peace, War, and Defense. He is the author of *Crowds and Soldiers in Revolutionary North Carolina: The Culture of Violence in Riot and War* (Florida, 2001), and numerous other works on early American and Native American warfare. His survey of cultural approaches to American military history was published by the *Journal of American History* in 2007. His next book studies the nature of violence and strategic calculation in English and American wars from 1500 to 1865, and will be published by Oxford University Press in 2011 under the title *Barbarians and Brothers: Restraint, and Atrocity in Anglo-American Warfare, 1500–1865*. He is currently editing two volumes on warfare, empires, and culture. He also works as an archaeologist and currently helps run a project in the mountains of northern Albania which, among other things, examines Ottoman recruitment of auxiliary troops from Catholic mountain tribes.

Brian McAllister Linn was born in Honolulu and educated in Hawaii, England, and Canada. He is a graduate of the University of Hawai'i and the The Ohio State University. He joined the Texas A&M University Department of History in 1989, was tenured in 1995, and promoted to professor in 1998. He is the author of four books, including *The Echo of Battle: The Army's Way of War, Guardians of Empire,* and *The Philippine War, 1899–1902*. He has twice received the Society for Military History's Distinguished Book Award. He has been an Olin Fellow at Yale University, the Susan Dyer Peace Fellow at the Hoover Institute, the Harold K. Johnson Visiting Professor of History at the Army War College, a John Simon Guggenheim Memorial Foundation Fellow, and a Woodrow Wilson International Center Fellow, and a Fulbright Fellow at the National University of Singapore. He was recently appointed the Ralph R. Thomas Professor in Liberal Arts and is the current president of the Society for Military History.

Specializing in United States military history, **Peter Maslowski** has taught at the University of Nebraska-Lincoln since January 1974, except for one year when he was the John F. Morrison Professor of Military History at the U.S. Army Command and General Staff College at Fort Leavenworth, Kansas. He has authored or co-authored four books, including *For the Common Defense: A Military History of the United States of America, Armed with Cameras: The American Military Photographers of World War II,* and *Looking for a Hero: Staff Sergeant Joe Ronnie Hooper and the Vietnam War,* and has written more than a dozen essays. He has received three distinguished teaching awards, including a University system-wide Outstanding Teaching and Creative Activity Award (OTICA) in 2002, and the Society for Military History's Samuel Eliot Morison Prize, which is awarded for "a spectrum of scholarly activity contributing significantly to the field," in 2010. Among his professional service activities, he has served on the Department of the Army's Historical Advisory Committee, the Society for Military History's Board of Trustees, and the Advisory

Board for the Gilder Lehrman Institute of American History. In addition, he co-edits a series entitled "War, Society, and the Military" for the University of Nebraska Press.

Roger J. Spiller holds a Ph.D. in History from Louisiana State University (1977). He is one of the founding members of the Combat Studies Institute, U.S. Army Command and General Staff College (USACGSC), where he first served on the faculty from 1978 to 1982. From 1982 to 1985, he was Special Assistant to the Commander in Chief, United States Readiness Command. From 1985 to 2005, he once again was on the faculty at USACGSC, first as Professor of Combined Arms Warfare, then as George C. Marshall Distinguished Professor of History. From 1992 to 1995, he served concurrently as Personal Historian to the Chief of Staff, United States Army. Since 2005, he has been an affiliated Professor of History at the University of Kansas. In 2007–2008, he was the Charles Boal Ewing Distinguished Visiting Professor of Military History at the United States Military Academy, West Point. He is the author or editor of numerous books, among them *An Instinct for War* (Harvard, 2005), and *In the School of War* (Nebraska, 2010).

Gerhard L. Weinberg was born in Germany and came to the USA in 1940. After service in the U.S. Army, he finished his BA in 1948 and then completed an MA in 1949 and Ph.D. in 1951 at the University of Chicago. After working on Columbia University's War Documentation Project, he taught at the Universities of Chicago, Kentucky, Michigan, and North Carolina, retiring in 1999. He established the program for microfilming the captured German documents, has published or edited eleven books and more than a hundred articles, chapters, and guides to records with an emphasis on Nazi Germany, World War II, and the Holocaust. He lives with his wife and a friendly dog in Efland, North Carolina.

Theodore A. Wilson earned a B.A. in History and Political Science from Indiana University in 1962, a M.A. in History from Indiana in 1963, and the Ph.D. in U.S. Diplomatic History from Indiana University in 1966. A member of the University of Kansas faculty since 1965, he teaches twentieth-century U.S. military and diplomatic history. He has served as Director of Graduate Studies and Chair of the Department of History, Associate Dean of the College of Liberal Arts and Sciences, Director of the Hall Center for the Humanities, and Director of the M.A. in International Studies Program. He has held visiting appointments at the U.S. Army Command and General Staff College, University College Dublin, and he served as Senior Research Fellow during 1989–91 at the U.S. Army Center of Military History. Since 1986, he has been General Editor of the University Press of Kansas series, Modern War Studies. Among his publications are *The First Summit: Roosevelt and Churchill at Placentia Bay, 1941* (1969; rev. ed., 1991); *The Marshall Plan, 1947–1951* (1977); *Three Generations in 20th Century America* (1976, rev. ed., 1981), and the edited and co-edited volumes: *D-Day 1944* (1994); *Victory in Europe 1945* (2000); *America in World War II: Critical Issues* (1998, rev. ed., 2004), and *Presidents, Diplomats, and Other Mortals* (2007). Wilson's research focuses on the intersections of politics, national security policies, and foreign affairs during the period 1940–1975. He has a forthcoming book on the selection and training of U.S. military forces in World War II, and his current project is a study of the U.S. military and civilian "occupation" of Britain during World War II.

About the Editor

Col. Matthew Moten is professor and deputy head of the Department of History at the United States Military Academy. A graduate of West Point, he has served in the U.S. Army for more than twenty-seven years, including assignments in the Pentagon, Germany, Kuwait, and Iraq. He specializes in the history of American political-military relations. His recent publications include an essay titled "A Broken Dialogue: Rumsfeld, Shinseki, and Civil-Military Tension," in *American Civil-Military Relations: The Soldier and the State in a New Era* (Johns Hopkins University Press, 2009) and a short monograph titled *The Army Officer's Professional Ethic—Past, Present and Future* (Strategic Studies Institute, February 2010). He is currently writing a history of American political-military relations to be published by Harvard University Press. Colonel Moten holds a doctorate in history from Rice University and is the author of *The Delafield Commission and the American Military Profession* (Texas A&M University Press, 2000). He and his wife, Margaret, have two grown children, Stephanie and Marshall.

Notes

SIX PROPOSITIONS

1. Thucydides, *The Peloponnesian War,* trans. Rex Warner, with an introduction by M. I. Finley (1952; London: Penguin Books, 1972), 75–76.
2. Ibid., 79–83.
3. Ibid., 81–82.
4. The phrase is Thucydides' (ibid., 495).
5. The British barrister and law scholar Coleman Phillipson's *Termination of War and Treaties of Peace* (London: Fisher Unwin, 1916) is usually considered the first study on this subject. Not until H. A. Callahan's *What Makes Wars End* (New York: Vanguard, 1944) did another scholarly work take war termination as its theme. Most of the scholarly work on the subject since the Vietnam War can be found in the pages of the *Journal of Peace Research* or the *Journal of Conflict Resolution.* The most useful surveys of this work can be found in William T. R. Fox, "How Wars End," in *The Annals of the American Academy of Political and Social Science,* ed. William T. R. Fox (Philadelphia: American Academy of Political and Social Science, 1970); Berenice A. Carroll, "How Wars End: An Analysis of Some Current Hypotheses," *Journal of Peace Research* 6, no. 4 (1969): 295–321.
6. James Reed, "Should Deterrence Fail: War Termination in Campaign Planning," *Parameters,* summer 1993, 41–52; Harry Summers, "Deter, Fight, Terminate: The Purpose of War Is a Better Peace," *Naval War College Review,* January–February 1986, 18–29.
7. Ardant du Picq, *Études sur le combat* (Paris: Librairie Hachette, 1880), 11: "L'homme ne va pas au combat pour la lutte, mais pour la victoire. Il fait tout ce qui depend de lui pour supprimer la premiere et assurer la seconde."
8. The negotiations at the end of the First Gulf War are discussed in detail by Andrew Bacevich's essay in this work.
9. Carl von Clausewitz, *On War,* trans. and ed. Michael Howard and Peter Paret (Princeton: Princeton University Press, 1976), 78.
10. Meredith Reid Sarkees and Fran Wayman, *Resort to War: 1816–2007,* 2010, www.correlatesofwar.org. This accounting is the latest in the long-standing Correlates of War Project, initiated in 1963 by David Singer at the University of Michigan.
11. Clausewitz, not surprisingly, had much to say about the checks imposed on the absolute military expression of a nation's resources. See, for instance, *On War,* 79.
12. See Joseph T. Glatthaar's essay in the present volume.

13. Allan R. Millett and Peter Maslowski, *For the Common Defense: A Military History of the United States of America* (New York: Free Press, 1994), 427–28.

14. Ibid., 432.

15. See in particular Alan Beyerchen, "Clausewitz and the Non-Linear Nature of Warfare," in *Clausewitz in the Twenty-First Century,* ed. Hew Strachan and Andreas Herberg-Rothe (Oxford: Oxford University Press, 2007), 45–56, especially 55.

16. Douglas Pike, "Conduct of the Vietnam War: Strategic Factors, 1965–1968," in *The Second Indochina War: Proceedings of a Symposium Held at Arlie, Virginia, 7–9 November 1984* (Washington: U.S. Army Center of Military History, 1986), 99–119.

17. This analysis is drawn principally from Tsuyoshi Hasegawa's *Racing the Enemy: Stalin, Truman, and the Surrender of Japan* (Cambridge: Harvard University Press, 2005); Edward J. Drea, *Japan's Imperial Army: Its Rise and Fall, 1853–1945* (Lawrence: University Press of Kansas, 2010); John W. Dower, *Embracing Defeat: Japan in the Wake of World War II* (New York: Norton, 1999); and Gerhard L. Weinberg's essay in the present volume.

18. The strategic revolution posed by the atomic bomb is surveyed by Lawrence Freedman, "The First Two Generations of Nuclear Strategists," and Colin S. Gray, "Strategy in the Nuclear Age: The United States, 1945–1991," both in *The Making of Strategy: Rulers, States, and War,* ed. Williamson Murray, MacGregor Knox, and Alvin Bernstein (Cambridge: Cambridge University Press, 1994), 735–78, 579–613.

19. Gavin is quoted in Russell Weigley, *The American Way of War: A History of United States Strategy and Policy* (New York: Macmillan, 1973), 368.

20. Geoffrey Blainey, *The Causes of War,* 267.

21. Traditional military knowledge was airily dismissed by these new strategists. One debate between Alain Enthoven and a senior officer ended with the all too representative remark, "General, I have fought just as many nuclear wars as you have." Fred Kaplan, *The Wizards of Armageddon* (New York: Simon and Schuster, 1983), 250–54.

22. See Marc Trachtenberg, "Strategic Thought in America, 1952–1966," *Political Science Quarterly* 104, no. 2 (1989): 301–34; Richard K. Betts, "Should Strategic Studies Survive?," *World Politics* 50, no. 1 (1997): 7–33; Bernard Brodie, "The Development of Nuclear Strategy," *International Security* 2, no. 4 (1978): 65–83.

23. T. C. Schelling, "The Retarded Science of International Strategy," *World Politics* 4, no. 3 (1960): 107–37. This article marked the debut of Schelling's thinking on conflict bargaining, which appeared in fuller form in his *Strategy of Conflict* (Cambridge: Harvard University Press, 1960).

24. See Wayne E. Lee's essay on the War of 1812 in the present volume.

25. On this early version of "signal sending," see Conrad C. Crane's essay on the Korean War in this volume.

26. Weigley, *The American Way of War,* 477.

27. On the ultimate effect of North Vietnam's Tet Offensive, see Gian P. Gentile's essay in this volume.

PLATTSBURGH 1814

1. Gordon S. Wood, *Empire of Liberty: A History of the Early Republic, 1789–1815* (New York: Oxford University Press, 2009), 659.

2. Jefferson to Adams, June 11, 1812, in *The Papers of Thomas Jefferson: Retirement Series,*

ed. J. Jefferson Looney, 6 vols. to date (Princeton: Princeton University Press, 2004–), 5:124

3. Madison to Congress, June 1, 1812, and Annual Message to Congress, November 4, 1812, in *A Compilation of the Messages and Papers of the Presidents, 1789–1898,* ed. J. D. Richardson (New York: Bureau of National Literature, 1896–98), 2:484–90, 499–506.

4. Bathurst to Prevost, June 3, 1814. This document was long missing but recently was discovered in a private collection and published in full in David G. Fitz-Enz, *The Final Invasion: Plattsburgh, the War of 1812's Most Decisive Battle* (New York: Cooper Square Press, 2001), 50–52.

5. W. H. Robinson to Mr. Clarkson, September 10, 1814, Public Archives of Canada, 24 I 21 MG, American War of 1812, quoted in Fitz-Enz, *Final Invasion,* 101.

6. Quoted in Fitz-Enz, *Final Invasion,* 119.

7. William Wood, ed., *Select British Documents of the Canadian War of 1812* (Toronto: Champlain Society, 1926), 3:399 ("Several wagons"); Prevost to Bathurst, September 22, 1814, in Wood, *Documents,* 3:364–66 ("Your Lordship").

8. Clay's Journal of the Negotiations, in *The Papers of Henry Clay,* ed. James F. Hopkins 10 vols. (Lexington: University Press of Kentucky, 1959–92), 1:1007.

9. Ibid., 1:968 ("The prospect"); R. D. Ross, "The Naval Officer, 1793–1815," *Army Quarterly* 78 (April 1959): 71–94, quoted in John K. Mahon, *The War of 1812* (Gainesville: University Press of Florida, 1972), 326 ("If we").

10. Quoted in Wood, *Empire of Liberty,* 698.

11. James Monroe to the House of Representatives, January 30, 1824, in *New American State Papers: Naval Affairs* I, (Wilmington, Del.: Scholarly Resources, Inc., 1981), 107–8 ("stop the enemy").

"A RECKLESS WASTE OF BLOOD AND TREASURE"

1. Jesup to the Secretary of War, March 14, 1838, in *The Territorial Papers of the United States: Florida Territory, 1834–1839,* ed. Clarence Edwin Carter (Washington: U.S. Government Printing Office, 1960), 25:495.

2. William P. DuVal to Thomas L. McKenney, February 22, 1826, in *American State Papers: Indian Affairs,* ed. Walter Lowrie and Walter S. Franklin (Washington: Gales and Seaton, 1834), 2:664.

3. Alexander C. W. Fanning to Duncan L. Clinch, November 27, 1835, in *Territorial Papers,* 25:201.

4. "Domestic Intelligence," *Army and Navy Chronicle* 2, no. 7 (1836): 99; Secretary of War to Scott, January 21, 1836, Presidential Message on Indian Hostilities in Florida, February 9, 1836, S. Doc. 152, 24th Cong., 1st sess., Serial 281, 15.

5. Quoted in Allan Peskin, *Winfield Scott and the Profession of Arms* (Kent, Ohio: Kent State University Press, 2003), 92; quoted in John K. Mahon, *History of the Second Seminole War, 1835–1842,* revised ed. (Gainesville: University of Florida Press, 1985), 161.

6. Scott to Adjutant General, April 30, 1836, Proceedings of a Military Court of Inquiry in Case of Major Generals Scott and Gaines, S. Doc. 224, 24th Cong., 2nd sess., Serial 299, 329.

7. Jesup to Poinsett, June 16, 1837, in *American State Papers: Military Affairs,* ed. Asbury Dickins and John W. Forney (Washington: Gales and Seaton, 1860), 7:876.

8. Jesup to Poinsett, February 11, 1838, and Poinsett to Jesup, March 1, 1838, quoted in

John T. Sprague, *The Origin, Progress, and Conclusion of the Florida War* (1848; Tampa: University of Tampa Press, 2000), 200–202.

9. Annual Report of the Secretary of War, November 30, 1839, H. Doc. 2/4, 26th Cong., 1st sess., Serial 363, 44; General Orders, Alexander Macomb, May 18, 1839, quoted in Sprague, *Origin,* 228.

10. Annual Report of the Secretary of War, November 30, 1839, H. Doc. 2/4, 26th Cong., 1st sess., Serial 363, 44; Message of Governor Reid to the Legislative Council, February 28, 1840, in *The Territorial Papers of the United States: Florida Territory, 1839–1845,* ed. Clarence Edwin Carter (Washington: U.S. Government Printing Office, 1973), 26:110.

11. "Florida War," *Army and Navy Chronicle* 11, no. 14 (1840): 220; Ethan Allen Hitchcock and W. A. Croffut, *Fifty Years in Camp and Field, Diary of Major-General Ethan Allen Hitchcock, U.S.A* (New York: G. P. Putnam's Sons, 1909), 124; Sprague, *Origin,* 248.

12. "Intelligence," *Army and Navy Chronicle* 13, no. 18 (1842): 281.

13. Scott to R. Jones, April 30, 1836, Proceedings of a Military Court of Inquiry in Case of Major Generals Scott and Gaines, S. Doc. 224, 24th Cong., 2nd sess., Serial 299, 329; Sprague, *Origin,* 274.

14. Worth to Call, August 17, 1841, quoted in Sprague, *Origin,* 403; Acting Adjutant General to William J. Worth, July 31, 1841, in *Territorial Papers,* 26:364.

15. Report of the Major General Commanding the Army, November 22, 1841, S. Doc. 1/4, 27th Cong., 2nd sess., Serial 395, 78, 79; Annual Report of the Secretary of War, December 1, 1841, S. Doc. 1/3, 27th Cong., 2nd sess., Serial 395, 60.

16. McCall to "My Dear M.," January 16, 1842, in George A. McCall, *Letters from the Frontiers: Written during a Period of Thirty Years' Service in the Army of the United States* (Philadelphia: J. B. Lippincott, 1868), 393; Sprague, *Origin,* 393.

17. *Savannah Republican,* February 2, 1842, quoted in *Army and Navy Chronicle* 13, no. 4 (1842): 59.

18. McCall to "My Dear E.," February 27, 1842, in McCall, *Letters from the Frontiers,* 396.

19. Sprague, *Origin,* 441.

20. Worth to Scott, February 14, 1842, H. Doc. 262, 27th Cong., 2nd sess., Serial 405, 11.

21. Sprague, *Origin,* 483; McCall to Father, May 11, 1842, in McCall, *Letters from the Frontiers,* 407.

22. Message from the President of United States Recommending Measures for the Suppression of Hostilities in Florida, May 11, 1842, 27th Cong., 2nd Sess., 1842, S. Doc. 295, Serial 398, 1–2.

23. McCall to Father, August 26, 1842, in McCall, *Letters from the Frontiers,* 411.

24. Message from the President of United States Recommending Measures for the Suppression of Hostilities in Florida, 1.

25. Vose to Adjutant General, September 29, 1842, in *Territorial Papers,* 26:552; Indians Remaining in Florida, January 26, 1844, H. Doc. 82, 28th Cong., 1st sess., Serial 442, 11.

26. Sherman to Ellen Boyle Ewing, September 7, 1841, in *Home Letters of General Sherman,* ed. M. A. De Wolfe Howe (New York: C. Scribner's Sons, 1909), 14; "Tactics," *Army and Navy Chronicle* 13, no. 11 (1842): 164.

THE U.S. WAR WITH MEXICO

1. James K. Polk, Inaugural Address, March 4, 1845, in *Messages and Papers of the Presidents,* compiled by James D. Richardson, 10 vols. (Washington: U.S. Government Printing Office, 1897), 4:379–81.

2. James K. Polk, Message to Congress, May 11, 1846, in ibid., 4:437–43.

3. Quotation on Polk's strategy in *The Diary of James K. Polk,* ed. Milo M. Quaile, 4 vols. (Chicago: McClurg, 1910), 1:400. For Polk's strategic outlook, see 1:384–90, 429, 438–39.

4. Ibid., 1:399–401.

5. Winfield Scott, *Memoirs of Lieut. General Scott,* 2 vols. (New York: Sheldon and Conway, 1864), 2:396. General Order No. 20 is quoted in full in Timothy D. Johnson, *A Gallant Little Army: The Mexico City Campaign* (Lawrence: University Press of Kansas, 2007), 293–95.

6. Winfield Scott, "Proclamation to the Good People of Mexico," April 11, 1847, in *House Executive Document No. 60,* 30th Congress, 1st Session, Serial 520, 937.

7. Winfield Scott to Zachary Taylor, April 24, 1847, in *House Executive Document No. 60,* 30th Congress, 1st Session, Serial 520, 948–49.

8. Scott's Proclamation, May 11, 1847, in *House Executive Document No. 60,* 30th Congress, 1st Session, Serial 520, 971–74, quotation on 974.

9. Robert R. Miller, ed., *The Mexican War Journal and Letters of Ralph W. Kirkham* (College Station: Texas A&M University Press, 1991), 57–58, quote on 57.

10. T. Harry Williams, ed., *With Beauregard in Mexico: The Mexican War Reminiscences of P. G. T. Beauregard* (Baton Rouge: Louisiana State University Press, 1956), 72.

11. Ibid., 88.

12. Scott's caution to his troops in George Ballentine, *Autobiography of an English Soldier in the United States Army,* 2 vols. (London: Hurst and Blackett, 1853), 2:271–72.

13. Scott to Col. Winston, October 13, 1847, in *House Executive Document No. 60,* 30th Congress, 1st Session, Serial 520, 1029.

14. Secretary of War Marcy to Scott, October 6, 1847, in *House Executive Document No. 60,* 30th Congress, 1st Session, Serial 520, 1006–9, quote on 1007.

15. Scott to Taylor, April 24, 1847, in *House Executive Document No. 56,* 30th Congress, 1st Session, 1848, Serial 518, 139; R. E. Lee to John Mackay, October 2, 1847, in Gary W. Gallagher, ed., "'We Are Our Own Trumpeters': Robert E. Lee Describes Winfield Scott's Campaign to Mexico City," *Virginia Magazine of History and Biography* 95 (July 1987): 363–75, quote on 369.

16. S. Compton Smith, *Chile Con Carne, or the Camp and the Field* (New York: Miller and Curtis, 1857), 359–60.

17. John R. Kenly, *Memoirs of a Maryland Volunteer: War with Mexico* (Philadelphia: Lippincott, 1873), 322–23, 327.

18. Ramón Alcaraz, *The Other Side* (1850; New York: Burt Franklin, 1970), 442.

19. Polk, Message to Congress, December 7, 1847, in Richardson, *Messages and Papers,* 4:537–44, especially 542–44.

20. Scott to Secretary of War Marcy, January 16, 1847, in Justin H. Smith, *War with Mexico,* 2 vols. (New York: Macmillan, 1919), 2:512–13.

21. Scott quoted in Erasmus Keyes, *Fifty Years Observations of Men and Events* (New York: Scribner's, 1884), 206.

22. Antoine Henri de Jomini, *The Art of War* (1862; Westport, CT: Greenwood Press, 1971), 387.

23. Marcy to Scott, October 6, 1847, in *House Executive Document No. 60,* 30th Congress, 1st Session, Serial 520, 1006–9, quote on 1007.

THE CIVIL WAR

1. Lincoln to Stanton, March 30, 1865, and Stanton to Lincoln, March 31, 1865, in *War of the Rebellion: Official Records of the Union and Confederate Armies* (Washington: U.S. Government Printing Office, 1880–1901), series 1, vol. 46, part 3, pp. 280, 332 (hereafter *OR*).

2. See Grant to Bowers, April 2, 1865, in *OR,* 1, 46, (3), 450.

3. Sheridan to Grant, April 6, 1865, in *OR,* 1, 46 (3), 610; Lincoln to Grant, April 7, 1865, in *Collected Works of Abraham Lincoln,* ed. Roy P. Basler (New Brunswick, NJ: Rutgers University Press, 1953–55), 8:392.

4. "Declaration of the Immediate Causes of Secession," in *Rebellion Record: A Diary of Events,* ed. Frank Moore (New York: Arno Press, 1977), 1:3–4; Journal of the Georgia Convention, in *OR,* 4, 1, 84; "A Declaration of the Immediate Causes Which Induce and Justify the Secession of the State of Mississippi from the Federal Union," *Journal of the State Convention and Ordinances and Resolutions Adopted in January 1861,* 86–88.

5. B. Jowett, *Thucydides: Translated into English, with Introduction, Marginal Analysis, Notes and Indices* (Oxford: Clarendon Press, 1881), 1:75.

6. Lincoln to Grant, August 9, 1863, in *OR,* 1, 24 (3), 584.

7. Stanton to Grant, March 3, 1865, in *OR,* 1, 46 (2), 802. Also see Grant to Stanton, March 3, 1865, Lee to Grant, March 2, 1865, and Grant to Lee, March 4, 1865,1, 46, (2), 801–2, 824–25.

8. Grant to Lee and Lee to Grant, April 9, 1865, in *OR,* 1, 46, (1), 57–58.

9. Lee to Grant, April 8 and 9, 1865, and Grant to Lee, April 8 and 9, 1865, in *The Papers of Ulysses S. Grant,* ed. John Y. Simon (Carbondale: Southern Illinois University Press, 1985), 14:367, 371–73; Edward Porter Alexander, *Fighting for the Confederacy,* ed. Gary W. Gallagher (Chapel Hill: University of North Carolina Press, 1989), 531–33.

10. Lee to Davis, April 20, 1865, Lee Letterbook No. 3, Robert E. Lee Papers, Library of Congress.

11. Sheridan to Grant, September 13, 1870, in *Papers of Grant,* 20, 216–17.

THE 300-YEARS WAR

1. I cannot remember the general's name, but he visited Fort Leavenworth during the 1986–87 academic year, when I was a visiting professor there.

2. John C. Ewers, "Intertribal Warfare as the Precursor of Indian-White Warfare on the Northern Great Plains," *Western Historical Quarterly* 6 (October 1975): 397.

3. Anthony McGinnis, *Counting Coup and Cutting Horses: Intertribal Warfare on the Northern Plains, 1738–1889* (Evergreen, CO: Cordillera Press, 1990), 37.

4. Francis Jennings, *The Invasion of America: Indians, Colonialism, and the Cant of Conquest* (New York: Norton, 1976), 150.

5. John Underhill, *News from America; Or, A New and Experimentall Discoverie of New England...*, ed. Paul Royster (1638), available from Electronic Texts in American Studies, 36.

6. Colin G. Calloway, "'The Only Way Open to Us': The Crow Struggle for Survival in the Nineteenth Century," *North Dakota History* 53 (summer 1986): 33.

7. Frank B. Linderman, *Pretty-Shield: Medicine Woman of the Crows* (Lincoln: University of Nebraska Press, 1972), 167.

8. Hiram Martin Chittenden and Alfred Talbot Richardson, eds., *Life, Letters and Travels of Father Pierre-Jean De Smet, S.J., 1801–1873,* 4 vols. (New York: Francis P. Harper, 1905), 3:948.

9. John E. Ferling, *A Wilderness of Miseries: War and Warriors in Early America* (Santa Barbara, CA: Greenwood Press, 1980), 41.

10. John Mason, *A Brief History of the Pequot War,* ed. Paul Royster (1736), available from Electronic Texts in American Studies, 8.

11. Underhill, *News from America,* 36.

12. Robert M. Utley, *The Indian Frontier, 1846–1890,* revised ed. (Albuquerque: University of New Mexico Press, 2003), 102.

13. "Our Indian Policy of Extermination," *Harper's Weekly,* March 19, 1870, 178.

14. *Owyhee Avalanche,* November 11, 1865.

15. Utley, *Indian Frontier,* 128.

16. Perry D. Jamieson, *Crossing the Deadly Ground: United States Army Tactics, 1865–1899* (Tuscaloosa: University of Alabama Press, 1994), 38.

17. Nelson A. Miles, *Serving the Republic: Memoirs of the Civil and Military Life of Nelson A. Miles* (New York: Harper and Brothers, 1911), 117–18.

18. Colin G. Calloway, *First Peoples: A Documentary Survey of American Indian History,* 2nd ed. (New York: Bedford/St. Martin's Press, 2004), 317.

19. John Gibbon, "Arms to Fight Indians," *United Service* 1 (April 1879): 240.

20. Jerome A. Greene, ed., *Lakota and Cheyenne: Indian Views of the Great Sioux War, 1876–1877* (Norman: University of Oklahoma Press, 1994), 7.

21. Ibid., 21.

22. Peter Nabokov, ed., *Native American Testimony: A Chronicle of Indian-White Relations from Prophecy to the Present, 1492–2000* (New York: Penguin, 1999), 109.

23. John G. Neihardt, *Black Elk Speaks: Being the Life Story of a Holy Man of the Oglala Sioux* (New York: William Morrow, 1932), 138.

24. Greene, *Lakota and Cheyenne,* 120.

25. Valerious Geist, *Buffalo Nation: History and Legend of the North American Bison* (Osceola, WI: Voyager Press, 1996), 101.

26. Peter Nabokov, *Two Leggings: The Making of a Crow Warrior* (Lincoln: University of Nebraska Press, 1982), 187, 197.

27. Peter Iverson, *"We Are Still Here": American Indians in the Twentieth Century* (Wheeling, IL: Harlan Davidson, 1998), 19.

BATANGAS

1. Transcript of meeting of officers at Batangas on December 1, 1901, reprinted in Robert D. Ramsey III, *A Masterpiece of Counterguerrilla Warfare: BG J. Franklin Bell in the Philippines* (Fort Leavenworth, KS: Combat Studies Institute Press, 2007), 32–43.

2. J. Franklin Bell to CO, Lucena, February 27, 1902, entry 2349, Record Group 395, National Archives.
3. William McKinley, "To the Senate and House of Representatives, 3 December 1900," in *Compilation of the Messages and Papers of the Presidents,* ed. James L. Richardson, 19 vols. (New York: Bureau of National Literature, 1897–1922), 10:216–22.
4. William P. Duvall to Adj. Gen., 1st District, Department of Northern Luzon, [1900], letter 1003, entry 2233, Record Group 395. Duvall was Johnston's commander and cited the results of Johnston's investigation in this letter.
5. Glenn A. May, *Battle for Batangas: A Philippine Province at War* (New Haven: Yale University Press, 1991), 6.
6. Miguel Malvar, "Guerrilla Warfare: Instructions," October 27, 1900, document 1132.4, Philippine Insurgent Records, National Archives.
7. William H. Wilhelm to Edgar Collins, May 27, 1901, entry 5489, Record Group 395.
8. Miguel Malvar, "Copy of a Reply to General Trias," April 19, 1901, exhibit 1155, in *The Philippine Insurrection against the United States, 1898–1903: A Compilation of Documents and Introduction,* ed. John R. M. Taylor, 5 vols. (1906: Pasay City, P.I.: Eugenio Lopez Foundation, 1971), 5:328–29.
9. Adna R. Chaffee to Henry C. Corbin, November 5, 1901, Box 1, Henry C. Corbin Papers, Library of Congress.
10. "Report of Major General Adna R. Chafee," *Report of the War Department,* 1902, vol. 1, part 9, p. 191 (Washington, DC: Government Printing Office, 1902).
11. Adna R. Chaffee to Henry C. Corbin, January 31, 1902, Corbin Papers.
12. Ramsey, *A Masterpiece of Counterguerrilla Warfare,* 41.
13. Adjutant General to William R. Green, March 6, 1922, Philippine Insurrection File 2159, Record Group 407, National Archives.
14. Frank McCoy to John P. Taylor, September 25, 1903, Box 10, Frank McCoy Papers, Manuscripts Division, Library of Congress.

THE MEUSE-ARGONNE OFFENSIVE

1. George Seldes, *Witness to a Century* (1987), 98–99.
2. Sir William Wiseman, interview with author.
3. Theodore Ropp, *War in the Modern World* (1956), 252.
4. John J. Pershing, *My Experiences in the World War* (1931), 2:320.
5. George Sylvester Viereck, ed., *As They Saw Us: Foch, Ludendorff and Other War Leaders Write Our War History* (1929), 286–87.
6. Bliss to March, October 14, 1918, box 75, Bliss Papers, Library of Congress.
7. John Milton Cooper, *Woodrow Wilson: A Biography* (2009), 491.
8. Winston S. Churchill, *The Gathering Storm: The Second World War* (1948), 7.
9. *Time,* November 15, 1943, 58.
10. Churchill, *The Gathering Storm,* 17.
11. Annual Report of the Secretary of War, 1923, 24; and the author's interviews with Anthony C. McAuliffe and J. Lawton Collins.
12. *Time,* November 15, 1943, 60.

GÖTTERDÄMMERUNG

1. Dwight D. Eisenhower to Combined Chiefs of Staff, November 20, 1944, in *The Papers of Dwight D. Eisenhower,* ed. Alfred D. Chandler Jr., 5 vols. (Baltimore: Johns Hopkins University Press, 1970), 4:2312.

2. Winston S. Churchill to Franklin D. Roosevelt, December 6, 1944, in *Churchill and Roosevelt: The Complete Correspondence,* ed. Warren F. Kimball, 3 vols. (Princeton: Princeton University Press, 1984), 3:434–35.

3. Pocket Diary, December 3, 1944, SMVL/1/35, Papers of Admiral Sir James Somerville, Churchill College Archives Centre, University of Cambridge, Cambridge, U.K.

4. Winston S. Churchill Speech to House of Commons, "We Shall Fight on the Beaches," June 4, 1940, in Charles Eades, comp., *The War Speeches of Rt. Hon. Winston Churchill* (London: Cassell, 1951), I, 93.

5. Atlantic Charter, August 4, 1941, in Samuel Rosenman, ed., *Public Papers and Addresses of Franklin D. Roosevelt,* 13 volumes (New York: Random House, 1938–1950), X, 314.

6. Gerhard Weinberg, *A World at Arms: A Global History of World War II* (New York: Cambridge University Press, 1994), 798.

7. Earl F. Ziemke, *The U.S. Army in the Occupation of Germany, 1944–1946* (Washington, DC: U.S. Army Center of Military History, 1975), 14–17.

8. Gen. Alan Brooke argued this scheme would subordinate the British, who possessed superior knowledge, organization, and experience, to Americans who were "still only beginners." Churchill supposedly replied: "We are no longer single but married," Arthur Bryant, *The Turn of the Tide* (London: Collins, 1957), 237.

9. Mark A. Stoler, *George C. Marshall: Soldier-Statesman of the American Century* (Boston: Twayne, 1989), 98–102; also see Forrest C. Pogue, *The Supreme Command* (Washington, DC: Office of the Chief of Military History, 1954), 112–13.

10. Warren F. Kimball, "The Ghost in the Attic: The Soviet Union as a Factor in Anglo-American Planning for Postwar Germany, 1943–1945," in *International Committee for the History of the Second World War, Politics and Strategy in the Second World War: Papers Presented Under the Auspices of the ICMH, San Francisco, August 26, 1975* (Manhattan, KS, Military Affairs Press, 1976), 210–35.

11. Gen. Albert Wedemeyer, quoted in Mark A. Stoler," The American Perception of British Mediterranean Strategy, 1941–45," in *New Aspects of Naval History,* Craigh L. Symonds, ed., (Annapolis, MD: Naval Institute Press, 1981), 326.

12. *U.S. Department of State, Foreign Relations of the United States: The Conferences at Washington, 1941–42, and Casablanca, 1943* (Washington, DC: GPO, 1968), 803–07.

13. T/3 Daniel Camp, ETOUSA Research Branch, Interview Notes, 2–3 October 1944, Box 1018-Entry 94, RG 94, NARA; a full discussion of these issues is in Peter Kindsvatter, *American Soldiers: Ground Combat in the World Wars, Korea, and Vietnam* (Lawrence: University Press of Kansas, 2003).

14. Message, Gen. Dwight D. Eisenhower to CCS, May 7, 1945, Records of the Combined Chiefs of Staff, RG 218, NARA.

15. Christian Johanassen, May 8, 1945, Columbus World War II Roundtable Collection, U.S. Army Military History Institute, Carlisle Barracks, PA.

16. Christian Herter, "Speech at Memorial Day Commemoration," May 30, 1945, box 1183, Christian Herter Papers, Houghton Library, Harvard University, Cambridge, MA.

17. Harry C. Butcher, *My Three Years with Eisenhower* (New York: Simon and Schuster, 1946), 855.
18. Henry A. Kissinger, *A World Restored*, new ed. (New York: Harper and Row, 1964), 109.

EXERTING AIR PRESSURE AND GLOBALIZING CONTAINMENT

1. Interview of Gen.(Ret.) Jacob Smart by Conrad Crane, Nov 2, 1997, Arlington, VA, with changes provided by letter from Gen. Smart on November 29, 1997; Col. R. L. Randolph and Lt. Col. B. I. Mayo, Staff Study for Deputy for Operations, FEAF, "The Application of FEAF Effort in Korea," April 12, 1952, in FEAF Historical Division, *FEAF Operations Policy, Korea, Mid-1952*, March 1955, file K720.01, 1952 (addendum), Air Force Historical Research Agency, Maxwell Air Force Base (hereafter AFHRA).
2. "The Application of FEAF Effort in Korea"; Smart interview with Crane.
3. Fifth Air Force Air Attack Program, in *5th AF Intelligence Summary, 16–31 July 1952*, file K730.607, AFHRA. There is some confusion on the actual date of the directive; some sources attribute it to July 10, others two days later.
4. Robert F. Futrell, *The United States Air Force in Korea 1950–1953*, revised ed. (Washington: U.S. Government Printing Office, 1983), 516–17, 525; Stephen E. Pease, *Psywar: Psychological Warfare in Korea, 1950–53* (Harrisburg, PA: Stackpole Books, 1992), 82–84; Memo, Brig. Gen. Jacob Smart to Commanding General, 5th AF, Targets in Pyongyang, in *History of the Far East Air Forces, 1 July–31 December 1952*, vol. 2, file K720.01; Minutes of FEAF Target Committee Meetings for August 12 and 21, 1952, file K720.151A, July 22–December 16 1952, AFHRA.
5. "Chinese Accuse U.S. Pilots: Raid across Yalu Reported" and "Korean Negotiations," *Times (London)*, July 14, 1952, 6–7; "Asians in UN Fear Raids Harm Truce," *New York Times*, July 12, 1952, 2; Telegram, Holmes to Dept. of State, July 23, 1952, in *Foreign Relations of the United States, 1952–1954*, vol. 15, *Korea* (Washington: U.S. Government Printing Office, 1984), part 1, p. 419; Lindesay Parrott, "Long UN Air Raid Pounds Pyongyang and Reds' Build-up," *New York Times*, July 12, 1952, 1–2; Lindesay Parrott, "Heaviest Air Blow of War Smashes Red Korea Capital," *New York Times*, August 30, 1952, 1–2; Universal International Newsreels, vol. 25, no. 582, July 28, 1952, Record Group 200, National Archives II, College Park, MD; "New Initiative in Korea," *New York Times*, June 24, 1953, 28.
6. Intelligence Summaries for July 16–31, 1952, pp. 57, 74–76, and for August 1–15, 1952, containing copies of the Strike leaflets, in *Fifth Air Force Intelligence Summaries*, file K730.607, AFHRA; Pease, *Psywar*, 82–84; Universal International Newsreels, vol. 25, no. 596, September 15, 1952, lead story, RG 200; Futrell, *The United States Air Force in Korea*, 518–19; entries for July 28 and August 7, 1952, Weyland Memoranda for Record, January 6, 1952–December 31, 1952, file 168.7104–6, AFHRA.
7. Entries for July 24 and 28 and August 1, 1952, Weyland Memoranda for Record, file 168.7104–6, AFHRA.
8. Memo, Banfill to Deputy for Operations, Utilization of Air Power in Korea, August 29, 1952, in *FEAF Operations Policy, Korea, Mid-1952*, file K720.01, 1952 (Addendum), AFHRA.
9. Memo, Smart to Deputy for Intelligence, Utilization of Air Power in Korea, September 16, 1952, in *FEAF Operations Policy, Korea, Mid-1952*, file K720.01, 1952 (Addendum), AFHRA.

10. See documents in *Foreign Relations of the United States, 1952–1954,* vol. 15, *Korea,* part 1, pp. 39, 436–42, 470, 527–28, 575, 650; Shu Guang Zhang, *Mao's Military Romanticism: China and the Korean War, 1950–1953* (Lawrence: University Press of Kansas, 1995), 180–81.

11. "Staff Study of Intelligence Requirements by Cdr, FEAF for the Present and the Future," p. 5, in *History of the Far East Air Forces, January–December 1953,* vol. 3, part 1, file K720.01, AFHRA; Message, JCS 915579, JCS to CINCFE, August 8, 1952, Geographic File, 1951–53, 383.21 Korea (3–19–45), section 109, box 40, RG 218, NA II.

12. Message, C62419, Clark to JCS, May 14, 1953, Incoming Messages, February 11–May 31, 1953, box 7, RG 218.

13. Minutes of the FEAF Formal Target Committee Meetings for April 7, May 12 and 26, 1953, in *FEAF Bomber Command History, January–27 July 1953,* vol. 3, file K713.01–39, and entries for May 7 and 8, Weyland Memoranda for Record, vol. 4, January 1, 1953–July 31, 1953, file 168.7104–7, AFHRA; Message, 62451, Clark to JCS, May 16, 1953, Incoming Messages, February 11–May 31, 1953, box 7, RG 218.

14. Though not so sure in 1953, Eisenhower did become convinced later that his threats had been successful. In early 1965 President Lyndon Johnson discussed the growing problem in Vietnam with Eisenhower, and the general remarked that he had ended the war in Korea by having the word passed through three different channels "telling the Chinese that they must agree to an armistice quickly, since he had decided to remove the restrictions of area and weapons if the war had to be continued." Notes by Andrew Goodpaster of a meeting between Johnson and Eisenhower, February 17, 1965, from the LBJ Library, copy furnished by Charles F. Brower IV.

VIETNAM

1. Richard M. Nixon, *The Memoirs of Richard Nixon* (New York: Filmways, 1978), 369.

2. James H. Wilbanks, *Abandoning Vietnam: How America Left and South Vietnam Lost Its War* (Lawrence: University Press of Kansas, 2004), 17.

3. Doris Kearns Goodwin, *Lyndon Johnson and the American Dream* (New York: St. Martin's Press, 1991), 251.

4. Hoang Ngoc Lung, *Strategy and Tactics* (Washington: U.S. Army Center for Military History, 1980), 129; Central Office for South Vietnam, Resolution No. 9, July 1969, available at U.S. Army Heritage and Education Center, Carlisle, PA (hereafter cited as AHEC); David W. P. Ellicot, *The Vietnamese War: Revolution and Social Change in the Mekong Delta, 1930–1975* (New York: M. E. Sharpe, 2003), 2:1279.

5. "Republic of Vietnam Pacification Program," January 1970, Robert M. Montague Papers, Box 7, AHEC.

6. Eric M. Bergerud, *The Dynamics of Defeat: The Vietnam War in Hua Nghia Province* (Boulder, CO: Westview Press, 1991), 314–15; Director CORDS, "MACORDS After Action Report," March 9, 1973, MACV Command Historian's Collection, Series II: Staff Sections: J3 CORDS, Reports, Briefings, 1967–73, AHEC. For a discussion of pacification in the Philippines, see Brian M. Linn's chapter in this volume. For observations very similar to Herrington's from a year prior, see Charles Benoit's RAND report, "Conversations with Rural Vietnamese," April 1970, RAND Corporation.

7. See "Viet Cong Evaluation of the Situation in Quang Dien," captured document from Viet Cong political officer, October 1968, Donald A. Seibert Papers, AHEC. In addi-

tion to current scholarship by the historian David Elliot on the war from the Vietnamese perspective, see his 1968 RAND study, coauthored with W. A. Stewart, "Pacification and the Viet Cong System in Dinh Tuong, 1966–1967."

8. Henry A. Kissinger, *White House Years* (Boston: Little, Brown, 1979), 444.

9. Jeffrey J. Clarke, *Advice and Support: The Final Years. The U.S. Army in Vietnam* (Washington, DC: Center of Military History, 1988), 401.

10. Jeffrey Kimball, *The Vietnam War Files: Uncovering the Secret History of Nixon-Era Strategy* (Lawrence: University Press of Kansas, 2004), 191.

11. Gen. Creighton Abrams discussion with Staff, Weekly Commander's Update, March 9, 1971, in Lewis Sorley, *Vietnam Chronicles: The Abrams Tapes, 1968–1972* (Lubbock: Texas Tech University Press, 2004), 558.

12. Kimball, *The Vietnam War Files*, 163.

13. Kissinger, *White House Years*, 1006; Nixon, *The Memoirs*, 606–7.

14. Kissinger, *White House Years*, 488.

15. William E. Le Gro, *Vietnam from Cease-Fire to Capitulation* (Washington, DC: Center of Military History, 1981), 171.

16. Kissinger, *White House Years*, 1006; David Broder, "Isolationist Sentiment Not Blind to Reality," *Washington Post*, March 22, 1975.

THE COLD WAR

1. Don Oberdorfer, *From the Cold War to a New Era: The United States and the Soviet Union, 1983–1991* (Baltimore, 1998), 381, 383.

2. Ronald Reagan, *An American Life* (New York, 1990), 611.

3. Lou Cannon, *President Reagan: The Role of a Lifetime* (New York, 2000), 667.

4. Ibid., 677.

5. Oberdorfer, *Cold War to New Era*, 299.

6. George C. Herring, *From Colony to Superpower: U.S. Foreign Relations since 1776* (New York, 2008), 904.

7. Melvyn P. Leffler, *For the Soul of Mankind: The United States, the Soviet Union and the Cold War* (New York, 2007), 436.

8. William C. Wohlforth, ed., *Witnesses to the End of the Cold War* (Baltimore, 1996), 263.

9. Walter LaFeber, *America, Russia, and the Cold War, 1945–1996*, 8th ed. (New York, 1997), 347.

10. Odd Arne Westad, *The Global Cold War: Third World Interventions and the Making of Our Times* (New York, 2007), 399.

THE UNITED STATES IN IRAQ

1. The briefing is available at www.youtube.com/watch?v=7BaSwaBPg6M, accessed April 2, 2010.

2. Richard M. Swain, *"Lucky War": Third Army in Desert Storm* (Fort Leavenworth, KS, 1994), 284. This account, written by a professional soldier who is also an accomplished historian, remains the best overall account of Operation Desert Storm from an American perspective.

3. Michael R. Gordon and Bernard E. Trainor, *The Generals' War: The Inside Story of the Conflict in the Gulf* (New York, 1994), 417.

4. Rick Atkinson, *Crusade: The Untold Story of the Persian Gulf War* (New York, 1993), 471.

5. George Bush and Brent Scowcroft, *A World Transformed* (New York, 1998), 484–85.

6. H. Norman Schwarzkopf, *It Doesn't Take a Hero* (New York, 1992), 468.

7. Ibid., 469.

8. Colin L. Powell, *My American Journey* (New York, 1995), 520.

9. Ibid., 521.

10. Ibid.

11. George H. W. Bush, "Address on the End of the Gulf War," February 27, 1991, http://millercenter.org/scripps/archive/speeches/detail/5530, accessed April 16, 2010.

12. Bush and Scowcroft, *A World Transformed,* 486–87.

13. Gordon and Trainor, *The Generals' War,* 429.

14. Powell, *My American Journey,* 518, 523; Gordon and Trainor, *The Generals' War,* 419; Atkinson, *Crusade,* 405–7, 426–27.

15. Atkinson, *Crusade,* 480.

16. Gordon and Trainor, *The Generals' War,* 431.

17. Atkinson, *Crusade,* 479.

18. Schwarzkopf, *It Doesn't Take a Hero,* 475.

19. Ibid., 480.

20. Ibid., 479, 483.

21. Ibid., 483.

22. Ibid., 488, 489.

23. Bob Woodward, *The Commanders* (New York, 1991). Powell's reluctance to use force is a recurring theme of this book, which recounts the Persian Gulf crisis up to the eve of Operation Desert Storm.

24. Dan Balz and Rick Atkinson, "Powell Vows to Isolate Iraqi Army and 'Kill It,'" *Washington Post,* January 24, 1991.

25. Powell, *My American Journey,* 523.

26. Atkinson, *Crusade,* 471.

27. Powell, *My American Journey,* 526.

28. Otto Friedrich, ed., *Desert Storm: The War in the Persian Gulf* (Boston, 1991), 1, 3. This book synthesized *Time's* coverage of the war.

29. "The President's Press Conference on the Persian Gulf Conflict," March 1, 1991, www.presidency.ucsb.edu/ws/index.php?pid=19352, accessed April 26, 2010.

30. Atkinson, *Crusade,* 5.

31. This war after the war continued without pause and little public notice until the Anglo-American invasion of Iraq in March 2003. During this period U.S. and British combat crews flew hundreds of thousands of sorties and launched thousands of weapons at Iraqi air defense sites, communications centers, and other targets. Terry Boyd, "Operation Northern Watch: Mission Complete," *Stars and Stripes,* March 31, 2003; "Operation Southern Watch," www.absoluteastronomy.com/topics/Operation_Southern_Watch, accessed April 26, 2010.

32. Robert Kagan, "Saddam's Impending Victory," *Weekly Standard,* February 2, 1998, 22–25.

33. The clearest expression of that consensus was the Iraq Liberation Act, passed by unanimous consent in the U.S. Senate and by a vote of 360–38 in the House of Representa-

tives. This legislation declared it the policy of the United States to oust Saddam Hussein from power. President Bill Clinton signed the bill into law on October 31, 1998.

34. "President Bush Declares End to Major Combat in Iraq," May 1, 1991, www.cbsnews.com/stories/2003/05/01/iraq/main551946.shtml, accessed April 27, 2010.

35. Articulated in President Jimmy Carter's State of the Union Address on January 23, 1980, the key proviso of the Carter Doctrine stated the following: "Let our position be absolutely clear: An attempt by any outside force to gain control of the Persian Gulf region will be regarded as an assault on the vital interests of the United States of America, and such an assault will be repelled by any means necessary, including military force." http://www.jimmycarterlibrary.org/documents/speeches/su80jec.phtml, accessed April 28, 2010.

36. "Security Structures: Gulf Crisis," January 21, 1991, Richard N. Haass Files, Office of the National Security Council, Bush Presidential Records, George Bush Library, College Station, TX (hereafter cited as Haass Files). At the time of the Persian Gulf crisis of 1990–91, Richard Haass was serving on the staff of the National Security Council as senior director for Near East and South Asian affairs, in effect the NSC point man for the region.

37. "War Termination," n.d. [January 1991], Robert M. Gates Files, Office of the National Security Council, Bush Presidential Records, Bush Library (hereafter cited as Gates Files). For more on the importance of incorporating Iraq into a restored Gulf balance of power, see U.S. Embassy Riyadh to Secretary of State, "U.S. and Coalition War Aims: Sacked Out on the Same Sand Dunes, Dreaming Different Dreams?," December 30, 1991, Haass Files. The U.S. ambassador to Saudi Arabia at the time was Charles W. Freeman.

38. Richard Haass, "Post-Crisis Security Arrangements in the Gulf," December 28, 1990, Gates Files.

39. Richard Haass, "Beyond the Gulf War," January 25, 1991, Gates Files.

40. "A Vision of the Future for the Middle East," n.d. [January 1991], Haass Files.

41. "Post-War Security Structures in the Gulf," February 8, 1991, Haass Files. This paper originated in the State Department.

42. "Think Piece: Dealing with a Post-Crisis Iraq," December 20, 1990, Haass Files. This memo is identified as the handiwork of the "J-5 Response Cell." For further JCS analysis along the same lines, see "Phase Seven: Iraq after the Crisis," January 7, 1991, Haass Files.

43. "The Middle East in the Post-War Period: Political Stability and Openness," n.d. [February 1991], Haass Files.

44. Ibid.

45. "Post-Crisis Economic Issues," February 8, 1991, Haass Files.

46. "Talking Points for Meeting with King Hassan," February 13, 1991, Haass Files.

47. Haass, "Post-Crisis Security Arrangements in the Gulf."

Permissions

Index

Page numbers in *italics* refer to maps.